GW00633839

Socio-Economic R_ _ _ _ _ _ _ _ _

What Would *Real* Recovery Look Like?

Securing Economic Development, Social Equity and Sustainability

Seán Healy, Adam Larragy, Ann Leahy, Sandra Mallon
Michelle Murphy, and Brigid Reynolds

Social Justice Ireland

Social Justice Ireland

Working to build a just society

ISBN No. 978-1-907501-08-1

First Published April 2013

Published by
Social Justice Ireland
Arena House
Arena Road
Sandyford
Dublin 18

www.socialjustice.ie

Tel: 01- 2130724

e-mail: secretary@socialjustice.ie

TABLE OF CONTENTS

1. Introduction

For some time there has been much discussion on when Ireland is likely to recover from the economic crisis that hit it in 2008. Government and many commentators insist that recovery is just 'around the corner' and all we have to do is persist with the current approach and all will be well in due course. This assertion, however, raises two questions that are not being addressed in a satisfactory manner i.e.

1. What would *real* recovery look like?
2. Is the pathway currently being travelled likely to produce such a recovery?

In this Review *Social Justice Ireland* challenges the dominant narrative on both of these questions. We believe that the future being offered is deeply unjust and does not constitute real recovery. Human dignity and the common good are not guiding policy decision-making. We also believe that the pathways being followed by Government seek to protect the rich at the expense of the rest of us. It is not acceptable that the major sacrifices in building the future should be borne by those on low to middle incomes or by future generations.

As individuals, when we are under pressure it can be difficult to distinguish between the urgent and the important. Any sense of purpose or direction tends to be swept aside in our panic to address what we see as immediate pressing problems. But when we are in this mode of thinking we simply do not recognise that much of our effort may merely be exacerbating current difficulties and storing up more, potentially even greater, problems for the future.

Societies tend to make the same mistakes. Policy-making in Ireland has tended to focus almost exclusively on the 'urgent' in recent years which may in part be understandable because of the serious nature of the series of crises that emerged since 2008. However, there has been a major failure to deal with these urgent issues within a broader framework of strategic thinking and planning. There has been no real guiding vision that would ensure choices were made on a consistent and integrated basis. Policy development has been extremely short-sighted and based on a series of unchallenged but invalid assumptions about the nature of the difficulties we now face and how they can best be resolved.

As a result Ireland has seen the single biggest transfer of resources from low and middle income people to the rich and powerful in its history. The main beneficiaries of this transfer have been parts of the corporate sector especially the bondholders and financial institutions who took little or no 'hit' for their gambling in Ireland's private banking sector. Other large corporates also benefitted as their privileged tax position continues to be protected and they are not asked to make any contribution towards Ireland's rescue.

At the same time, poverty rose, unemployment rose, emigration rose dramatically, waiting lists for social housing rose, child poverty, long-term unemployment and the numbers working poor also rose. Simultaneously employment fell dramatically as did domestic demand and investment. Public services were reduced significantly. Costs were introduced for many services while costs were increased in many areas. Funding for the community and voluntary sector was cut disproportionately at the very moment when the demand for their services was increasing.

Social Justice Ireland fully acknowledges Ireland's difficult fiscal position. We also accept that Ireland must pay its way. However, we believe strongly that there are alternatives to the present approach which would protect the vulnerable while rescuing the economy and doing this in a sustainable manner.

This Review argues that Ireland needs to recognise the essentially complementary nature of economic and social development – two sides of the one reality. Economic development is essential to provide the resources necessary for social development. But social development, in turn, is essential because there can be no lasting economic development of any substance without the provision of social services and infrastructure. All one has to do is reflect on the importance of a good education system for the development of a 'hi-tech, hi-spec, smart' economy.

At the same time we argue that both economic development and social development must be sustainable if it is to be of lasting value. All development must be sustainable economically, socially and environmentally. Otherwise it should not be accepted as development. Recognising the importance of sustainability presents new challenges which must be addressed, not ignored, in the rush to address the urgent rather than the important.

It is time to put a stop to short-termism. We must ask ourselves as a society where we are right now and, more importantly, where we want to be in the future. As we outline in the following chapters of this Review, many Government initiatives since the current crisis began have been deeply flawed. It is of immense concern that, to the extent that they reflect any kind of vision of the future, it is one that is not sustainable and highly questionable, anyway, in terms of its underlying values.

The financial crisis of recent years has led to a widespread belief worldwide amongst academics, policymakers and even business people that the neo-liberal version of capitalism itself is in a serious crisis. Such debate is no longer confined to a radical fringe but is rightly now part of mainstream thinking. A vision for a sustainable future needs to be articulated.

Social Justice Ireland advocates a vision for Ireland based on the core values of justice, human dignity, equality, human rights, solidarity, sustainability and the pursuit of the common good.

To move towards this vision five key policy areas must be addressed urgently. These are:

- **macroeconomic stability**
- **just taxation**
- **social protection**
- **governance**
- **sustainability.**

Social Justice Ireland offers this analysis and critique together with its proposals as a contribution to the public debate that is urgently required on the central question of what real recovery would look like. All responses are most welcome.

2. IRELAND TODAY – A NARRATIVE

In this chapter we set the scene for this *Socio-Economic Review*. We outline what happened over recent decades to bring Ireland to where it is today, where exactly Ireland finds itself now, where Ireland should go in the future and what it needs to do to get there. The remainder of this review will address key policy areas, present a detailed analysis and highlight the key policy initiatives that are required if Ireland is to emerge from the current series of crises.

Given the space constraints, it has not been possible in this review to address every issue that should be tackled or to present extensive detail in respect of every policy area. Our focus in this chapter is on the broad socio-economic reality that has emerged. We do not accept many of the assumptions that have informed much of the commentary in public and policy-making arenas in recent times. The analysis of the past that seems to have underpinned decision-making is flawed and inaccurate. While some of the policy decisions that have been adopted did move in the right direction, many initiatives since the current crisis emerged:

- have been deeply flawed and are producing growing inequality;
- are built on a vision of the future that is unsustainable;
- fail to put human dignity and the common good at the core of the policy-making process; and
- appear to be guided by a questionable vision of Ireland's future.

The scale and severity of the crises Ireland is currently facing raise obvious questions about how they came about. This chapter provides a commentary on the background to these events. It also asks how Ireland can recover from these crises and, more importantly, how we can shape a future Ireland that cares for the well-being of its entire people and protects the environment.

The chapter is structured in four parts:

2.1 How Ireland got here: the background to the crises
2.2 Ireland in 2013: the context
2.3 The need for vision: where is Irish society going?
2.4 Priorities for a New Ireland

2.1 How Ireland got here: the background to the crises

There are international, European and national roots to the current crises. This understanding has not always been recognised or acknowledged. All three dimensions are significant.

2.1.1 The international background

The origin of the global financial crisis can be traced to policy responses to the economic crises of the 1970s. During that decade the existing international monetary regime collapsed and economies suffered high inflation and high unemployment. During the Second World War, the victorious allies had agreed at Bretton Woods to establish new international economic institutions to avoid another Great Depression. The Bretton Woods system was heavily influenced by John Maynard Keynes and the New Dealers in the United States. A fixed currency regime based upon a 'dollar standard' – meaning the dollar was convertible into a fixed quantity of gold – was established, with capital controls employed to maintain the stability of the system. One prominent scholar has identified this system as a type of 'embedded liberalism', in which international economic institutions were constructed to encourage the creation of welfare states and achievement of full employment through demand management (Ruggie, 1982). The period 1950-1973 – the 'Golden Age' of capitalism – was characterised by rapid growth, rising living standards and wages and full employment, facilitated by strong state intervention and demand management. The aims of monetary and fiscal policy were the maintenance of the stability of the Bretton Wood system and full employment. It was the era of the Keynesian state.

However, during the 1970s a hitherto unseen problem emerged: the combination of inflation and high unemployment, known colloquially as 'stagflation'. During the 1960s economic policy had come to be guided by the Phillips curve, which posited an inverse relationship between unemployment and inflation (Gordon, 2011: 12-14). The unexpected simultaneous occurrence of both was exacerbated by the 1973 Oil Shock, which caused a massive shift in the cost of production of industrial and, to a lesser extent, agricultural goods and the collapse of the Bretton Woods system. In the case of the latter, the US was faced with the 'Triffin dilemma'; its domestic economic policy conflicted with the dollar's role as an international reserve currency (Triffin, 1960). This had been anticipated by Keynes at Bretton Woods in 1944, who had advocated a separate international reserve currency instead of the dollar (Skidelsky, 2000). However, the American delegation, led by Harry Dexter White, had overruled him and so in the early 1970s the US was faced with a dollar under huge external pressure.

American private investment and public investment through the Marshall Plan had built up large quantities of dollars outside the regulation of the Federal Reserve. Lax regulation allowed such 'Eurodollars' to be deposited in international branches of US banks – particularly in the City of London – at higher rates than those allowable by the Federal Reserve (Helleiner, 1994). The Eurodollars, in turn, could circumvent capital controls on the host country's currency and be used to hedge currency risk. Massive US military expenditure in South-East Asia led to an increasing trade deficit and currency speculators could use freely tradable Eurodollars to put pressure on the US dollar. The US, the anchor of the Bretton Woods system, was unwilling to reduce public expenditure to maintain the international monetary system and instead presided over the dissolution of Bretton Woods.

In 1971 Richard Nixon suspended the link between the dollar and gold, effectively ending the Bretton Woods monetary system, and imposed emergency import tariffs and price and wage controls (Kirschner, 2003: 651). The oil crisis of 1973 vastly increased the quantity of dollars outside the United States. These 'petrodollars' were recycled through private financial markets as OPEC residents placed their dollars with investment banks and were used to purchase developing countries' government debt or invested in the money markets.

Efforts at creating a new international monetary system failed, though the collapse of Bretton Woods spurred the European Community to attempt to create its own regional monetary system. To manage a chaotic international economic environment, high inflation and unemployment, different states adopted new strategies. Incomes policies were introduced to control inflation through wage and price controls; in the Nordic countries the public sector was expanded to reduce unemployment and expand services; and Keynesian demand management was used to mitigate unemployment by stimulating the economy. However, in the early 1970s Keynesian deficit spending was often blamed for further increasing unemployment, though incomes policy had some effect in mitigating the inflationary effects of government spending and oil price rises. Moreover, the collapse of the Bretton Woods system confronted policymakers with an uncertain international economic environment.

A school of economic theorists, the 'monetarists', blamed lax monetary policy and fiscal policy for increasing inflation and unemployment. They argued in favour of strict controls of the money supply through monetary policy, balancing of the budget deficit, reducing the state's role in the economy, reducing taxes on capital and income and expansion of free trade. In the UK the Thatcher government briefly flirted with the monetarists' prescriptions for monetary policy but abandoned them in its second term in office (Smith, 1986). However, the other policies recommended by the monetarists were pursued by the Thatcher and Reagan governments in the 1980s and soon spread to influence, to varying degrees, governments throughout the world. Since the late 1970s, the 'embedded liberalism' of the Keynesian state and Bretton Woods system – whose origins lay in the New Deal and post-war welfare states of Europe – has been replaced by the 'neo-liberalism' currently in place (Glyn, 2006). Two broad approaches have been pursued by governments in the neo-liberal era – neoliberal restructuring and financialisation. The problems produced by financialisation are the immediate cause of the crisis in the financial system in recent years.

Neo-Liberal Restructuring: During the 1980s governments, particularly in the United States and Britain, claimed that they could control inflation, increase employment and raise the standard of living. They attempted to do this through:

- removing state constraints on the growth, use and flow of capital and wealth;
- privatising state assets and contracting out core state services to the private sector;
- using high interest rates and wage squeezes to control inflation;
- redistributing income from the poor and middle classes to the rich by shifting the burden of taxation from capital and income taxes to consumption taxes and user charges, in the belief that the wealthy and high income earners would then be motivated to reinvest their additional income and reignite economic growth.

This theory was incorrect. Global growth, which had averaged 3.5 per cent a year in the 1960s and 2.4 per cent in the 1970s, when state interventionist policies were the accepted norm, only averaged 1.4 per cent in the 1980s and 1.1 per cent in the 1990s. This neo-liberal approach redistributed income to the rich and seriously damaged the incomes of the poor and the middle classes. In his study of global economic growth, Angus Maddison (2005: 6) noted that GDP per capita grew at a faster rate during the 'Golden Age' (1950-1973) than at any other time in human history (see Table 2.1).

Table 2.1 Annual average compound growth rate of GDP per capita, 1950-2001

	1950-1973	1973-2001
Western Europe	4.05	1.88
Western offshoots (e.g. USA)	2.45	1.84
Japan	8.06	2.14
West	**3.72**	**1.95**
Asia (excluding Japan)	2.91	3.55
Latin America	2.58	0.91
E. Europe and f. USSR	3.49	-0.05
Africa	2	0.19
Rest	**2.83**	**1.75**
World	**2.92**	**1.41**

Source: Maddisson, 2005: 10.

Moreover, the implicit abandonment of full employment as a policy objective, to be replaced by the control of inflation, led to persistent unemployment in many communities, particularly those that had traditionally worked in industry. Western European nations have been particularly blighted by persistent unemployment in the neo-liberal era (see Chart 2.1). John Kenneth Galbraith pithily summed up 'the doctrine of the eighties, namely that the rich were not working because they had too little money, the poor because they had too much'. However, despite the failure of many neo-liberal policies, neo-liberal ideas gained great prestige within academia, business and political parties.

The efforts to control inflation led to the use of extremely high interest rates in Britain and the US. One knock-on effect of the Federal Reserve's 'Volcker Shock' – a massive hike in the US interest rate – was to increase the interest rate of developing countries' dollar denominated debts. This forced many to turn to the IMF in the 1980s and 1990s for emergency funding to service their dollar deb.; In return they were forced to accept IMF mandated 'structural adjustment programmes', which were based on neo-liberal policy prescriptions of privatisation, the liberalisation of private capital markets and labour market flexibility. These programmes reduced economic growth in those countries, exposed them to economic volatility and increased the precariousness of their workers. By the late 1990s there was increasing scepticism about the efficacy of the policy measures proscribed by the IMF, the US Treasury Department and the World Bank (the 'Washington Consensus') among economists and senior policymakers in both the Fund and the Bank (Florio, 2002).

Chart 2.1 Unemployment rate in the EU-15, US and Japan, 1960-2010

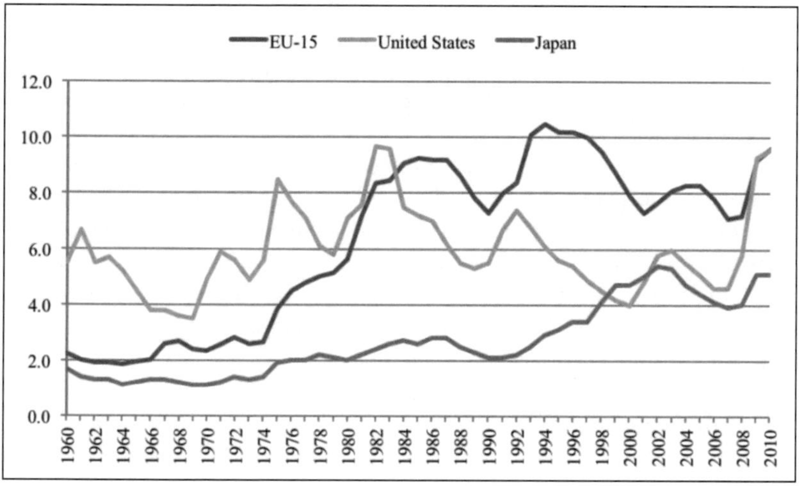

Source: AMECO, 2013.

Financialisation:

The other great economic process that has characterised the era has been 'financialisation'. In 2001 US economist Gerald Epstein defined the term as referring 'to the increasing importance of financial markets, financial motives, financial institutions, and financial elites in the operation of the economy and its governing institutions, both at the national and international level' (Epstein 2001, p.1) At an international level countries have removed capital controls and other restrictions on the flow of capital internationally, often with the imprimatur of international economic institutions such as the OECD, IMF and European Commission which came to embrace the idea of the freedom of movement of capital (Abdelal, 2007). At the same time, the regulation of the financial sector was

---

[1] The IMF has recently reconsidered its position on capital controls.

transformed by the removal of the legal barriers between different financial functions. For example, the 'Big Bang' of 1987 removed traditional distinctions within the City of London's stockbroking community while repeal of the Glass-Steagall Act in 1999 removed the New Deal-era legal separation of investment and retail banks. Financialisation originated in the late 1970s and became almost universally applied in the 1990s.

The liberalisation of capital markets and the creation of a global capital market encouraged firms – particularly in the Anglo-American countries – to rely for financing on bond markets and stock markets rather than their traditional banks. This provided a large market in which pension funds and other types of savings vehicles could invest and equity markets became increasingly important outlets for global savings. This led firms to increasingly view their share price as their key indicator of performance – particularly as executive remuneration is often tied to share price. However, this form of 'shareholder capitalism' has induced a short-termism in the behaviour of firms reliant on the stock-market, with a short-term fixation on share price and boosting short-term profitability leading to long-term problems (Hutton, 2003). This has been a particular problem in the financial sector, where assets mature over long periods of time.

A crisis of financialisation
With the changes in regulation, removal of capital controls, reduction in capital taxes and the creation of global capital market, debt rapidly expanded. Financial markets integrated more participants and offered a wider range of financial 'products'. This led to more liquidity within the market and financial firms assumed that they could access money easily and at rates of interest close to central bank rates. Many of these new financial products were 'derivatives'– financial products without an intrinsic value of their own and whose value is based on the performance of underlying market factors, such as exchange rates or stock market indices. Such products were originally designed to help manage the risk of investing in a particular type of asset, such as residential property, for example.

However, in practice this led to 'compounding bubbles'– first in equities and later in residential and commercial property – as capital, freed from constraints, moved into asset classes whose prices were rising rapidly (Blyth, 2008). This had particularly deleterious effects on developing countries that had liberalised their capital controls and their financial sectors. The Asian Financial Crisis of 1997 was partly caused by investors borrowing in foreign currencies and gambling on domestic equities and property prices. The lack of control over their capital accounts meant that Asian policymakers could not control the inflows of 'hot money' taking advantage of liberalisation and high domestic interest rates (Stiglitz, 2002). Those countries in East Asia that employed capital controls and had less financialised economies were the least affected.

However, it was not only developing countries that were affected by a crisis of financialisation. As the state retreated from key sectors of the economy, such as housing, and as incomes for middle and lower-income groups in many developed countries – particularly in the United States – stagnated, consumers increasingly came to rely on debt to fund the purchase of houses, cars and consumer durables (see Charts 2.2 and 2.3). The liberalisation of finance increased the capacity and willingness of banks to extend credit. This led to increases in house prices, which in turn encouraged further lending as homeowner's collateral rose. Those countries with the most liberalised banking sectors and housing markets witnessed the greatest increase in house prices and mortgage debt (Schwartz, 2009). Prudential standards fell, particularly in those countries with liberal mortgage markets, loan to income ratios and deposit requirements were both reduced and new mortgage products, including 100 per cent mortgages, were advanced.

Chart 2.2 – Share of total household income growth attributable to various income groups in the US, 1979-2007

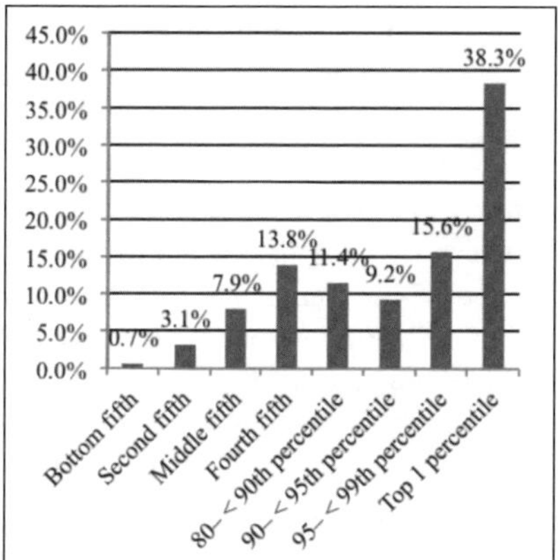

Chart 2.3 – Percentage of Income Accruing to the top 10% of earners in the United States, 1928-2011

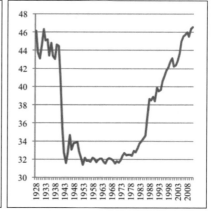

Source: State of Working America, 12th Edition.

Source: Piketty and Saez (2007), updated by authors.

The expansion in debt was only possible due to the emergence of 'securitisation'. Securitisation emerged as a legal possibility in eighteenth-century Prussia and the 'Pfandbriefe' market remains an important aspect of European finance today, particularly in Denmark and Germany. However, in contrast to the Pfandbriefe model, the securitisation instruments most commonly used in the US and liberal economies – Residential Mortgage-Backed Securities (RMBS) and Collateralised Mortgage Obligations (CMO) – are do not appear in the issuer's balance sheet. This allowed US mortgage originators to issue mortgages of questionable debt quality and to bundle them together as 'collateralised debt obligations'. These were then being sold on to international financial institutions that were unaware of the dubious quality of some of the underlying mortgages. Following the New Deal of the 1930s the US mortgage securitisation market had been controlled by the Federal National Mortgage Association (Fannie Mae), which pooled mortgages, securitised them, and then sold those RMBS on in an attempt to increase liquidity in the US mortgage market and ultimately expand home ownership in the US.

However, during the 1990s private mortgage securitisation – those not insured by agencies such as Fannie Mae – had become increasingly important in the US due to deregulation of the finance and mortgage market and changes in status to US government-owned companies that had previously dominated the market (see Chart 2.4). This facilitated the creation of a 'sub-prime market' – the extension of mortgages to people who might previously have been deemed credit risks, often on extremely onerous terms that only became clear to borrowers following two years of paying interest on 'teaser rates'. This market was dominated by 'non agency' issuers, including prestigious US investment banks such as Lehman Brothers and Goldman Sachs.

An essential part of financialisation was the belief that markets could correctly price risk. There was a firm belief that markets in financial derivatives (which were merely bets about the future) would bring in all the necessary information and thus could accurately predict the future. This in turn led to the belief that there was no uncertainty about the future. But uncertainty about the future was a central message of Keynes and was one of the reasons for financial regulation. Thus while financial markets were deregulated, the agencies in charge of monitoring and regulating banks and other financial institutions stopped doing their jobs. In the US for example Alan Greenspan, chair of the Federal Reserve, argued that fraud on Wall Street should not be the responsibility of government regulators. He and most of the other regulators and central bankers felt that the market and self-regulation was enough.

Chart 2.4 Total Outstanding RMBS and CMO debt by issuer in $bn, 2002-2008

Chart 2.5 – Total Debt Outstanding in non-financial sectors of the US Economy as a % of US GDP, 1950-2011

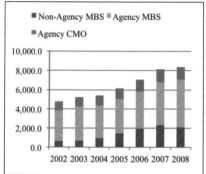

Source: Securities Industry and Financial Markets Association (2013).

Source: US Federal Reserve (2013).

This lack of government oversight and regulation led to major financial institutions being turned into enterprises where fraud was at the heart of their business model. Securitisation of the residential mortgage market increased both the liquidity and volatility of the market. Many of originators of residential mortgages engaged in fraud by falsely presenting mortgages with high default risks as repayable. These mortgages were then packaged into triple-A securities and sold to international investors.

Former employees from Ameriquest, which was United States's leading wholesale lender, described a system in which they were pushed to falsify mortgage documents and then sell the mortgages to Wall Street banks eager to make fast profits[2]. Richard Bowen, chief underwriter of Citigroup's consumer division, was demoted with 218 of his 220 employees reassigned allegedly for attempting to inform several senior executives that over 80 percent of their mortgages violated Citigroup's own standards. (Ferguson 2012: 104) It is clear that such mortgage fraud was part of the cause of the crisis.

---

[2] *Road to Ruin: Mortgage Fraud Scandal Brewing*, May 13, 2009 by American News Project hosted by 'The Real News'

The massive growth in the derivative markets (over \$500 trillion by some estimates) made capital markets more volatile, but the underlying questionability in how derivative contracts were constructed and in fixing the triggers is what cause the international financial system to freeze after Lehman Brothers failed as no bank wanted to lend to other banks because they all feared that the other banks were acting as they were. Similar problems concerning the fraudulent basis for so many of its mortgage calculations played a key role in the financial crashes in Ireland and Iceland.

The interaction of two pervasive trends – the stagnation of the incomes of lower and middle-income groups and financialisation – precipitated the financial crisis of 2008. Rising interest rates, both from central banks and from the terms of many sub-prime mortgages themselves, led to increasing defaults amongst homeowners in the US. This led to the realisation that the true values of many MBS were significantly lower than their face values. Financial institutions, however, were already highly leveraged and many simply did not have the reserves to meet the losses they were now facing. From the summer of 2007 onwards growing mistrust between financial institutions – many of whom suspected others of holding assets worth less than their face value – led to a 'liquidity crisis', as banks and financial institutions became wary of lending to each other.

Believing that lack of liquidity was the underlying problem, central banks attempted to boost liquidity. However, by September 2008 it became clear that many banks were simply insolvent. The collapse of the US investment bank Lehman Brothers threatened a cascade of defaults and bank failures. The crisis was compounded when one large insurance company, the American Insurance Group (AIG), had to be rescued through nationalisation when it emerged that it was unable to meet its obligations in respect of a derivative known as a credit default swap (CDS). This was a peculiar paradox as the instrument had – ostensibly been created to hedge against the risk of default of a particular security or company and AIG had played a leading role in its creation. The US government reacted to the crisis by nationalising large segments of the US banking and financial system – particularly those relating to mortgage finance – and the US Federal Reserve engaged in massive intervention in the US financial system, significantly expanding its balance sheet in an effort to reduce long-term interest rates and encourage US financial institutions to lend again.

The financial crisis has led to a widespread belief that the capitalism itself – or at least the neo-liberal variant – is in a serious crisis. This is not confined to a radical fringe, but rather is a subject of debate amongst academics, policymakers and businesspeople. Some – particularly senior European policymakers – see the solution to the crisis in a combination of additional financial regulation, fiscal austerity and the imposition of further neo-liberal reforms in public services and labour markets (see e.g Rehn, 2013). Yet others, such as prominent Keynesian economists in the United States and Europe, have argued that some combinations of fiscal stimulus and greater income redistribution are required (Krugman, 2012; Eichengreen & O'Rourke: 2012; De Grauwe and Ji: 2013; Stiglitz, 2012; Holland and Portes, 2012). Even those wary of outright Keynesian arguments and explanations have become extremely worried about income inequality, viewing it as lying at the core of the crisis as credit was used to maintain consumption in lieu of broad-based income growth in the United States (Rajan: 2010).

Mark Blythe (2002: 6) has referred to the transition to neo-liberal institutions, practices and ideas in the late 1970s and early 1980s as a 'Great Transformation' which brought back many of the nostrums discredited in the 1930s:

'… both classical liberalism and neoliberalism are characterized by high capital mobility, large private capital flows, market-conforming tools of macroeconomic management, a willingness to ride out balance of payments and other disequilibria by deflation, and a view of the rate of re-employment as dependent upon the market-clearing price of labour.'

At present, throughout the European Union the 'austerity-focused' neo-liberal perspective is dominant. However, as in the late 1970s, intellectual trends and practices in economic policy can shift rapidly in response to economic crises. Another 'Great Transformation' in economic ideas and practices is required.

2.1.2 The European background

In September 2008 there was a perception amongst some senior European policy makers that, in the words of German finance minister Peer Steinbrück, 'the financial crisis is above all an American problem'. This reflected a belief amongst continental policymakers and commentators that Western and Central Europe had a less liberalised financial sector and that continental economies were thus more stable than 'Anglo-Saxon' economies. However, in the following months European governments were forced into limited recapitalisation of their banking sectors, while systemic weaknesses in the Euro became apparent between 2009 and the present. The response of European policymakers to the financial crisis has reflected both national traditions – particularly the often-quoted German attachment to *ordoliberalism* – but also a pervasive neo-liberalism, albeit one more cautiously applied than it has been in the US and Britain. The response has also been entirely counterproductive, condemning peripheral European economies to conditions of mass unemployment and transferring private financial sector debt to the public sector and, in some cases, to the European Central Bank's balance sheet. This section will examine the specifically European origins of the financial crisis, explain how many of the reactions of many European policymakers have compounded the crisis and explore the role of the European single currency in the crisis.

While some of the champions of early European integration, including Jean Monet, anticipated a European single currency, the Treaty of Rome in 1957 only contained references to an eventual abolition of capital controls within the Community (Padoa-Schioppa, 2000: 26-44). The political desire for a common European currency only received an impetus when the Bretton Woods system began to slowly disintegrate in the late 1960s. The placatory pay settlement following May 1968 in France led to devaluation of the Franc and revaluation of the Deutschemark. This, in turn, led to fears that intra-European trade could contract due to monetary instability and that the Common Agricultural Policy, based on common prices, could be endangered. The Council of Ministers accepted the Werner Report of 1971, which advocated fixed currencies with free movement of capital (Swann, 2000: 205). However, the 'Nixon Shock' of 1971 led to an effort to stabilise the international monetary system and instead the 'snake in the tunnel' was adopted. European currencies were fixed to the DM within a common band and a common band between European currencies and the dollar was maintained. This proceeded under the rubric of the Smithsonian Agreement, which devalued the dollar by 9%, allowing the US room to drop emergency import surtaxes.

The 'snake in the tunnel' could not survive the divergent reactions of European governments to the economic conditions of the 1970s. These reactions were heavily conditioned by domestic institutions. The German government was heavily constrained by the German Central Bank, which was completely independent from government under the Bundesbank Law of 1957 (Heisenberg, 1999). Only exchange rate policy remained under the remit of the Chancellor of Germany. The Bundesbank was a firm believer in 'sound money' policies, and prized price stability above all else. In contrast, the French government believed that if unemployment rose above a certain point, France would become ungovernable. Even the French liberal President Valery Giscard d'Estaing refused to allow the Banque de France shadow the DM, which would have required unacceptably high interest rates.

Instead, protected by capital controls, French monetary policy was geared towards maintaining full employment (Levy, 1999).

German and French policymakers in the 1970s continued to believe that stagflation was exacerbated by currency fluctuations. So a renewed attempt at co-operation was initiated in 1979, the European Monetary System (EMS), which fixed participating currencies within a margin of +/- 2.25%, and established a European Currency Unit (ECU), based on a basket of European currencies. However, this was likely made possible by the German Chancellor Helmut Schmidt's decision to reluctantly agree to President Carter's request that Germany, with its balance of payments surplus and low inflation and budget deficits, play a part in reflating the world economy through an expansionary fiscal programme. However, when the rate of inflation rose to 5.8% in Germany, the Bundesbank raised interest rates rapidly. By 1981 Germany, the US, and Britain were all pursuing strategies of disinflation through – in the cases of Germany and Britain – budgetary cutbacks and high interest rates. In contrast, the newly elected government of Francois Mitterand attempted to reflate the French economy through a programme of nationalisations and increased public spending. Given the timing, with France's main trading partners in austerity programmes, much of the increased French demand leaked abroad. The franc was subject to speculative attacks and the French were forced to disguise devaluations of the franc as DM revaluations to sustain the EMS. The French cabinet split on what path to pursue: to use temporary import surtaxes and draconian capital controls, effectively abandoning the EMS and many tenets of European integration; or to attempt to direct European integration in a manner that would protect the French social and economic model. President Mitterand and finance minister Jacques Delors choose the latter option and France liberalised its financial sector and capital account while maintaining a strong franc to shadow the DM and reduce domestic inflation. This reduced the strains that had developed in the relationship with Germany's conservative chancellor Helmut Kohl, who had been unwilling to allow the French continually devalue against the DM, particularly as it strained his relationship with the Bundesbank,

Following the French U-turn in 1983, European economic and political integration was given a new impetus. Jacques Delors, appointed President of the EU Commission in 1985, stated that he wanted Europe to become a regional economic bloc capable 'of perpetuating a European model of society' (Ross, 1995: 4). The Single European Act completed the Common Market – the largest free trade area in the world – and enforced the liberalisation of all capital controls by 1990 at the latest. The acceptance of the Single European Market and removal of capital controls had an inexorable logic that was recognised by Delors and senior policymakers at the time. One of those policymakers, Tommaso Padoa-Schioppio, argued that capital liberalisation within the Community inevitably led to monetary union. The 'inconsistent quartet' of free trade, free capital mobility, fixed exchange rates and autonomous national monetary policies could not exist at the same time for any one country (Padoa-Schioppa, 2000: 183).

Under the EMS participating countries had forgone their right to pursue autonomous monetary policies, being forced instead to shadow the Bundesbank in order to maintain fixed exchange rates. France and Italy faced a particular dilemma: they could maintain the EMS or they could attempt to achieve additional monetary sovereignty by creating a common currency, which they could at least influence. A compromise position was first flagged in the Delors Report, a document written by central bankers that recommended an independent European central bank on the Bundesbank model with price stability as its primary objective. The Maastricht Treaty gave legal effect to the agreed institutions, and the agreed convergence criteria, which reflected the Bundesbank's belief in fiscal conservatism.

The institutions that underpinned European Monetary Union (EMU) thus reflected a compromise between the trio at the heart of monetary integration; the German and French governments and the Bundesbank. Domestic fiscal policy was heavily constrained by the Growth & Stability Pact agreed in 1995, monetary policy was vested in an independent European Central Bank, which was solely committed to price stability, and national regulators were to remain responsible for regulating resident financial institutions. The central bankers who designed the Euro feared that member states' would run up large deficits. Following the adoption of the Euro, therefore, European policymakers, particularly in the European Commission and European Central Bank, were focused on imposing fiscal rigour and implementing neo-liberal labour market and social security reforms which they believed would increase employment and growth.

However, European policymakers – particularly politicians active in domestic politics – also prided themselves on the distinctiveness of their economic models. They frequently championed neo-liberal measures as means by which domestic welfare states and institutions could be protected. The liberalisation of the financial sector was pursued as a good in itself and cross-border European financial flows were viewed as a benign result of monetary integration and capital liberalisation (See Chart 2.6). Following the adoption of the Euro, financial institutions in the 'core' – with their large balance of payments surpluses – had lent large sums to banks in the periphery, particularly in Spain and Ireland, which were experiencing housing booms (see Chart 2.7). It was in precisely this sector that the financial crisis of 2008 emerged.

Chart 2.6 - External claims (loans and deposits) of BIS Reporting Banks (March 1999 = 100)

Chart 2.7 - Private debt in % of GDP - non consolidated in select Eurozone countries, 2001-2010

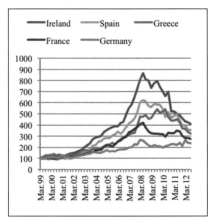

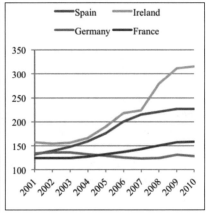

Source: BIS Locational Statistics Table 7A   Source: Eurostat (2013).

The European response to the crisis: Socialising debt, austerity and structural reform: Many European banks had invested heavily in US RMBS and other financial products that plummeted in value after August 2007. Many of these were effectively bailed-out by the US government through its extensive nationalisations of European banks' counter-parties and were heavily supported by the US Federal Reserve through its asset purchase programmes. These measures either preserved the value of the assets the US government had agreed to pay at face value or ensured dollars could be swapped for dollar denominated MBS with a minimal write-down. [3] European governments reluctantly nationalised some of their more egregiously exposed financial institutions in September 2008. However, many governments, particularly in France and Germany, simply refused to acknowledge

---

[3] http://www.bloomberg.com/data-visualization/federal-reserve-emergency-lending/#/overview/?sort=nomPeakValue&group=none&view=peak&position=0&comparelist=&search

the solvency crisis their banking sectors faced. Lacking a European policy and legal framework on banking resolution which would have provided for the winding up of a collapsed financial institution (some countries, such as Ireland, did not have any domestic framework at all for banking resolution), the European Central Bank argued that no bank should be allowed to default.

The structure of inter-European lending – with 'core' banks and financial institutions holding bonds issued by 'peripheral' banks, particularly Spanish and Irish ones – meant that peripheral governments and citizens were required to re-capitalise domestic banks in the interest of protecting the position of foreign bondholders. The ECB feared a 'contagion' resulting from a defaulting bank could collapse the European financial system. However, a concomitant commitment from 'core' countries to buttress their own financial institutions was not required. Essentially, this 'no bondholder left behind' policy was a massive socialisation of the debt accumulated by private banks – arguably representing the largest transfer of wealth, from citizens to private creditors in Europe's history.

There has been one exception to the 'no bondholder left behind' policy – Greece. The crisis in Greece is unique in some respects as it is a genuine fiscal crisis whose origins lie in both a failure of Greek institutions and the Greek political elite. However, instead of recognising and addressing Greece's difficulties the European response has compounded them and contributed to a severe social crisis in Greece. At the same time it has drawn incorrect conclusions which it has sought to apply elsewhere. The Greek fiscal crisis emerged in 2009 when it emerged that the Greek state had falsified its level of national debt with the aid, of US investment banks and others. When the true debt and deficit levels became known Greek bond yields rose precipitously. European policymakers viewed the crisis as entirely a result of Greek profligacy and Greece became the first country to enter an IMF/EU/ECB 'troika' financial aid programme.

In return, the troika demanded that Greece embark on an austerity programme, entailing fiscal consolidation and 'structural reforms' of the Greek state. Some of these were understandable, such as reform of the statistics agency. But others, such as a labour market reform, merely increased job insecurity and unemployment. Two key characteristics of the Greece's institutional problems were ignored: the high level of tax evasion amongst the country's elite and its high level of economic inequality, which is the greatest in the EU. Despite repeated warnings *from some prominent economists* that the austerity programme would precipitate a deep depression and a profound social crisis, European policymakers and the IMF forged ahead. However, the latter at least recognised the impossibility of Greek recovery given the size of its debt burden. Eventually, the European Central Bank and German government came to an agreement and private sector involvement in a write-down of Greek public sector debt was secured.

The nature of the Greek crisis has led to a common conception that the problems arising throughout the Eurozone have been fundamentally problems of public debt. However, this is misleading, as Ireland and Spain ran low deficits, and even surpluses, throughout early 2000s. The current large budget deficits are a result of the economic collapse in the peripheral countries, which is related to the overhang of private debt. Efforts to address rising public debt through tax rises and expenditure cuts have not just failed; they have exacerbated the fall-out from private debt crises in the periphery. The creation of the European Financial Stability Facility (EFSF), which was used to fund the Greek, Irish and Portuguese programmes, and the European Stability Mechanism (ESM), a new permanent facility which will recapitalise the Spanish banking sector and potentially fund the Cypriot programme, has secured funding for peripheral countries. They have been accompanied, however, by conditional austerity programmes.

The current European strategy involves a series of measures:

- reducing deficits throughout the EU through fiscal consolidation;
- lending to distressed countries and requiring they undertake programmes;
- creating a banking union to centralise regulation of European banks and provide a banking resolution scheme;
- creating supervisory structures for the European Commission and other member-states to monitor state's budgets; and
- the writing of a fiscal rule into the law of each member state.

The strategy is informed by a particular analysis of the crisis which puts the blame for it on a combination of lax regulation of the banking sector and insufficient fiscal rigour. However, Greece is the only example of the latter. Based on this erroneous analysis, a disastrous imposition of austerity is leading to high unemployment and stagnation within the Eurozone, even as the ECB and European authorities insist that excessive public debt and deficits are the problem and that 'socialised' private debt must be repaid.

Box 2.1 - The 'Sixpack' and the Fiscal Compact – Solving the wrong problem

The Treaty on Stability, Coordination and Governance, otherwise known as the Fiscal Compact, entered into force on 1 January 2013. An intergovernmental treaty rather than an EU treaty, it was subject to a referendum in Ireland. Many of the provisions within the Treaty were already contained in the 'Sixpack' measures agreed by the European Parliament and Council in 2011. These measures increased budgetary surveillance of member-states within the Excessive Deficit Procedure (EDP). The Stability and Growth Pact rules require government deficits to be 3% or less; government debt to GDP ratio to be 60% or less; Government structural deficits to be 0.5% or less;. They do permit the structural deficit to be up to 1% if debt to GDP is significantly below 60% and they require a 1/20th reduction in debt per year if a country has a debt to GDP ratio above 60%. However, there is an allowance that a member-state can deviate from the need to implement adjustment under 'exceptional circumstances'. The Fiscal Compact upon which the Irish people voted required countries to transpose automatic mechanisms into national law. *Social Justice Ireland* welcomed greater budgetary monitoring but expressed concern that the Treaty would not address the economic crisis, nor prevent future economic crises.

Social Justice Ireland continues to argue that this is a crisis caused by accumulations of private debt – except for the unique Greek example. The fiscal compact would not have prevented Ireland or Spain from experiencing a fiscal crisis, as both countries ran budget surpluses before the crisis (See Chart 2.1.1). The structural deficit measure, which is meant to measure the deficit as a % of potential GDP and take account of cyclical changes in the economy, is notoriously indeterminate, given disagreements on the measurement of potential GDP. Moreover, *Social Justice Ireland* is still concerned that placing fiscal policy on a statutory footing restricts the role of democratic deliberation in making economic decisions. If the Fiscal Compact is not accompanied by investment programmes and a generous interpretation of structural deficit figures it has the potential to become, in the words of Nobel prize-winning economist Joseph Stiglitz, a 'suicide pact' (Moore, 2012).

Chart 2.1 – General Government Deficit as % of GDP, 2002-2009

While European policymakers have agreed to reduce the interest rates on ESFS and EMS loans to programme countries, there has been little debt relief agreed with Ireland and Portugal. In June 2012 the Euro Area Group and European Council, though reaffirming a European commitment to structural reforms and fiscal consolidation, agreed to recapitalise banks directly through the ESM. They also agreed that the link between bank debt and national debt should be broken, raising the possibility of relief for Spain and Ireland. Recognising that banking debt is a European problem and that Spanish citizens should not bear sole responsibility for the actions of their private banks, Spanish banks may be recapitalised directly by the ESM. However, senior national politicians in Europe have questioned whether the agreement could or should apply retrospectively to the recapitalisation of Irish banks.

The European strategy has also raised serious questions about the democratic nature of EU institutions. In particular, the crisis has placed the ECB – an unelected institution – in an extremely powerful position *vis-à-vis* Euro area member-states and other European institutions. Guaranteed independence by the European treaties, the ECB has played a dominant role in dictating the European response. It has chosen to support private bank borrowing – and arguably in the Greek debt write-down to support private banks' prerogatives over those of the Greek state and people – rather than state borrowing up to 2012. Debates within the ECB about the appropriate role of monetary policy have remained opaque and citizens and parliamentarians rely on interviews given by executives and Board members. The ECB announced plans in August 2012 for unlimited purchases in secondary bond markets of selected government bonds in the event of yields rising above a certain level through an Outright Monetary Transactions (OMT) mechanism. This announcement has produced a reduction in the bond yields of non-programme peripheral countries. However, the ECBs commitment to purchasing government debt on secondary markets has yet to be tested. Furthermore, the inclusion of a conditionality clause puts additional question marks over the legitimacy of the ECB interfering in domestic policy and its role in furthering European integration in this way.

During the early 1990s some commentators – particularly economist historians – expressed doubts about the viability of creating a common currency union along the model of the Eurozone (see e.g. Krugman, 1994: 182-187; von Hagen and Eichengreen, 1996). Economists argued that the Euro area was not and is still not an 'optimal currency union' (OCU). In practice, language and cultural barriers still restrict labour mobility and each member-state still retains distinctive economic institutions (see Mundell, 1961 for the original concept). Therefore, while economic recessions may remain local phenomena, countries are deprived of monetary policy tools, such as devaluation, which have traditionally been used to combat such recessions. Using the conceptual framework of an OCU, it is arguable that a fiscal union can smooth exogenous shocks, possibly negating the problems of factor immobility (Cooper & Hempf, 2004). Yet efforts to introduce redistribution between Eurozone members through the use of commonly issued Eurobonds have been rejected. Some leaders believed that this would lead to a 'transfer union', with stronger members permanently subsidising weaker ones – although this view ignores the cyclical nature of market economies.

The President of the ECB has argued that what is required is 'the collective commitment of all governments to reform the governance of the euro area'. This means completing economic and monetary union along four key pillars: (i) a financial union, with a single supervisor at its heart, to re-unify the banking system; (ii) a fiscal union with enforceable rules to restore fiscal capacity; (iii) an economic union that fosters sustained growth and employment; and (iv) political union, in which the exercise of shared sovereignty is rooted in political legitimacy' (James, 2013). As Professor Harold James noted in the 2013 T.K Whitaker lecture in Dublin, this is an extraordinarily uncomfortable proposal for many Europeans. Yet European institutions – at least for those within the EMU – are currently unable to face the crisis. The monetary union is now somewhat akin to the 19th century gold standard (even though that was more flexible than popularly imagined), with the burden of economic adjustment falling entirely on the populations of countries with budget deficits. As Dr. Draghi and European policymakers recognise, this is unsustainable. It is also unsustainable that such decisions are taken without consulting European citizens. Ireland needs to debate publicly the trajectory of the European Union. Such a debate must reach beyond even the immediate and pressing concerns surrounding the link between Ireland's private bank and national debt burdens and focus instead on what type of European Union Irish citizens seek for the future.

Whenever he was challenged about the role of the ECB and the dangers of monetary union in the early 1990s, Jacque Delors used to reply that 'social Europe is coming'. Unfortunately, the response to the crisis has ignored 'social Europe'. Indeed, the European response has been to dismantle many of the social protections that Delors considers to constitute the pinnacle of European achievement. The role of a 'social Europe' in the coming debate on Ireland's place in Europe must be central. This will require Irish politicians to take a hard look at their own role in promoting or dismantling 'social Europe' over the last 20 years.

International and European developments since the crisis have given rise to a number of important questions:
- What is needed to ensure effective and efficient regulation – at both national and international level – of the world's financial systems and how can the current situation of moral hazard be eliminated?

- Will the June 2012 agreement on breaking the link between banking debt and sovereign debt be honoured?
- How is democracy to be protected within the European Union when the unaccountable European Central Bank has taken a leading role in questions of fiscal and social policy? What role will the ECB play in a member state's political affairs if that state requires the implementation of the Outright Monetary Transactions mechanism?
- What kinds of institutions are required in the European Union to preserve and expand a 'Social Europe', and ensure the stability of EMU?
- How is rising income inequality in the developed world to be addressed?
- What needs to be done to ensure that economic development and social development are given equal priority in countries across the world?
- How is the environment to be protected and sustainability secured?

2.1.3 The Irish background

Ireland is a small open economy, one of the most open in the world, and an international recession was bound to have implications for this country's economic growth, jobs and trade. Consequently, the severity of the recent international recession would of itself have had serious implications for Ireland and ensured that this country experienced a contraction in economic activity. However, the recession experienced since 2008 has been far more severe and protracted than it might have been otherwise due to an array of national policies and decisions over recent decades. Ireland may have been unfortunate to have experienced national and international recession at the same time but domestic economic problems would have led a substantial economic slowdown, notwithstanding international developments. This section examines the economic and social background to Ireland's economic crisis.

The early years of the independent Irish state were characterised by a stagnant economy and a government committed to low taxes, low spending, a balanced budget, a minimal state, retention of the link with sterling and sustaining cattle exports to the Britain. The election of new government in 1932 saw more interventionist economic policies, a limited commitment to increase social security spending and an attempt to industrialise Ireland by encouraging native capitalists behind tariff barriers. However, despite this change policymakers were focused on maintaining a balance of payments surplus, which tended to dictate fiscal policy. Even after the adoption of the Keynesian distinction between capital and current spending in 1948, a balance of payments surplus remained the key policy goal, leading to a series of severely contractionary budgets, such as that of 1952.

The 1950s were a particularly dark time in Ireland's economic history. Persistent emigration, reflecting the lack of employment opportunities, meant that Ireland's population reached its lowest level since the pre-Famine high in 1958. Ireland did not share in the Golden Age economic growth of Western Europe. In the following years Ireland's economic policy was significantly re-orientated along the lines outlined in *Economic Development*, a tentative document written by a T.K.Whitaker, secretary of the Department of Finance. As a result, Ireland in the 1960s pursued a policy of indicative planning, removing protectionist barriers, investment in public education and public services and an industrial policy which gave tax concessions to induce foreign owned firms to set up industries in Ireland. Emigration halted during this decade and it seemed as if Ireland could eventually converge with other Western European nations.

The economic environment in the 1970s was as difficult for Ireland as for other countries and governments engaged in deficit spending to sustain employment and economic expansion. Despite a difficult global environment, Ireland seemed well-placed to achieve sustained economic growth by joining the European Union, despite concerns about protected industry; pursuing well-focused industrial policies; reaping the benefits of strong investment in education since the mid-1960s and by having a favourable geographic location for European markets and an English speaking labour force. In an attempt to restart growth, the new government elected in 1977 pursued a strongly expansionary fiscal policy. The programme was strongly influenced by electoral considerations rather than strategic priorities, however, and expected growth and employment targets were missed. Ireland's largest trading partner remained Britain and when that country embarked on a heavily deflationary fiscal and monetary contraction in 1979 Ireland was badly affected. As happened in France in the early 1980s, the effectiveness of fiscal measures in Ireland were severely constrained by external economic conditions.

In 1979 Ireland joined the EMS, breaking the link with sterling. Successive devaluations within the exchange rate mechanism (ERM) of the EMS provided some respite. During the 1980s governments were committed to fiscal contraction, with increased income and consumption taxes between 1982 and 1984. A declining economy, however, led to increased social spending, which threw this effort off course. In 1987 a particularly sharp contraction was attempted, with a large part of the effect felt in government capital spending (See Box 2.2). In many respects Ireland was fortunate that the Lawson Boom in Britain mitigated some of the deleterious effects of this policy, but key services were badly affected and emigration between 1987 and 1989 reached levels not seen again until 2009. The Social Partnership process begun in 1987 – a stronger, more cohesive effort than previous attempts at an Irish incomes policy – provided a framework to secure stability and industrial peace.

Box 2.2 - Learning the wrong lessons from the 1980s – The Myth of an 'Expansionary Fiscal Contraction'

Some policymakers, including former ECB President Jean-Claude Trichet, have argued that Ireland's fiscal contraction in the late 1980s constituted a so-called 'expansionary fiscal contraction' (EFC) (Trichet, 2004). A paper published by Giavazzi and Pagano (1990) declared that Ireland's 1987-1989 contraction was expansionary – in other words, it caused the economy to grow – because they assumed that households and firms increased consumption in response to a credible fiscal policy that promised deficit reduction and thus lower future taxation. This is based on the theory of rational expectations – that individuals and firms all seek to maximise utility and profits – and the associated 'Ricardian equivalence', which assumes that higher spending will not change individual behaviour because citizens will assume the tax burden will increase in the future. Barry and Devereux (2003: 2) have noted that this view was characteristic of the German 'Treasury' position in the early 1980s. Alesina and Ardagna (2010) updated the thesis, arguing that fiscal contractions that concentrated on the spending side could be expansionary. While this idea gained some credence in the 1990s it has been disproved by the events of the last five years, and policymakers – albeit not in the ECB – have moved away from it. However, it did prove very influential in European policymakers' initial response to the crisis and it has unfortunately created a pervasive myth in Irish public life. This led some policymakers to believe that if they are just 'tough' enough with public spending the economy will eventually rebound. It has also led to persistent underestimation of the effect of fiscal contractions by some Irish policymakers. This 'just one more austerity budget and we will turn the corner' attitude leads to short-term policy decisions based on a profoundly mistaken view of the recent past.

In fact, while many Irish economists agree that the fiscal contraction of the 1980s was desirable, they have generally observed that no expansionary fiscal contraction actually occurred. Using similar theoretical assumptions to Giavazza and Pagano (1990), Bradley and Whelan (1997), for example, argued that the contractionary fiscal policy of the late 1980s was contractionary, and that expansionary fiscal policy in Britain – the 'Lawson Boom' – mitigated the effects of Irish fiscal policy. Honohan and Walsh (2002: 15) noted that the idea of 'the confidence story underlying the simplified version of the EFC hypothesis has an uphill struggle to find empirical support in Ireland'. Kinsella (2012: 234) has recently argued that the combined effects of a devaluation in

August 1986 following a depreciation of sterling, growth in the international economy from 1987, low corporate taxes, fiscal transfers from the EU, high emigration (which reduced the social security bill), real wage increases, and a bumper tax yield produced by the tax amnesty all point to a 'proto-Keynesian' story of convergence. O'Gráda's (2011) analysis is broadly similar: 'The Irish economy had failed to grow at all between 1980 and 1986; then, spurred on by well-executed currency devaluations, a booming UK economy, a successful tax amnesty and the beginnings of social partnership, in the following decade it would grow by more than five per cent annually'. Internationally, a former advocate of EFC has argued that he was mistaken, and that all the countries he had studied – apart from Denmark –owed their expansions to a combination of currency devaluations and an incomes policy (Perotti, 2011).

As O'Gráda (2011) has pointed out, Ireland lacks many of the policy options it had in the late 1980s. Irish policymakers must acknowledge this and recognise the increased risks of 'front-loading' austerity. Irish advocates of increasing the pace of fiscal consolidation tend to argue that it will increase debt sustainability and/or creditworthiness, rather than that it would expand the economy (Irish Fiscal Advisory Council, 2012: 60).

Neo-liberal policies have often been adopted unevenly, with distinct varieties conditioned by domestic institutions but all influenced by common trends, such as intellectual shifts within the discipline of economics, and by the effects of the liberalisation of trade and capital markets and globalisation of production. Ireland adapted to these processes – the policy framework adopted since 1987 can be termed 'neo-liberal'. The income accruing to the top 10% has moved accordingly (Chart 2.8). A low corporate tax regime and a highly educated workforce encouraged the siting of multinational manufacturing facilities in Ireland, contributing to employment growth and tax revenue (perhaps more through additional income tax receipts than corporate income *per se*). The liberalisation of capital enabled the development of an Irish Financial Services Centre in the Dublin Docklands. However, these developments were not without disadvantages, some of which have become particularly obvious during the last five years.

In terms of domestic institutions, Ireland moved towards private sector, mortgage finance driven provision of housing, while social and affordable housing was side-lined. In a process familiar internationally, income taxes and capital taxes were reduced while user charges were increasingly relied upon to fund specific services. Public services were increasingly moved into the private sector and semi-state corporations were privatised. While these processes were indicative of neo-liberal trends globally, Ireland also included quite specific institutions. Social Partnership provided a framework in which otherwise excluded groups gained an input into public policy and industrial peace was secured through negotiated pay rounds.

Chart 2.8 – Share of total income earned by the top 10% of income-earners, 1975-2009[4]

Chart 2.9 – Irish Unemployment, 1960-2011

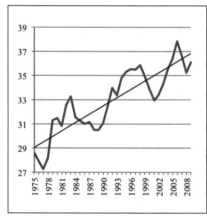

Source: Nolan, (2007), updated by author.   Source: AMECO, 2013

Ireland's extremely high unemployment in the 1980s slowly began to fall in the mid to late 1990s (see Chart 2.9). Ireland's employment patterns and GDP per capita rapidly converged towards developed country norms. Honohan and Walsh (2002) have persuasively argued that the rapid growth rates of the mid to late 1990s were a sign of Ireland belatedly enjoying the growth rates of the 'Golden Age' of European capitalism (Chart 2.10 and Chart 2.11). During the late 1980s and early 1990s growth had been export-led and, although employment in the export manufacturing sector grew, unemployment remained stubbornly high. Moreover, the tight fiscal policy of the late 1980s was not conducive to employment growth. The collapse of the ERM of the EMS in 1993 led to the punt being placed on a

---

[4] The methodology used in Nolan's calculations differs from that used in our chapter on income distribution.

managed float, which in turn led to lower real interest rates than there would have been in the ERM.

Chart 2.10 – Convergence: Ireland and the Netherlands GDP per capita at constant prices (2005) in '000, 1960-2002

Chart 2.11 – Irish Growth in GDP per capita, 1960-2010 in relation to the EU-15 (EU-15 = 100)

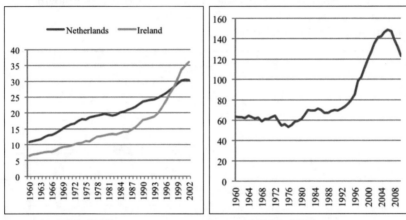

Source: AMECO (2013).   Source: AMECO (2013).

From the mid-1990s Ireland's employment patterns were transformed in three ways. Firstly, the proportion of Ireland's population that was employed converged with the levels experienced elsewhere in Europe and the OECD. In 1989 only 31 per cent of Ireland's population was in employment. This proportion climbed to over 45 per cent by the end of the following decade. Secondly, the proportion of the labour force that was employed grew dramatically in the decade and a half from the early 1990s while the proportion unemployed fell dramatically after a period of jobless growth in the early 1990s. Thirdly, the labour force itself grew dramatically, increasing by over 900,000 during the 1990s. A key change in all of this was the increase in female participation in the labour force. Between 1990 and 2000 the number of females in the Irish labour force increased by almost 250,000 and the female labour force participation rate rose from 44 per cent to 56 per cent (OECD Labour Force Database, 2010).

This labour force driven growth was complemented by a very strong growth in productivity, as measured by average output, during the 1990s. Though some of this was illusory, produced by the practice of transfer pricing by multinational corporations, productivity growth was a reality. Productivity growth is the main determinant of long-term, sustained economic growth and contributed heavily to Ireland's rapid economic expansion in the 1990s. However, as Ireland's productivity levels converged towards that of world-leading countries the underlying pace of such growth slowed.

From 2000/2001, growth was driven by population growth and an extraordinary credit boom, which financed speculation and construction activity in the residential and commercial property sectors. This population growth and the consequent increase in labour supply and economic activity was supported by a huge increase in immigration and it was unlikely that it would be sustainable over a long period. By 2000/2001 Ireland had lost focus on productivity growth as the key to improving living standards and focussed simply on economic growth.

Three false conclusions
In effect, Ireland had reached three false conclusions: that economic growth was a good in itself and could be pursued through the construction sector; that deregulated finance was both more efficient and more stable; and that lower taxation was conducive to long-term growth and could still be used to finance social security and public investment. Each of these played a role in exacerbating the severity of the financial crisis.

Government became fixated with economic growth. It became convinced that economic growth was good in itself and that the higher the rate of economic growth, therefore, the greater the benefits that would accrue to the Irish people as a whole. It followed that whatever was believed to support economic growth was to be facilitated and whatever restricted economic growth was to be resisted. Consequently, Ireland followed a very questionable pathway, putting considerable faith in the ability of a highly incentivised property and construction sector to maintain the high growth levels enjoyed in previous years.

For several years, commencing in 2000/2001, growth in housing activity masked Ireland's deteriorating 'fundamentals'[5]. As Ireland's per-capita income grew, so too did the demand for housing. As we detail in chapter 7 of this review, Ireland's housing construction rose from 19,000 completions in 1990 to a peak of over 93,000 completions in 2006. While there were 48,413 households on local

---

[5] We examine Housing and Accommodation issues in more detail in chapter 7 of this review.

authority waiting lists for social housing in 2002, this level of housing construction was unsustainable. Most of the new construction was for private housing. Of the 57,695 houses completed in 2002, 51,932 were private housing. Of the 93,419 completed in 2006, 88,211 were private housing. Overall, the number of houses in Ireland rose from 1.2 million homes in 1991 to 1.4 million in 2000 and then exploded to 1.9 million in 2008. By 2007, construction accounted for 13.3 per cent of all employment, the highest share in the OECD (OECD, 2010). The property bubble produced over-priced housing, the product of foolish lending, irrational borrowing and unrealistic profit expectations.[6] The legacy of this policy disaster was empty housing units, many of them in inappropriate locations, negative equity and high numbers of unemployed construction workers.

This level of construction was encouraged and supported by many factors. Three key factors were:

- Very low interest rates. Ireland's entry into the Euro area eliminated currency risks. Moreover, low inflation and growth rates in the Euro – particularly in the 'core' – led to the ECB to set low interest rates. This allowed Irish banks to borrow heavily from 'core' banks at relatively low rates, and lend to Irish firms and households.
- Large tax incentives for construction provided by the Irish Government and lax planning regulations.
- Unsustainable house price and commercial property price inflation and profiteering. Ireland's largest developers and senior bankers formed strong alliances, and their perceived successes were highly praised by the media and prized by politicians.

The fixation on economic growth was combined with a second false conclusion – a deep faith in the capability of deregulated finance to provide credit for investment in housing and business. Since Irish independence there had been, and remains, a certain deference towards Irish banking institutions. Moreover, global trends in the liberalisation of finance influenced the intellectual culture amongst policy makers so that there was a particular predisposition to less regulation of finance. This deference and the intellectual adherence to neo-liberal ideas contributed to the idea that finance should not be regulated and that market solutions to questions such as the supply of housing maximised human welfare.

---

[6] See Drudy, Healy, Reynolds and Collins (2011) who discuss this further.

Irish policymakers had entered the Euro with the knowledge that interest rates would be determined by inflation figures in the largest Eurozone economies. As such, they should have put in place tax policies, regulatory policies and housing policies that would have had the effect of restricting the growth of credit in the property sector. House price inflation could have been ameliorated by public provision of housing and commercial property growth could have been controlled through planning regulations.

Box 2.3 – The Construction and Property Bubble – A Failure of Housing policy.
Countries whose housing policies were orientated towards expanding home-ownership through the private financing and construction of housing witnessed a rapid appreciation of house prices up to 2007 (See Graph).

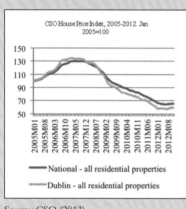

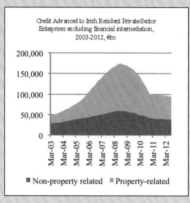

Source: CSO (2013).   Source: Central Bank of Ireland (2013).

In the European Union, Ireland and Spain were at the forefront of this development. This led to a rapid expansion of property related debt as a % of GDP and concomitantly the expansion of construction activity and employment. It is now widely accepted – by a series of banking reports – that the banking sector was subject to 'light-touch' regulation and that the directors and management of banks behaved recklessly (Regling &Watson, 2010; Commission of Investigation into the Banking Sector in Ireland, 2011; Honohan, 2010). Credit was increasingly directed at construction-related Irish firms (see Graph), towards households forced to secure a home on the private market and towards individuals seeking to speculate in the housing market.

Despite the high level of activity, housing policy actually led to lower levels of owner-occupancy, while leaving an excess of vacant houses. While speculative activity was also focused on the commercial sector, particularly on the construction of buildings whose functions attracted extensive tax reliefs, such as hotels and hospitals, the failure of housing policy was particularly egregious and it has left many people who sought only to purchase their own homes in negative equity, or far more seriously, in unable to make full repayments on their mortgages.

Similarly, the International Financial Services Centre (IFSC) came to play an increasingly important role in the eyes of policymakers. Here, too, the regulation of branches of international banks was minimal. The perceived benefit accruing to professional services firms, namely the legal and accounting professions, and subsequent employment growth in those sectors was one factor influencing on lax regulation of the IFSC and the creation of an accommodating tax code. This has led to the IFSC having a disproportionate influence on policymaking in Ireland, which has had a negative influence on Ireland's relations with the major Euro area nations. Ireland came to be regarded as the 'Financial Wild West' of Europe and its policymakers' reactive defence of the IFSC and opposition to such measures as the Financial Transactions Tax (FTT) has often antagonised key allies (Lavery & O'Brien, 2005). Moreover, the long-term effect of maintaining what a US Congressional report classes as a 'tax-haven' has been to facilitate the growth of the global shadow-banking industry which deprives both developed and developing countries' of tax revenue and contributes to global financial instability (Gravelle, 2013).

During this period Ireland had reached a third false conclusion in relation to taxation[7]. It had come to believe that low taxation was good in itself and that reducing tax rates would lead inevitably to an increase in tax revenues. The theory was that 'giving people back their own money', through the reduction of capital and income taxes, was far better than investing that money in developing and improving infrastructure and services. The reduction of capital taxes and provision of pension tax relief in particular benefited the wealthiest in society. The result of these beliefs was that by the end of the Celtic Tiger years Ireland had one of the lowest total tax-takes in the EU. At the same time, while there had been some

---

[7] We review these issues in greater detail in chapter 4 of this review.

improvements in areas such as housing, public transport and social welfare during those years, many aspects of Ireland's infrastructure and social services remained far below EU-average levels. A strong assumption persisted that infrastructure and social services could be improved to EU-average levels at the same time as one of the lowest total tax-takes in the EU was maintained. This belief endured despite the very strong efforts of some policy analysts to convince Government and policy-makers otherwise.

By 2007 Ireland had 'run out of road', with no scope for any further substantial improvement in the population/labour force/employment situation. The labour market had become over-heated and was relying on inward migration to sustain supply. At the same time, productivity was weakening, the tax-base was narrowing and economic activity was concentrated on the construction and property sector, while government had become reliant on revenue from property-related transactions. Yet, even with a serious slowdown inevitable, the General Election of 2007 was still fought on the generally accepted assumption that growth would average 4.5 per cent per year over the 2007-2012 period. All political parties, with just one exception, drew up their manifestos on this basis. Those who challenged this assumption of continued growth were rejected, often with derision.

Eight false assumptions
Overall, Ireland's policy-making during this period was underpinned by a series of false assumptions and conclusions. These included:

* Economic growth was good in itself and the higher the rate of economic growth the better it would be for Ireland.
* Everyone would enjoy the benefits of economic growth, which would trickle down automatically.
* Infrastructure and social services at an EU-average level could be delivered with one of the lowest total tax-takes in the EU.
* The growing inequality and the widening gaps between the better-off and the poor that followed from this approach to policy-development were not important because 'a rising tide lifts all boats'.
* Low taxation was an unqualified good.
* Reducing tax rates would lead inevitably to an increase in tax revenues.
* 'Giving people back their own money', through reducing taxes was far better than investing that money in developing and improving infrastructure and services. The sum of individual decisions would produce greater and more lasting prosperity than the collective decisions of the Irish people.

- Ireland had a great deal to teach the rest of the world, particularly about how it could reach full employment, generate rapid and sustained economic growth and provide for all the society's needs while having one of the lowest total tax-takes in the Western world.

Eight policy failures

Arising from this series of false policy conclusions and false assumptions, there were many resulting policy failures. Among these were:

- Failure to take action to broaden the tax base by, for example:
  - introducing a property tax;
  - removing existing tax exemptions which have no demonstrated benefit-cost advantage;
- Failure to promote tax equity by, for example, introducing Refundable Tax Credits.
- Failure to overcome infrastructure deficiencies, such as in broadband, public transport, primary health care, water, energy, social housing and waste.
- Failure to adequately address high energy costs.
- Failure to create a universal health service based on need.
- Failure to address income inequality.
- Failure to appropriately regulate the banking, financial and professional services sector.
- Failure to manage the growth of personnel numbers in the public service.

2.2 Ireland in 2013: the context

In this section we analyse where Ireland stands today. We assess various dimensions of the current crisis and subsequently explore the present context in economic, social, political and cultural terms.

2.2.1 The Emergence of the Crisis

Irish policymakers were initially slow to realise the consequences of the liquidity problems that emerged in global financial markets in August 2007. This was largely due to the false assumptions of the bubble years and intellectual dominance of neo-liberalism. As a result, there was a widespread belief that 'light-touch' regulation ensured that bank runs and insolvencies were unthinkable. Moreover, Irish bank's exposure was not to international capital markets but to the domestic and British commercial and residential property markets. Despite preparation following the bank run on Northern Rock in the UK, senior policymakers were taken by surprise when informed by the Irish banks that they required funds to meet the obligations to pay for maturing liabilities because international money markets were unwilling to lend to Irish banks. This led to the decision to guarantee all domestic bank liabilities in September 2008, which pledged the taxpayer to pay all bank liabilities in full at face value, whether they were deposits – ordinarily guaranteed up to a certain limit by governments – or bonds.

This precipitous and unwise decision to socialise the banking debt accumulated throughout the bubble years surprised many of Ireland's trading partners; though the 'no bondholder left behind' was later affirmed as a Euro area policy by the European Central Bank.[8] By January 2009 the government was forced to nationalise one of the guaranteed banks, Anglo-Irish Bank, given the sheer scale of its insolvency, and to re-capitalise two others using the National Pension Reserve Fund. Government was loath to nationalise the remaining banks. The intellectual antipathy towards nationalisation remained too strong amongst policymakers and during 2009 and early 2010 government was willing to allow private ownership of insolvent private banks whose liabilities had been guaranteed in full.

The rapid downturn in the construction sector and credit freeze precipitated by the crisis led to a rapid fall in tax revenues. As unemployment rose – initially job losses focused in the construction sector – social expenditure rose. Policymakers had come to view the economic crisis of the 1980s as a public finance crisis. Consequently, it was believed that a rapid fiscal consolidation enacted in Budget 2009 would prevent a repeat of the experience of the 1980s. However, policymakers failed to appreciate that, as with the 1980s, the economic problems facing Ireland were multifaceted. The bank guarantee had joined the fate of the Irish state, economy and society to that of the Irish private banking sector.

The dangers of attempting an austerity policy in the face of a 'balance-sheet' recession – characterised by private firms and households holding debts larger than the value of the underlying assets – have been highlighting by many economic commentators and the effects of Irish austerity have borne them out. Output has contracted rapidly, partly under the pressure of austerity, reducing government's tax revenue. This has led to remarkably little reduction in Ireland's deficit to GDP

---

[8] There remains considerable confusion about the events leading up to and immediately after the bank guarantee was issued on the night of the 29th September. No definitive account of the events has yet emerged.

figures, due to a combination of successive bank bailouts, leading to an onerous interest schedule, and the reduction of GDP due to austerity. Between 2008 and 2010 the policy of austerity failed to increase market and investor confidence and the continuing insolvency of Ireland's banks led to increasing doubts about the future solvency of the Irish state, as reflected by steadily rising bond yields on Irish government debt. Attempts were made to enforce some kind of burden sharing on those who held the debt of Irish private banks. However, the European Central Bank insisted that there could be no write-downs on any Euro area bank debt, even as unemployment rose rapidly in Ireland and the country came under severe pressure on international debt markets.

Though the Irish state had raised significant cash reserves, in September and November 2010 European leaders placed considerable pressure on Irish leaders to be placed in an IMF/EU programme. It was feared that high bond yields on Irish government debt would have a contagion effect on other vulnerable Euro area economies. Senior Irish policymakers – both elected and unelected – appeared to be publicly at odds during this period, though the government eventually accepted entry into an IMF/EU programme. However, the confusion surrounding the decision to seek a loan from the IMF and EU has yet to be dispelled. Ireland's IMF/EU programme required fiscal consolidation to bring the deficit to GDP ratio below the 3% prescribed in the Growth and Stability Pact. In addition, a structural adjustment programme comprising reforms to social security and the labour market and privatisation of public utilities was agreed as part of the programme. Ireland has now entered its third year of the programme and its sixth year of austerity.

2.2.2 Ireland's Five-part Crisis

Today, Ireland remains in crisis. At the beginning of this period the National Economic and Social Council (NESC, 2009) summarised this crisis as having five closely related dimensions, summarised below. These provide an important analytical framework for addressing the Irish crisis. Although it has been nearly five years since NESC formulated its analysis, these crises have persisted, with some becoming more severe than others.

A banking crisis in which the taxpayer has responsibility for rescuing all the major banks and financial institutions from the consequences of the dishonesty and incompetence of individuals and institutions which were responsible for managing and regulating our financial system. So far, the socialisation of debt has been unrelenting, though a significant breakthrough was achieved in June 2012 at the

Euro area meeting, holding out the prospect of the ESM purchasing the Irish governments shares in private banks.

However, the only result of that meeting so far has been a decision, taken in early February 2013, to liquidate Irish Resolution Bank Corporation (IRBC), redistribute its assets and liabilities and convert the promissory note used to fund the bank to long-term government debt, which will yield some Exchequer savings. This arrangement needs to go further in terms of interest rates and maturities. The June 2012 decision on bank debt should be fully respected so that additional relief is granted in relation to the IRBC promissory note.

Some of the questions addressed by NESC (2009) have become even more pressing:

- The need to ensure that policy measures provide protection to the increasing number of households with mortgage arrears. In September 2012, 86,146 (11.3 per cent) private residential mortgage accounts for principal dwelling houses were in arrears of over 90 days (Central Bank of Ireland, 2012);
- The need to ensure that those who led Irish financial institutions into their current reliance on the state, and who were major beneficiaries of the boom, are being held accountable and are bearing their share of the adjustment burden;
- The need to persuade our EU partners, other international institutions and participants in the global financial market that a new regulatory regime and governance culture is being created in Ireland.

A public finance crisis – because we are borrowing far more than we are collecting in taxes. To bring Ireland back into line with our EU/IMF commitments, major budgetary adjustments have been required and will be required over the next few years. We discuss the nature of these changes later in this chapter. However, as the NESC has noted, these fiscal adjustments need to be considered and implemented, not just with regard to how they address the gap between taxes and spending but also with regard to the impact these adjustments may have on the other dimensions of Ireland's challenges, such as the economic crisis, the social crisis and the country's reputation. (NESC, 2009: x).

Social Justice Ireland also believes that the pace of fiscal consolidation has been too great, and that both government and the EU/IMF have underestimated the damaging effects of sharp budget cuts and tax rises, which have contributed sharp reductions in domestic demand and investment, and subsequently to the stagnation of Ireland's economy. Government and the EU/IMF should take account of international evidence which points to the dangers of rapid fiscal consolidation, particularly when such a strategy is in concert with major trading partners and fellow EU member-states. Greater consideration should be given to the role of economic stimulus in spurring investment, which increases the rate of economic growth and thus reduces the budget deficit as a percentage of GDP.

An economic crisis – because we have lost many jobs and, throughout much of the last decade, undermined our competitiveness. The speed, depth and nature of Ireland's economic decline demands a policy response which collectively addresses what NESC described as "a difficult set of overlapping and competing objectives and factors" (NESC, 2009: *xi*). These include:

- the employment situation – particularly the threat of further unemployment and, in particular, large levels of long-term unemployment;
- Ireland's loss of competitiveness over the past decade;
- the evolution of prices, including policy instruments that influence input costs to business, professional fees and rents;
- the level of domestic demand;
- the state of the public finances, which are directly affected by public sector pay developments and indirectly influenced by wider unemployment, economic and income developments; and
- the burden of mortgage debt, particularly on those who become unemployed, and social solidarity, encompassing the whole of Irish society, not just those whose incomes are determined through collective bargaining.

Unemployment is now the greatest challenge facing Irish society.

A social crisis – because our social services and social infrastructure are being eroded, unemployment has dramatically increased, incomes are falling, debt levels are rising and the prospect of a sustained period of high long-term unemployment levels now seems unavoidable. While the economic crisis and, in particular, the collapse of private construction provides some opportunities to address the social housing deficit (see chapter 7), policy makers need to be keenly aware that their responses to the other crises should not further undermine the vulnerable in Irish society and the social services and infrastructure on which they depend. The nature of this social crisis is described in greater detail later in this chapter.

A reputational crisis – because our reputation around the world has been damaged for several reasons (NESC, 2009: *xii*):

- The perception that, along with a number of other countries, Ireland has had a lax and ineffective system of regulation of the financial sector;
- The perception that Ireland's response to the banking crisis may not include sufficient change in governance and personnel.

Social Justice Ireland would also add that;
- Ireland's reputation as engaging in tax haven style behaviour damages its reputation with many larger European partners;

The perception that Ireland continues to sees its interests as intimately connected with those of large financial firms – as indicated by governments opposition to the Financial Transactions Tax – perpetuates the idea of Ireland as a 'wild west' of financial deregulation.

2.2.3 The economic context

The dramatic and sudden turnaround in Ireland's economic experiences since 2007 must be considered in the context of its economic growth and expansion throughout the last decade. Clearly, as indicated earlier, there have been a number of major policy failures behind some of this growth – for example, the excessive fuelling of the construction industry and an unregulated banking sector, which represent a massive misallocation of capital. As table 2.3 shows, Ireland's Gross Domestic Product (GDP) and Gross National Income (GNI) have increased significantly since 1997.[9] The final column of the table shows the per-capita value of GNI over the last decade. In the early years it increased in real-terms (after taking account of price changes) by over 30 per cent.[10] However, the current economic slowdown has brought per capita income levels to below the levels experienced in the early years of this century.

---

[9] GDP is calculated as the value of all economic activity that occurs in Ireland. GNI is calculated as GDP minus the net outflow of income from Ireland (mainly involving foreign multinationals repatriating profits), minus EU taxes and plus EU subsidies (for further information see CSO, 2008:76).
[10] We examine the distribution of this income, which was far from even, in chapter 3.

Table 2.3 – Gross Domestic Product (GDP), Gross National Income (GNI), and GNI per capita, 1997-2011

Year	GDP (€b)	GNI (€b)	GNI per capita €*
1997	68.2	60.9	n/a
1998	78.7	69.8	n/a
1999	90.7	78.1	n/a
2000	105.8	91.3	n/a
2001	117.6	99.6	30,488
2002	130.9	108.7	28,854
2003	140.8	120.5	29,755
2004	150.2	129.1	30,391
2005	163.0	141.0	31,393
2006	177.7	155.8	32,645
2007	188.7	163.4	33,136
2008	178.9	154.9	31,927
2009	161.3	134.3	29,200
2010	156.5	131.3	29,368
2011	C159.0	128.3	28,557

Source:AMECO and CSO online database

Note: * Gross National Income per capita at constant 2010 prices;

The speed and severity of Ireland's economic decline is also visible in Chart 2.12. It shows the strength of economic growth between 1995 and 2006 (a period in which most developed world countries experienced 2 to 3 per cent growth per annum) and the rapid decrease between 2007 and 2010. The IMF has forecast a modest increase in world output in 2013 – from 3.2 per cent to 3.5 per cent. But the Euro area economy is expected to continue to contract – by 0.2 per cent – under the influence of fiscal consolidation programmes and deep uncertainty within the Eurozone (IMF, 2013: 2). The IMF expects the Irish economy to expand by 1.1 per cent of GDP in 2013, while the Department of Finance believes it will grow by 1.5 per cent of GDP (IMF, 2012; Department of Finance, 2012).

The scale of the international recession had an impact on the level of exports, which fell by almost 3 per cent in 2009. During that period both the number of workers and hours worked per worker fell as production declined. Exports have subsequently increased, growing by 6 per cent in 2010, 4.6 per cent in 2011 and by 1 per cent in 2012 (CSO, 2012). The rate of export growth has fallen as growth in the Euro area has stalled. Additionally, the 'patent cliff' – a positive development from a developing country perspective – faced by pharmaceutical manufacturers has contributed to a large fall in the value pharmaceutical exports, which dropped by over 7 per cent in 2012 (CSO, 2013).

Chart 2.12: Ireland's GDP Growth, 1995-2015 (%)

Source: OECD (2013); Department of Finance (2012).

The combined effect of these changes on the public finances has been dramatic. Over the decade to 2008 the state had become heavily dependent on tax revenue derived from construction related activities. Indeed, the report by the Governor of the Central Bank estimated that cyclical taxes (Corporation Tax, Stamp Duty and Capital Gains Tax) rose from accounting for 7 per cent of the total tax take in 1987 to 30 per cent in 2006 (Honohan, 2010: 29). In addition, VAT receipts on construction related activity were a temporary boon to the Exchequer. Table 2.4 shows that as the economy declined these revenues rapidly declined. Overall, total tax receipts fell from over €59 billion in 2007 to €43.3 billion in 2010. They rose to €45.3bn in 2011, largely due to the introduction of the Universal Social Charge and a temporary levy on pension funds.[11]

---

[11] In these calculations we have included items such as social insurance contributions that do not appear in the usual Budget calculations on taxation.

Table 2.4 The Changing Nature of Ireland's Tax Revenue, 2007-2011 (€m)

	2007	2008	2009	2010	2011
Taxes on income and wealth					
Income tax (including surtax)	13,563	13,148	11,801	11,315	14,010
Corporation tax	6,393	5,071	3,889	3,944	3,751
Motor tax - Estimated portion paid by households etc.	526	583	582	563	556
Other taxes	5	6	5	8	5
Fees under the Petroleum and Minerals Development Acts	5	10	2	3	3
Training and Employment Levy	411	414	373	310	317
Social Insurance contribution	9,053	9,259	8,924	8,701	7,532
Total Taxes on income and wealth	29,957	28,491	25,575	24,843	26,174
Taxes on capital					
Estate, etc. duties	0	0	0	0	0
Capital gains tax	3,097	1,424	545	345	416
Capital acquisitions tax	391	343	256	237	244
Pension fund levy	0	0	0	0	463
Total Taxes on capital	3,488	1,767	801	582	1,123
Taxes on expenditure					
Custom duties	30	21	11	23	38
Excise duties including VRT	5,993	5,547	4,909	4,824	4,886
Value added tax	14,057	12,842	10,175	9,862	9,588
Residential property tax	0	0	0	0	0
Rates	1,267	1,353	1,471	1,504	1,499
Motor tax - Estimated portion paid by businesses	431	477	476	461	455
Stamps (excluding fee stamps)	3,244	1,763	1,003	962	936
Broadcasting licence fee	23	23	24	27	27
Other fees	171	219	201	259	250
Total taxes on expenditure	25,216	22,246	18,271	17,922	17,678
EU Taxes	519	484	359	400	416
Total Taxation	59,157	52,964	44,861	43,301	45,391

Source: CSO, 2012.

The policy of socialising Ireland's bank debt has imposed large costs on the Exchequer and a large opportunity cost – and potential cost – in terms of the recapitalisation of the banking sector through the National Pension Reserve Fund (NPRF). Table 2.5 details the total cost of the funding of the Irish bank rescue by source of funding. The NPRF, established to meet the future costs of the public sector and contributory state pension bill, has been used as a rescue vehicle for the state's banking sector. This has deprived the state of one of the main resources it had for introducing a counter-cyclical investment policy. The total cost of the banking rescue has been €62.8bn, €16.5bn of which was directed to the banks under the Prudential Capital Assessment Review mandated under the EU/IMF Programme.

In February 2013 a decision was taken to wind up IRBC and substitute the promissory notes for long-dated government date. While the potential to ease austerity is welcome, the transformation of the promissory notes into sovereign debt copper-fastens the transfer of wealth from low and middle-income citizens to those who profited from the decision to rescue Anglo-Irish Bank. Furthermore, the decision is contrary to the June 2012 agreement to retrospectively recognise the principle that bank bondholders should share part of the burden when banks collapse.

Table 2.5 Total Cost of Irish Banking Rescue by Source of Funding and Year (€bn)

	2009	2010	2011	Total
NPRF	7	3.7	10	20.7
Promissory Notes		30.7		30.7
Exchequer	4	0.9	6.5	11.4
Total	11	35.3	16.5	62.8

Source: http://debates.oireachtas.ie/dail/2012/04/18/00157.asp

As shown above, the interaction of falling tax revenues and rising public expenditure brought on by the recession and the cost of the bank bailout led to the EU/IMF Programme. The primary aim of the programme is to reduce the General Government Balance (GGB), a metric used by the European Union to ascertain the budget deficit. This supposes that if the GGB is reduced to a level viewed as sustainable by purchasers of government debt – broadly assumed to be the 3% of GDP outlined in the Stability and Growth Pact – then Ireland can once again fund itself independently. Under the Memorandum of Understanding, which runs till 2015, a deficit reduction programme is set out. Table 2.6 outlines the GGB targets laid out by the Memorandum of Understanding and the nominal targets the government believes necessary to achieve it.

Table 2.6 Planned and Actual GGB reduction path, 2009-2015

	2009	2010	2011	2012	2013	2014	2015
Actual GGD (% of GDP)	-13.9	-30.9	-13.4	-8.3	-7.5	-5	-2.9
Target GGD (% of GDP)	n/a	n/a	-10.1	-8.4	-7.5	-5	-2.9
GGB €m		22,519	-48,607	-21,256	-13,470	-12,645	-8,770	-5,345

Source: AMECO; Medium Term Fiscal Statement, 2012: 26, 91

The IMF, EU and Government initially agreed – in line with both Government and the EU/IMF approach to the economic crisis before 2010 – that deficit reduction should be pursued through a rapid fiscal consolidation weighted towards expenditure cuts. Alternative arguments were initially dismissed and it appeared some policymakers continued to believe in the possibility of an 'expansionary fiscal consolidation', provided adjustment was 'frontloaded'. However, the EU, IMF and Government underestimated the effect of the domestic programme and international austerity on economic growth. The Programme projections included in the IMF's First and Second Review published in May 2011 have deteriorated significantly. Weisbrot and Jorgenson's (2013) analysis of the IMF advice to the EU-27 shows that underestimation of the effects of an austerity programme been a recurring theme in the IMF's initial response to the crisis.

Table 2.7 A Changing Programme: Comparing MoU Projections, April 2011 and December 2012

	2011	2012	2013	2014	2015
MoU 2011 Real GDP Growth	0.6	1.9	2.4	2.9	3.3
MoU 2012 Real GDP Growth	1.4	0.4	1.1	2.2	2.8
MoU 2011 Unemployment (%)	14.5	13.9	13.2	12.3	11.3
MoU 2012 Unemployment (%)	14.6	14.8	14.7	14.2	13.4
MoU 2011 Fiscal Consolidation (€bn)	6	3.6	3.1	n/a	n/a
MoU 2012 Fiscal Consolidation (€bn)	6	3.8	3.5	3.1	2

Source: IMF, 2011; 2012.

Table 2.7 shows the additional fiscal consolidation required to meet the deficit targets agreed with the IMF. If the GGB target is to be met, a lower growth rate requires even greater fiscal consolidation. However, the IMF has signalled that it is worried about the effects of 'fiscal drag' on the recovery of the Irish economy, particularly domestic demand, and has argued that additional austerity should be deferred if the economy continues to deteriorate (IMF, 2012: 11, 15).

Table 2.8 Budgetary Adjustments 2008-2015 (€m)

Adjustment Description	Taxation	Expenditure	Total	Running Total
Adjustment July	2008	1,000	1,000	**1,000**
Budget 2009	1,215	€747	1,962	**2,962**
Adjustments Feb/March 2009		2,090	2,090	**5,052**
Supplementary Budget 2009	3,621	1,941	5,562	**10,614**
Budget 2010	23	4,051	4,074	**14,688**
Budget 2011	1,409	4,590	5,999	**20,687**
Budget 2012	1,600	2,200	3,800	**24,487**
Budget 2013	1,432	1,940	3,372	**27,859**
Budget 2014★	1,100	2,000	3,100	**30,959**
Budget 2015★	700	1,300	2,000	**32,959**
Total of Adjustments	**11,100**	**22,859**		
% Division of Adjustments	**33.68%**	**66.32%**		

Note: ★ indicates projected adjustment from Medium Term Fiscal Review Nov. 2012

Budget 2013 marked the eighth fiscal adjustment to the Irish economy since the beginning of the current economic crisis in 2008. Increases in taxes and decreases in public expenditure brought the total adjustment to date to almost €28 billion. This is equivalent to nearly 15% of the 2007 level of GDP – the highest year of output the Irish economy has experienced. Table 2.8 shows the cumulative impact of tax increases and expenditure cuts since the fiscal consolidation process began in July 2008 and includes the projected consolidation contained in the Memorandum of Understanding. Government has indicated that it intends to remove a further €8.6 billion from the economy over three Budgets from 2013-2015. If these plans are implemented, the overall sum of the adjustments from 2008-2015 will total nearly €33 billion – equivalent to 18 per cent of the GDP forecast for 2015.

The implications of these large and harsh adjustments can be seen in the continued extension of the adjustment plan, the sustained high level of unemployment and the persistent doubts concerning the Irish economy's recovery. Spending cuts and tax increases have meant that households are spending less, investment is falling and it is only export growth – which is entirely driven by non-domestic demand factors – that is pulling the economy out of recession. The effects of a balance-sheet recession compound this effect. Many households are giving priority to punishing repayment schedules on debts incurred over the past decade that mainly relate to the purchase of the family home.

How sustainable is this policy approach? Austerity has led to persistent unemployment and renewed emigration. A recent IMF working paper that found frontloading consolidations during a recession seems to aggravate the costs of fiscal adjustment in terms of output loss and to greatly delay the reduction in the debt-to-GDP ratio. This, in turn, can exacerbate market sentiment towards a country at times of low confidence, defying fiscal austerity efforts altogether (Batini, Callegari and Melina, 2012: 32). *Social Justice Ireland* believes that Government needs to adopt policies to stimulate the economy rather than induce economic stagnation. Domestic demand should be given a chance to recover through policies which promote investment on a much larger scale than that currently planned while further building domestic economic confidence through addressing the unemployment crisis. The latter can be done through such initiatives as our Part Time Job Opportunities proposal to take thousands of unemployed people off the dole queues (outlined in chapter 5).

Achieving these targets will be very challenging given the continuing decline in domestic demand and the difficulties being experienced at international level by Ireland's main trading partners. The Government's projections also assume that the on-going banking crisis does not require the exchequer to further invest in the banks and that the excessive budgetary cuts in recent years do not damage the economy to such an extent that it remains stuck in recession – a risk we have continually highlighted. Given developments locally and internationally, it remains open to question whether Ireland will reach the 3 per cent of GDP borrowing threshold, which is the cornerstone the bailout agreement, by the target date of 2015.

Table 2.9 presents a summary of projections for Ireland over the years 2013-2015. Most of this data is derived from the Department of Finance's Budget 2013 documentation and, where appropriate, we highlight those projections we consider unreliable given the economic and banking events that have occurred since the Budget was presented in December 2012.

Table 2.9: Ireland's Economic Position, 2013-2015	
National Income	
GDP in 2013 (€m)[#]	167,725
GNP in 2013 (€m) [#]	133,900
GDP growth in 2013[#]	1.5%
GNP growth in 2013[#]	0.9%
GDP growth 2013-2015 (average) [#]	2.3% per annum
GNP growth 2013-2015 (average) [#]	1.6% per annum
Exchequer Budgetary Position	
Current Budget Balance, 2013 (€m)[##]	- 9,610
Net Capital Investment, 2013 (€m)	7,810
Capital Investment paid from current resources, 2013 (€m)	Zero
Capital Investment paid from borrowing, 2013 (€m)	All
Exchequer Borrowing, 2013 (€m)	15,400
General Government Balance (%GDP)	-7.5%
Current Budget Balance 2014 (€m)	- 5,955
Current Budget Balance 2014 (€m)	- 2,320
Net Capital Investment 2013-2015 (€m)	7,280 (average)
Exchequer Borrowing 2013-2015 (€m)	11,500 (average)
National Debt 2013 % GDP[*]	117.6%
National Debt 2015 % GDP[*]	116.8%
Inflation and the Labour Market	
HICP inflation in 2012	1.7%
HICP inflation 2013-2015 (average)	1.8% per annum
Unemployment rate in 2013	14.6%
Employment growth in 2013	0.2%
Unemployment rate 2013-2015 (average)	13.9%
Employment growth 2013-2015 (average)	0.8%

Source: Department of Finance, Budget 2013 (various tables) and separate calculations where indicated.

Notes: [*] Adjusted upwards to account for subsequent CSO revisions to GDP and borrowing to fund capital injections into the banks.

[#] This is a Department of Finance Budget 2013 estimate and the actual number is likely to be smaller.

Social Justice Ireland has not only been concerned by the size and speed of the adjustments, but also by their composition. As Table 2.8 shows, one-third of the total adjustment over the period 2008-2015 will be on the spending side. Apart from objections to the size of the consolidation, there are two other important questions about this decision. Are there large and discernible effects observable from the decision to opt for tax rises and new taxes over spending cuts? What type of tax system and social security system would Ireland like to have?

Many commentators have advocated spending cuts over tax rises when attempting to reduce a budget deficit. For example, Alesina and Giavazzi (2012) have argued that there is empirical evidence to support their view that spending cuts are less recessionary than tax cuts. They base this on a belief that spending cuts lead to a permanent expectation of lower taxes in the future, that higher taxes cause entrepreneurs' confidence to fall, thereby influencing investment decisions negatively, which in turn causes output to fall. It also assumes that direct taxes distort otherwise optimal economic behaviour, causing output to fall. This position is similar to that underpinning the idea of 'expansionary fiscal contraction'. However, others have warned – along more traditional Keynesian lines – that cutting public expenditure can have deeper impacts than tax rises on economic output, particularly through drops in consumption amongst financially-constrained households (Batini, Callegari and Melina, 2012).

More importantly, the question of whether to cut the deficit through spending cuts or tax rises reflects a country's priorities. Table 2.10 shows Ireland's position relative to other EU members in terms of its total tax take. Ireland is near the bottom of the rankings.

Of the EU-27 states, the highest tax ratios can be found in Denmark, Sweden, Belgium, Italy, France and Italy while the lowest appear in Latvia, Romania, Slovakia, Bulgaria, Lithuania and Ireland. Overall, Ireland possesses the third lowest tax-take at 28.2 per cent, some 7.4 percentage points below the EU average. The increase in the overall level of taxation between 2002 and 2006 can be explained by short-term increases in construction related cyclical taxation sources (in particular stamp duty and construction related VAT) rather than any underlying structural increase in taxation levels. Ireland's economic adjustment will bring tax take as a proportion of GDP up to 31.7 per cent - still 3.9 percentage points below the 2010 EU average (Department of Finance, 2012).

Table 2.10: Total tax revenue as a % of GDP, for EU-27 Countries in 2010

Country	% of GDP	+/- from average	Country	% of GDP	+/- from average
Denmark	47.6	12.0	Estonia	34.2	-1.4
Sweden	45.8	10.2	Ireland GNP	33.9	-1.7
Belgium	43.9	8.3	Czech Rep	33.8	-1.8
France	42.5	6.9	Malta	33.3	-2.3
Italy	42.3	6.7	Spain	31.9	-3.7
Finland	42.1	6.5	Poland	31.8	-3.8
Austria	42.0	6.4	Portugal	31.5	-4.1
Netherlands	38.8	3.2	Greece	31.0	-4.6
Germany	38.1	2.5	Ireland GDP	28.2	-7.4
Slovenia	38.0	2.4	Slovakia	28.1	-7.5
Hungary	37.7	2.1	Bulgaria	27.4	-8.2
Luxembourg	37.1	1.5	Latvia	27.3	-8.3
Cyprus	35.7	0.1	Romania	27.2	-8.4
United Kingdom	35.6	0.0	Lithuania	27.1	-8.5

Source: Eurostat (2012:180) and CSO National Income and Expenditure Accounts (2012:3)
Notes: All data is for 2010. EU-27 average is 35.6 per cent.

In the context of the figures in Table 2.10 the question needs to be asked: If we expect our economic and social infrastructure to catch up with the rest of Europe, how can we do this while simultaneously gathering less taxation income than it takes to run the infrastructure already in place in most of those other European countries we wish to emulate? In reality, we will never bridge the social and economic infrastructure gaps unless we gather a larger share of our national income and invest it in building a fairer and more successful Ireland.

Social Justice Ireland believes that Ireland should increase its total tax-take to 34.9 per cent of GDP by 2015 – which would still leave Ireland as a low-tax economy as defined by Eurostat).

Another important question is which countries should we choose to benchmark against? Which countries do we wish to emulate, in terms of public services, pensions, social welfare payments and private and public wage rates? Are Latvia, Lithuania, Romania, Slovakia and Bulgaria to be our new benchmark countries?

2.2.4 The social context

Ireland's social context is addressed throughout this review. This section provides a brief overview.

The ramifications for Ireland's citizens of the recent economic turmoil have been severe. Most notably, one of the great achievements of recent years has been reversed in a short period of time. Unemployment has returned as a widespread phenomenon.[12] In late 2006, 90,300 people were recorded as unemployed by the CSO's quarterly national household survey (QNHS). This figure represented 4.2 per cent of the labour force. Six years later, the number of people unemployed had more than tripled to 294,600, equal to approximately 14.2 per cent of the labour force (CSO, 2013). In a relatively short period Ireland returned to levels of unemployment not experienced since the mid-1980s. Behind each of these figures are people and families – the society-wide impact of these increases cannot be over-estimated.

The scale of this unemployment crisis and the simultaneous collapse in employment opportunities has resulted in many people becoming stranded in unemployment. Consequently long-term unemployment, defined as those unemployed for more than one year, has rapidly increased. By late 2012, 176,400 people were recorded as long-term unemployed, a rate equal to 8.2 per cent of the entire labour force (CSO, 2013). It is of considerable concern that a large proportion of the newly long-term unemployed possess skills for which there is likely to be limited demand over the next few years. In particular, large numbers of males who formerly worked in the construction sector have joined this group and they will require significant assistance and retraining before many of them can return to employment.[13]

Rhetoric that seeks to divide society and demonise the unemployed has made a return in some sections of the media. This should have no place in Irish political discourse; it demoralises those who have lost their jobs in a recession caused and compounded by both government policy and international factors outside of their control.

Another of the social ghosts of the 1980s and 1990s has also returned – emigration. Preliminary estimates from the CSO Population and Migration Estimates, April

---

[12] The data cited in this section comes from the CSO's QNHS, the official measure of employment and unemployment. We analyse the live register figures in chapter 5.

[13] We analyse the issues of unemployment, employment and work in chapter 5.

2011, suggest that net outmigration was running at over 34,000 a year in 2011 and 2012 (CSO, 2012: 2) In 2012 preliminary estimates suggested that over 87,100 emigrated, of whom 46,500 were Irish, a sharp increase on 2009, when 19,200 of the 70,000 who emigrated were Irish. As Ireland's employment is not expected to grow until domestic demand and investment increase substantially and the international economy recovers, it is expected that emigration will remain at these high levels, with a large outflow of young and skilled Irish-born people, for a number of years to come.

As noted above, seven successive budgets have cut public spending; in 2008, twice in 2009, and in 2010, 2011, 2012 and 2013. Throughout this review we highlight and critique many of the cuts in social spending, including the unacceptable cut in many social welfare payments delivered in the 2010, 2011 and 2012 budgets.

Cuts in both national and local social services and support initiatives are being made at a particularly difficult time, just when demand for these services is rising. All too often decisions made in times of crisis focus on short-term gains and savings with no regard for their potentially negative long-term consequences. Cutting funding for particular disability services, for example, may save money in the short term but can also effectively imprison people with a disability in their own homes and subsequently result in increased acute hospital costs. In reality, many decisions made during the current series of crises are set to have such negative effects.

Many public services are provided by community and voluntary organisations. These have come under huge pressure in recent years as the recession has forced an ever-growing number of people to seek their help on a wide range of fronts. But, just at the very moment when the demand for their services increased, Government has reduced the funding available to many of these organisations. It is noticeable that the scale of cutbacks by Government in the funding for provision of public services by the community and voluntary sector is proportionately much larger than for public services provided directly by the public sector. There has been no adequate explanation for this inequitable disparity.

The impact of these cuts and the threats of further similar ones continue to undermine the social structures within Irish society and their ability to cope in the present circumstances.

The collective implications of these actions were well summarised by Magdalena Sepulveda, the UN independent expert on Human Rights and Extreme Poverty, who visited Ireland following an invitation from Government in January 2011.[14] She stated in her report that "the current economic and financial crisis poses a disproportionate threat to those who did not benefit much from the Irish economic boom and is a serious threat to the milestones achieved in social protection". This is further reflected in the experience of the Society of St Vincent de Paul which reported that throughout the last few years calls for its assistance increased dramatically. Many of these came from 'first-timers' struggling to cope with the impact of the current crisis. In some cases very vulnerable people have turned to money-lenders as a last resort, making their long-term situation worse in the process.

The proportions of the population at risk of poverty or in consistent poverty and the deprivation rate all declined despite commitments by government to increase social security payments to the most vulnerable during the mid-2000s. This progress has been reversed during the recession (see Table 2.11). This has particularly affected extremely vulnerable groups; in 2011 56% of children in lone parent households suffered two or more types of enforced deprivation, up from 44.1% in 2009. The quintile share ratio – measuring the difference between the average equivalised income of the top 20% of households from the bottom 20% - in 2011 was 4.9, up from 4.3 in 2009,

Table 2.11 Poverty and Deprivation Rates, 2008-2011				
	2008	2009	2010	2011
At risk of poverty rate (%)	14.4	14.1	14.7	16.0
Deprivation Rate (%)	13.8	17.1	22.6	24.5
Consistent poverty rate (%)	4.2	5.5	6.3	6.9

Source: CSO (2013: 1).

Social Justice Ireland has strongly objected to the budgetary strategy from 2008 to 2013, though it does recognise differences in approach between those various budgets. An analysis by the ESRI (Callan et. al., 2012) examined the effects of changes in direct taxes, direct welfare payments and some indirect taxes and found that the changes in budgets between 2008 and 2009 were progressive, taking more proportionately from those higher up the income distribution. This analysis did not include the impact of cuts to service provision, which have the greatest effects on those most reliant on public services – usually the poorest.

---

[14] *Social Justice Ireland* held a detailed meeting with the UN delegation in January 2011.

While budgetary policy may have been progressive between 2008 and 2009, it became regressive subsequently, and this trend has continued. Callan et. al. (2012) showed that the budgetary changes in Budget 2012 took proportionately more from those on the lowest incomes than from those on the highest. It must be remembered that the ESRI analysis does not include the impact of cuts in some services. Both the ESRI and *Social Justice Ireland* concluded that Budget 2013 was also a regressive budget. This has become a particularly worrying trend in budgetary policy which will make Irish society more unequal.

As mentioned above, the CSO's EU-SILC data release only includes changes up to 2011 and has measured an increase in inequality. Given the change in budgetary stance since Budget 2010 – which came into effect in 2011 – and the increases in unemployment, we can expect to see increases in inequality when figures for 2012 and 2013 are released. Government policy, particularly in its budgetary decision-making, should also seek to reduce inequality. Inequality damages social solidarity, fractures social cohesion and contradicts the egalitarian instincts of the majority of the Irish people.

A special CSO Quarterly National Household Survey module on the impacts of the recession on households was published in February 2012. It showed that 30 per cent of households headed by a person who is unemployed had borrowed money from family or friends to pay for basic goods and services. In addition, half of such households had missed paying household bills and more than one quarter had missed loan repayments. Two thirds of households headed by a person with a job and two thirds of those headed by an unemployed person had reduced the amount they saved.

However, households headed by an unemployed person were far more likely to have spent some or all of their savings. Almost 64 per cent of these households had spent savings to pay for basic goods and services in the two years prior to the survey, compared with 46 per cent of households headed by a person who was employed.

In addition to the economic and social problems discussed above, an alarming number of people, of all ages, have literacy difficulties. We still have schools with leaking roofs and 'temporary' portacabins. Ireland's two-tier health system has persisted through the crisis and availability of many services remains related to income rather than need. Clearly, in the Ireland of 2013 the social crisis continues.

2.2.4 The Political Context

The 2011 General Election produced a new government with a large majority and a mandate to address the broad economic and social problems outlined above. The *Programme for Government* covered a wide range of issues at different levels. It contained very welcome commitments on some issues but was exceptionally vague on how it proposed to address others. It contains very few numbers or target dates. This Government has introduced two regressive budgets so far. *Social Justice Ireland* urges the Government to change its approach to budgets and to place protection of the vulnerable and promotion of the common good at the core of its decision making.

The issue of governance is of major importance for society at large. There is a substantial role for civil society in the huge task that Ireland currently faces. Social dialogue is a critically important component of effective decision-making in a modern democracy. Recently the process of consultation and society-wide cooperation has been undermined, even demonised, and its significant positive contributions ignored. The severity of Ireland's current situation is reminiscent of the late 1980s, a time when social dialogue was seen as the key to economic and social recovery; the lessons learnt then should be remembered now.

The Europe 2020 Strategy places an onus on the Irish government to include all stakeholders in framing, developing and delivering Ireland's National Reform Programme. This programme is intended to set out how Ireland proposes to meet its commitments towards achieving the Europe 2020 Strategy targets. By including all stakeholders and civil society, it is believed that these targets will be 'owned' and that all will work for their achievement. *Social Justice Ireland* believes this is a sensible and desirable approach.

Much work has been done in recent years by the Council of Europe on how such an approach might be formalised and benefit all concerned. From that has come a new draft Charter on Shared Social Responsibilities which was finalised by the Council of Europe in late 2011. This charter argues that having a well-defined deliberative process can ensure, among other things, that individual preferences are reconciled with widespread priorities in the field of social, environmental and intergenerational justice. It can also reduce the 'imbalances of power between stakeholders and neutralise its impact on the construction of knowledge and on decision-making' (Council of Europe, 2011: 24).

It is apparent to *Social Justice Ireland* that in the on-going framing, development and implementation of policy in areas such as the National Reform Programme there is a need for Government to move towards a deliberative approach. In a deliberative process all stakeholders would address the evidence together, independent of the traditional power differentials between the stakeholders. The evidence would be presented and discussed with a view to providing the most accurate 'reading' of the issues being addressed.

Stakeholders would collaboratively identify:
* the current situation and how it emerged;
* the most desirable future that could be achieved; and
* the means by which to move towards such a future.

Were this process evidence-based it would go some way towards ensuring that the most appropriate manner in which to address issues would be identified and agreed. Such an approach requires a high level of accountability from stakeholders and encourages them to take responsibility for decisions and the subsequent implementation of the actions required.

Social Justice Ireland believes governance along these lines can be developed in Ireland. Such engagement would reflect the value of social dialogue and the need for good governance characterised by transparency, accountability and inclusion.

2.2.5 The cultural context (assumptions, values and attitudes)

At times of crisis strategic thinking and planning are often set-side. This has been quite obvious in Ireland since the current crisis began. Its most visible manifestation has been the widespread acceptance of a series of largely unchallenged assumptions that are not valid, as already outlined in this report. These include:

* that the economy should have priority over everything else;
* that preventing all the major banks from collapse is the major economic priority; and
* that cutting public expenditure is the key solution.

These assumptions fail to acknowledge that, far from being mutually exclusive, economic development and social development are complementary. Economic development is required to provide resources for social development. On the other hand, social development is essential if economic development is to be successful.

There can be no lasting economic development of substance without the provision of social services and infrastructure. For example, it will not be possible to promote a smart, green, hi-tech economy without having an education system that ensures people are capable of taking up jobs in these areas. Similarly, infrastructure in areas such as public transport and Information and Communication Technology (ICT) are essential for a successful economy in the 21st century. Thinking we can have economic development first and follow up with social development later is to ignore many of the major lessons that have been learned over the past two decades.

Other assumptions that are only half true are repeated like mantras in policy discussion and commentary. These include the admonition that 'everybody should make a contribution to the adjustment required' and that, while fairness is important, cuts are more effective than tax increases.

Social Justice Ireland agrees everyone should make a contribution –as far as they can. However, we cannot accept that some people should be driven into poverty by the contribution that is demanded of them. This would be attempting to solve one problem by creating a deeper and more long-lasting one. We reject any proposal; to solve Ireland's problems by increasing inequality or by forcing the most vulnerable members of the population into a situation where they do not have the resources to live life with dignity. It is also profoundly wrong that poor people should carry a major burden while senior bond-holders, who carry a significant part of the responsibility for Ireland's implosion, make no contribution whatsoever. Nor do we believe that Ireland's socio-economic situation can be rectified fairly if we persist in prioritising expenditure cuts at the same time as retaining one of the lowest total tax-takes in the EU.

We reject other regularly repeated mantras, too, such as the notion that the solutions lie in getting better value for public expenditure and in reforming the public sector.

The widely quoted assumptions listed in this chapter have been adopted with limited consideration of their meaning or implications. Consequently, those that are not valid generate ill-considered policies which are met with widespread opposition and anger. As a society we lack a coherent set of guiding values and assumptions to shape the policies and actions for the decade to come.

But that is not all. Developments over the past decade and more and the response to the multi-faceted crises Ireland has been encountering have produced a situation which is dominated by individualism, anxiety and greed.

Individualism, in the sense of people being seen as isolated, self-sufficient, economic individuals, has grown dramatically in recent years. Increasingly the individual has come to be seen as the primary unit of social reality while community connectedness is played down.

In practice, policy has done much to undermine this community dimension. Autonomy, self-sufficiency and self-reliance have increasingly been seen as virtues. This kind of individualism is seen almost exclusively in economic terms. It resonates with the 'Celtic Tiger' rhetoric of the decade before the crisis, which favoured low taxation as a supposed stimulus to entrepreneurial activity. As noted above, this was based on the false premise that the combined spending and investment decisions of individuals would produce far better results for Ireland than allowing collective institutions determine national spending and investment priorities. This notion is demonstrably wrong. Furthermore, this focus on individualism has had another equally negative effect on Irish society, the emergence of anxiety as a constant in Ireland's core.

Anxiety accompanies the growing realisation that the individualism described above can never provide an adequate basis for either the long-term progress of society or a guarantee of the individual's well-being. The autonomous individual championed in much current economic theory becomes caught in a never satisfied quest for achievement that ultimately produces a bottomless pit of anxiety – about the markets, about performance in all spheres of activity and even about fundamental self-worth.[15] This anxiety, in turn, leads many people to experience feelings of growing insecurity, pressure and threat. The individual experiencing anxiety often responds by seeking to have more in an effort to have control over the future. This often leads to greed, which feeds into the wider society.

Greed generates what Brueggemann (2009) calls "ravenous acquisitiveness" so that life becomes a passionate pursuit of every form of security and self-worth, especially through money. This may explain why people who have the most often think they do not have enough. The effective legitimisation of avariciousness amongst those already well off not surprisingly stimulates similar desires in those with less. With financial institutions suspending their own critical judgements in the quest for profits, it is not difficult to see why borrowers were also persuaded to suspend any normal sense of caution in respect of borrowing and investing. This situation was

---

[15] For further development of these points cf. Walter Brueggemann, *From Anxiety and Greed to Milk and Honey*, Sojourners, http://www.sojo.net/

exacerbated by a culture of extremely large 'bonus' payments for some which stimulated envy and greed in others. Greed, at both corporate and individual levels, has been an important contributory factor in the recent crises, not just in Ireland but worldwide.

The series of developments which produced the growth of individualism, anxiety and greed is one of the core reasons why Ireland, and much of the Western world, is where it is today. A route out of this morass is needed. That pathway should be guided by a vision of Irish society, a New Ireland.

2.3 The need for vision: what does recovery look like?

The economic crisis confronting Ireland is not a result of the failure of any one political party, or of the mischief of a faction. It is the result of the failure of an economic and social philosophy that exalted private greed above the common good. The response to the crisis has been guided and underpinned by many of the mistaken assumptions of the Tiger Years. Many of the progressive social programmes introduced during the previous 20 years have been eroded or abandoned and the state remains committed to the ultra-low tax model of the early 2000s.

Alternative economic proposals are dismissed out of hand while economic decisions are imposed without consultation with citizens and with little examination of the impact of those decisions. While this is not due to any malice on the part of those who govern Ireland it is closely linked to an absence of vision and a lack of imagination. A lazy reliance on outworn neo-liberal dogmas is disguised by frequent declarations that 'there is no alternative'.

Social Justice Ireland believes that Ireland cannot continue to be guided by the failed ideologies of the past. Ireland's crisis demands both an immediate policy response – for example the investment programme advocated by *Social Justice Ireland* and a debt reduction pact with the European Union – and also the development of a vision of a New Ireland. We must ask the question: what does recovery look like? Will it be characterised by gains in wealth for the few, and stagnation for the many? Will our citizens access to healthcare continue to be determined by the size of their bank accounts? Will one in every five Irish children continue to live in poverty? Will long-term unemployment continue for years to come, while a lucky few see their incomes soar?

Addressing these questions and challenges cannot be postponed until after the IMF/EU programme comes to end and they cannot wait for the next electoral cycle. They demand an immediate response and immediate answers. The decisions taken now will shape the recovery to come and the shape of Irish society over the next decades.

Social Justice Ireland believes that an alternative vision of Ireland's future is urgently needed. This vision should prioritise the common good and provide economic and social security for all the people of Ireland while ensuring that all policy decisions are focused of delivering a future that is sustainable economically, environmentally and socially. Such a vision requires radically different policies to those pursued by Government and the IMF/EU/ECB; alternative policies which *Social Justice Ireland* has advocated for many years. Ireland is still a wealthy country, despite its recent challenges, and still has the resources and skills to achieve 'liberty, justice and equality for all its citizens', in the words of the Democratic Programme of the first Dail (1919). What has been missing is the resolve, the will and the vision to achieve a New Ireland.

A guiding vision for a New Ireland

In this section we explain *Social Justice Ireland's* vision and later we set out the practical measures necessary to put it into effect. *Social Justice Ireland* advocates a new guiding vision to shape the future direction of Irish society. We believe that Ireland should be guided by a vision of becoming a just society in which human rights are respected, human dignity is protected, human development is facilitated and the environment is respected and protected. The core values of such a society would be human dignity, equality, human rights, solidarity, sustainability and the pursuit of the common good.

Human dignity is central to our vision. It demands that all people be recognised as having an inherent value, worth and distinction regardless of their nationality, gender, ethnicity, culture, sexual orientation or economic and social position. *Social Justice Ireland* believes that in a New Ireland human dignity must be respected and that the State must uphold and promote human dignity, treating all citizens and non-citizens alike with dignity and respect.

The need for greater equality is closely linked to the recognition of human dignity and the desire for social justice. Great disparities in wealth and power divide society into the rich and the poor, which weakens the bond between people and divides society between the lucky and the left-out, between the many and the few. A commitment to equality requires society to give priority to this value so that all people can achieve their potential.

The development and recognition of human rights has been one of the great achievements of the 20th century. In the 21st century human rights are moving beyond civil and political rights to embrace social, economic and cultural rights. In this context *Social Justice Ireland* believes that every person has seven core rights that should be part of our vision of the future i.e. the right to sufficient income to live life with dignity; the right to meaningful work; the right to appropriate accommodation; the right to relevant education; the right to essential healthcare; the right to real participation and the right to cultural respect. Policy decisions should be moving towards the achievement of each of these rights, not moving in the opposite direction.

Solidarity is the recognition that we are all bound, as human beings, one to another, within nations, between nations and across generations. Many policy decisions taken in recent years are unjust to future generations. Solidarity requires all people and all nations to recognise their duties to one another and to vindicate the rights of their fellow members of society. Solidarity enables people and communities to become the shapers of their own destiny.

Sustainability is a central motif for economic, social and environmental policy development. Central to this is the recognition that economic development, social development and environmental protection are complementary and interdependent. None of these objectives can be achieved by ignoring any of the others. Respect for the natural environment is not a luxury to be indulged in but an imperative that cannot be ignored.

A commitment to the common good is also critical. The right of the individual to freedom and personal development is limited by the rights of other people. The concept of the 'common good' originated over 2,000 years ago in the writings of Plato, Aristotle and Cicero. More recently, the philosopher John Rawls defined the common good as 'certain general conditions that are...equally to everyone's advantage' (Rawls, 1971 p.246).

Social Justice Ireland understands the term 'common good' as being 'the sum of those conditions of social life by which individuals, families and groups can achieve their own fulfilment in a relatively thorough and ready way' (Gaudium et Spes, 1965 no.74). This understanding recognises the fact that the person develops his or her potential in the context of society where the needs and rights of all members and groups are respected (Healy and Reynolds, 2011). The common good, then, consists primarily of having the social systems, institutions and environments on which we all depend work in a manner that benefits all people simultaneously and in solidarity. A study by NESC states that 'at a societal level, a belief in a "common good" has been shown to contribute to the overall wellbeing of society. This requires a level of recognition of rights and responsibilities, empathy with others and values of citizenship' (NESC, 2009, p.32).

This raises the issue of resources. The goods of the planet are for the use of all people – not just the present generation but for generations still to come. The present generation must recognise it has a responsibility to ensure that it does not damage but rather enhances the goods of the planet that it passes on – be they economic, cultural, social or environmental. The structural arrangements regarding the ownership, use, accumulation and distribution of goods are disputed areas. However it must be recognised that these arrangements have a major impact on how society is shaped and how it supports the wellbeing of each of its members in solidarity with others.

Social Justice Ireland believes that the values outlined above must be at the core of the vision for a nation in which all men, women and children have what they require to live life with dignity and to fulfil their potential, including sufficient income, access to the services they need and active inclusion in a genuinely participatory society.

There are many policy areas that are outside Ireland's control at the present time and this has contributed to a sense of helplessness amongst Irish people. However, even within the confines of the EU/IMF/ECB programme there are real choices to be made about the amount of resources that our health service and our welfare state should receive, the distribution of wealth and power in our society and the level of taxation required to furnish the resources necessary for a compassionate and civilised society. There must be a serious debate in Irish society about our economic and social priorities. If there is not, policy will continue along the current trajectory with regressive budgets, cuts to vital services and a continued low-tax policy. *Social Justice Ireland* believes this vision of a New Ireland should guide policy development and decision-making in the period ahead.

2.4 Five priority areas to move towards our vision

To move towards our vision five key policy areas must be addressed urgently. These are in the areas of macroeconomic stability, taxation, social security, governance and sustainability.

Ensure Macroeconomic Stability	Move Towards Just Taxation	Enhance Social Protection	Reform Governance	Create a Sustainable Ireland
Reduce Ireland's debt burden	Bring tax-take to European average	Protect services by adjusting deficit reduction	Reform policy evaluation	Combat climate change
Financial and fiscal stability	Increase tax level equitably	Combat unemployment	Develop a rights-based approach	Balanced regional development
Investment programme	Reduce income inequality	Reduce poverty	Promote social dialogue	Indicators of progress and wellbeing

2.4.1 Ensuring Macroeconomic Stability

Ensuring macroeconomic stability requires a reduction in Ireland's debt burden, the launching of a substantially larger investment programme than currently envisaged and the restoration of fiscal and financial stability. All of these measures are connected. An investment programme will contribute to jobs and recovery which in turn will help lower Ireland's deficit and real debt burden. Financial stability will ensure that additional bank bailouts do not threaten Ireland's fiscal stability and provide Irish firms with greater credit facilities. A reduction in Ireland's debt burden will increase confidence in Ireland's capacity to grow and exit the EU/IMF programme, thus reducing yields on Irish government debt.

i) Reducing Ireland's debt burden

The Irish Fiscal Advisory Council (2012: 35-36) has forecast that debt-to-GDP levels will peak at 120 per cent of GDP during 2013, while the Department of

Finance (2012: 91) has assumed it will peak at 121.4 per cent of GDP in the same year. However, the Council also warned that if Ireland's recession follows the trajectory of a 'balance sheet recession' then debt-to-GDP levels will continue to rise. This is because balance sheet recessions induce 'L-shaped' growth patterns in which GDP falls rapidly and then stagnates. Without growth, Ireland's real debt burden will continue to increase.

A large proportion of Ireland's debt was accumulated in the course of rescuing the Irish banking sector in a manner which resulted in a much lower sharing of the financial burden by investors than would have been expected if the rescue was of any other business sector. In addition, the loss of confidence in Ireland during 2009–2010 was a direct result of fixed-asset analysts and other observers of the government bond market viewing Ireland's assumption of banking debt as unsustainable. The total cost of the banking rescue has been €62.8bn, of which €11.4bn has come directly from the Exchequer, €30.7bn through promissory notes and €20.7bn from the National Pension Reserve Fund.

This part of Ireland's debt represents a direct subsidy by the Irish public of international bondholders and the European banking system. In June 2012 the Eurogroup appeared to recognise this, holding out the possibility that the European Stability Mechanism (ESM) would retrospectively recapitalise the Irish banking sector by purchasing the Irish government's bank equities. However, following this agreement key member-states appear to have withdrawn their agreement to recognise this principle.

In 2013 the Irish Government appeared to secure an agreement on the status of the promissory notes granted to Anglo-Irish Bank (the now liquidated IRBC) by the government in 2010. Unfortunately this agreement does not appear to be in the spirit of the June 2012 agreement. Instead it has transferred the promissory notes to the status of sovereign debt, confirming that Irish citizens must bear the responsibility for the mistakes of the Irish banks and for the rescue of international bondholders.

Ireland's economy will only expand again if the debt burden is reduced. . Such expansion is essential if it is to contribute to a European recovery and to ensure that all *public* funds lent to Ireland through the Troika's programme are returned in full.

To reduce Ireland's debt burden in 2013 the European authorities must uphold their agreement to retrospectively recapitalise Irish banks. If this is done through the ESM – which would take ownership of the majority of the Irish banking sector as a result – this decision must take account of Irish mortgage holders and the need to secure credit availability in the Irish economy. The ESM must also be prepared to further recapitalise the Irish banking sector if necessary. European authorities should also consider further changes to the status of the government bonds which will be issued to replace the promissory notes, including further extending the maturity and applying a lower interest rate to them. Such measures could also be applied to the loans received under the EU/IMF programme. This would lead to a less onerous repayment schedule and boost confidence in Ireland.

ii) Financial stability

The stability of Ireland's financial system remains of great concern. Credit supply is reported to be extremely tight. The Central Bank of Ireland published research by two of its economists indicating that 'the Irish rejection rate for credit applications is the second highest in the euro area, while Irish SMEs are among the most likely to have faced increased collateral requirements, increased interest rates, or lower loan quantities'. At the same time Ireland had almost double the amount of discouraged borrowers – those who do not even apply for loans – than the euro area average (Holton and McCann, 2012). A banking sector that does not supply adequate credit to those firms seeking to invest and expand inhibits economic growth.

It is recognised by Irish policymakers that the Irish banking sector is unprepared for widespread losses on distressed mortgages (e.g Honohan, 2013). This raises the possibilities of further demands by the banks for capital on the basis of the Prudential Capital Assessment Review (PCAR) targets imposed by the Troika. *Social Justice Ireland* believes that government must ensure that additional demands for recapitalisation by banks are met by the EMS in line with the June 2012 decision and ensure a flow of credit to Irish firms.

At the same time it is crucial that Ireland pay its way and that its annual budget is brought back into balance. While this is a core feature of current government policy it is highly unlikely that such a balance will be achieved without a reduction in Ireland's debt burden and the development of a substantially larger investment programme than currently envisaged.

iii) An investment programme

Since the onset of the recession Ireland's GDP has declined by just over 16 per cent, GNP by nearly 23 per cent and domestic demand by 28 per cent (CSO, 2012). Unemployment remains at 14.2 per cent, despite a small rise in employment in the fourth quarter of 2012 (CSO, 2013). Both the Troika and Department of Finance believe that the domestic economy will remain stagnant and rely on a rise in exports to boost growth. Increased investment in the domestic economy is urgently needed to provide employment and much-needed infrastructure. This would reduce unemployment and increase the long-term productivity of the Irish economy.

It is essential to bear in mind that without investment there will be no jobs. Without jobs there will be no recovery and without recovery Ireland will be stuck in austerity for the foreseeable future. *Social Justice Ireland* believes that there must be an off-balance sheet investment programme between 2013 and 2015 of €7bn, along the lines outlined in its *Budget Choices* Policy Briefings in recent years. This would enhance growth and contribute to a reduction in the deficit by, among other things, reducing unemployment and increasing tax returns.

2.4.2 Towards a Just Taxation System

The American jurist Oliver Wendell Holmes once said that 'taxes are the price we pay for a civilized society'. *Social Justice Ireland* has long argued that Ireland's total tax-take is simply too low to pay for the services and social security provision that is necessary to ensure human dignity for all. *Social Justice Ireland* also believes that the incidence of taxation falls too much on the shoulders of the poorest in society. In chapter 4 on taxation we examine Ireland's taxation system in depth. Below are three immediate priorities.

i) Bring taxes towards the European average

Ireland's tax-take in 2010 was 28.2 per cent of GDP, some 7.4 per cent below the European average. The Department of Finance believes that taxation as a percentage of GDP will rise to 31.7 per cent of GDP by 2015. *Social Justice Ireland* believes that Ireland should raise the total tax-take (which includes all taxes and social insurance payments) to 34.9 per cent. This would still keep Ireland as a low-tax economy as defined by Eurostat, while raising significant revenue.

Table 2.12 compares the Department of Finance's targets for taxation as a percentage of GDP, as announced in the Medium Term Fiscal Statement released before Budget 2013, with the level of taxation that would be raised were Ireland to increase its tax take to 34.9 per cent of GDP.

Table 2.12 Potential Irish Total Tax Revenues, 2011-2015

Year	GDP (€bn)	DoF GDP %	DoF Tax (€bn)	Tax@34.9% (€bn)	Difference (€bn)
2011	158,993	30.4	48,334	55,489	7,155
2012	163,150	30.4	49,598	56,939	7,342
2013	167,725	30.9	51,827	58,536	6,709
2014	174,100	31.5	54,842	60,761	5,919
2015	181,400	31.7	57,504	63,309	5,805

Source: Department of Finance (2012: 87).

The reliance on a relatively low level of taxation to fund vital public services contributed to the scale of the crisis in the public finances. Ireland can never hope to address its longer-term deficits in infrastructure and social provision if it continues to collect substantially less tax income than that required by other European countries it seeks to emulate. *Social Justice Ireland* recommends moving towards a total tax take of 34.9 per cent, which would keep Ireland as a low-tax country while remaining below the EU average. There should also be a public debate on the appropriate level of taxation required over the next 20 years to fund its public service and social security system. Future policy development may possibly involve increasing public spending and tax levels. These questions should be openly debated instead of avoided by policymakers.

ii) Increase taxes equitably

An increase in total tax-take must be done in a fair and equitable manner. As detailed later in chapter 4, *Social Justice Ireland* believes that these tax reforms should not be attained through increasing income tax rates but rather via reforming and broadening the tax base so that Ireland's taxation system becomes fairer. This would involve shifting taxation towards wealth, ensuring those who benefit the most from Ireland's economic system contribute the most, in the most efficient manner. Changes in taxation since 2010 have been regressive, with the increase in VAT impacting particularly significantly on those with the lowest incomes. In future tax changes should be progressive.

iii) Reduce income inequality

Income inequality, gender inequality and inequality of opportunity represent a key problem in Irish society. They produce a range of negative outcomes for those who are poor and/or excluded. Growing inequality, which has been the norm for some time, exacerbates the negative effects on people who are poor and/or excluded.

The 'gini coefficient', a measure of income inequality, has risen from a low in 2009 of 29.3 to 31.1 in 2011 (CSO, 2013). Reducing inequality must be a core objective of Government policy.

The key mechanism through which income inequality is reduced is redistribution via the tax system. Since Budget 2010 government policy has redistributed income from those who earn less to those with more. Moreover, particular measures such as cuts in the lone-parent allowance particularly affect women. Government should proof its annual budget to ensure it reduces poverty and inequality. This should be a statutory responsibility of Government which would enlighten public debate. In the Budget 2013 documentation the Department of Finance attempt to obfuscate the effect of its measures by selectively citing research conducted by the ESRI among others (Department of Finance, 2012: B40). This should not happen.

2.4.3 Enhancing Social Protection

There have been significant cuts to social services and welfare payments since 2008. *Social Justice Ireland* believes many of these cuts have been socially destructive and counterproductive. They have reduced demand in the economy and many have been imposed without an adequate examination of their likely impact. Moreover, in reducing the budget deficit the balance between cuts and taxes has been incorrect. As *Social Justice Ireland* has consistently argued, taxation should be increased towards the European average while social services and payments should be protected. Throughout this volume we propose specific priority areas for investment. Below are three immediate priorities for government.

i) Protect services by adjusting deficit reduction

Since 2008 the government has cut spending by €18,559m while increasing taxes by €9,300m: a ratio of €2 in spending cuts for €1 in tax rates rises. By the projected end of the EU/IMF programme in 2015 taxation will have contributed €11,000m and spending cuts €21,859m to the total budgetary adjustments; the ratio of tax increases to spending cuts is set to remain unaltered. *Social Justice Ireland* believes that this ratio should be reversed. Measures must be taken to reduce the deficit but they should not fall upon the most vulnerable in society. Cuts to services and social protection payments ensure that they do. *Social Justice Ireland* recommends that the ratio of spending cuts to tax increases should be reversed. This will go some way to taking account of the excess burden placed on the spending side in the attempt to reduce the budget deficit.

ii) Combat unemployment

Unemployment has risen rapidly since 2008 and by the fourth quarter of 2012 stood at 294,600, or 14.2 per cent, of the labour force (CSO, 2013). While it fell by 19,200 in the fourth quarter, employment only grew by 1,200, reflecting the level of discouraged workers and emigration. Long-term unemployment is at 8.2 per cent of the labour force, lower than the third quarter of 2013, but this decrease may also be due to emigration and discouraged workers. The IMF (2012) estimates that unemployment will still be 13.4 per cent in 2015.

Unemployment is the gravest crisis facing Ireland at the present time. It has a corrosive effect on people and communities throughout society. The proposal for an investment programme for Ireland has been mentioned above. *Social Justice Ireland* also proposes the introduction of *Part Time Job Opportunities Programme* which would create thousands of jobs for those who are long-term unemployed. These proposals are covered at greater length in chapter 5 on work, unemployment and job creation.

iii) Reduce poverty

There is a real danger that Irish society will permit those on the lowest incomes, and in particular those dependent on social welfare, to fall behind once again, as it did in the late 1990s (see chapter 3). From 2006, Ireland's poverty levels had been slowly falling, driven by the increases in social welfare payments delivered in the Budgets of 2005-2007. These increases compensated only partly for the extent to which social welfare rates had fallen behind other incomes in society over the preceding two decades. However, these advances have been reversed. The 'at-risk-of-poverty' rate rose from a low of 14.1 per cent in 2009 to 16 per cent in 2011, consistent poverty rose from a low of 4.2 per cent in 2008 to 6.9 per cent in 2011 and the deprivation rate rose from a low of 11.8 per cent in 2007 to 24.5 per cent in 2011 (CSO, 2013:1). In 2011 the single largest demographic group at-risk-of-poverty was children, with nearly one in five at risk of poverty (CSO, 2013).

It would be a great mistake for Irish policy makers to repeat the mistakes of the late 1990s. At that time economic growth benefited only those who were employed while others, such as those dependent on pensions and social welfare payments, slipped further and further behind. *Social Justice Ireland* believes that policy in the future should provide equity in social welfare rates across genders while providing adequate payments for children and those with a disability. These issues are examined in greater detail in chapter 3.

2.4.4 Reforming Governance

It has been widely recognised that Ireland's governance was poor in certain areas prior to the economic crisis, particularly in relation to financial regulation. Moreover, the economic crisis has led to government making rash and hasty decisions without consultation, whether in relation to financial or budgetary policy. These have been recognised as damaging or – as in the case of the bank guarantee – catastrophic. Reforming governance and widening participation are a necessity and this issue is addressed in chapter 11. Below are three immediate priorities.

i) Reform policy evaluation

Policy evaluation has been extremely poor in some cases throughout the crisis. *Social Justice Ireland* welcomes the steps taken by Government to increase its research and evaluative capacity. However, we believe that Government should also take steps to increase the transparency of budgetary and other important decisions, which are often opaque. Government should publish its analysis of the impact of budgetary measures and engage in public debate in the light of that analysis.

ii) A rights-based approach

Social Justice Ireland believes strongly in the importance of developing a rights-based approach to social, economic and cultural issues. The need to develop these rights is becoming ever more urgent for Ireland in the context of achieving recovery. Such an approach would go a long way towards addressing the growing inequality Ireland has been experiencing. Social, economic and cultural rights should be acknowledged and recognised, just as civil and political rights have been. We believe seven basic rights that are of fundamental concern to people who are socially excluded and/or living in poverty should be acknowledged and recognised. These are the rights to sufficient income to live life with dignity, meaningful work, appropriate accommodation, relevant education, essential healthcare, cultural respect and real participation in society.

iii) Social dialogue

Government must engage more extensively with all sectors of Irish society, particularly those most affected by cuts in particular areas. Government has provided a high-level forum called the IFSC Clearing House Group for the financial industry, and 23 changes were made in the Finance Act 2012 to accommodate this group (McGee, 2012). This contrasts with the treatment of bodies representing vulnerable groups in Irish society. These do not have access to the senior civil servants or ministers and have been unable to secure changes in legislation. We have already seen the damaging effects to Ireland when one sector's voice is prioritised by government in policymaking. Government should engage in wide-ranging consultation on budgetary measures, consulting with those groups which will be particularly affected by each proposed measure and sharing its own impact assessment of the proposed measure.

Of particular concern in this context is the community and voluntary sector which has seen a huge increase in the demand for its services as the crisis continues but whose funding has been reduced proportionately more than other sectors'.

2.4.5 Creating a Sustainable Ireland

Sustainable development is development which meets the needs of the present while not compromising the needs of the future. In this regard financial, environmental, economic and social sustainability are all key areas that Ireland must prioritise. In chapter 12 we outline these issues in greater depth. Here we identify three immediate priorities.

i) Combat climate change

Climate change remains the largest long-term challenge facing Ireland and the wider world today. The challenge of reducing Ireland's fossil fuel emissions should not be postponed in the face of the current recession. *Social Justice Ireland* believes that Ireland should adopt ambitious statutory targets regarding the limitation of fossil fuel emissions and introduce the taxation measures necessary to achieve this.

ii) Balanced regional development

A sustained recovery requires balanced regional development. During the recession, particular regions of Ireland have suffered worse than others. In chapter 13 we look specifically at rural development. While the numbers in employment in Dublin have grown since the first quarter of 2012 historically less developed regions continue to witness reductions in the numbers in employment (CSO, 2013). Rural areas have been severely impacted by cuts in services. *Social Justice Ireland* believes that policy must ensure balanced regional development through the provision of services and through capital spending projects.

iii) New indicators

Creating a sustainable Ireland requires the adoption of new indicators to measure progress and wellbeing. We analyse these issues in chapter 12. GDP alone as a measure of progress is unsatisfactory, as it only describes the monetary value of gross output, income and expenditure in an economy. The *Report by the Commission on the Measurement of Economic Performance and Social Progress*, led by Nobel prize winning economists Amartya Sen and Joseph Stiglitz and established by President Sarkozy, argued that new indicators measuring environmental, financial sustainability, wellbeing and happiness are required. *Social Justice Ireland* believes that government should adopt such benchmarks against which Ireland can measure its substantial progress in these areas (Reynolds and Healy, 2009).

2.4.6 Keeping People at the Centre of the Policy-making Process – *The Developmental Welfare State*

Any development of policy must take place in a framework that places the needs of the person at its heart. Within the broader framework set out above, one useful approach would be to use the core structure developed by the NESC in its report on *The Developmental Welfare State* (NESC, 2005). Chart 2.13 presents the core structure of the NESC model. It proposed that every person in Ireland should have what is required to secure human dignity in three interrelated areas: (i) services, (ii) income supports and (iii) innovative measures that would secure active inclusion.

Chart 2.13: The Core Structure of the Developmental Welfare State

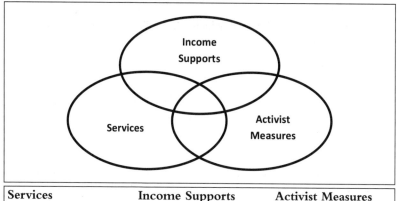

Services	Income Supports	Activist Measures
• Childcare	• Progressive child	• Social inclusion
• Education	income support	• Area-based strategies
• Health	• Working age income	• Particular community
• Eldercare	for participation	/group projects
• Housing	• Minimum pension	• Emerging new needs
• Transport	guarantee	• Novel approaches
• Employment services	• Capped tax	
• Training	expenditures	

Source: NESC (2005:144, 156)

NESC argued that in building the developmental welfare state Irish society should take a 'life-cycle' approach to ensuring that all three dimensions were delivered. As table 2.13 shows, such an approach would focus on identifying the needs of children, young adults, people of working age, older people and people challenged in their personal autonomy, such as those in care or with a disability. The council suggested that for each group, policy should focus on securing an effective combination of income supports, services and active inclusion measures.

Table 2.13:NESC Life-cycle approach to delivering the Developmental Welfare State

Who?	What?	How?	
0-17yrs	Integration of services, income support and activist measures	Governance and leadership	Standards and rights
18-29yrs			
30-64yrs			
65+ yrs			
People challenged in their personal autonomy			

Source: NESC (2005:147)

Successfully implementing this approach would underscore the ability of each of these groups to play a real and sustained role in Irish society and thereby play an important part in tackling social exclusion. This approach provides each sector involved with key challenges if the best options are to be taken and if the approach is to be successfully developed as a template for policy.

Conclusion

What are the implications for policy in Ireland flowing from this analysis? What are the specific issues to be addressed in areas such as taxation or education or rural development? What specific policy initiatives should Government take in areas such as income distribution or healthcare or unemployment? The following 12 chapters address these and similar questions. Each chapter addresses one specific area:

- Income Distribution
- Taxation
- Work, Unemployment and Job creation
- Public Services
- Housing and Accommodation
- Rural Development

- Education and Education Disadvantage
- Migration & Intercultural issues
- Participation
- Healthcare
- The Developing World

On each of these issues we propose a core policy objective. We also provide an analysis of the present situation, review relevant initiatives and outline key policy priorities aimed at securing a fair and just Ireland. In doing this, we clearly indicate the choices *Social Justice Ireland* believes should be made in the years immediately ahead. In chapter 15 we set out the values-base from which we provide this analysis and critique.

3. Income Distribution

High rates of poverty and income inequality in Ireland require greater attention
than they currently receive. Tackling these problems effectively is a multifaceted
task. It requires action on many fronts, ranging from healthcare and education to
accommodation and employment. However, the most important requirement in
tackling poverty is the provision of sufficient income to enable people to live life
with dignity. No anti-poverty strategy can possibly be successful without an
effective approach to addressing low incomes.

This chapter addresses the issue of income in four parts. The first (section 3.1)
examines the extent and nature of poverty in Ireland today while the second
(section 3.2) profiles our income distribution. The final two sections address
potential remedies to these problems by (section 3.3) outlining the issues and
arguments surrounding achieving and maintaining an adequate social welfare
income and (section 3.4) the introduction of a basic income.

3.1 Poverty

While there is still considerable poverty in Ireland, there has been much progress
on this issue over recent years. Driven by increases in social welfare payments, in
particularly payments to the unemployed, the elderly and people with disabilities,
the rate of poverty significantly declined between 2001 and 2009. However, the
most recent data, analysed in this section, indicates that poverty has once again
begun to increase. It climbed from a record low level in 2009 to a higher level in
2010 and 2011, driven by recent budgetary policy which has reversed earlier social
welfare increases. [16]

---

[16] Irish household income data has been collected since 1973 and all surveys up to the period 2008-
2010 recorded poverty levels above 15 per cent.

Data on Ireland's income and poverty levels are now provided by the annual *SILC* survey *(Survey on Income and Living Conditions)*. This survey replaced the *European Household Panel Survey* and the *Living in Ireland Survey* which had run throughout the 1990s. Since 2003 the *SILC / EU-SILC* survey has collected detailed information on income and living conditions from up to 130 households in Ireland each week; giving a total sample of between 4,000 and 6,000 households each year.

Social Justice Ireland welcomes this survey and in particular the accessibility of the data produced. Because this survey is conducted simultaneously across all of the EU states, the results are an important contribution to the on-going discussion on relative income and poverty levels across the EU member states. It also provides the basis for informed analysis of the relative position of the citizens of member states. In particular, this analysis is informed by a set of agreed indicators of social exclusion which the EU Heads of Government adopted at Laeken in 2001. These indicators (known as the updated-Laeken indicators) are calculated from the survey results and cover four dimensions of social exclusion: financial poverty, employment, health and education.[17]

What is poverty?
The National Anti-Poverty Strategy (NAPS) published by government in 1997 adopted the following definition of poverty:

> *People are living in poverty if their income and resources (material, cultural and social) are so inadequate as to preclude them from having a standard of living that is regarded as acceptable by Irish society generally. As a result of inadequate income and resources people may be excluded and marginalised from participating in activities that are considered the norm for other people in society.*

This definition was reiterated in the 2007 *National Action Plan for Social Inclusion 2007-2016 (NAPinclusion)*.

Where is the poverty line?
How many people are poor? On what basis are they classified as poor? These and related questions are constantly asked when poverty is discussed or analysed.

In trying to measure the extent of poverty, the most common approach has been to identify a poverty line (or lines) based on people's disposable income (earned

---

[17] For more information on these indicators see Nolan (2006:171-190).

income after taxes and including all benefits). In recent years the European Commission and the UN, among others, have begun to use a poverty line located at 60 per cent of median income. The median income is the income of the middle person in society's income distribution. This poverty line is the one adopted in the *SILC* survey and differs from the Irish poverty line up to 2003, which was set at 50 per cent of mean, or average, income. This switch to median income removes many of the technical criticisms that had been levelled against the use of relative income measures to assess poverty.[18] In cash terms, however, there is very little difference between the poverty line drawn at either 60 per cent of median income or 50 per cent of mean income.[19] While the 60 per cent median income line has been adopted as the primary poverty line, alternatives set at 50 per cent and 70 per cent of median income are also used to clarify and lend robustness to assessments of poverty.

The most up-to-date data available on poverty in Ireland comes from the 2011 *SILC* survey, conducted by the CSO. In that year the CSO gathered data from a statistically representative sample of more than 4,300 households containing 11,005 individuals. The data gathered by the CSO is very detailed. It incorporates income from work, welfare, pensions, rental income, dividends, capital gains and other regular transfers. This data was subsequently verified anonymously using PPS numbers.

According to the CSO, the median disposable income per adult in Ireland during 2011 was €18,148 per annum or €348.05 per week. Consequently, the income poverty lines for a single adult derived from this are:

50 per cent line	€174.03 a week
60 per cent line	€208.84 a week
70 per cent line	€243.65 a week

Updating the 60 per cent median income poverty line to 2013 levels, using the ESRI's (Duffy, Durkan, Timoney and Casey, 2012:iii) predicted changes in wage levels for 2012 (+1.1 per cent) and 2013 (+1.2 per cent) that produces a relative income poverty line of €213.67 for a single person. In 2013, any adult below this weekly income level will be counted as being at risk of poverty. It is noteworthy

---

[18] In particular the use of median income ensures that it is possible to eliminate poverty (a rate of 0 per cent), a feature that was theoretically impossible when poverty lines were calculated using mean income.
[19] For example, in 2011 the CSO's data indicates that the annual 60 per cent median income line was €169 higher (€3.24 per week) than the 50 per cent mean income line.

that the value of the 2013 poverty line is little different to the 2011 figure shown above and is lower than the poverty line value for 2009 (€231.37). This is because wages fell in 2009 and 2010 and increased by only 0.1 per cent in 2011 while throughout that period taxes have increased and most social welfare rates of payment have decreased. Taken together, these factors have had a negative impact on disposable income and, because the poverty line is a relative measure, it is adjusted accordingly.

Table 3.1 shows what income corresponds to the poverty line for a number of household types. The figure of €213.67 is an income per adult equivalent figure. It is the minimum weekly disposable income (after taxes and including all benefits) that one adult needs to be above the poverty line. For each additional adult in the household this minimum income figure is increased by €141.02 (66 per cent of the poverty line figure) and for each child in the household the minimum income figure is increased by €70.51 (33 per cent of the poverty line).[20] These adjustments reflect the fact that as households increase in size they require more income to meet the basic standard of living implied by the poverty line. In all cases a household below the corresponding weekly disposable income figure is classified as living at risk of poverty. For clarity, corresponding annual figures are also included.

Table 3.1: The Minimum Weekly Disposable Income Required to Avoid Poverty in 2013, by Household Types

Household containing:	Weekly poverty line	Annual poverty line
1 adult	€213.67	€11,141
1 adult + 1 child	€284.18	€14,818
1 adult + 2 children	€354.70	€18,495
1 adult + 3 children	€425.21	€22,172
2 adults	€354.70	€18,495
2 adults + 1 child	€425.21	€22,172
2 adults + 2 children	€495.72	€25,848
2 adults + 3 children	€566.23	€29,525
3 adults	€495.72	€25,848

One immediate implication of this analysis is that most weekly social assistance rates paid to single people are more than €25 below the poverty line.

---

[20] For example the poverty line for a household with 2 adults and 1 child would be calculated as €213.67 + €141.02 + €70.51 = €425.20.

How many have incomes below the poverty line?

Table 3.2 outlines the findings of various poverty studies since detailed poverty studies commenced in 1994. Using the EU poverty line set at 60 per cent of median income, the findings reveal that 16 out of every 100 people in Ireland were living in poverty in 2011. The table shows that the rates of poverty decreased significantly after 2001, reaching a record low in 2009. These decreases in poverty levels were welcome. They were directly related to the increases in social welfare payments delivered over the Budget's spanning these years.[21] However poverty increased again in 2010 and 2011 as the effect of budgetary changes to welfare and taxes, as well as wage reductions and unemployment, drove more low income households into poverty.

Table 3.2: Percentage of population below various relative income poverty lines, 1994-2011

	1994	1998	2001	2005	2007	2009	2010	2011
50% line	6.0	9.9	12.9	10.8	8.6	6.9	7.6	8.5
60% line	**15.6**	**19.8**	**21.9**	**18.5**	**16.5**	**14.1**	**14.7**	**16.0**
70% line	26.7	26.9	29.3	28.2	26.8	24.5	24.7	24.1

Source: CSO (2013:12) and Whelan et al (2003:12), using national equivalence scale.
Note: All poverty lines calculated as a percentage of median income.

Because it is sometimes easy to overlook the scale of Ireland's poverty problem, it is useful to translate the poverty percentages into numbers of people. Using the percentages for the 60 per cent median income poverty line and population statistics from CSO population estimates, we can calculate the numbers of people in Ireland who have been in poverty for a number of years between 1994 and 2012. These calculations are presented in table 3.3. The results give a better picture of just how significant this problem really is in Ireland today.

The table's figures are telling. Over the past decade just over 110,000 people have been lifted out of poverty. Furthermore, over the period from 2004-2008, the period corresponding with consistent Budget increases in social welfare payments, almost 140,000 people left poverty. Despite this, since the onset of the recession and its associated implications for incomes (earnings and welfare), the number in poverty has increased once again, rising by 90,000 since 2009.

---

[21] See table 3.8 below for further analysis of this point.

Table 3.3: The numbers of people below relative income poverty lines in Ireland, 1994-2011

	% of persons in poverty	Population of Ireland	Numbers in poverty
1994	15.6	3,585,900	559,400
1998	19.8	3,703,100	733,214
2001	21.9	3,847,200	842,537
2003	19.7	3,978,900	783,843
2004	19.4	4,045,200	784,769
2005	18.5	4,133,800	764,753
2006	17.0	4,232,900	719,593
2007	16.5	4,375,800	722,007
2008	14.4	4,485,100	645,854
2009	14.1	4,533,400	639,209
2010	14.7	4,554,800	669,556
2011	16.0	4,574,900	731,984

Source: Calculated using CSO on-line database population estimates, Whelan et al (2003:12) and CSO SILC results for various years.
Note: Population estimates are for April of each year.

Furthermore, the fact that there are now just over 730,000 people in Ireland living life on a level of income that is this low remains a major concern. As shown above (see table 3.1) these levels of income are low and those below them clearly face difficulties in achieving what the NAPS described as "*a standard of living that is regarded as acceptable by Irish society generally*".

Annex 3 provides a more detailed profile of those groups in Ireland than are living in poverty.

The incidence of poverty

Figures detailing the incidence of poverty reveal the proportion of all those in poverty that belong to particular groups in Irish society. Tables 3.4 and 3.5 report all those below the 60 per cent of median income poverty line, classifying them by their principal economic status. The first table examines the population as a whole, including children, while the second table focuses exclusively on adults (using the ILO definition of an adult as a person aged 16 years and above).

Table 3.4 shows that in 2011, the largest group of the population who are poor, accounting for 25.8 per cent of the total, were children. The second largest group were those working in the home (17.5 per cent). Of all those who are poor, 30.8 per cent were in the labour force and the remainder (64.4 per cent) were outside the labour market.[22]

Table 3.4: Incidence of persons below 60% of median income by principal economic status, 2003-2010

	2003	2005	2006	2007*	2010	2011
At work	16.0	15.7	16.1	16.8	13.5	14.2
Unemployed	7.6	7.5	8.3	9.2	15.1	16.6
Students/school	8.6	13.4	15.0	14.1	12.3	14.7
On home duties	22.5	19.7	18.4	18.7	17.3	17.5
Retired	9.0	7.5	5.8	7.1	4.4	4.3
Ill/disabled	9.1	7.9	8.0	7.4	5.4	4.8
Children (under 16 years)	25.4	26.8	26.6	25.9	29.2	25.8
Other	1.9	1.6	1.8	0.8	2.8	2.1
Total	**100.0**	**100.0**	**100.0**	**100.0**	**100.0**	**100.0**

Source: Collins (2006:141), CSO SILC Reports (2007:19; 2009:48; 2013:15).
Note: * Data for 2007 not excluding SSIA effect as not published by CSO.

Table 3.5 looks at adults only and provides a more informed assessment of the nature of poverty. This is an important perspective as children depend on adults for their upbringing and support. Irrespective of how policy interventions are structured, it is through adults that any attempts to reduce the number of children in poverty must be directed. The table shows that in 2011 almost one-fifth of Ireland's adults with an income below the poverty line were employed. Overall, 41.5 per cent of adults at risk of poverty in Ireland were associated with the labour market.

The incidence of being at risk of poverty amongst those in employment is particularly alarming. Many people in this group do not benefit from Budget changes in welfare or tax. They would be the main beneficiaries of any move to make tax credits refundable, a topic addressed in chapter 4.

---

[22] This does not include the ill and disabled, some of whom will be active in the labour force. The SILC data does not distinguish between those are temporally unable to work due to illness and those permanently outside the labour market due to their illness or disability.

Table 3.5: Incidence of adults (16yrs+) below 60% of median income by principal economic status, 2003-2010

	2003	2005	2006	2007★	2010	2011
At work	21.4	21.4	21.9	22.7	19.1	19.1
Unemployed	10.2	10.2	11.3	12.4	21.3	22.4
Students/school	11.5	18.3	20.4	19.0	17.4	19.8
On home duties	30.1	26.9	25.1	25.2	24.4	23.6
Retired	12.0	10.2	7.9	9.6	6.2	5.8
Ill/disabled	12.2	10.8	10.9	10.0	7.6	6.5
Other	2.5	2.2	2.5	1.1	4.0	2.8
Total	**100.0**	**100.0**	**100.0**	**100.0**	**100.0**	**100.0**

Source: Calculated from Collins (2006:141), CSO SILC Reports (2007:19; 2009:48; 2013:15).

Note: ★ Data for 2007 not excluding SSIA effect as not published by CSO.

Finally, table 3.6 examines the composition of poverty by household type. Given that households are taken to be the 'income receiving units' (income flows into households who then collectively live off that income) there is a value in assessing poverty by household type. *Social Justice Ireland* welcomes the fact that the CSO has, at our suggestion, begun to publish the *SILC* poverty data broken down by household category, even though this data has yet to be released for the 2010 and 2011 SILC.[23] From a policy making perspective this information is crucial as anti-poverty policy is generally focused on households (households with children, pensioner households, single person households etc.). The 2009 data shows that 22.8 per cent of households who were at risk of poverty were headed by somebody who was employed. Almost 44 per cent of households at risk of poverty were found to be headed by a person outside the labour force.[24]

---

[23] This data is due to be published by the CSO on their website in mid 2013.

[24] Those on home duties, students and school attendees, retired plus a proportion of the ill and disabled.

Table 3.6: Households below 60% of median income classified by principal economic status of head of household, 2004-2009					
	2004	2006	2007*	2008*	2009
At work	29.8	29.5	31.3	39.6	22.8
Unemployed	12.0	14.7	12.3	11.5	26.0
Students/school	2.8	4.6	5.1	4.1	5.4
On home duties	28.0	30.7	28.7	25.7	26.7
Retired	13.5	8.5	10.9	7.9	6.6
Ill/disabled	12.0	11.5	11.2	10.1	10.9
Other	1.9	0.7	0.4	1.1	1.6
Total	**100.0**	**100.0**	**100.0**	**100.0**	**100.0**

Source: CSO SILC Reports (2007:39; 2008:36; 2009:49; 2010:49)
Note: * Data for 2007 and 2008 not excluding SSIA effect as not published by CSO.

The Scale of Poverty - Numbers of People
As the three tables in the last section deal only in percentages it is useful to transform these proportions into numbers of people. Table 3.3 revealed that 731,984 people were living below the 60 per cent of median income poverty line in 2011. Using this figure, table 3.7 presents the number of people in poverty in that year within various categories. Comparable figures are also presented for 2005, 2009 and 2010.

The data in table 3.7 is particularly useful in the context of framing anti-poverty policy. Groups such as the retired and the ill/disabled, although carrying a high risk of poverty, involve much smaller numbers of people than groups such as adults who are employed (the working poor), people on home duties and children/students. The primary drivers of the 2005-09 poverty reductions were increasing incomes among those who are on home duties, those who are classified as ill/disabled, the retired and children. Between 2005 and 2009 the numbers of workers in poverty declined while the numbers of unemployed people in poverty notably increased. This reflected the rise in unemployment in the labour market as a whole during those years. As the table shows, the increase in poverty between 2009 and 2011 can be principally explained by the increase in poverty among people with jobs, people who are unemployed and children.

Table 3.7:Poverty Levels Expressed in Numbers of People, 2005-2011				
	2005	**2009**	**2010**	**2011**
Overall	764,753	639,209	669,556	731,984
Adults				
On home duties	150,656	115,058	115,833	128,097
Unemployed	57,356	82,458	101,103	121,509
Students/school	102,477	93,325	82,355	107,602
At work	120,066	91,407	90,390	103,942
Ill/disabled	60,415	40,909	36,156	35,135
Retired	57,356	30,043	29,460	31,475
Other	12,236	9,588	18,748	15,372
Children				
Children (under 16 yrs)	204,954	176,422	195,510	188,852
Children (under 18 yrs)	n/a	223,084	226,979	232,039

Source: Calculated using CSO SILC Reports (2013:15; 2006:13) and data from table 3.3.

Poverty and social welfare recipients

Social Justice Ireland believes in the very important role that social welfare plays in addressing poverty. As part of the *SILC* results the CSO has provided an interesting insight into the role that social welfare payments play in tackling Ireland's poverty levels. It has calculated the levels of poverty before and after the payment of social welfare benefits.

Table 3.8 shows that without the social welfare system almost 51 per cent of the Irish population would have been living in poverty in 2011. Such an underlying poverty rate suggests a deeply unequal distribution of direct income – an issue we address further in the income distribution section of this chapter. In 2011, the actual poverty figure of 16 per cent reflects the fact that social welfare payments reduced poverty by almost 35 percentage points.

Looking at the impact of these payments on poverty over time, it is clear that the increases in social welfare over the period 2005-2007 yielded noticeable reductions in poverty levels. The small increases in social welfare payments in 2001 are reflected in the smaller effects achieved in that year. Conversely, the larger increases, and therefore higher levels of social welfare payments, in subsequent years delivered greater reductions. This has occurred even as poverty levels before social welfare increased. *Social Justice Ireland* warmly welcomed these social welfare increases and the CSO's data proves the effectiveness of this policy approach.

Table 3.8: The role of social welfare (SW) payments in addressing poverty

	2001	2005	2007	2009	2010	2011
Poverty pre SW	35.6	40.1	41.0	46.2	50.2	50.7
Poverty post SW	21.9	18.5	16.5	14.1	14.7	16.0
The role of SW	-13.7	-21.6	-24.5	-32.1	-35.5	-34.7

Source: CSO SILC Reports (2006:7; 2013:12) using national equivalence scale.

As social welfare payments do not flow to everybody in the population, it is interesting to examine the impact they have on alleviating poverty among certain groups, such as older people, for example. Using data from SILC 2009, the CSO found that without any social welfare payments 88 per cent of all those aged over 65 years would have been living in poverty. Benefit entitlements reduce the poverty level among this group to 9.6 per cent in 2009. Similarly, social welfare payments (including child benefit) reduce poverty among those under18 years of age from 47.3 per cent to 18.6 per cent – a 60 per cent reduction in poverty risk (CSO, 2010:47). [25] These findings, combined with the social welfare impact data in table 3.8, underscore the importance of social transfer payments in addressing poverty; a point that needs to be borne in mind as Government continues to address Ireland's on-going crisis.

Analysis in Annex 3 (see table A3.1 and the subsequent analysis) has shown that many of the groups in Irish society which experienced increases in their poverty levels over the last decade have been dependent on social welfare payments. These include pensioners, the unemployed, lone parents and those who are ill or disabled. Table 3.9 presents the results of an analysis of five key welfare recipient groups performed by the ESRI using poverty data for five of the years between 1994 and 2001. These are the years that the Irish economy grew fastest and the core years of the famed 'Celtic Tiger' boom. Between 1994 and 2001 all categories experienced large growth in their poverty risk. For example, in 1994 only five out of every 100

---

[25] This data has not been updated in the SILC publication for 2011 or the CSO revision of SILC for 2010.

old age pension recipients were in poverty. In 2001 this had increased ten-fold to almost 50 out of every 100. The experience of widow's pension recipients is similar.

Table 3.9: Percentage of persons in receipt of welfare benefits/assistance who were below the 60 per cent median income poverty line, 1994/1997/1998/2000/2001

	1994	1997	1998	2000	2001
Old age pension	5.3	19.2	30.7	42.9	49.0
Unemployment benefit/assistance	23.9	30.6	44.8	40.5	43.1
Illness/disability	10.4	25.4	38.5	48.4	49.4
Lone Parents allowance	25.8	38.4	36.9	42.7	39.7
Widow's pension	5.5	38.0	49.4	42.4	42.1

Source: Whelan et al (2003: 31)

Table 3.9 highlights the importance of adequate social welfare payments to prevent people becoming at risk of poverty. Over the period covered by these studies groups similar to *Social Justice Ireland* repeatedly pointed out that these payments had failed to rise in proportion to earnings elsewhere in society. The primary consequence of this was that recipients slipped further and further back and as a consequence more and more fell into poverty. It is clear that adequate levels of social welfare need to be maintained and we outline our proposals for this later in this chapter.

The poverty gap

As part of the 2001 Laeken indicators, the EU asked all member countries to begin measuring their relative "at risk of poverty gap". This indicator assesses how far below the poverty line the income of the median (middle) person in poverty is. The size of that difference is calculated as a percentage of the poverty line and therefore represents the gap between the income of the middle person in poverty and the poverty line. The higher the percentage figure, the greater the poverty gap and the further people are falling beneath the poverty line. As there is a considerable difference between being 2 per cent and 20 per cent below the poverty line this approach is significant.

Table 3.10: The Poverty Gap, 2003-2011							
	2003	2004	2005	2006	2007*	2009	2011
Poverty gap size	21.5	19.8	20.6	17.5	17.4	16.2	19.6

Source: CSO SILC reports (2008:16; 2013:12)
Note: * Data for 2007 not excluding SSIA effect as not published by CSO.

The *SILC* results for 2011 showed that the poverty gap was 19.6 per cent, compared to 17.7 per cent in 2010 (not in table) and 16.2 per cent in 2009. Over time the gap had decreased from a figure of 21.5 per cent in 2003. The 2011 poverty gap figure implies that 50 per cent of those in poverty had an equivalised income below 80.4 per cent of the poverty line. As the depth of poverty is an important issue, we will monitor closely the movement of this indicator in future editions of the *SILC*. It is crucial that, as part of Ireland's approach to addressing poverty, this figure declines in the future. It is of concern that recent figures once again record increases.

Poverty and deprivation
Income alone does not tell the whole story concerning living standards and command over resources. As we have seen in the NAPS definition of poverty, it is necessary to look more broadly at exclusion from society because of a lack of resources. This requires looking at other areas where 'as a result of inadequate income and resources people may be excluded and marginalised from participating in activities that are considered the norm for other people in society' (NAPS, 1997). Although income is the principal indicator used to assess wellbeing and ability to participate in society, there are other measures. In particular, these measures assess the standards of living people achieve by assessing deprivation through use of different indicators. To date assessments of deprivation in Ireland have been limited and confined to a small number of items. While this is regrettable, the information gathered is worth considering.

Deprivation in the SILC survey
Since 2007 the CSO has presented 11 measures of deprivation in the *SILC* survey, compared to just eight before that. While this increase is welcome, *Social Justice Ireland and* others have expressed serious reservations about the overall range of measures employed. We believe that a whole new approach to measuring deprivation should be developed. Continuing to collect information on a limited

number of static indicators is problematic in itself and does not present a true picture of the dynamic nature of Irish society.

The details presented in table 3.11, therefore, should be seen in the context of the above reservation. The table shows that in 2011 the rates of deprivation recorded across the set of 11 items varied between 2 and 21 per cent of the Irish population. Overall 59.8 per cent of the population were not deprived of any item, while 15.7 per cent were deprived of one item, 9.2 per cent were without two items and 15.4 per cent were without three or more items. It is of interest that from 2007 onwards, as the economic crisis unfolded, the proportion of the population who experienced no deprivation has fallen steadily from 75.6 per cent in 2007 to 63.9 per cent in 2010 and 59.8 per cent in 2011. Simultaneously, the proportion of the population experiencing deprivation of two or more items has more than doubled, increasing from 11.8 per cent in 2007 to 24.5 per cent in 2011 (CSO, 2013:13).

Table 3.11: Levels of deprivation for eleven items among the population and those in poverty, 2011 (%)		
	Total Population	Those in Poverty★
Without heating at some stage in the past year	12.2	21.7
Unable to afford a morning, afternoon or evening out in the last fortnight	21.1	35.8
Unable to afford two pairs of strong shoes	3.1	5.2
Unable to afford a roast once a week	6.7	9.3
Unable to afford a meal with meat, chicken or fish every second day	2.8	5.8
Unable to afford new (not second-hand) clothes	7.3	16.3
Unable to afford a warm waterproof coat	2.2	4.6
Unable to afford to keep the home adequately warm	6.8	11.9
Unable to replace any worn out furniture	21.7	34.3
Unable to afford to have family or friends for a drink or meal once a month	14.8	26.5
Unable to afford to buy presents for family or friends at least once a year	5.8	13.3

Source: CSO (2013:14)

Note: ★ Poverty as measured using the 60 per cent median income poverty line.

Deprivation and poverty combined: consistent poverty

'Consistent poverty' combines deprivation and poverty into a single indicator. It does this by calculating the proportion of the population simultaneously experiencing poverty and registering as deprived of two or more of the items in table 3.11. As such, it captures a sub-group of the poor.

The 2007 *SILC* data marked an important change for this indicator. Coupled with the expanded list of deprivation items, the definition of consistent poverty was changed. From 2007 onwards, to be counted as experiencing consistent poverty individuals must be both below the poverty line and experiencing deprivation of at least two items. Up to 2007 the criteria was below the poverty line and deprivation of at least one item. The *National Action Plan for Social Inclusion 2007-2016* (*NAPinclusion*) published in early 2007 set its overall poverty goal using this earlier consistent poverty measure. One of its aims was to reduce the number of people experiencing consistent poverty to between 2 per cent and 4 per cent of the total population by 2012, with a further aim of totally eliminating consistent poverty by 2016. A revision to this target was published as part of the Government's *National Reform Programme 2012 Update for Ireland* (2012). The revised poverty target is to reduce the numbers experiencing consistent poverty to 4 per cent by 2016 and to 2 per cent or less by 2020. *Social Justice Ireland* participated in the consultation process on the revision of this and other poverty targets. While we agree with the revised 2020 consistent poverty target (it is not possible to measure below this 2 per cent level using survey data) we have proposed that this target should be accompanied by other targets focused on the overall population and vulnerable groups.[26] These are outlined at the end of this chapter.

Using these new indicators and definition, the 2011 *SILC* data indicates that 6.9 per cent of the population experience consistent poverty, an increase from 4.2 per cent in 2008 and 5.5 per cent in 2009 (CSO, 2013:12). In terms of the population, the 2011 figures indicate that just over 315,000 people live in consistent poverty. Over time, the reality of the current recession and its austerity measures are pushing Ireland further away from these targets.

Annex 3 also examines the experience of people who are in food poverty, fuel poverty alongside an assessment of the research on minimum incomes in Ireland.

---

[26] See also Leahy et al (2012:61).

Moving to Persistent Poverty

Social Justice Ireland is committed to using the best and most up-to-date data in its on-going socio-economic analysis of Ireland. We believe that to do so is crucial to the emergence of accurate evidence-based policy formation. It also assists in establishing appropriate and justifiable targeting of state resources.

At the intergovernmental conference in Laeken in 2001 the EU adopted a set of commonly measured indicators to monitor socio-economic progress across all of the member states. Data for these measures is to be collected annually in the *SILC* survey. The availability of annual data on poverty, incomes and living conditions is an important move. It facilitates a more informed and timely assessment of these issues than was achievable in the past. It will also allow people to track changes more closely over time and to make accurate comparisons across all 27 EU member states.

Among the Laeken indicators is an indicator of persistent poverty. This indicator measures the proportion of those living below the 60 per cent of median income poverty line in the current year and for two of the three preceding years. Persistent poverty, therefore, identifies those who have experienced sustained exposure to poverty which is seen to harm their quality of life seriously and to increase their levels of deprivation. To date the *SILC* survey has not produced any detailed results and breakdowns for this measure (although the survey has run for more than four full years and it is therefore possible to provide this insight). The CSO had indicated that it would publish such a breakdown; however to date this has not occurred due to sampling reasons. We regret this delay and hope that the technical impediments to the publication of this data are overcome. *Social Justice Ireland* believes that this data should be used as the primary basis for setting poverty targets and monitoring changes in poverty status. Existing measures of relative and consistent poverty should be maintained as secondary indicators. As the persistent poverty indicator will identify the long-term poor, wwe believe that the CSO should produce comprehensive breakdowns of those in persistent poverty, similar to the approach it currently takes with relative income poverty.

Poverty: a European perspective

It is helpful to compare Irish measures of poverty with those elsewhere in Europe. Eurostat, the European Statistics Agency, produces comparable 'at risk of poverty' figures (proportions of the population living below the poverty line) for each EU member state. The data is calculated using the 60 per cent of median income poverty line in each country. Comparable EU-wide definitions of income and equivalence scale are used.[27] The latest data available is for the year 2011.

As table 3.12 shows, Irish people experience a below average risk of poverty when compared to all other EU member states. Eurostat's 2008 figures marked the first time Ireland's poverty levels fell below average EU levels. This phenomenon was driven, as outlined earlier in this review, by sustained increases in welfare payments in the years prior to 2008. Ireland's poverty levels remained below average EU levels in 2009 and 2010, although over that time poverty rates increased. In 2010, across the EU the highest poverty levels were found in the recent accession countries of Bulgaria and Romania and countries caught up in the EU-wide economic crash: Spain and Greece. The lowest levels were in Austria, the Netherlands and the Czech Republic.

Table 3.12: The risk of poverty in the European Union in 2011

Country	Poverty Risk	Country	Poverty Risk
Bulgaria	22.3	Belgium	15.3
Romania	22.2	Cyprus	14.5
Spain	21.8	France	14.0
Greece	21.4	Sweden	14.0
Lithuania	20.0	Hungary	13.8
Italy	19.6	Finland	13.7
Latvia	19.1	Luxembourg	13.6
Portugal	18.0	Slovenia	13.6
Poland	17.7	Denmark	13.0
Estonia	17.5	Slovakia	13.0
United Kingdom	16.2	Austria	12.6
IRELAND	**16.1**	Netherlands	11.0
Germany	15.8	Czech Republic	9.8
Malta	15.4	**EU-27 average**	**16.9**

Source: Eurostat online database

Note: Table uses the most up-to-date comparable data available for countries and corresponds to the year 2011 for all countries except Ireland where the value is for 2010.

---

[27] Differences in definitions of income and equivalence scales result in slight differences in the poverty rates reported for Ireland when compared to those reported earlier which have been calculated by the CSO using national definitions of income and the Irish equivalence scale.

The average risk of poverty in the EU-27 for 2011 was 16.9 per cent. Chart 3.1 further develops the findings of table 3.12 and shows the difference between national poverty risk levels and the EU-27 average.

Chart 3.1: Percentage difference in National Poverty risk from EU-27 average

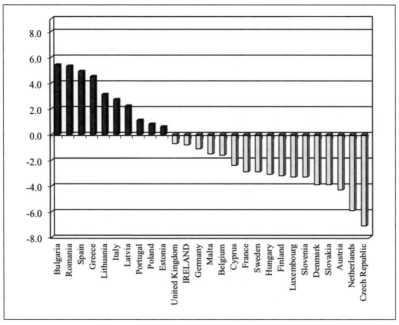

Source: Eurostat online database

Note: Chart uses the most up-to-date comparable data available for countries and corresponds to the year 2011 for all countries except Ireland where the value is for 2010.

While there have been some reductions in poverty in recent years across the EU, the data does suggest that poverty remains a large and on-going EU-wide problem. In 2011 the average EU-27 level implies that 83.5 million people are in poverty across the EU.

Europe 2020 Strategy – Risk of Poverty or Social Exclusion
As part of the Europe 2020 Strategy, European governments have begun to adopt policies to target these poverty levels and are using as their main benchmark the

proportion of the population at risk of poverty or social exclusion. This indicator has been defined by the European Council on the basis of three indicators: the aforementioned 'at risk of poverty' rate after social transfers, an index of material deprivation[28] and the percentage of people living in households with very low work intensity.[29] It is calculated as the sum of persons relative to the national population who are at risk of poverty or severely materially deprived or living in households with very low work intensity, where a person is only counted once even if recorded in more than one indicator.[30]

Table 3.13 summarises the latest data on this indicator for Europe and chart 3.2 summarises the latest Irish data (which is for 2010). While *Social Justice Ireland* regrets that the Europe 2020 process shifted its indicator focus away from an exclusive concentration on the at risk of poverty rate, we welcome the added attention at a European level to issues regarding poverty, deprivation and joblessness. Together with Caritas Europa, we have initiated a process to monitor progress on this strategy over the years to come (Mallon and Healy, 2012 and Leahy et al, 2012). However, it is clear already that the austerity measures which are being pursued in many EU countries will result in the erosion of social services and lead to the further exclusion of people who already find themselves on the margins of society. This is in direct contradiction to the inclusive growth focus of the Europe 2020 Strategy. It is reflected in the figures in table 3.13 which show an increase in risk levels in 2010 and 2011.

Table 3.13: People at risk of poverty or social exclusion, Ireland and the EU 2007–2011

	2007	2009	2010	2011
Ireland % Population	23.1	25.7	29.9	n/a
Ireland 000s people	1,005	1,150	1,335	n/a
EU % Population	24.4	23.1	23.6	24.2
EU 000s people	119,281	113,767	116,300	119,566

Source: Eurostat online database
Note: 2011 data for Ireland has yet to be submitted by the CSO to Eurostat.

---

[28] Material deprivation covers indicators relating to economic strain and durables. Severely materially deprived persons have living conditions severely constrained by a lack of resources. They experience at least 4 out of 9 listed deprivations items. (Eurostat, 2012)

[29] People living in households with very low work intensity are those aged 0-59 living in households where the adults (aged 18-59) work less than 20% of their total work potential during the past year (Eurostat, 2012)

[30] See European Commission (2011) for a more detailed explanation of this indicator.

Chart 3.2: Population at risk of poverty or social exclusion, Ireland 2010

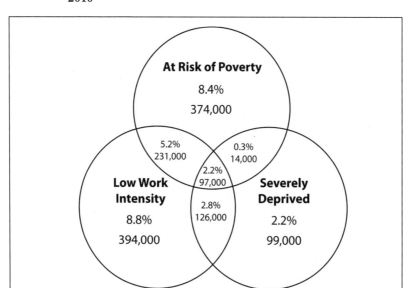

Source: Compiled from Eurostat online database
Note: 2011 data for Ireland has yet to be submitted by the CSO to Eurostat.

3.2 Income Distribution

As previously outlined, despite some improvements poverty remains a significant problem. The purpose of economic development should be to improve the living standards of all of the population. A further loss of social cohesion will mean that large numbers of people continue to experience deprivation and the gap between them and the better-off will widen. This has implications for all of society, not just those who are poor.

Analysis of the annual income and expenditure accounts yields information on trends in the distribution of national income. However, the limitations of this accounting system need to be acknowledged. Measures of income are far from perfect gauges of a society. They ignore many relevant non-market features, such as volunteerism, caring and environmental protection. Many environmental factors, such as the depletion of natural resources, are registered as income but not seen as a cost. Pollution is not registered as a cost but cleaning up after pollution is seen as income. Increased spending on prisons and security, which are a response to crime, are seen as increasing national income but not registered as reducing human well-being.

The point is that national accounts do not include items that cannot easily be assigned a monetary value. But progress cannot be measured by economic growth alone. Many other factors are required, as we highlight elsewhere in this review.[31] However, when judging economic performance and making judgements about how well Ireland is really doing, it is important to look at the distribution of national income as well as its absolute amount.[32]

Ireland's income distribution: latest data

The most recent data on Ireland's income distribution, from the 2011 SILC survey, was published in early 2013. While the publication provided considerable detail on poverty figures (see earlier in this chapter) it provided limited details on the structure of the income distribution. Further data from the CSO is due to be released in mid-2013. However, the report did show that over recent years Ireland's income distribution has widened – a point we return to later.

Chart 3.3 shows the most comprehensive data on the income distribution available, which was published by the CSO in late 2010. It examines the income distribution by household deciles, starting with the 10 per cent of households with the lowest income (the bottom decile) up to the 10 per cent of households with the highest income (the top decile). The data presented is for disposable income. This is the amount of money households have in their pocket to spend after they have received any employment/pension income, paid all their income taxes and received any welfare entitlements.

In 2009, the top 10 per cent of Irish households received 25.83 per cent of the total disposable income while the bottom decile received 2.39 per cent. Collectively, the poorest 50 per cent of households received a very similar share (25.02 per cent) to the top 10 per cent. Overall the share of the top 10 per cent is nearly 11 times the share of the bottom 10 per cent. Table 3.14 outlines the cash values of these income shares in 2009. It shows that the top 10 per cent of

---

[31] We return to critique National Income statistics in chapter 12. There, we also propose some alternatives.

[32] We examine the issue of the world's income and wealth distribution in chapter 14.

households receive an average weekly disposable income (after all taxes and having received all benefits) of €2,276 while the bottom decile receives €210 per week. In 2009 the average household disposable income was €880 a week / €45,926 per annum (CSO, 2010: 24-25). While the nominal value of these shares is likely to have declined since 2009, the spread of income reflected in the table has become more unequal according to the CSOs 2011 SILC report.

Chart 3.3: Ireland's Income Distribution by 10% (decile) group, 2009

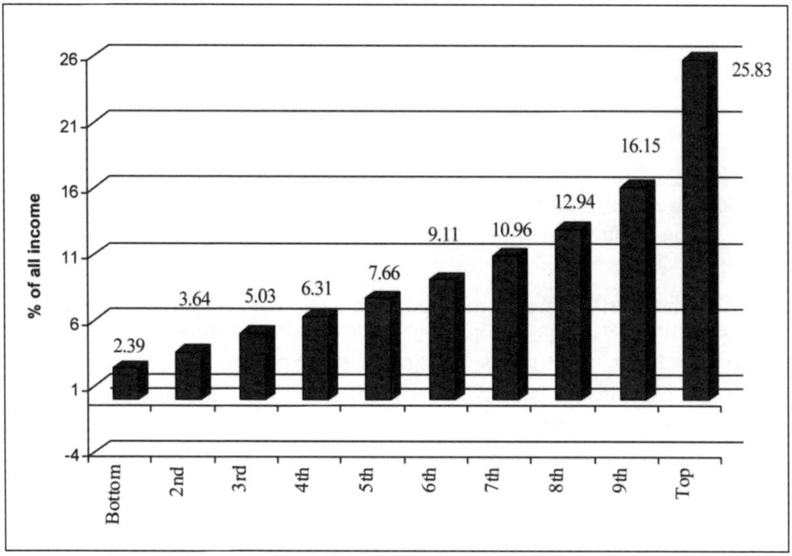

Source: Calculated from CSO, 2010:24-25

An examination of income distribution over the period from 1987-2010 is provided in annex 3.

Table 3.14: Amounts of disposable income, by decile, in 2009		
Decile	**Weekly disposable income**	**Annual disposable income**
Bottom	€210.45	€10,973
2nd	€320.37	€16,705
3rd	€443.07	€23,103
4th	€555.88	€28,985
5th	€675.19	€35,206
6th	€802.53	€41,846
7th	€965.83	€50,361
8th	€1,140.49	€59,468
9th	€1,422.84	€74,191
Top	€2,276.00	€118,677

Source: Calculated from CSO (2010:24–25)
Note: Annual figures are rounded to the nearest Euro to ease interpretation.

Direct income distribution

It is noteworthy that Ireland's disposable income distribution (after redistribution through taxes and transfers) has been largely static despite improvements in welfare payments which reduced poverty, as highlighted in table 3.8. The implication of this is that simultaneous with improvements in welfare payments and redistributive taxes, the underlying distribution of direct or market income has become more unequal. Collins and Kavanagh (2006: 155, 162) highlighted the 'marked increase in the level of direct income inequality' over the period from 1973 to 2004.

Table 3.15 suggests that the level of direct income inequality has continued to widen. Over the period from 1987 to 2009 the direct income shares of all deciles except the top two have declined. Compared to the situation in 1987 the gap between the bottom and top deciles has dramatically widened. By 2009 the share of the top 10 per cent was almost four times that of the bottom 50 per cent. While the role of the redistribution system is to intervene and address this inequality via taxation and welfare payments, the fact that the underlying income inequality continues to worsen suggests that the challenges faced by the redistribution system have become much greater over time.

Table 3.15: The distribution of household direct income, 1987-2009 (%)			
Decile	**1987**	**2004**	**2009**
Bottom	0.38	0.19	0.23
2nd	1.00	0.48	0.71
3rd	1.40	1.05	1.35
4th	3.30	2.64	2.57
5th	6.10	5.70	4.69
6th	8.70	8.65	7.69
7th	11.60	11.49	10.68
8th	15.09	14.96	14.47
9th	20.08	19.54	21.02
Top	32.46	35.31	36.59
Total	**100.00**	**100.00**	**100.00**
Bottom 20%	1.38	0.67	0.94
Bottom 50%	12.08	10.06	9.55
Top 10:Bot 10	85 times	185 times	160 times

Source: Collins and Kavanagh (2006:155) and CSO (2010: 24-25).
Note: Data for 1987 is from the Household Budget Survey, 2004 and 2009 data from SILC.

Income changes – a 25 year assessment

It has been suggested in recent times that there should be a reduction in the basic social welfare payment, the jobseekers allowance. It has been asserted by some that this rate increased too fast and reached too high a level during the last decade. The earlier analysis (see tables 3.8 and 3.9) highlighted that over the period since 2000 welfare increases were essentially attempting to catch up, given the dramatic worsening of the position of those dependent on social welfare relative to the rest of society. This was most significantly demonstrated by the large increases in the poverty levels of welfare recipients between 1994 and 2001. However, it is worth broadening this perspective to compare the income gains of those on welfare compared to a range of others in Irish society over the past quarter of a century. Chart 3.4 presents the results of such an analysis undertaken by *Social Justice Ireland* for the years between 1986 and 2012 (incorporating all changes to earnings and take home pay in Budget 2011).

The following should be noted about the calculations:

- Taxation is calculated on a single person basis under normal rules as this yields the lowest net pay. It could be calculated differently, which would result in the net weekly pay increase being higher for those in paid employment included in the table.
- Irish punt values have been converted to euros.
- The pay for a TD in 2011 is the rate paid after the General Election of that year which set all TDs salaries at €92,672 a year.
- To allow like-for-like comparison, the figures do not take account of pension contributions or deductions as these are neither available nor comparable across sectors. In this context it should be noted that those at the higher income range have a much greater gain for their pension contributions compared to the others listed in the table.

Chart 3.4: Increases in weekly pay, 1986-2011

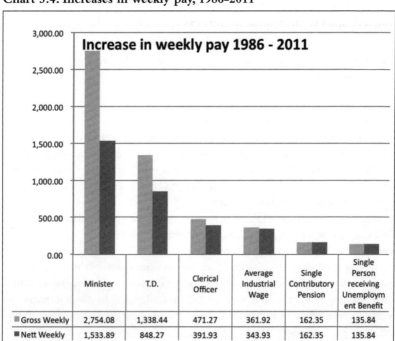

	Minister	T.D.	Clerical Officer	Average Industrial Wage	Single Contributory Pension	Single Person receiving Unemployment Benefit
Gross Weekly	2,754.08	1,338.44	471.27	361.92	162.35	135.84
Nett Weekly	1,533.89	848.27	391.93	343.93	162.35	135.84

The analysis shows that over the quarter century 1986-2011 the take-home pay of TDs rose by €848 a week while jobseekers benefit rates for a single person only increased by €136 a week in the same period. Government ministers' take-home pay rose by more than €1,533 a week in the same period. Similarly, the take-home pay of clerical officers in the public sector rose by €392 a week; the take-home pay of a person on the average industrial wage rose by €344 a week; and the contributory old age pension for a single person rose by €162.35 a week.

These are dramatic numbers in the context of the on-going calls for welfare and pension cuts. As we have pointed out in various publications over recent years, other choices exist that would have enabled Government not to cut social welfare rates. These choices should have been taken in the past and should be taken in the period ahead. The figures also underscore the massive increases in direct income inequality over recent decades demonstrated earlier in this review.

Income distribution: a European perspective

Another of the 18 indicators adopted by the EU at Laeken assesses the income distribution of member states by comparing the ratio of equivalised disposable income received by the bottom quintile (20 per cent) to that of the top quintile. This indicator reveals how far away from each other the shares of these two groups are – the higher the ratio the greater the income difference. Table 3.16 presents the most up-to-date results of this indicator for the 27 states that were members of the EU in 2011. The data indicate that the Irish figure increased to 5.3 from a ratio of 4.2 in 2009, reflecting the already noted increase in income inequality in 2011. Ireland now has a ratio above the EU average and, given recent economic and budgetary policy, this looks likely to persist and may even worsen. Overall, the greatest differences in the shares of those at the top and bottom of income distribution are found in many of the newer and poorer member states. However, some EU-15 members, including the UK, Italy, Spain, Greece and Portugal, also record large differences.

A further measure of income inequality is the Gini coefficient, which ranges from 0 to 100 and summarises the degree of inequality across the entire income distribution (rather than just at the top and bottom).[33] The higher the Gini coefficient score the greater the degree of income inequality in a society. As table 3.17 shows, over time income inequality has been reasonably static in the EU-27, although within the EU there are notable differences. Countries such as Ireland

---

[33] See Collins and Kavanagh (2006: 159-160) who provide a more detailed explanation of this measure.

cluster around or just above the average EU score and differ from other high-income EU member states which record lower levels of inequality. As the table shows, the degree of inequality is at a notably lower scale in countries like Finland, Sweden and the Netherlands. Ireland's Gini coefficient for 2010 has been revised downwards by the CSO to 31.6 and is at 31.1 for 2011 (CSO: SILC, 2013: 3). These adjustments have not yet been incorporated into the Eurostat data. However, these adjustments do not change our key point i.e. that despite the aforementioned role of the social transfer system, the underlying degree of direct income inequality dictates that our income distribution remains much more unequal than in many of the EU countries we wish to emulate in term of economic and social development.

Table 3.16: Ratio of Disposable Income received by bottom quintile to that of the top quintile in the EU-27

Country	Ratio	Country	Ratio
Spain	6.8	Denmark	4.4
Latvia	6.6	Cyprus	4.3
Bulgaria	6.5	Malta	4.1
Romania	6.2	Luxembourg	4.0
Greece	6.0	Belgium	3.9
Lithuania	5.8	Hungary	3.9
Portugal	5.7	Netherlands	3.8
Italy	5.6	Austria	3.8
Estonia	5.3	Slovakia	3.8
IRELAND	**5.3**	Finland	3.7
United Kingdom	5.3	Sweden	3.6
Poland	5.0	Czech Republic	3.5
France	4.6	Slovenia	3.5
Germany	4.5	**EU-27 average**	**5.1**

Source: Eurostat online database

Note: Chart uses the most up-to-date comparable data available for countries and corresponds to the year 2011 for all countries except Ireland where the value is for 2010.

Table 3.17: Gini coefficient measure of income inequality for selected EU states, 2005-2011

	2005	2007	2008	2009	2010	2011
EU-27	30.6	30.6	30.8	30.4	30.5	30.7
IRELAND	31.9	31.3	29.9	28.8	33.2	n/a
UK	34.6	32.6	33.9	32.4	33.0	33.0
France	27.7	26.6	29.8	29.9	29.8	30.8
Germany	26.1	30.4	30.2	29.1	29.3	29.0
Sweden	23.4	23.4	24.0	24.8	24.1	24.4
Finland	26.0	26.2	26.3	25.9	25.4	25.8
Netherlands	26.9	27.6	27.6	27.2	25.5	25.8

Source: Eurostat online database
Notes: The Gini coefficient ranges from 0-100 with a higher score indicating a higher
          level of inequality.
The table uses the most up-to-date comparable data available for countries and corresponds to the year 2011 for all countries except Ireland, where the value is for 2010.

3.3 Maintaining an Adequate Level of Social Welfare

From 2005 onwards there was major progress on benchmarking social welfare payments. Budget 2007 benchmarked the minimum social welfare rate at 30 per cent of Gross Average Industrial Earnings (GAIE). This was a key achievement and one that we correctly predicted would lead to reductions in poverty rates, complementing those already achieved and detailed earlier.

The process of benchmarking social welfare payments centred on three elements: the 2001 *Social Welfare Benchmarking and Indexation Working Group* (SWBIG), the 2002 *National Anti-Poverty Strategy (NAPS) Review* and the *Budgets 2005-2007*.

Social welfare benchmarking and indexation working group

In its final report the SWBIG agreed that the lowest social welfare rates should be benchmarked. A majority of the working group, which included a director of *Social Justice Ireland*, also agreed that this benchmark should be index-linked to society's standard of living as it grows and that the benchmark should be reached by a definite date. The working group chose Gross Average Industrial Earnings (GAIE) to be the index to which payments should be linked. The group further urged that provision be made for regular and formal review and monitoring of the range of issues covered in its report.[34] The group expressed the opinion that this could best be accommodated within the structures in place under the NAPS and the *National Action Plan for Social Inclusion* (now combined as *NAPinclusion*). The SWBIG report envisaged that such a mechanism could involve:

- the review of any benchmarks/targets and indexation methodologies adopted by government to ensure that the underlying objectives remain valid and were being met;
- the assessment of such benchmarks/targets and indexation methodologies against the various criteria set out in the group's terms of reference to ensure their continued relevance;
- the assessment of emerging trends in the key areas of concern, e.g. poverty levels, labour market performance, demographic changes, economic performance and competitiveness, and
- identification of gaps in the area of research and assessment of any additional research undertaken in the interim.

National Anti-Poverty Strategy (NAPS) review 2002

In 2002, the NAPS review set the following as key targets:

To achieve a rate of €150 per week in 2002 terms for the lowest rates of social welfare to be met by 2007 and the appropriate equivalence level of basic child income support (i.e. Child Benefit and Child Dependent Allowances combined) to be set at 33 per cent to 35 per cent of the minimum adult social welfare payment rate.

Social Justice Ireland and others welcomed this target. It was a major breakthrough in social, economic and philosophical terms. We also welcomed the reaffirmation of this target in *Towards 2016*. That agreement contained a commitment to 'achieving the NAPS target of €150 per week in 2002 terms for lowest social welfare rates by 2007' (2006:52). The target of €150 a week was equivalent to 30 per cent of Gross Average Industrial Earnings (GAIE) in 2002.[35]

---

[34] The group recommended a benchmark of 27 per cent although *SJI* argued for 30 per cent.
[35] GAIE is calculated by the CSO on the earnings of all individuals (male and female) working in all industries. The GAIE figure in 2002 was €501.51 and 30 per cent of this figure equals €150.45 (CSO, 2006: 2).

Table 3.18 outlines the expected growth rates in the value of €150 based on this commitment and indicates that the lowest social welfare rates for single people should have reached €185.80 by 2007.

Table 3.18: Estimating growth in €150 a week (30% GAIE) for 2002-2007						
	2002	**2003**	**2004**	**2005**	**2006**	**2007**
% Growth of GAIE -	+6.00	+3.00	+4.50	+3.60	+4.80	
30% GAIE	150	159.00	163.77	171.14	177.30	185.80

Source: GAIE growth rates from CSO Industrial Earnings and Hours Worked (September 2004:2) and ESRI Medium Term Review (Bergin et al, 2003:49).

Budgets 2005-2007

The NAPS commitment was very welcome and was one of the few areas of the anti-poverty strategy that was adequate to tackle the scale of the poverty, inequality and social exclusion being experienced by so many people in Ireland today.

In 2002 *Social Justice Ireland* set out a pathway to reaching this target by calculating the projected growth of €150 between 2002 and 2007 when it is indexed to the estimated growth in GAIE. Progress towards achieving this target had been slow until Budget 2005. At its first opportunity to live up to the NAPS commitment the government granted a mere €6 a week increase in social welfare rates in Budget 2003. This increase was below that which we proposed and also below that recommended by the government's own tax strategy group. In Budget 2004 the increase in the minimum social welfare payment was €10. This increase was again below the €12 a week we sought and at this point we set out a three-year pathway (see table 3.19).

Table 3.19: Proposed approach to addressing the gap, 2005-2007			
	2005	**2006**	**2007**
Min. SW. payment in €'s	148.80	165.80	185.80
€ amount increase each year	14.00	17.00	20.00
Delivered	✓	✓	✓

Following Budget 2004 we argued for an increase of €14 in Budget 2005. The Government's decision to deliver an increase equal to that amount in that Budget marked a significant step towards honouring this commitment.. Budget 2006 followed suit, delivering an increase of €17 per week to those in receipt of the minimum social welfare rate. Finally, Budget 2007's decision to deliver an increase of €20 per week to the minimum social welfare rates brought the minimum social welfare payment up to the 30 per cent of the GAIE benchmark.

Social Justice Ireland believes that these increases, and the achievement of the benchmark in Budget 2007, marked a fundamental turning point in Irish public policy. Budget 2007 was the third budget in a row in which the government delivered on its NAPS commitment. In doing so the government moved to meet the target so that in 2007 the minimum social welfare rate increased to €185.80 per week; a figure equivalent to the 30 per cent of GAIE.

We warmly welcomed this achievement. It marked major progress and underscored the delivery of a long overdue commitment to sharing the fruits of this country's economic growth since the mid-1990s. An important element of the NAPS commitment to increasing social welfare rates was the acknowledgement that the years from 2002-2007 marked a period of 'catch up' for those in receipt of welfare payments. Once this income gap had been bridged, the increases necessary to keep social welfare payments at a level equivalent to 30 per cent of GAIE became much smaller. In that context we welcomed the commitment by Government in *NAPinclusion* to 'maintain the relative value of the lowest social welfare rate at least at €185.80, in 2007 terms, over the course of this Plan (2007-2016), subject to available resources' (2007:42). Whether or not 30 per cent of GAIE is adequate to eliminate the risk of poverty will need to be monitored through the SILC studies and addressed when fresh data on persistent poverty emerges.

Setting a Benchmark: 2011 onwards
In late 2007 the CSO discontinued its *Industrial Earnings and Hours Worked* dataset and replaced it with a more comprehensive set of income statistics for a broader set of Irish employment sectors. The end of that dataset also saw the demise of the GAIE figure from Irish official statistics. It has been replaced with a series of measures, including a new indicator measuring average earnings across all the employment sectors now covered. While the improvement to data sources is welcome, the end of the GAIE figure poses problems for continuing to calculate the social welfare benchmark. To this end, *Social Justice Ireland* commissioned a report in late 2010 to establish an appropriate way of continuing to calculate this benchmark.

A report entitled 'Establishing a Benchmark for Ireland's Social Welfare Payments' (Collins, 2011) is available on Social Justice Ireland's website. It established that 30 per cent of GAIE is equivalent to 27.5 per cent of the new average earnings data being collected by the CSO. A figure of 27.5 per cent of average earnings is therefore the appropriate benchmark for minimum social welfare payments and reflects a continuation of the previous benchmark using the new CSO earnings dataset.

Table 3.20 applies this benchmark using CSO data for third quarter of 2012 (published February 2013). The data is updated using ESRI projections for wage growth in 2013 (1.2 per cent) and 2014 (1.5 per cent). In 2013 27.5 per cent of average weekly earnings equals €192.56, marginally more than the current minimum social welfare rate of €188. It increases to €195.45 in 2014. As a consequence of this benchmark, Social Justice Ireland believes that the appropriate budgetary policy in 2014 would be to increase minimum social welfare rates to ensure it is equivalent to 27.5 per cent of average weekly earnings. This would address some of the losses in buying power over recent years and maintain the benchmark. We will develop this proposal further in our pre-Budget submission in mid-2013.

Table 3.20: Benchmarking Social Welfare Payments for 2013 and 2014 (€)		
Year	Average Weekly Earnings	27.5% of Average Weekly Earnings
2012	691.93	190.28
2013	700.23	192.56
2014	710.74	195.45

Notes: 2012 data from Quarter 3 2012 (CSO, February 2013).
Earnings growth rates for 2012 and 2013 from ESRI QEC Winter 2012.

Individualising social welfare payments

The issue of individualising payments so that all recipients receive their own social welfare payments has been on the policy agenda in Ireland and across the EU for several years. Social Justice Ireland welcomed the report of the Working Group, Examining the Treatment of Married, Cohabiting and One-Parent Families under the Tax and Social Welfare Codes, which addressed some of the individualisation issues.

At present the welfare system provides a basic payment for a claimant, whether that be, for example, for a pension, a disability payment or a job-seeker's payment. It then adds an additional payment of about two-thirds of the basic payment for the second person. For example, following Budget 2013 a couple on the lowest social welfare rate receive a payment of €312.80 per week. This amount is approximately 1.66 times the payment for a single person (€188). Were these two people living separately they would receive €188 each; giving a total of €376. Thus by living as a household unit such a couple receive a lower income than they would were they to live apart.

Social Justice Ireland believes that this system is unfair and inequitable. We also believe that the system as currently structured is not compatible with the Equal Status Acts (2000-2004), a point we strongly made in a submission to the *Department of Social and Family Affairs Review of the Social Welfare Code* with regard to its compatibility with the Equal Status Acts. People, often women, are disadvantaged by living as part of a household unit because they receive a lower income. We believe that where a couple is in receipt of welfare payments, the payment to the second person should be increased to equal that of the first. Such a change would remove the current inequity and bring the current social welfare system in line with the terms of the Equal Status Acts (2000-2004). An effective way of doing this would be to introduce a basic income system which is far more appropriate for the world of the 21st century.

3.4 Basic Income

Over the past 12 years major progress has been achieved in building the case for the introduction of a basic income in Ireland. This includes the publication of a *Green Paper on Basic Income* by the Government in September 2002 and the publication of a book by Clark entitled *The Basic Income Guarantee* (2002). A major international conference on basic income was also held in Dublin during summer 2008 at which more than 70 papers from 30 countries were presented. These are available on *Social Justice Ireland*'s website. More recently, Healy et al (2012) have provided an initial set of costing for a basic income and new European and Irish Basic Income networks have emerged.[36]

---

[36] These networks are the European Citizens' Initiative for Unconditional Basic Income and BIEN Ireland.

The case for a basic income

Social Justice Ireland has long argued that the present tax and social welfare systems should be integrated and reformed to make them more appropriate to the changing world of the 21st century. To this end we have sought the introduction of a basic income system. This proposal is especially relevant at the present moment of economic upheaval.

A basic income is an income that is unconditionally granted to every person on an individual basis, without any means test or work requirement. In a basic income system every person receives a weekly tax-free payment from the Exchequer while all other personal income is taxed, usually at a single rate. The basic-income payment would replace income from social welfare for a person who is unemployed and replace tax credits for a person who is employed.

Basic income is a form of minimum income guarantee that avoids many of the negative side-effects inherent in social welfare payments. A basic income differs from other forms of income support in that:

- it is paid to individuals rather than households;
- it is paid irrespective of any income from other sources;
- it is paid without conditions; it does not require the performance of any work or the willingness to accept a job if offered one; and
- it is always tax free.

There is real danger that the plight of large numbers of people excluded from the benefits of the modern economy will be ignored. Images of rising tides lifting all boats are often offered as government's policy makers and commentators assure society that prosperity for all is just around the corner. Likewise, the claim is often made that a job is the best poverty fighter and consequently priority must be given to securing a paid job for everyone. These images and claims are no substitute for concrete policies to ensure that all are included. Twenty-first century society needs a radical approach to ensure the inclusion of all people in the benefits of present economic growth and development. Basic income is such an approach.

As we are proposing it, a basic income system would replace social welfare and income tax credits. It would guarantee an income above the poverty line for everyone. It would not be means tested. There would be no 'signing on' and no restrictions or conditions. In practice, a basic income recognises the right of every person to a share of the resources of society.

The Basic Income system ensures that looking for a paid job and earning an income, or increasing one's income while in employment, is always worth pursuing, because for every euro earned the person will retain a large part. It thus removes the poverty traps and unemployment traps in the present system. Furthermore, women and men would receive equal payments in a basic income system. Consequently the basic income system promotes gender equality because it treats every person equally.

It is a system that is altogether more guaranteed, rewarding, simple and transparent than the present tax and welfare systems. It is far more employment friendly than the present system. It also respects other forms of work besides paid employment. This is crucial in a world where these need to be recognised and respected. It is also very important in a world where paid employment cannot be permanently guaranteed for everyone seeking it. There is growing pressure and need in Irish society to ensure recognition and monetary reward for such work. Basic income is a transparent, efficient and affordable mechanism for ensuring such recognition and reward.

Basic income also lifts people out of poverty and the dependency mode of survival. In doing this, it also restores self-esteem and broadens horizons. Poor people, however, are not the only ones who should welcome a basic income system. Employers, for example, should welcome it because its introduction would mean they would not be in competition with the social welfare system. Since employees would not lose their basic income when taking a job, there would always be an incentive to take up employment.

Costing a basic income

During 2012 Healy et al presented an estimate for the cost of a basic income for Ireland. Using administrative data from the Census, social protection system and taxation system, the paper estimated a cost where payments were aligned to the existing social welfare payments (children = €32.30 per week; adults of working age = €188.00 per week; older people aged 66-80 = €230.30 per week; and older people aged 80+ = €240.30 per week). The paper estimated a total cost of €39.2 billion per annum for a basic income and outlined a requirement to collect a total of €41 billion in revenue to fund this. It is proposed that the revenue should be raised via a flat 45 per cent personal income tax and the continuance of the existing employers PRSI system (renamed a 'social solidarity fund'). It is important to remember that nobody would have an effective tax rate of 45 per cent in this system as they would always receive their full basic income and it would always be tax-free. Healy et al also outline further directions for research in this area in the future and are likely to contribute future inputs into the evolving Irish and European basic income networks.

Ten reasons to introduce basic income

- It is work and employment friendly.
- It eliminates poverty traps and unemployment traps.
- It promotes equity and ensures that everyone receives at least the poverty level of income.
- It spreads the burden of taxation more equitably.
- It treats men and women equally.
- It is simple and transparent.
- It is efficient in labour-market terms.
- It rewards types of work in the social economy that the market economy often ignores, e.g. home duties, caring, etc.
- It facilitates further education and training in the labour force.
- It faces up to the changes in the global economy.

Key policy priorities on income distribution

- If poverty rates are to fall in the years ahead, *Social Justice Ireland* believes that the following are required:
  - benchmarking of social welfare payments,
  - equity of social welfare rates,
  - adequate payments for children,
  - refundable tax credits,
  - a universal state pension, and
  - a cost of disability payment.

Social Justice Ireland believes that in the period ahead Government and policy-makers generally should:

- Acknowledge that Ireland has an on-going poverty problem.
- Adopt targets aimed at reducing poverty among particular vulnerable groups such as children, lone parents, jobless households and those in social rented housing.
- Carry out in-depth social impact assessments prior to implementing proposed policy initiatives aimed at achieving the fiscal adjustments required by the EU/IMF bailout and the Government's multi-year budgetary plan.

- Change the ratio of expenditure cuts to tax increases in forthcoming budgets. Tax increases should account for two thirds of the required fiscal adjustment.
- Examine and support viable, alternative policy options aimed at giving priority to protecting vulnerable sectors of society.
- Provide substantial new measures to address long-term unemployment. This should include programmes aimed at re-training and re-skilling those at highest risk.
- Recognise the problem of the 'working poor'. Make tax credits refundable to address the situation of households in poverty which are headed by a person with a job.
- Introduce a cost of disability allowance to address poverty and social exclusion of people with a disability.
- Poverty-proof all public policy initiatives and provision.
- Recognise the reality of poverty among migrants and adopt policies to assist this group. In addressing this issue also reform and increase the 'direct provision' allowances paid to asylum seekers.
- Accept that persistent poverty should be used as the primary indicator of poverty measurement once this data becomes available.
- Move towards introducing a basic income system. No other approach has the capacity to ensure all members of society have sufficient income to live life with dignity.

4. Taxation

> ## CORE POLICY OBJECTIVE:
> ## TAXATION
> To collect sufficient taxes to ensure full participation in society for all, through a fair tax system in which those who have more, pay more, while those who have less, pay less.

The fiscal adjustments made in response to the economic crisis have underscored the centrality of taxation in budget deliberations and policy development at both macro and micro levels. Taxation plays a key role in shaping Irish society through funding public services, supporting economic activity and redistributing resources to enhance the fairness of society. Consequently, it is crucial that clarity exist with regard to both the objectives and instruments aimed at achieving these goals. To ensure the creation of a fairer and more equitable tax system, policy development in this area should adhere to our core policy objective outlined above. In that regard, *Social Justice Ireland* is committed to increasing the level of detailed analysis and debate addressing this area.[37]

This chapter first considers Ireland's present taxation position and outlines the anticipated future taxation needs of the country. Given this, we outline approaches to reforming and broadening the tax base and proposals for building a fairer tax system.

Ireland's total tax-take: current and future needs
The need for a wider tax base is a lesson painfully learnt by Ireland during the past number of years. A disastrous combination of a naïve housing policy, a failed regulatory system and foolish fiscal policy and economic planning combined to cause a collapse in exchequer revenues. It is only through a determined effort to reform Ireland's taxation system that these mistakes can be addressed and avoided in the future. The narrowness of the Irish tax base resulted in almost 25 per cent of tax revenues disappearing, plunging the exchequer and the country into a series of fiscal policy crises. As shown in table 4.1, tax revenues collapsed from over €59 billion in 2007 to €44 billion in 2010, fractionally recovering to €45 billion in 2011.

---

[37] We present our analysis in this chapter and in the accompanying annex 4.

Table 4.1: The changing nature of Ireland's tax revenue (€m)

	2007	2008	2009	2010	2011
Taxes on income and wealth					
Income tax	13563	13148	11801	11315	14010
Corporation tax	6393	5071	3889	3944	3751
Motor tax - households★	526	583	582	563	556
Other taxes	5	6	5	8	5
Fees – Petroleum & Minerals Dev. Acts	5	10	2	3	3
Various Levies on income	411	414	373	310	317
Social Insurance contribution	9053	9259	8924	8701	7532
Total taxes on income and wealth	**29957**	**28491**	**25575**	**24843**	**26174**
Taxes on capital					
Capital gains tax	3097	1424	545	345	416
Capital acquisitions tax	391	343	256	237	244
Total taxes on capital	**3488**	**1767**	**801**	**582**	**1123**
Taxes on expenditure					
Custom duties	30	21	11	23	38
Excise duties including VRT	5993	5547	4909	4824	4886
Value added tax	14057	12842	10175	9862	9588
Rates	1267	1353	1471	1504	1499
Motor tax★★ - businesses	431	477	476	461	455
Stamps (excluding fee stamps)	3244	1763	1003	962	936
Other fees and levies	194	242	226	286	277
Total taxes on expenditure	**25216**	**22246**	**18271**	**17922**	**17678**
EU Taxes	**519**	**484**	**359**	**400**	**416**
Total Taxation★★★	**59180**	**52988**	**45006**	**43747**	**45391**

Source: CSO On-line database table N1022:T22.

Notes: ★Motor tax is an estimate of the portion paid by households.

★★Motor tax is an estimate of the portion paid by business.

★★★Total taxation is the sum of the rows in bold.

While a proportion of the decline in overall taxation revenue is related to the recession, a large part is structural and requires policy reform. As detailed in chapter 2, *Social Justice Ireland* believes that over the next few years policy should focus on increasing Ireland's tax-take to 34.9 per cent of GDP, a figure defined by Eurostat as 'low-tax' (Eurostat, 2008:5). Such increases are certainly feasible and are unlikely to have any significant negative impact on the economy in the long term. As a policy objective, Ireland should remain a low-tax economy – but not one incapable of adequately supporting the economic, social and infrastructural requirements necessary to support our society and complete our convergence with the rest of Europe.

Looking to the years immediately ahead, Budget 2013 provided some insight into the expected future shape of Ireland's current taxation revenues and this is shown in table 4.2. The Budget provided a detailed breakdown of current taxes for 2012 and 2013 and overall projections for 2014-2015. Over the next three years, assuming these policies are followed, overall current revenue will climb to €43.2 billion.

Table 4.2: Projected current tax revenues, 2012-2015				
	2012 €m	2013 €m	2014 €m	2015 €m
Customs	245	250		
Excise Duties★		4,615	4,920	
Capital Gains Tax	375	420		
Capital Acquis. Tax	275	375		
Stamp Duties	1,415	1,180		
Income Tax ★★	15,040	15,860		
Corporation Tax	4,010	4,135		
Value Added Tax	10,190	10,560		
Property Tax	0	250		
Total Tax Receipts#	**36,165**	**37,950**	**40,705**	**43,175**

Source: Department of Finance, Budget 2013: C12, C18.
Notes: ★ Excise duties include carbon tax and motor tax revenues.
          ★★Including USC.
          #These figures do not incorporate other tax sources including revenues to the social insurance fund and local government charges. These are incorporated into the totals reported in table 4.4 below.

The Governments Medium Term Fiscal Statement (November 2012) also set out projections for the overall scale of the national tax-take (as a proportion of GDP) up to 2015. These figures are reproduced in table 4.3 and have been used to calculate the cash value of the overall levels of tax revenue expected to be collected. While the estimates in this table are based on the tax-take figures from the Medium Term Fiscal Statement and the national income projections in that document and Budget 2013, both documents provided only limited details on the nature and composition of these figures. It should be borne in mind that over recent years the Department's projections for the overall taxation burden have continually undershot the end-of-year outcomes. However, even taking the Department's projections as the likely outcome, chart 4.1 highlights just how far below average EU levels (assuming these remain at a record low of 35.6 per cent of GDP) and the *Social Justice Ireland* target (34.9 per cent of GDP) these taxation revenue figures are.

Table 4.3:Ireland's projected total tax take, 2010-2015 (% GDP)*			
Year	GDP (nominal)	Tax as % GDP	Total Tax Receipts
2011	158,993	30.4	48,334
2012	163,150	30.4	49,598
2013	167,725	30.9	51,827
2014	174,100	31.5	54,842
2015	181,400	31.7	57,504

Source: Department of Finance, Budget 2013: C10 and Medium Term Fiscal Statement (2012:8).

Note: * Total tax take = current taxes (see table 4.1 and 4.2) + Social Insurance Fund income + charges by local government.

Future taxation needs

Government decisions to raise or reduce overall taxation revenue needs to be linked to the demands on its resources. These demands depend on what Government is required to address or decides to pursue. The effects of the current economic crisis and the way it has been handled have significant implications for Ireland's future taxation needs. The rapid increase in national debt, driven by the need to borrow both to replace disappearing taxation revenues and to fund emergency 'investments' in the failing commercial banks, has increased the on-going annual costs associated with servicing the national debt.

Chart 4.1: Ireland's Projected Taxation Levels to 2015 and comparisons with EU-27 averages and Social Justice Ireland target

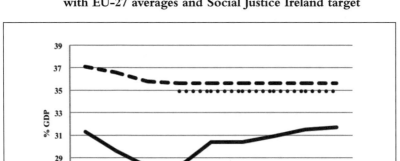

Source: Calculated from Eurostat (2012:180), Department of Finance, Budget 2013: C10 and Medium Term Fiscal Statement (2012:8).

National debt has increased from a level of 25 per cent of GDP in 2007, low by international standards, to 118 per cent of GDP in 2012. Taking account of the February 2013 restructuring of the Anglo Irish promissory notes, the national debt is expected to peak at 122 per cent in 2013. Despite favourable lending rates and payback terms, there remains a recurring cost to service this large national debt – costs which have to be financed by current taxation revenues. Furthermore, the erosion of the National Pension Reserve Fund (NPRF) through its use for funding various bank rescues (over €20 billion) has transferred the liability for future public sector pensions onto future exchequer expenditure. Again, this will require additional taxation resources.

These new future taxation needs add to those which already exist for funding local government, repairing and modernising our water infrastructure, paying for the health and pension needs of an ageing population, paying EU contributions and purchasing any carbon credits that are required. Collectively, they mean that Ireland's overall level of taxation has to rise significantly in the years to come – a reality Irish society and the political system need to begin to seriously address.

Research by Bennett et al (2003) has also provided some insight into future exchequer demands associated with healthcare and pensions in Ireland in the years 2025 and 2050. As the population ages these figures will increase substantially, almost doubling between 2002 and 2050 from 8.9 to 16.7 per cent of GDP. Dealing purely with the pension issue, an ESRI study reached similar conclusions and projected that social welfare spending that is focused on older people will rise from 3.1 per cent in 2004 to 5.5 per cent in 2030 and to 9.3 per cent in 2050. The 2008 OECD Economic Survey of Ireland reached similar conclusions, suggesting a 2050 peak of 11.1 per cent of GDP (2008:80-84).[38]

Table 4.4: Projected Costs of Healthcare and Pensions in Ireland, as % GDP			
	2002	**2025**	**2050**
Healthcare	6.0	6.3	8.8
Pensions	2.9	4.5	7.9
Healthcare + Pensions	**8.9**	**10.9**	**16.7**

Source: Bennett et al (2003)

Is a higher tax-take problematic?

Suggesting that any country's tax take should increase normally produces negative responses. People think first of their incomes and increases in income tax, rather than more broadly of reforms to the tax base. Furthermore, proposals that taxation should increase are often rejected with suggestions that they would undermine economic growth. However, a review of the performance of the British and US economies over recent years sheds a different light on this issue.

In the years prior to the current international economic crisis, Britain achieved low unemployment and higher levels of growth compared to other EU countries (OECD, 2004). These were achieved simultaneously with increases in its tax/GDP ratio. In 1994 this stood at 33.7 per cent and by 2004 it had increased 2.3 percentage points to 36.0 per cent of GDP. Furthermore, in his March 2004 Budget the then British Chancellor Gordon Brown indicated that this ratio would reach 38.3 per cent of GDP in 2008-09 (2004:262). His announcement of these increases was not met with predictions of economic ruin or doom for Britain and its economic growth remained high compared to other EU countries (IMF, 2004 & 2008).

---

[38] The 2010 National Pensions Strategy suggested a higher overall cost of pensions in 2050 as equivalent to 15.5% of GDP but provided no verifiable explanation for this forecast and why it differs so much from other research on the topic.

Taxation and competitiveness

Another argument made against increases in Ireland's overall taxation levels is that it will undermine competitiveness. However, the suggestion that higher levels of taxation would damage Ireland's position relative to other countries is not supported by international studies of competitiveness. Annually the World Economic Forum publishes a *Global Competitiveness Report* ranking the most competitive economies across the world.

Table 4.5 outlines the top 15 economies in this index for 2012-13 as well as the ranking for Ireland (which comes 31st). It also presents the difference between the size of the tax-take in these, the most competitive economies in the world, and in Ireland for 2010.[39]

Table 4.5: Differences in taxation levels between the world's 15 most competitive economies and Ireland.		
Competitiveness Rank	**Country**	**Taxation level versus Ireland**
1	Switzerland	+0.4
2	Singapore	*not available*
3	Finland	+14.9
4	Sweden	+17.9
5	Netherlands	+11.1
6	Germany	+8.4
7	United States	-2.8
8	United Kingdom	+7.2
9	Hong Kong SAR	*not available*
10	Japan	0.0
11	Qatar	*not available*
12	Denmark	+20.0
13	Taiwan, China	*not available*
14	Canada	+3.4
15	Norway	+15.3
31	**IRELAND**	–

Source: World Economic Forum (2012:13)

Notes: a) Taxation data from OECD (2012) for the year 2010

            b) For some countries comparable data is not available.

            c) The OECD's estimate for Ireland in 2010 = 27.635 per cent of GDP

---

[39] This analysis updates that first produced by Collins (2004:15-18).

Only the US reports a lower taxation level than Ireland. All the other leading competitive economies collect the same (Japan) or a greater proportion of national income in taxation. Over time Ireland's position on this index has varied, most recently falling from 22nd to 31st. When Ireland has slipped back the reasons stated for Ireland's loss of competitiveness included decreases in economic growth and fiscal stability, poor performances by public institutions and a decline in the technological competitiveness of the economy (WEF, 2003: xv; 2008:193; 2011: 25-26; 210-211). Interestingly, a major factor in that decline is related to underinvestment in state funded areas such as education, research, infrastructure and broadband connectivity. Each of these areas is dependent on taxation revenue and they have been highlighted by the report as necessary areas of investment to achieve enhanced competitiveness.[40] As such, lower taxes do not feature as a significant priority; rather it is increased and targeted efficient government spending.

A similar point was expressed by the Nobel Prize winning economist Professor Joseph Stiglitz while visiting Ireland in June 2004. Commenting on Ireland's long-term development prospects he stated that 'all the evidence is that the low tax, low service strategy for attracting investment is short-sighted' and that 'far more important in terms of attracting good businesses is the quality of education, infrastructure and services.' Professor Stiglitz, who chaired President Clinton's Council of Economic Advisors, added that 'low tax was not the critical factor in the Republic's economic development and it is now becoming an impediment'.[41]

Reforming and broadening the tax base

Social Justice Ireland believes that there is merit in developing a tax package which places less emphasis on taxing people and organisations on what they earn by their own useful work and enterprise, or on the value they add or on what they contribute to the common good. Rather, the tax that people and organisations should be required to pay should be based more on the value they subtract by their use of common resources. Whatever changes are decided upon should also be guided by the need to build a fairer taxation system, one which adheres to our already stated core policy objective.

There are a number of approaches available to Government in reforming the tax base. Recent Budgets have made some progress in addressing some of these issues while the 2009 Commission on Taxation Report highlighted many areas that

---

[40] A similar conclusion was reached in another international competitiveness study by the International Institute for Management Development (2007).

[41] In an interview with John McManus, Irish Times, June 2nd 2004.

require further reform. A short review of the areas we consider a priority are presented below across the following subsections:

Tax Expenditures / Tax Reliefs
Minimum Effective Tax Rates of Higher Earners
Corporation Taxes
Site Value Tax
Second Homes
Taxing Windfall Gains
Financial Transactions Tax
Carbon Taxes

Tax Expenditures / Tax Reliefs

Part eight of The Commission on Taxation's Report details all the tax breaks (or 'tax expenditures' as they are referred to officially). For years *Social Justice Ireland* have sought to have published the full list of these tax breaks and their actual cost. However, despite our best endeavours neither the Department of Finance nor the Revenue Commissioners have been either able or willing to produce such a list. Subsequently, two members of the Commission have produced a detailed report for the Trinity College Policy Institute which offered further insight into this issue (Collins and Walsh, 2010). Table 4.6 reproduces their findings which highlight that the annual cost of tax expenditures in 2006 (the year where most data was available) totalled in excess of €11.5b per annum and that of the 131 tax expenditures in the Irish system, cost estimates are only available for 89 of them (68 per cent). Given the scale of public expenditure involved, this is a bizarre and totally unacceptable situation.

Some welcome progress has been made in addressing and reforming these tax breaks in recent Budgets. However, despite this both the 2012 and 2013 Finance Bills (Department of Finance, 2012 and 2013) introduced new tax breaks targeted at high earning multinational executives and research and development schemes – with no accompanying documentation evaluating the cost, distributive impacts or appropriateness of these proposals.

There is further potential to reduce the cost of this area. Recipients of these tax expenditures use them to reduce their tax bills, so it needs to be clearly understood that this is tax which is being forgone. *Social Justice Ireland* has highlighted a number of these reforms in our pre-Budget Policy Briefings, *Budget Choices*, and will further address this issue in advance of Budget 2014. We will have particular regard to the need to reform the most expensive tax break, which is associated with pensions.[42] *Social Justice Ireland* believes that reforming the tax break system would make the tax system fairer. It would also provide substantial additional resources which would contribute to achieving the adjustment Government has proposed for the years to come.

Tax Expenditures relating to:	No. of tax expenditures	No. with available costs	Estimated Cost €m
Children	8	8	723
Housing	6	6	3,256
Health	10	7	579
Philanthropy	16	7	89
Enterprise	28	12	457
Employment	28	18	2,816
Savings and investment	8	6	2,995
Age-related and other	7	5	144
Property investment	20	20	435
Total	**131**	**89**	**11,494++**

Table 4.6: Estimate of the Annual Cost of Ireland's Tax Expenditures

Source: Collins and Walsh (2010:4).

Both the Commission on Taxation (2009:230) and Collins and Walsh (2010:20-21) have also highlighted and detailed the need for new methods for evaluation/introducing tax reliefs. We strongly welcome these proposals, which are similar to the proposals the directors of *Social Justice Ireland* made to the Commission in written and oral submissions. The proposals focus on prior evaluation of the costs and benefits of any proposed expenditure, the need to collect detailed information on each expenditure, the introduction of time limits for expenditures, the creation of an annual tax expenditures report as part of the Budget process and the regular scrutiny of this area by an Oireachtas committee. *Social Justice Ireland* believes that these proposals should be adopted as part of the necessary reform of this area.

---

[42] See Social Justice Ireland Budget 2013 *Policy Briefing* on 'Budget Choices' (2012: 14).

Minimum Effective Tax Rates for Higher Earners
The suggestion that it is the better-off who principally gain from the provision of tax exemption schemes is underscored by a series of reports published by the Revenue Commissioners entitled *Effective Tax Rates for High Earning Individuals* (2002, 2005, 2006 and 2007). These reports provided details of the Revenue's assessment of the top 400 earners in Ireland and the rates of effective taxation they faced.[43] The reports led to the introduction of a minimum 20 per cent effective tax rate as part of the 2006 and 2007 Finance Acts for all those with incomes in excess of €500,000. Subsequent budgets have revised upwards the minimum effective rate and revised downwards the income threshold at which it applies. These are necessary and long-overdue reforms. Most recently, the 2010 Finance Bill introduced a requirement that all earners above €400,000 pay a minimum effective rate of tax of 30 per cent. It also reduced the income threshold at which restrictions on the use of tax expenditures to decrease income tax liabilities commence from €250,000 to €125,000.

Table 4.7: The Distribution of Effective Tax Rates among those earning in excess of €125,000 in 2010 (% of total)

Effective Tax Rate	Individuals with incomes of €400,000+	Individuals with incomes of €125,000 – €400,000
0%–5%	0%	1.56%
5% < 10%	0%	13.14%
10% < 15%	0%	18.06%
15% < 20%	0%	18.50%
20% < 25%	0%	21.95%
25% < 30%	16%	26.10%
30% < 35%	84%	0.69%
35%< 40%	0%	0%
> 40%	0%	0%
Average effective rate	**30.72%**	**18.97%**
Total Cases	**387**	**1,157**

Source: Revenue Commissioners (2012)

During 2012 the Revenue Commissioners published an analysis of the operation of these new rules using data for 2010 (Revenue Commissioners, 2012). Table 4.7

---

[43] The effective taxation rate is calculated as the percentage of the individual's total pre-tax income paid in taxation.

gives the findings of that analysis for 387 individuals with income in excess of €400,000. The report also includes information on the distribution of effective tax rates among the 1,157 earners with incomes between €125,000 and €400,000.

Social Justice Ireland welcomed the introduction of this scheme, which marked a major improvement in the fairness of the tax system. However, it should be noted that the average effective tax rate faced by earners above €400,000 in 2010 (30.72 per cent) was equivalent to the amount of income tax paid by a single PAYE worker with a gross income of €60,000 in that year. Similarly, the average effective tax rate faced by people earning between €125,000 and €400,000 in 2010 (18.97 per cent) was equivalent to the amount of income tax paid by a single PAYE worker with a gross income of approximately €35,000 in that year. The contrast in these income levels for the same overall rate of income taxation brings into question the fairness of the taxation system as a whole.

Social Justice Ireland believes that it is important that Government continues to raise the minimum effective tax rate so that it is in-line with that faced by PAYE earners on equivalent high-income levels. Following Budget 2013 a single individual on an income of €120,000 gross will pay an effective tax rate of 42.9 per cent; a figure which suggests that the minimum threshold for high earners has potential to adjust upwards over the next few years.

Corporation Taxes

In Budget 2003 the standard rate of corporation tax was reduced from 16 per cent to 12.5 per cent, at a full year cost of €305m. This followed another reduction in 2002, which had brought the rate down from 20 per cent to 16 per cent. At the time the total cost in lost revenue to the exchequer of these two reductions was estimated at over €650m per annum. Serious questions remain concerning the advisability of pursuing this policy approach. Ireland's corporation tax rate is now considerably below the corresponding rates in most of Europe. Windfall profits are flowing to a sector that is already extremely profitable. Furthermore, Ireland's low rate of corporation tax is being abused by multinational companies which channel profits through units, often very small units, in Ireland to avail of the lower Irish rate of tax. In many cases this is happening at a cost to fellow EU member's exchequers and with little benefit in terms of jobs and additional real economic activity in Ireland. Understandably, Ireland is coming under increasing pressure to reform this system.

There is no substantive evidence in any of the relevant literature to support the contention that corporations would leave if the corporate tax rate were higher – at 17.5 per cent for example. Furthermore, the logic of having a uniform rate of corporation tax for all sectors is questionable. David Begg of ICTU has stated, 'there is no advantage in having a uniform rate of 12.5 per cent corporation tax applicable to hotels and banks as well as to manufacturing industry' (2003:12). In the last few years there has been some improvement in this situation with special, and higher, tax rates being charged on natural resource industries. *Social Justice Ireland* welcomes this as an overdue step in the right direction.

As the EU expands corporation tax competition is likely to intensify. Already Estonia and the Isle of Man have introduced zero per cent corporation tax rates, Cyprus and Bulgaria have set their rates at 10 per cent and others continue to reduce their headline rates and provide incentives targeted at reducing the effective corporate tax rate. Over the next decade Ireland will be forced to either ignore tax rates as a significant attraction/retention policy for foreign investors, which would be a major change in industrial policy, or to follow suit, despite the exchequer costs, and compete by further cutting corporation tax. Sweeney has warned of a dangerous situation in which Ireland could end up 'leading the race to the bottom' (2004:59). The costs of such a move, in lost exchequer income, would be enormous.

An alternative direction could be to agree a minimum effective rate for all EU countries. Given the international nature of company investment, these taxes are fundamentally different from internal taxes and the benefits of a European agreement which would set a minimum effective rate are obvious. They include protecting Ireland's already low rate from being driven even lower, protecting jobs in industries which might move to lower taxing countries and protecting the revenue generated for the exchequer by corporate taxes. *Social Justice Ireland* believes that an EU wide agreement on a minimum effective rate of corporation tax should be negotiated and this could evolve from the current discussions around a Common Consolidated Corporate Tax Base (CCCTB). *Social Justice Ireland* believes that the minimum rate should be set well below the 2011 EU-27 average rate of 23.1 per cent but above the existing low Irish level.[44] A rate of 17.5 per cent seems appropriate. Were such a rate in place in Ireland in 2012, corporate tax income would have been between €1.25 billion and €1.6 billion higher – a significant sum given the current economic challenges.

---

[44] Data from Eurostat (2011:130).

While a reform of the headline corporate tax rate is not currently favoured by the major political parties, an interim measure would be to address the manner by which companies avail of tax breaks to reduce their effective corporate tax rate. A 2011 study by Stewart examined data derived from company accounts to estimate effective corporate tax rates among companies operating in Ireland. He found that indigenous companies such as Ryanair and Grafton Group experienced effective corporate tax rates of 7 per cent and 4.2 per cent respectively in the financial year ending in 2009. His examination of the accounts of multinational companies cite examples including Boston Scientific which had an effective tax rate of less than 0.6 per cent, over the period 2001-03; Forest Laboratories, which had a rate of just over 6 per cent for the period 2005-07; and Symantic, which had a 0 per cent rate for the period 2004-05. Overall, Stewart found that US multinationals had effective corporate tax rates in Ireland that averaged 6.6 per cent in 2006, 7.4 per cent in 2007 and 7.3 per cent in 2008 (2011: 4-7). *Social Justice Ireland* believes that Government should adopt policies to ensure that corporations pay a minimum effective corporate tax rate of 10 per cent. This would mean that corporations would have to pay a *minimum* of 10 per cent of their profits in tax in Ireland. This reform would simultaneously maintain Ireland's low corporate tax position and provide additional revenues to the exchequer.

Site Value Tax

Taxes on wealth are minimal in Ireland, which is unique amongst developed countries in having no tax on immovable property. Revenue is negligible from capital acquisitions tax (CAT) because it has a very high threshold in respect of bequests and gifts within families and the rates of tax on transfers of family farms and firms are very generous (see tax revenue tables at the start of this chapter). While recent increases in the rate of CAT are welcome, the likely future revenue from this area remains limited given the tax's current structure.

The requirement, as part of the EU/IMF/ECB bailout agreement, to introduce a recurring property tax led Government in Budget 2012 to introduce an unfairly structured flat €100 per annum household charge and a value based property tax in Budget 2013. While we welcome the overdue extension of the tax base to include a recurring revenue source from property, we believe that a Site Value Tax, also known as a Land Rent Tax, would be a more appropriate and fairer approach.

The issue of site value taxation is one that has received considerable attention over the past few years. Two papers at a 2004 Social Policy Conference directly addressed this issue (O'Siochru, 2004:23-57; and Dunne, 2004:93-122) and the Chambers of Commerce of Ireland has published a report entitled *Local Authority Funding – Government in Denial* (2004) which called for an annual site tax. More recently, Collins and Larragy (2011) have outlined how such a charge could work, using the Property Registration Authority of Ireland's (PRAI) database as the basis for operation of the tax. In 2012 a detailed study of site value tax was published entitled 'The Fair Tax' edited by O'Siochru (O'Siochru, 2012).

A 'land value', 'land rent' or 'site-value' tax (all three names are used to describe the same concept) is based on the annual rental value of land. The annual rental site value is the rental value that a particular piece of land would have if there were no buildings or improvements on it. It is the value of a site, as provided by nature and as affected for better or worse by the activities of the community at large. The tax falls on the annual value of land at the point where it enters into economic activity, before the application of capital and labour to it.

The arguments for a land rent tax are to do with fairness and economic efficiency. While the owners of land receive most of the reward of rising land values they do not incur most of the costs associated with such rises. This is because rising land values – for example, in prosperous city centres or prime agricultural areas – are largely created by the activities of the community as a whole and by government regulations and subsidies. This often results in land owners retaining unused sites in the hope of selling them later when land values will have risen. Speculation on rising land values distorts land prices, generally making them significantly higher than they would be otherwise. NESC (2003:96) points out that given the immobility of land the introduction of a tax on development land would have minimal economic effects.

A land value tax is positive on both efficiency and equity grounds. From an efficiency perspective, a site value tax would be a major step toward securing the tax base as it could not move to any location providing greater tax reductions. In doing this it would move the tax away from a transaction, such as stamp duty, which can make the tax base vulnerable because it is dependent on maintaining and increasing the scale of the transactions, and switch it instead to an immovable physical asset which is a much securer base. It would have other efficiency impacts, such as ensuring that derelict sites are developed and that land would not be held over, as appears to be the situation at present, in an attempt to increase its value by creating artificial scarcity of land for development.

A land value tax is also positive on equity grounds. High land values in urban areas of Ireland are mainly a product of the economic and social activity in those areas. Consequently, it can be argued that a substantial portion of the benefits of these land values should be enjoyed by all the members of the community and not just the site owners. In addition, increasing site values are closely linked to the level of investment in infrastructure those areas have received. Much of that investment has been paid for by taxpayers. It can be argued, therefore, that a substantial portion of the benefits of the increasing site value should go to the whole community through the taxation system. After all, the site owner may well have made little or no contribution to the investment that produced the increased value in the first place.

Social Justice Ireland believes that the introduction of a site value tax would be a better alternative than the current Government value based local property tax. A site value tax would lead to more efficient land use within the structure of social, environmental and economic goals embodied in planning and other legislation.

Second Homes

A feature of the housing boom of the last decade was the rapid increase in ownership of holiday homes and second homes. For the most part these homes remain empty for at least nine months of the year. It is a paradox that many were built at the same time as the rapid increases in housing waiting lists (see chapter 7).

Results from Census 2011 indicated that since 2006 there had been a 19 per cent increase in the number of holiday homes, with numbers rising from 49,789 in 2006 to 59,395 in 2011. The Census also found that overall the number of vacant houses on Census night was 168,427 (April 2011) – some of which are also likely to be second homes.

What is often overlooked when the second home issue is being discussed is that the infrastructure to support these houses is substantially subsidised by the taxpayer. Roads, water, sewage and electricity infrastructure are just part of this subsidy which goes, by definition, to those who are already better off as they can afford these second homes in the first place. *Social Justice Ireland* supports the views of the ESRI (2003) and the Indecon report (2005:183-186; 189-190) on this issue. We believe that people purchasing second houses should have to pay these full infrastructural costs, much of which is currently borne by society through the Exchequer and local authorities. There is something perverse in the fact that the taxpayer should be providing substantial subsidies to the owners of these unoccupied houses at a time when so many people do not have basic adequate accommodation.

The second house issue should be addressed so that priority can be given to supplying needed accommodation which will be lived in all year round. The introduction of the Non Principal Private Residence (NPPR) charge in 2009 was a welcome step forward. However, notwithstanding subsequent increases, the charge is still very low relative to the previous and continuing benefits that are derived from these properties. Despite the new local property tax (from mid-2013), the charge should therefore be increased and the NPPR retained as a separate substantial second homes payment.

Table 4.8: Illustrative examples of the operation of an 80% Windfall Gain Tax on rezoned land					
Agricultural Land Value	Rezoned Value	Profit	Tax @ 80%	Post-Tax Profit	Profit as % Original Value
€50,000	€400,000	€350,000	€280,000	€70,000	140%
€100,000	€800,000	€700,000	€560,000	€140,000	140%
€200,000	€1,600,000	€1,400,000	€1,120,000	€280,000	140%
€500,000	€4,000,000	€3,500,000	€2,800,000	€700,000	140%
€1,000,000	€8,000,000	€7,000,000	€5,600,000	€1,400,000	140%

Note: Calculations assume an eight-fold increase on the agricultural land value upon rezoning.

Taxing Windfall Gains

The vast profit made by property speculators on the rezoning of land by local authorities was a particularly undesirable feature of the recent economic boom. For some time *Social Justice Ireland* has called for a substantial tax to be imposed on the profits earned from such decisions. While this may not be an issue in Ireland at this time of austerity, it is best to make the system fairer before any further unearned gains are reaped by speculators. Rezonings are made by elected representatives, supposedly in the interest of society generally. It therefore seems appropriate that a sizeable proportion of the windfall gains they generate should be made available to local authorities and used to address the on-going housing problems they face (see chapter 7). In this regard, *Social Justice Ireland* welcomes the decision to put such a tax in place. The windfall tax level of 80 per cent is appropriate and, as table

4.8 illustrates, this still leaves speculators and land owners with substantial profits from these rezoning decisions. The profit from this process should be used to fund local authorities. We fear that when the property market recovers in years to come there will be lobbying for this tax to be reduced or removed. Government should anticipate and resist this.

Financial Transactions Tax

As the international economic chaos of the past few years has shown, the world is now increasingly linked via millions of legitimate, speculative and opportunistic financial transactions. Similarly, global currency trading increased sharply throughout recent decades. It is estimated that a very high proportion of all financial transactions traded are speculative currency transactions which are completely free of taxation.

An insight into the scale of these transactions is provided by the Bank for International Settlements (BIS) Triennial Central Bank Survey of Foreign Exchange and Derivatives Market Activity (December 2010). The key findings from that report were:

- In April 2010 the average daily turnover in global foreign exchange markets was US$3.98 trillion; an increase of almost 20 per cent since 2007 and 160 per cent since 2001.
- The major components of these activities were: $1.490 trillion in spot transactions, $475 billion in outright forwards, $1.765 trillion in foreign exchange swaps, $43 billion currency swaps, and $207 billion in options and other products.
- 65 per cent of trades were cross-border and 35 per cent local.
- The vast majority of trades involved four currencies: US Dollar, Euro, Japanese Yen and Pound Sterling.
- Most of this activity (55 per cent) occurred in the US and UK, as did most activity involving interest rate derivatives (71 per cent).

The Tobin tax, first proposed by the Nobel Prize winner James Tobin, is a progressive tax, designed to target only those profiting from speculation. It is levied at a very small rate on all transactions but, given the scale of these transactions globally, it has the ability to raise significant funds.

Social Justice Ireland regrets that Budget 2013 did not commit Government to supporting recent European moves to introduce a Financial Transactions Tax (FTT) or Tobin Tax. The October 2011 EU Commission proposal for an FTT proposes that it would be levied on transactions between financial institutions if at least one party to the transaction is located in the EU. The exchange of shares and bonds would be taxed at a rate of 0.1% and derivative contracts at an even lower rate of 0.01%. Overall, the Commission projects that the FTT would raise €57 billion per annum.

To date 11 of the 27 EU member states have signed up to this tax and *Social Justice Ireland* believes that Ireland should join this group. In our opinion, the tax offers the dual benefit of dampening needless and often reckless financial speculation and generating significant funds. We believe that the revenue generated by this tax should be used for national economic and social development and international development co-operation purposes, in particular funding Ireland and other developed countries to fund overseas aid and reach the UN ODA target (see chapter 14). According to the United Nations, the amount of annual income raised from a Tobin tax would be enough to guarantee to every citizen of the world basic access to water, food, shelter, health and education. Therefore, this tax has the potential to wipe out the worst forms of material poverty throughout the world.

Social Justice Ireland believes that the time has come for Ireland to adopt a financial transactions tax.

Carbon Taxes

Budget 2010 announced the long-overdue introduction of a carbon tax. This had been promised in Budget 2003 and committed to in the *National Climate Change Strategy* (2007). The tax has been structured along the lines of the proposal from the Commission on Taxation (2009: 325-372) and is linked to the price of carbon credits which was set at an initial rate of €15 per tonne of CO_2 and subsequently increased in Budget 2012 to €20 per tonne. Budget 2013 extended the tax to cover solid fuels on a phased basis from May 2013, with the full tax applying from May 2014. The taxes are based on the levels of the emission the products create.

While *Social Justice Ireland* welcomed the introduction of this tax, we regret the lack of accompanying measures to protect those most affected by it, in particular low income households and rural dwellers. *Social Justice Ireland* believes that as the tax increases the Government should be more specific in defining how it will assist these households. Furthermore, there is a danger that given the difficult fiscal circumstances Ireland now finds itself in, any increases in the carbon tax over the next few years may divert from the original intention, to encourage behavioural change, towards a focus on raising revenue.

Building a fairer taxation system

The need for fairness in the tax system was clearly recognised in the first report of the Commission on Taxation more than 25 years ago. It stated:

'...in our recommendations the spirit of equity is the first and most important consideration. Departures from equity must be clearly justified by reference to the needs of economic development or to avoid imposing unreasonable compliance costs on individuals or high administrative costs on the Revenue Commissioners.' (1982:29)

The need for fairness is just as obvious today and *Social Justice Ireland* believes that this should be a central objective of the current reform of the taxation system. While we recognise that many of the reforms below can only occur once the current crisis in the exchequer's finances has been resolved, we include them here because they represent necessary reforms that would greatly enhance the fairness of Ireland's taxation system. This section is structured in eight parts:

- Standard rating discretionary tax expenditures
- Keeping the minimum wage out of the tax net
- Favouring changes to tax credits rather than tax rates
- Favouring changes to tax credits rather than tax bands
- Introducing Refundable Tax Credits
- Introducing a Refundable Tax Credit For Children
- Reforming individualisation
- Making the taxation system simpler

Standard rating discretionary tax expenditures

Making all discretionary tax reliefs/expenditures only available at the standard 20 per cent rate would represent a crucial step towards achieving a fairer tax system. If there is a legitimate case for making a tax relief/expenditure available, then it should be made available in the same way to all. It is inequitable that people on higher incomes should be able to claim certain tax reliefs at their top marginal tax rates while people with less income are restricted to claim benefit for the same relief at the lower standard rate of 20 per cent. The standard rating of tax expenditures, otherwise known as reliefs, offers the potential to simultaneously make the tax system fairer and fund the necessary developments they are designed to stimulate without any significant macroeconomic implications.[45] Recent Budgets have made substantial progress towards achieving this objective and we welcome these developments. Furthermore, we encourage the Government to standard rate the tax relief on pension contributions. This is an overdue reform with an ability to generate almost €700m per annum in savings for the exchequer (Collins and Walsh, 2010:22).

Keeping the minimum wage out of the tax net

The decision by the Minister for Finance to remove those on the minimum wage from the tax net was a major achievement of Budget 2005. This had an important impact on the growing numbers of working-poor and addressed an issue with which *Social Justice Ireland* is highly concerned.

The fiscal and economic crisis of 2008-13 lead to Government reversing this policy, first by way of the income levy in second Budget 2009 then via the Universal Social Charge (USC) in Budget 2011 and a PRSI increase in Budget 2013. Since Budget 2012 the USC is charged on all the income of those who earn more than €10,036 per annum. Using the unadjusted minimum wage of €8.65 per hour, the threshold implies that a low-income worker on the minimum wage and working more than 23 hours per week (earning €199 per week) is subject to the tax. *Social Justice Ireland* believes that this threshold is far too low and unnecessarily depresses the income and living standards of the working poor. Budget 2012 raised the entry point for the USC from €4,004 per annum to €10,036 per annum, a move welcomed by Social *Justice Ireland*. However, the imposition of the USC at such low income levels raises a very small amount of funds for the exchequer. Forthcoming Budgets should continue to raise the point at which the USC commences and in the years to come, as more resources hopefully become available to the Exchequer, *Social Justice Ireland* will urge Government to restore the policy of keeping the minimum wage fully outside the tax net.

Favouring changes to tax credits rather than tax rates

Social Justice Ireland believes that any future income tax changes should be restricted to changes in tax credits or tax bands rather than tax rates. This is more desirable in the context of achieving fairness in the taxation system.

To emphasise this point, we start by comparing a change in tax credits against a change in tax rates (the next section makes a comparison with tax bands). One of

---

[45] See O'Toole and Cahill (2006:215) who also reach this conclusion.

the initiatives announced in Budget 2007 was a cut in the top tax rate of one per cent (from 42 to 41 per cent). In his Budget speech the Minister indicated that the full year cost of this change was €186m. The Budget documentation also indicated that the full-year cost of a €90 increase in the tax credits of every taxpayer equalled €185m. Therefore, both policy changes have roughly the same exchequer cost. Chart 4.2 compares these two changes and the increased income they delivered to earners across the income distribution.

An increase in tax credits would provide the same value to all taxpayers across the income distribution, provided they are earning sufficient to pay more than €90 in income taxes. Therefore, the increased income received by an earner on €25,000 and on €80,000 is the same – an extra €90. However, a decrease in the top tax rate only benefits those paying tax at that rate. Therefore, the earner on €25,000 gains nothing from this change while those on €50,000 gain €160 per annum and those on €80,000 gain €460 per annum. The higher the income, the greater the gain.

Chart 4.2: Comparison of a 1% cut in the top tax rate and an increase in tax credits of €90 for each taxpayer

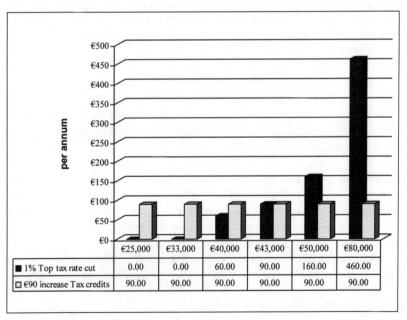

	€25,000	€33,000	€40,000	€43,000	€50,000	€80,000
■ 1% Top tax rate cut	0.00	0.00	60.00	90.00	160.00	460.00
□ €90 increase Tax credits	90.00	90.00	90.00	90.00	90.00	90.00

As chart 4.2 shows, all single people earning less than €43,000 would have gained more from an increase in tax credits rather than a decrease in the top tax rate. For a couple (not shown in the diagram), all those earning less than €86,000 would have been better off had the government used the same money to deliver an increase in tax credits rather than a decrease in the top tax rate. In terms of fairness, changing tax credits is a fairer option than changing tax rates.

Favouring changes to tax credits rather than tax bands

In reforming income taxation policy over the years and decades to come, Government should always seek to enhance fairness. The following example, based on numbers from Budget 2008, illustrates the choices between changing either tax credits or tax bands.

If €535 million were available for distribution in a Budget it could be used to either increase the 20 per cent tax band by €5,000 (full year cost €536.1m) or increase personal tax credits by €250 a year (full-year cost €533.75m).[46] While the exchequer cost of these two alternatives is roughly the same, their impact is notably different:

Increasing the 20 per cent tax band by €5,000 would be of no benefit to anyone with incomes at or below the top of that band (i.e. €35,400 for a single person) but would provide a benefit of €1,000 a year to a single person earning more than €40,400. Single people with incomes in the €35,400–€40,400 range would benefit by a proportion of the €1,000. (The thresholds for married people with one or two incomes are different but the impacts are along the same lines as those identified here for single people).

Increasing the tax credit by €250 a year would mean that every earner with a tax bill in excess of €250 a year would benefit by that amount.

In terms of fairness, increasing tax credits is a better option than widening the standard rate tax band. Government should always take this option when it has money available to reduce income taxes. It has the additional advantage of helping to address the 'working poor' issue which, as we have highlighted earlier, is emerging as a growing problem that requires a policy response.

---

[46] Figures from Department pre-Budget 2008 income tax ready reckoner.

Introducing refundable tax credits

The move from tax allowances to tax credits was completed in Budget 2001. This was a very welcome change because it put in place a system that had been advocated for a long time by a range of groups. One problem persists however. If a low income worker does not earn enough to use up his or her full tax credit then he or she will not benefit from any tax reductions introduced by government in its annual budget.

Making tax credits refundable would be a simple solution to this problem. It would mean that the part of the tax credit that an employee did not benefit from would be 'refunded' to him/her by the state.

The major advantage of making tax credits refundable lies in addressing the disincentives currently associated with low-paid employment. The main beneficiaries of refundable tax credits would be low-paid employees (full-time and part-time). Chart 4.3 displays the impacts of the introduction of this policy across various gross income levels. It clearly shows that all of the benefits from introducing this policy would go directly to those on the lowest incomes.

Chart 4.3: How much better off would people be if tax credits were made refundable?

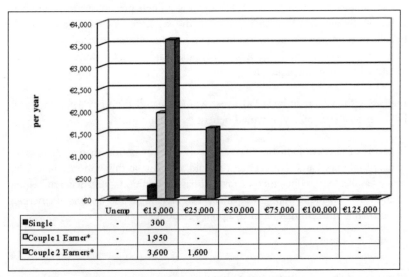

	Unemp	€15,000	€25,000	€50,000	€75,000	€100,000	€125,000
■Single	-	300	-	-	-	-	-
□Couple 1 Earner*	-	1,950	-	-	-	-	-
▣Couple 2 Earners*	-	3,600	1,600	-	-	-	-

Note: * Except where unemployed as there is no earner

With regard to administering this reform, the central idea recognises that most people with regular incomes and jobs would not receive a cash refund of their tax credit because their incomes are too high. They would simply benefit from the tax credit as a reduction in their tax bill. Therefore, as chart 4.3 shows, no change is proposed for these people and they would continue to pay tax via their employers, based on their net liability after deduction of their tax credits by their employers on behalf of the Revenue Commissioners. For other people on low or irregular incomes, the refundable tax credit could be paid via a refund by the Revenue at the end of the tax year. Following the introduction of refundable tax credits, all subsequent increases in the level of the tax credit would be of equal value to all employees.

To illustrate the benefits of this approach, charts 4.4 and 4.5 compare the effects of a €100 increase in the personal tax credit before and after the introduction of refundable tax credits. Chart 4.4 shows the effect as the system is currently structured – an increase of €100 in credits, but these are not refundable. It shows that the gains are allocated equally to all categories of earners above €50,000. However, there is no benefit for those workers whose earnings are not in the tax net.

Chart 4.4: How much better off would people be if tax credits were increased by €100 per person?

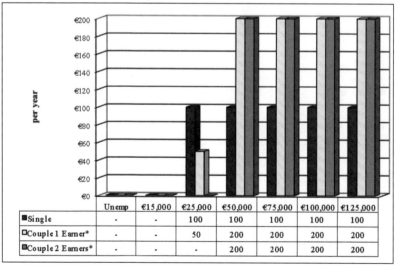

	Unemp	€15,000	€25,000	€50,000	€75,000	€100,000	€125,000
■Single	-	-	100	100	100	100	100
□Couple 1 Earner*	-	-	50	200	200	200	200
■Couple 2 Earners*	-	-	-	200	200	200	200

Note: * Except where unemployed, as there is no earner

Chart 4.5 shows how the benefits of a €100 a year increase in personal tax credits would be distributed under a system of refundable tax credits. This simulation demonstrates the equity attached to using the tax-credit instrument to distribute budgetary taxation changes. The benefit to all categories of income earners (single/couple, one-earner/couple, two-earners) is the same. Consequently, in relative terms those earners at the bottom of the distribution do best.

Chart 4.5: How much better off would people be if tax credits were increased by €100 per person and this was refundable?

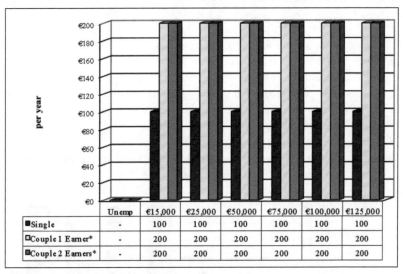

	Unemp	€15,000	€25,000	€50,000	€75,000	€100,000	€125,000
■Single	-	100	100	100	100	100	100
□Couple 1 Earner*	-	200	200	200	200	200	200
■Couple 2 Earners*	-	200	200	200	200	200	200

Note: * Except where unemployed, as there is no earner

Overall the merits of adopting this approach are that every beneficiary of tax credits could receive the full value of the tax credit, the system would improve the net income of the workers whose incomes are lowest, at a modest cost, and there would be no additional administrative burden placed on employers.

The refundable tax credits approach has enjoyed increasing attention outside Ireland, including a detailed Brooking Policy Briefing on the issue published in the United States in late 2006 (see Goldberg et al, 2006). In reviewing this issue in the Irish context Colm Rapple stated that 'the change is long overdue' (2004:140).

During late 2010 *Social Justice Ireland* published a detailed study on the subject of refundable tax credits. Entitled *Building a Fairer Tax System: The Working Poor and the Cost of Refundable Tax Credits*, the study identified that the proposed system would benefit 113,000 low-income individuals in an efficient and cost-effective manner.[47] When children and other adults in the household are taken into account the total number of beneficiaries would be 240,000. The cost of making this change would be €140m. The *Social Justice Ireland* proposal to make tax credits refundable would make Ireland's tax system fairer, address part of the working poor problem and improve the living standards of a substantial number of people in Ireland. The following is a summary of that proposal:

Making tax credits refundable: the benefits
- Would address the problem identified already in a straightforward and cost-effective manner.
- No administrative cost to the employer.
- Would incentivise employment over welfare as it would widen the gap between pay and welfare rates.
- Would be more appropriate for a 21st century system of tax and welfare.

Details of Social Justice Ireland proposal
- Unused portion of the Personal and PAYE tax credit (and only these) would be refunded.
- Eligibility criteria in the relevant year.
- Individuals must have unused personal and/or PAYE tax credits (by definition).
- Individuals must have been in paid employment.
- Individuals must be at least 23 years of age.
- Individuals must have earned a minimum annual income from employment of €4,000.
- Individuals must have accrued a minimum of 40 PRSI weeks.
- Individuals must not have earned an annual total income greater than €15,600.
- Married couples must not have earned a combined annual total income greater than €31,200.
- Payments would be made at the end of the tax year.

---

[47] The study is available on our website: www.socialjustice.ie

Cost of implementing the proposal

- The total cost of refunding unused tax credits to individuals satisfying all of the criteria mentioned in this proposal is estimated at €140.1m.

Major findings

- Almost 113,300 low income individuals would receive a refund and their disposable income would increase as a result of the proposal.
- The majority of the refunds are valued at under €2,400 per annum, or €46 per week, with the most common value being individuals receiving a refund of between €800 to €1,000 per annum, or €15 to €19 per week.
- Considering that the individuals receiving these payments have incomes of less than €15,600 (or €299 per week), such payments are significant to them
- Almost 40 per cent of refunds flow to people in low-income working poor households who live below the poverty line.
- A total of 91,056 men, women and children below the poverty threshold benefit either directly through a payment to themselves or indirectly through a payment to their household from a refundable tax credit.
- Of the 91,056 individuals living below the poverty line that benefit from refunds, over 71 per cent receive refunds of more than €10 per week and 32 per cent receive in excess of €20 per week.
- A total of 148,863 men, women and children above the poverty line benefit from refundable tax credits, either directly through a payment to themselves or indirectly through a payment to their household. Most of these beneficiaries have income less than €120 per week above the poverty line.
- Overall, some 240,000 individuals (91,056 + 148,863) living in low-income households would experience an increase in income as a result of the introduction of refundable tax credits, either directly through a refund to themselves or indirectly through a payment to their household.

Once adopted, a system of refundable tax credits as proposed in this study would result in all future changes in tax credits being equally experienced by all employees in Irish society. Such a reform would mark a significant step in the direction of building a fairer taxation system and represent a fairer way for Irish society to allocate its resources.

Reforming individualisation

Social Justice Ireland supports individualisation of the tax system. However, the process of individualisation followed to date has been deeply flawed and unfair. The cost to the exchequer of this transition has been in excess of €0.75 billion and almost all of this has gone to the richest 30 per cent of the population. A significantly fairer process would have been to introduce a basic income system that would have treated all people fairly and ensured that a windfall of this nature did not accrue to the best off in this society (see chapter 3).

Given the current form of individualisation, couples with one partner losing his/her job end up even worse off than they would have been had the current form of individualisation not been introduced. Before individualisation was introduced, the standard-rate income-tax band was €35,553 for all couples. After that they would start paying the higher rate of tax. Now, the standard-rate income-tax band for single-income couples is €32,800, while the band for dual-income couples is €65,600. If one spouse (of a couple previously earning two salaries) leaves a job voluntarily or through redundancy, the couple loses the value of the second tax band.

Making the taxation system simpler

Ireland's tax system is not simple. Bristow (2004) argued that 'some features of it, notably VAT, are among the most complex in the world'. The reasons given to justify this complexity vary but they are focused principally around the need to reward particular kinds of behaviour seen as desirable by legislators. This, in effect, is discrimination either in favour of one kind of activity or against another. There are many arguments against the present complexity and in favour of a simpler system.

Discriminatory tax concessions in favour of particular positions are often very inequitable, contributing far less to equity than might appear to be the case. In many circumstances they also fail to produce the economic or social outcomes which are being sought and sometimes they even generate very undesirable effects. At other times they may be a complete waste of money, since the outcomes they seek would have occurred without the introduction of a tax incentive. Having a complex system has other downsides. It can, for example, have high compliance costs both for taxpayers and for the Revenue Commissioners.

For the most part, society at large gains little or nothing from the discrimination contained in the tax system. Mortgage interest relief, for example, and the absence of any residential or land-rent tax contributed to the rise in house prices up to 2007. Complexity makes taxes easier to evade, invites consultants to devise avoidance schemes and greatly increases the cost of collection. It is also inequitable because those who can afford professional advice are in a far better position to take advantage of that complexity than those who cannot. A simpler taxation system would better serve Irish society and all individuals within it, irrespective of their means.

Key Policy Priorities on Taxation
- *Social Justice Ireland* believes that Government should:
  - increase the overall tax take;
  - adopt policies to broaden the tax base; and
  - develop a fairer taxation system.

Policy priorities under each of these headings are listed below.

Increase the overall tax take
- Move towards increasing the total tax take to 34.9 per cent of GDP (i.e. a level below the low tax threshold identified by Eurostat).

Broaden the tax base
- Continue to reform the area of tax expenditures and put in place procedures within the Department of Finance and the Revenue Commissioners to monitor on an on-going basis the cost and benefits of all current and new tax expenditures.
- Continue to increase the minimum effective tax rates on very high earners (those with incomes in excess of €125,000) so that these rates are consistent with the levels faced by PAYE workers.
- Move to negotiate an EU wide agreement on minimum corporate taxation rates (a rate of 17.5 per cent would seem fair in this situation).
- Adopt policies to ensure that corporations based in Ireland pay a minimum effective corporate tax rate of 10 per cent.
- Introduce a site-value tax as a fairer form of property taxation.
- Impose charges so that those who construct or purchase second homes pay the full infrastructural costs of these dwellings.
- Retain the 80 per cent windfall tax on the profits generated from all land re-zonings.
- Join with other EU member states to adopt a financial transactions tax (FTT).
- Adopt policies which further shift the burden of taxation from income tax to eco-taxes on the consumption of fuel and fertilisers, waste taxes and a land rent tax. In doing this, government should avoid any negative impact on people with low incomes.

Develop a fairer taxation system
- Apply only the standard rate of tax to all discretionary tax expenditures.
- Adjust tax credits and the USC so that the minimum wage returns to being outside the tax net.
- Make tax credits refundable.
- Ensure that individualisation in the income tax system is done in a fair and equitable manner.
- Integrate the taxation and social welfare systems.
- Begin to monitor and report tax levels (personal and corporate) in terms of effective tax rates.
- Develop policies which allow taxation on wealth to be increased.
- Ensure that the distribution of all changes in indirect taxes discriminate positively in favour of those with lower incomes.
- Adopt policies to simplify the taxation system.
- Poverty-proof all budget tax packages to ensure that tax changes do not further widen the gap between those with low income and the better off.

5. Work, Unemployment and Job Creation

CORE POLICY OBJECTIVE:
WORK, UNEMPLOYMENT AND JOB CREATION
To ensure that all people have access to meaningful work

The severity of the 2008-2010 economic collapse resulted in a reversion to the phenomenon of widespread unemployment in Ireland. Since then, despite the attention given to the banking and fiscal collapse, the transition from near full employment to high and static unemployment has been the most telling characteristic of this recession. The implications for people, families, social cohesion and the exchequer's finances have been serious and the effects are likely to be felt for many years to come. CSO data and economic forecasts for the remainder of 2013 indicate that unemployment will stabilise at an annual rate of just under 15 per cent of the labour force in 2013, having been 4.7 per cent before the recession in 2007. There can be little doubt that we are in a very challenging period in which a high level of long-term unemployment has once again become a characteristic of Irish society.

This chapter reviews the evolution of this situation and considers the implications and challenges which arise for Government and society.[48] It also looks at the impact on various sectors of the working-age population and outlines a series of proposals for responding to this unemployment crisis. *Social Justice Ireland* considers that the response to date has been slow and limited and that the scale and nature of our unemployment crisis deserves greater attention. The chapter concludes with some thoughts on the narrowness of how we consider and measure the concept of 'work'.

Recent trends in employment and unemployment
The nature and scale of the recent transformation in Ireland's labour market is highlighted by the data in table 5.1. Over the six years from 2007-2012 the labour force decreased by almost 5 per cent, participation rates dropped, full-time employment fell by over 20 per cent, representing some 380,000 jobs, while part-time employment increased by over 14 per cent. By the third quarter of 2012 the

---

[48] The analysis complements information on the measurement of the labour market and long-term trends in employment and unemployment detailed in annex 5.

number of underemployed people, defined as those employed part-time but wishing to work additional hours, had increased to 147,600 people – almost 7 per cent of the labour force. Over this period unemployment increased by over 215,000 people, bringing the unemployment rate up from 4.7 per cent to 15 per cent.

Table 5.1: Labour Force Data, 2007 - 2012

	2007	2010	2012	Change 07-12
Labour Force	2,277,100	2,196,700	2,165,800	-4.9%
LFPR %	64.7	61.0	60.2	-4.5%
Employment %	69.8	59.8	59	-10.8%
Employment	2,169,600	1,886100	1,841,300	-15.1%
Full-time	1,779,400	1,459700	1,395,000	-21.6%
Part-time	390,200	426,400	446,300	+14.4%
Underemployed	..	112,500	147,600	–
Unemployed %	4.7	14.1	15.0	+10.3%
Unemployed	107,500	310,600	324,500	201.9%
LT Unemployed %	1.4	6.9	8.9	+7.5%
LT Unemployed	31,800	152,600	193,000	+506.9%

Source: CSO, QNHS on-line database.
Notes: All data is for quarter 3 of the reference year.
         LFPR = Labour force participation rate measures the percentage of the adult population who are in the labour market.
         Underemployment measures part-time workers who indicate a desire to work additional hours which are not currently available.
         Comparable underemployment data is not available for 2007.
         LT = Long Term (12 months or more).

This transformation in the labour market has significantly altered the nature of employment in Ireland when compared to the pre-recession picture in 2007. Overall, employment fell 15 per cent between 2007-2012 and table 5.2 traces the impact of this fall across various sectors, groups and regions. Within the CSO's broadly defined employment sectors, industrial employment has seen the biggest fall of over 42 per cent while there have been sizeable, but smaller, falls in agriculture and services. Job losses have had a greater impact on males versus females, with male employment down 20 per cent since 2007 while female employment decreased by 8 per cent. The proportional impact of the crisis has hit employment levels for employees and self-employed in much the same way; although there are many more of the former and the actual job losses among employees is significantly higher.

Table 5.2: Employment in Ireland, 2007 – 2012

	2007	2010	2012	Change 07-12
Employment	2,169,600	1,886,100	1,841,300	-15.1%
Sector				
Agriculture	112,200	89,900	85,600	-23.7%
Industry	578,200	361,800	332,100	-42.6%
Services	1,474,000	1,426,900	1,420,800	-3.6%
Gender				
Male	1,236,100	990,200	986,100	-20.2%
Female	933,500	855,500	855,100	-8.4%
Employment Status				
Employees	1,799,700	1,543,300	1,546,400	-14.1%
Self-Employed	352,000	292,300	279,700	-20.5%
Assisting relative	17,900	10,000	15,200	-15.1%
Region				
Border	221,900	185,100	172,400	-22.3%
Midlands	127,700	101,700	105,300	-17.5%
West	207,200	180,900	181,900	-12.2%
Dublin	640,500	543,500	548,400	-14.4%
Mid-East	255,600	226,600	223,500	-12.6%
Mid-West	173,400	154,000	150,900	-13.0%
South-East	225,900	183,800	183,800	-18.6%
South-West	317,400	270,100	274,900	-13.4%

Source: CSO, QNHS on-line database.

The consequence of all these job losses has been the sharp increase in unemployment and emigration. Table 5.3 shows how unemployment has changed between 2007 and 2012, a period when the numbers unemployed increased by over 200 per cent. Male unemployment increased by almost 150,000 people and female unemployment by 68,000. Most of the unemployed, who had been employed in 2007 and before it, are seeking to return to a full-time job and less than 9 per cent of those unemployed in 2012 were seeking part-time employment. The impact of the unemployment crisis was felt right across the age groups, and it is only in the age groups below 34 years than any recent decrease has been recorded – a phenomenon almost entirely explained by emigration.

Table 5.3:Unemployment in Ireland, 2007 - 2011				
	2007	**2010**	**2011**	**Change 07-11**
Unemployment	107,500	310,600	324,500	201.9%
Gender				
Male	64,300	209,700	213,300	231.7%
Female	43,200	101,000	111,200	157.4%
Employment sought				
Seeking FT work	88,800	274,400	282,000	217.6%
Seeking PT work	15,200	24,200	29,000	90.8%
Age group				
15-19 years	12,100	21,100	20,700	71.1%
20-24 years	24,000	55,000	53,300	122.1%
25-34 years	32,100	94,300	92,200	187.2%
35-64 years	38,900	139,400	157,700	305.4%
Region				
Border	14,100	30,200	37,200	163.8%
Midlands	4,900	22,800	22,200	353.1%
West	10,300	34,300	32,800	218.4%
Dublin	31,700	76,200	81,300	156.5%
Mid-East	10,500	31,400	35,900	241.9%
Mid-West	10,400	30,300	30,000	188.5%
South-East	12,500	41,500	44,300	254.4%
South-West	12,900	44,000	40,800	216.3%
Duration				
Unemp. less than 1 yr	74,800	155,500	128,500	71.8%
Unemp. more than 1 yr	31,800	152,600	193,000	506.9%
LT Unemp. as % Unemp	29.6%	49.1%	59.5%	

Source: CSO, QNHS on-line database (see table 5.1)

The rapid growth in the number and rates of long-term unemployment are also highlighted in table 5.3 and in chart 5.1. The number of long-term unemployed was less than 32,000 in 2007 and has increased since, reaching 193,000 in 2012. QNHS data relating to late 2010 indicated that for the first time long-term unemployment accounted for more than 50 per cent of the unemployed. By third quarter 2012 the long-term unemployed represented just under 60 per cent of the unemployed. The transition to these high levels has been rapid since 2007 – see chart 5.1. The experience of the 1980s showed the dangers and long-lasting implications of an unemployment crisis characterised by high long-term unemployment rates. It remains a major policy failure that Ireland's level of long-term unemployment has been allowed to increase so rapidly in recent years. Furthermore, it is of serious concern that to date Government policy has given limited attention to the issue.

Chart 5.1: The increased presence of long-term unemployed in Ireland, 2007-2012

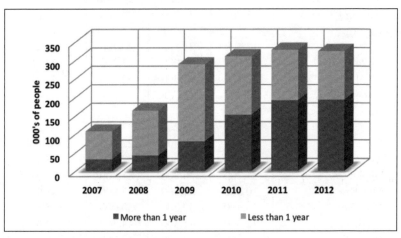

Source: CSO, QNHS on-line database.

Addressing a crisis such as this is a major challenge and we outline our suggestions for urgent policy action later in the chapter. However, as table 5.4 shows, it is clear that reskilling many of the unemployed, in particular those with low education levels, will be a key component of the response. Using the latest data, for 2011, 178,000 of the unemployed, almost 60 per cent, had no more than second level education, with 95,000 not having completed more than lower secondary (equivalent to the junior certificate). At the other extreme, the scale and severity of the recession has resulted in high levels of third-level graduates being unemployed, with 12 per cent of all those unemployed having at least a degree or higher qualification. While Government should not ignore any group in its overdue attempts to address the unemployment crisis, major emphasis should be placed on those who are most likely to become trapped in long term unemployment – in particular those with the lowest education levels.

Table 5.4: Unemployment by highest education attained		
	2010	**2011**
Primary or below	26,100	28,800
Lower secondary	64,100	66,200
Higher secondary	84,600	91,900
Post leaving cert	48,300	52,100
Third level non degree	30,300	29,200
Third level degree or above	35,800	38,700
Other	9,000	7,500
Total persons aged 15 to 64	**299,000**	**314,700**

Source: CSO, QNHS on-line database, table S9a, data not updated by CSO for 2012.

Previous experiences, in Ireland and elsewhere, have shown that many of those under 25 years old and many of those over 55 find it challenging to return to employment after a period of unemployment. This highlights the danger of large increases in long-term unemployment and suggests a major commitment to retraining and re-skilling will be required. In the long-run Irish society can ill afford a return to the long-term unemployment problems of the 1980s. In the short-term the new unemployed will add to the numbers living on low income in Ireland and this, in turn, will continue to have a negative effect on future poverty figures (see chapter 3).

Table 5.5: Numbers on the Live Register (unadjusted), Jan 2007 - 2013				
Year	**Month**	**Males**	**Females**	**Total**
2007	January	95,824	62,928	158,752
2008	January	116,160	65,289	181,449
2009	January	220,412	105,860	326,272
2010	January	291,648	145,288	436,936
2011	January	292,003	150,674	442,677
2012	January	283,893	155,696	439,589
2013	January	273,627	155,769	429,396

Source: CSO Live Register on-line database.

The Live Register
While the live register is not an accurate measure of unemployment, it is a useful barometer of the nature and pace of change in employment and unemployment. Increases in the register suggest a combination of more people unemployed, more people on reduced employment weeks and consequently reductions in the

availability of employment hours to the labour force. Table 5.5 shows that the number of people signing on the live register increased rapidly following the onset of the economic crisis in 2007. By January 2013 the numbers signing-on the live register had increased more than 270,000 compared to four years earlier.

Youth unemployment

While the increase in unemployment has been spread across people of all ages and sectors (see table 5.3), table 5.6 highlights the very rapid increase on the live register of those aged less than 25 years. The numbers in this group doubled between January 2008 and January 2009 and subsequently peaked at just over 89,000 in September 2009. Since then some decreases have occurred and, although we have limited empirical knowledge of the reasons for these decreases, a large part of the decrease is probably due to emigration.

Table 5.6: Persons under 25 yrs on the Live Register, Jan 2008 – Jan 2013

Month and Year	Numbers	Month and Year	Numbers
January 2008	36,945	January 2011	82,237
September 2008	53,666	September 2011	80,870
January 2009	70,268	January 2012	75,345
September 2009	89,810	September 2012	73,698
January 2010	85,910	January 2013	68,364
September 2010	88,663		

Source: CSO Live Register on-line database.

To complement the analysis in table 5.6, table 5.7 shows those on the live register by their last occupation and also examines the differences between those over and under 25 years. The figures once again highlight the need for targeted reskilling of people who have skills in sectors of the economy that are unlikely to ever return to the employment levels of the early part of the last decade.

Table 5.7: Persons on Live Register by last occupation – January 2013			
Occupational group	Overall	Under 25 yrs	Over 25 yrs
Managers and administrators	17,668	628	17,040
Professional	24,453	2,032	22,421
Associate prof.& technical	12,326	1,407	10,919
Clerical and secretarial	40,557	3,416	37,141
Craft and related	97,932	10,381	87,551
Personal and protective service	51,789	9,267	42,522
Sales	45,528	12,061	33,467
Plant and machine operatives	69,974	9,458	60,516
Other occupation	49,111	10,388	38,723
Never worked / not stated	20,058	9,326	10,732
Total	429,396	68,364	361,032

Source: CSO Live Register on-line database.

Responding to the unemployment crisis

The scale of these increases is enormous and it is crucial that Government, commentators and society in general remember that each of these numbers represents people who are experiencing dramatic and, in many cases, unexpected turmoil in their lives and their families' lives. As Irish society comes to terms with the enormity of this issue, we believe that this perspective should remain central.

To date, the policy response to this crisis has been limited, comprising announcements of apprenticeship schemes, 'Job Initiative' (2011) reforms, two Action Plans (2012, 2013) and the 'Pathways to Work' (2012) programme. Each of these has targeted small reforms and had limited success given the scale of the unemployment crisis. In responding to this situation *Social Justice Ireland* believes that the Government should:

- Launch a major investment programme focused on creating employment and prioritise initiatives that strengthen social infrastructure, such as the school building programme, primary care programme and the social housing programme.
- Resource the up-skilling of those who are unemployed and at risk of becoming unemployed through integrating training and labour market programmes.
- Maintain a sufficient number of active labour market programme places available to those who are unemployed.

- Adopt policies to address the worrying trend of youth unemployment. In particular, these should include education and literacy initiatives as well as retraining schemes.
- Recognise that many of the unemployed are skilled professionals who require appropriate support other than training.
- Resource a targeted re-training scheme for those previously employed in the construction industry, recognising that this industry is never likely to recover to the level of employment it had prior to 2007.
- Recognise the scale of the evolving long-term unemployment problem and adopt targeted policies to begin to address this.
- Ensure that the social welfare system is administered efficiently to minimise delays in paying the newly unemployed the social welfare benefits to which they are entitled.

In addition to these measures Government needs to adopt a strategy of making large scale job-creation interventions into the labour market. Without such action the current high levels of unemployment will only be eroded by further emigration and marginally reduced by the recently announced job creation schemes. *Social Justice Ireland* believes that the Government's current strategy is unlikely to bring unemployment down to 13 per cent of the labour force by 2015. This is the Government's projection in Budget 2013 – three percentage points higher than its Budget 2012 target for unemployment in 2015. The prospect of a decade long unemployment crisis is, therefore, very high. We propose that in addition to its current measures, Government makes two large-scale interventions which will significantly address the unemployment crisis and we outline the nature of these in the remainder of this section.

A Major Investment Programme

The depressed nature of the domestic economy, and in particular domestic demand (see discussion in chapter 2), highlights the extent of Ireland's dependency on external economic growth and exports for economic recovery and job creation prospects. *Social Justice Ireland* believes that, given the current weakness of the economy, Government needs to adopt policies which will stimulate it. This should be achieved through the adoption of a major capital investment programme on a substantially larger scale than currently proposed by Government.[49]

---

[49] This investment stimulus initiative is discussed in more detail in chapter 2.

Such a multi-billion euro programme, implemented over the next three to four years, would offer the prospect of simultaneously creating employment and addressing some of the socio-economic deficits that persist in Irish society. The focus should be on initiatives that strengthen social infrastructure such as school building, social housing, a nationwide high-speed broadband network, water-system investment (e.g. pipes and meters), green energy, childcare and rural transport.

A large-scale capital investment programme is attractive because it would create new economic activity and jobs, particularly in the supressed construction sector. Furthermore, pursuing justifiable investment projects which make good long-term socio-economic sense is especially appropriate given the current economic and unemployment crisis. The scale and ambition of the stimulus programme announced by Government in mid-2012 is far short of what is needed to make a real, long overdue impact on the socio-economic deficits and the unemployment crisis.

Part Time Job Opportunities Programme

In a series of documents and briefings to Government, political parties and the Oireachtas over the past three years, *Social Justice Ireland* has outlined a proposal for a *Part Time Job Opportunities Programme* (PTJO). We proposed that the government introduce this programme to ensure real employment at the going hourly rate for the job is available to 100,000 people currently long-term unemployed. We believe that participation must be on a voluntary basis and that the scheme should be modelled on the *Part-Time Job Opportunities Programme* that was piloted in the 1994–1998 period.[50] Details of that pilot programme are outlined below.

The proposed programme would enable unemployed people to be employed on a part-time basis by local authorities, the HSE, education authorities, voluntary and community organisations or groups. They would be employed voluntarily in work of public or social value which is either being done only partially or not at all at present. Participants would be remunerated at the established hourly 'going rate for the job' for as many hours as would give them a net income equivalent to what they were receiving from jobseekers allowance plus an additional €20 a week. They would be employed for a minimum of eight hours and a maximum of 19.5 hours per week and the person taking up the new position would lose none of his/her other social welfare entitlements. Once the required number of hours had been worked, the person would be free to do whatever she/he wished for the remainder

---

[50] The current directors of *Social Justice Ireland* led this pilot programme.

of the week. The money paid to the person filling the new position would be reallocated to the employing organisation by the Department for Social Protection and the employer would be encouraged to give extra hours to the worker, who would be taxed accordingly. If the person received further income from another job, this income would be assessed for tax purposes in the normal way. To protect against any 'deadweight effect', no position under the programme would be created if a person had been employed to do this particular work at any time during the previous two years.

The voluntary nature of the programme is considered very important from the point of view of the worker and the employer. It must not have any of the characteristics of 'workfare'.

- From the viewpoint of the worker, he/she must freely choose to come on the programme and must be free to leave if he/she chooses, subject only to normal requirements with regard to notice to the employer.
- From the point of view of the employer, there must be free choice in selecting workers from among those eligible for the programme. The employer should also be free to select the number of workers required. This ensures that the employment offered is real. The PTJO pilot programme showed that there would be more demand for these jobs than there were positions to accommodate them.

To protect the voluntary nature of the programme and to ensure that the employment is real the following would be expected:

- Positions should be advertised publicly by the employing body, through local media, or any other method used in the local area.
- A job description would be provided.
- Workers should be interviewed for the positions.
- Written job contracts should be provided.
- Employers would not be pressured to take more workers than they need.
- Leaving a particular job would not prejudice a worker seeking to participate in another project or training programme.
- Employers could replace workers immediately they left the programme.

Paying the 'going rate for the job' is an important concept in valuing the work done under the PTJO programme. It is the value which is placed on work in the market economy. In the pilot programme the programme's manager liaised with trade unions, professional organisations, employment agencies and personnel departments in an effort to arrive at a reasonable hourly rate for the various jobs created. To reflect incremental scales in many areas of employment, lower and higher level rates were provided in many instances, within which employers were free to negotiate the actual rate.

Social Justice Ireland estimates that thousands of positions can be created in the community, voluntary and public sectors using this PTJO approach. Funding currently being spent on social welfare payments to participants on this programme would be switched to their new employers. The additional funding required would be relatively low and would provide welcome, real jobs for people with relevant skills who are long-term unemployed.

Social Justice Ireland welcomes the growing support for this proposal and we note the February 2013 recommendation from the Joint Oireachtas Committee on Jobs, Enterprise and Innovation that Government should consider this proposal as part of its response to the jobs crisis (2013: 13).

Box 5.1 - Part Time Job Opportunities (PTJO) Pilot Programme, 1994-98

The early 1990s brought high unemployment levels to Ireland and little prospect of jobs being available for some time to come, even though the economy was beginning to recover. Jobless growth was the reality. A proposal made by the current directors of *Social Justice Ireland* was formally adopted by the Irish Government and announced in Budget 1994.

The proposal sought to create real part-time jobs in the community and voluntary sector principally. Long-term unemployed people could access these jobs on a voluntary basis. They were paid the going rate for the job and they worked the number of hours required to earn the equivalent of their social welfare payment with a small top up. The going rate for the job was agreed with the relevant trade unions and employers.

This programme was piloted in six very different areas: Finglas/Blanchardstown, Co. Laois, Waterford City, four towns in South Tipperary (Clonmel, Carrick-on-Suir, Cashel and Tipperary Town), North Kerry and the offshore islands.

The programme was adopted by 162 organisations and was extremely successful. Five hundred of the original 1,000 employees left during the course of the programme – almost all of these to take up full-time employment. These positions were all replaced by others who fitted the criteria for participation.

The market economy is unable to provide anywhere near the number of jobs required to reduce unemployment in the immediate future. This programme contributes to *Social Justice Ireland*'s view that public policy should change so that it recognises that people have a right to work, that unemployed people should not be forced to spend their lives doing nothing when traditional jobs do not exist and that all meaningful work should be recognised.

Work and people with disabilities

Results from Census 2011 have provided new data on the scale and nature of disability in Ireland. In a report published in November 2012, the CSO reported that there were 595,335 people with a disability in Ireland, equivalent to 13 per cent of the population. The most common disability was a difficulty with pain, breathing or other chronic illness or condition, which was experienced by 46.2 per cent of all people with disability. This was followed by a difficulty with basic physical activities, experienced by 41.1 per cent. The report found that both of these disabilities were closely related to age. It also showed that 1.1 per cent of the population were blind or had a sight related disability (51,718 people), 1.3 per cent (57,709 people) suffered from an intellectual disability, 2 per cent (92,060 people) were deaf or had a hearing related disability, 2.1 per cent (96,004 people) had a psychological or emotional condition, 3 per cent (137,070 people) had a difficulty with learning, remembering or concentrating; 5.3 per cent (244,739 people) had a difficulty with basic physical activities and 6 per cent (274,762 people) had a disability connected with pain, breathing or another chronic illness or condition (CSO, 2012: 45, 51-53).[51]

The Census 2011 data also revealed that there were 162,681 people with a disability in the labour force, representing a participation rate of 30 per cent. This is less than half that for the population in general. These findings are in line with results from the 2006 National Disability Survey (CSO, 2008 and 2010) and a 2004 QNHS special module on disability (CSO, 2004). This low rate of employment among

---

[51] Note, some individuals will experience more than one disability and feature in more than one of these categories.

people with a disability is of concern. Apart from restricting their participation in society, it also forces them into state dependent low-income situations. Therefore, it is not surprising that Ireland's poverty figures reveal that people who are ill or have a disability are part of a group at high risk of poverty (see chapter 3).

Social Justice Ireland believes that further efforts should be made to reduce the impediments faced by people with a disability to obtain employment. In particular, consideration should be given to reforming the current situation in which many such people face losing their benefits, in particular their medical card, when they take up employment. This situation ignores the additional costs faced by people with a disability in pursuing their day-to-day lives. Many people with disabilities are denied the opportunity to take up employment and they are trapped in unemployment, poverty or both.

Some progress was made in Budget 2005 to increase supports intended to help people with disabilities access employment. However, sufficient progress has not been made and recent Budgets have begun to reduce these services. New policies, including that outlined above, need to be adopted if this issue is to be addressed successfully. It is even more relevant today, given the growing employment challenges of the past few years.

Asylum seekers and work

Social Justice Ireland is very disappointed that the government continues to reject any proposal to recognise the right to work of asylum seekers. Along with other agencies, we have consistently advocated that asylum seekers should be automatically granted this right whenever Government fails to meet its own stated objective of processing their asylum applications within six months. Detaining people for an unnecessarily prolonged period in such an excluded state is completely unacceptable. Recognising asylum seekers' right to work would assist in alleviating poverty and social exclusion in one of Ireland's most vulnerable groups.[52]

The need to recognise all work

The current labour-market situation raises major questions about the assumptions underpinning culture and policy making in this area. The priority given to paid employment over other forms of work is one such assumption. Most people recognise that a person can be working very hard outside a conventionally accepted

---

[52] We examine this issue in further detail in chapter 10.

"job". Much of the work carried out in the community and in the voluntary sector, for example, comes under this heading. So, too, does much of the work done in the home. *Social Justice Ireland*'s support for the introduction of a basic income system comes, in part, because it believes that all work should be recognised and supported (see chapter 3).

The need to recognise voluntary work has been acknowledged in the Government White Paper, *Supporting Voluntary Activity* (Department of Social, Community and Family Affairs, 2000). The report was prepared by Government and representatives of numerous voluntary organisations in Ireland to mark the UN International Year of the Volunteer 2001. The report made a series of recommendations to assist in the future development and recognition of voluntary activity throughout Ireland. A 2005 report presented to the Joint Oireachtas Committee on Arts, Sport, Tourism, Community, Rural and Gaeltacht Affairs also provided an insight into this issue. It estimated that the cost to the state of replacing the 475,000 volunteers working for charitable organisations would be at least €205 million and could be as high as €485 million per year.

Social Justice Ireland believes that government should recognise in a more formal way all forms of work. We believe that everyone has a right to work, to contribute to his or her own development and that of the community and the wider society. However, we believe that policy making in this area should not be exclusively focused on job creation. Policy should recognise that *work* and a *job* are not always the same thing.

The work of carers
Ireland's carers receive minimal recognition despite the essential role they play in society. Recent results from the 2011 Census offer a new insight into the scale of their commitments, which save the state large costs which it would otherwise have to bear.

Census 2011 found that 4.1 per cent of the population aged over 15 provided some care for sick or disabled family members or friends on an unpaid basis. This figure equates to 187,112 people. The dominant caring role played by women was highlighted by the fact that 114,113 (61 per cent) of these care providers were female.[53] When assessed by length of time, the census found that a total of 6,287,510

---

[53] A CSO QNHS special module on carers (CSO, 2010) and a 2008 ESRI study entitled '*Gender Inequalities in Time Use*' found similar trends (McGinnity and Russell, 2008:36, 70).

hours of care were provided by carers each week, representing an average of 33.6 hours of unpaid help and assistance each. Two thirds of this volume of care was provided by female carers (CSO, 2012: 71-77). Using the minimum wage as a simple (and unrealistically low) benchmark to establish the benefit which carers provide each year suggests that Ireland's carers provide care valued at more than €2.8bn per annum.

Social Justice Ireland welcomed a commitment in *Towards 2016,* and more recently in the Fine Gael/Labour Party *Programme for Government* (2011), to develop a National Carers Strategy. However, progress has been slow and despite significant work on this strategy in 2008 the commitment to complete and publish it has been lacking. Given the above data from Census 2011, we strongly urge Government to complete and publish this strategy because it is essential that policy reforms be introduced to reduce the financial and emotional pressures on carers., These should focus, in particular, on addressing the poverty experienced by many carers and their families as well as increasing the provision of respite care for carers and for those for whom they care. In this context, the 24 hour responsibilities of carers contrast with the improvements over recent years in employment legislation setting limits on working-hours of people in paid employment.

Key policy priorities on work, unemployment and job creation
- Adopt the following policy positions in responding to the recent rapid increase in unemployment:
  - Launch a major investment programme focused on creating employment and prioritise initiatives that strengthen social infrastructure, such as the school building programme and the social housing programme.
  - Resource the up-skilling of those who are unemployed and at risk of becoming unemployed through integrating training and labour market programmes.
  - Maintain a sufficient number of active labour market programme places available to those who are unemployed.
  - Adopt policies to address the worrying trend of youth unemployment. In particular, these should include education and literacy initiatives as well as retraining schemes.
  - Recognise that many of the unemployed are skilled professionals who require appropriate support other than training.
  - Resource a targeted re-training scheme for those previously unemployed in the construction industry, recognising that this industry

is never likely to recover to the level of employment it had prior to 2007.

- Recognise the scale of the evolving long-term unemployment problem and adopt targeted policies to begin to address this.
- Ensure that the social welfare system is administered to ensure minimal delays in paying the newly unemployed the social welfare benefits to which they are entitled.

- Introduce a *Part Time Job Opportunities Programme* to create real part-time jobs for people who are long-term unemployed.
- Funded programmes supporting the community should be expanded to meet the growing pressures arising from the current economic downturn.
- A new programme should be put in place targeting those who are very long-term unemployed (i.e. 5+ years).
- Seek at all times to ensure that new jobs have reasonable pay rates and adequately resource the inspectorate.
- As part of the process of addressing the working poor issue, reform the taxation system to make tax credits refundable.
- Develop employment-friendly income-tax policies which ensure that no unemployment traps exist. Policies should ease the transition from unemployment to employment.
- Adopt policies to address the obstacles facing women when they return to the labour force. These should focus on care initiatives, employment flexibility and the provision of information and training.
- Reduce the impediments faced by people with a disability in achieving employment. In particular, address the current situation in which many face losing their benefits when they take up employment.
- Recognise the right to work of all asylum seekers whose application for asylum is at least six months old and who are not entitled to take up employment.
- Recognise that the term 'work' is not synonymous with the concept of 'paid employment'. Everybody has a right to work, i.e. to contribute to his or her own development and that of the community and the wider society. This, however, should not be confined to job creation. *Work* and a *job* are not the same thing.
- Request the CSO to conduct an annual survey to discover the value of all unpaid work in the country (including community and voluntary work and work in the home). Publish the results of this survey as soon as they become available.

- Give greater recognition to the work carried out by carers in Ireland and introduce policy reforms to reduce the financial and emotional pressures on carers. In particular, these should focus on addressing the poverty experienced by many carers and their families as well as on increasing the provision of respite opportunities to carers and to those for whom they care.

6. PUBLIC SERVICES

CORE POLICY OBJECTIVE: PUBLIC SERVICES

To ensure the provision of, and access to, a level of public services regarded as acceptable by Irish society generally

Earlier chapters have outlined how a focus on austerity as the solution to the economic crisis has resulted in a social crisis, with negative effects in such areas as employment and unemployment. Later chapters will review the spiral of decline in such areas as housing and accommodation, healthcare and education.

This chapter, however, looks at public services in a range of areas not addressed elsewhere. These include public transport, library services, financial services, information and communications technology, telecommunications, free legal aid, sports facilities and regulation.

It is important to note that 'public services' is not synonymous with 'public sector'. While the public sector delivers a wide spectrum of public services, such services are also delivered by the community and voluntary sector and by the business sector in a variety of combinations with the public sector.

As noted in chapter 2, public services and infrastructure have been eroded since the crisis of 2008. At both national and local level, social services and related initiatives have been cut just as the demands for these services are increasing. We have also noted that particular budgetary decisions may provide a short-term gain or saving for Government but have huge negative long-term consequences. *Social Justice Ireland* is very concerned that many decisions made during the current series of crises will have negative long-term effects. Government's continuing insistence on prioritising expenditure cuts over increasing taxation in Ireland has serious implications for public services and negative effects on Ireland's low and middle-income individuals and households.

Many public services provided by community and voluntary organisations have come under huge pressure in recent years as the recession has forced an ever-growing number of people to seek their help. But, just at the very moment when the demand for their services increased, Government reduced the funding being made available to many such organisations. We will return to this issue in chapter 11.

Increasingly, Ireland is being identified as a country whose public services are underdeveloped. Because poorer people rely on public services more than those who are better off, it is they who are most acutely affected by this shortage.

This issue was examined by the National Economic and Social Forum (NESF). In its report entitled *Improving the Delivery of Quality Public Services* it recommended a series of developments (2006:112-117). *Social Justice Ireland* believes that the Government should implement the approach outlined in the NESF report for the delivery of public services.

Public transport

'The provision of adequate and affordable public transport will not only address the needs of those who are isolated from services or employment, it will contribute to reduced traffic and environmental pollution and better public health' (Farrell et al. 2008: 44). Increased car dependency compounds issues relating to social isolation, increasing obesity and health hazards connected to heavy traffic and environmental pollution. Coupled with this, access in terms of transport to jobs, health services, education and other facilities is a major factor in ensuring social inclusion (Lucas, et al, 2001; Wilkinson & Mormot, 2003; Considine & Dukelow, 2009). Consequently public transport is an important component of any strategy to address issues such as health and to ensure social inclusion.

In Ireland 'over the last 20 years the percentage of total journeys undertaken by public transport has declined and public transport also accounts for a declining share of overall transport' (Department of Transport 2009: 40). Since 2007 the main public transport provider, CIE, suffered a decline in passenger journeys of 21 per cent over the period to 2011 (Department of Transport Tourism and Sport, 2011).

The Department of Transport (2009), acknowledged that in creating a sustainable transport system it was necessary to ensure that alternatives to car transport were available. Improving public transport systems, along with investment in cycling and walking, are a central means by which this will be achieved. According to the European Commission 'Public transport has to gain a higher share than today in the transport mix, become easily accessible for everyone and fully integrated with non-motorised modes' (2011:24).

However, the increase in car dependency and the decline in the use of public transport in Ireland suggests that public transport provision is not adequate or of a sufficient quality. In a consultation report for *A Sustainable Transport Future: a New*

Transport Policy for Ireland 2009 – 2020, concerns were highlighted in regard to a range of issues including the availability and quality of public transport in Ireland, lack of integration, lack of capacity, overcrowding, poor availability and design of routes.

Further to this, *The European Green City Index* report carried out in 2009 ranked Dublin last out of 30 cities in the transport category. The length of its public transport network and the extent of its cycle lanes are well below the average. According to this report less than 20 per cent of people take public transport to work; nearly 61 per cent use private cars (Economist Intelligence Unit, 2009). This data does not take cognisance of recent welcome developments such as the 'Dublin Bikes' scheme, cross-city cycle lanes and the rollout of integrated public transport ticketing (the 'Leap' card) (The National Competitiveness Council, 2012). It is apparent, however, that issues with public transport provision still remain.

For instance, in 2011, the Environmental Protection Agency, (EPA) highlighted that one of the most significant barriers to achieving sustainable transport in Ireland relates to 'lack of reliable and efficient public transport and cycling facilities, particularly in low-density rural areas and residential neighbourhoods' (Browne et al. 2011: vii).

The Department of Transport Tourism and Sport acknowledges the 'need to rebalance transport policy to favour public transport' (2011:33). While it has been necessary to re-schedule some public transport initiatives that had been planned, it is crucial that Government continues to give priority to public transport over private transport in allocating capital funding in the years ahead.

The issue of affordability in relation to public transport is important if people are to be encouraged to use this form of transport. In 2012, as a result of reductions in the subsidies for public transport, there were fare increases across all public transport operators – Dublin Bus, Iarnród Éireann, Bus Éireann and Luas. With continuing reductions envisaged, it is essential that affordability is maintained.

In light of the discussion relating to the role public transport plays in underpinning social inclusion it is also essential that continued support is provided for the development and maintenance of the rural transport programme.[54] It should also

---

[54] Issues specifically related to the provision of public services in rural areas are addressed in chapter 13.

be recognised that public transport in Ireland generally falls short of the quality levels usually associated with a developed society.

Library services

Libraries play an important role in Irish society, performing a valuable community service and ensuring access to reading, information and learning. 'They provide a focal point for community and intergenerational contact, and enable access to learning and an ever-expanding range of information for a wide constituency through an increasingly broad and varied range of media' (Mc Grath et al, 2010: 6).

Recent research by the Carnegie Trust (2012) indicated that overall more than three quarters (79 per cent) of those in Ireland said that libraries were 'very important' or 'essential' for communities, this was higher than any other jurisdiction included in this research (i.e. Wales, England, Scotland and Northern Ireland).

Statistics provided for 2010 further underscore the important function that libraries play in Ireland. In that year registered membership of libraries increased by .02 per cent from 809,032 to 809,169. Fractionally under one in five of the population (19.1 per cent) are registered as members of the public library service. Children's membership of the library increased by 1.6 per cent in 2010 to 316,800 while adult membership in the same period declined 1.0 per cent to 492,369. Visits to full-time branches increased by 1.4 per cent to 14.7 million and visits to all branches increased by the same percentage to 16.3 million. (An Chomhairle Leabharlanna, 2010).

'Branching Out' (Department of Environment, Heritage and Local Government, 2008) was a major review of library services in Ireland and built on a publication of the same name undertaken in 1998 (Department of Environment, Heritage and Local Government, 1998). Between 1998 and 2008, when this review of policy was published, there were significant improvements in the services provided by libraries. These included improvements in book collections, ICT infrastructure and electronic services and building infrastructure. According to the review, it is imperative that the improvements made in the library service to date are maintained. This is particularly important given the continued growth in demand on library services.

While the 2012 local authority expenditure estimates indicated that library expenditure as a percentage of the total spent on all services would increase slightly, overall investment in public libraries is being reduced. Local authorities estimated that they would invest €137.0 million of their revenue budgets on public library services in 2012.[55] This represented a decrease of 2.6 per cent on the 2011 figure of €140.6 million. Total local authority expenditure on library stock was set to decrease by 12.1 per cent on the 2011 figure. The reduced funding for stock is of particular concern in light of the growing demand for the service. If quality is to be maintained then funding for stock must be preserved (An Comhairle Leabharlanna, 2012).

A further issue highlighted in An Chomhairle Leabharlanna's 2010 annual report is the increase in annual charges being levied on adult users of the service. The issue of fees is viewed as a serious barrier to use, with the agency concluding that the benefits of free access outweigh the value of the money gained. This is a particularly important point in the current economic climate and *Social Justice Ireland* urges local authorities to reconsider this measure.

Public libraries play a crucial role in Irish society and have the potential to play an even more important role into the future. *Social Justice Ireland* believes that, as part of our commitment to providing a continuum of education provision from early childhood to third level and throughout the life-cycle, Ireland needs to recognise the potential that the library service offers. This requires ready availability and easy access to information. Coupled with this is the need for easy access to modern means of communication. Libraries are obvious centres with potential to support these objectives. To play this potential role, continued support for and expansion of the library service is essential.

Financial services
Financial exclusion refers to a household's difficulty in accessing and using financial services. This has particular implications as we move towards an increasingly cashless society because groups already financially excluded will become more marginalised. A 2011 study by the ESRI examined four dimensions of financial exclusion: access to a bank current account, access to credit, ability to save and access to housing insurance (Russell et al, 2011). Of these, access to a bank current account was considered the most fundamental because exclusion from basic banking services means households may face difficulties carrying out everyday transactions such as paying bills, receiving earnings or welfare benefits, transferring funds or purchasing goods and services.

---

[55] The actual out-turn for 2012 was not available at the time of writing.

This research highlighted serious deficiencies in the ability of Irish households to access these basic financial services. In 2008 it was found that 20 per cent of Irish households did not have a bank current account – a figure that is almost three times higher than the average for the EU15. The proportion without a bank current account rose to 40 per cent among those with low education qualifications, 38 per cent in households in the bottom 20 per cent of the income distribution, 50 per cent among local authority tenants, 52 per cent among those who are ill or disabled and 27 per cent among those aged over 55 years (Russell et al 2011:126-127).

The *Strategy for Financial Inclusion* published in 2011 demonstrated that a binding requirement on banks in other EU countries to address the issues faced by people who are financially excluded yielded positive results. 'As a significant first step in this direction, a binding requirement to support the provision of a BPA (basic payment account) was introduced for Allied Irish Banks and Bank of Ireland in 2009 as part of the recapitalisation of those banks, and this commitment was extended to the remainder of the domestic banking sector in a package of sector-wide commitments which was agreed with the European Commission in 2010 as part of its Decision on the Bank of Ireland Restructuring Plan' (Steering Group on Financial Inclusion, 2011: 7).

While the provision of a basic payment account does not address all elements of financial exclusion, it is considered to be the most important initial requirement. A pilot project to introduce a basic payment account commenced during 2012.

The potential role for post offices in providing an access point has also been emphasised as an effective tool in addressing financial exclusion and deserves consideration.

Information and communications technology

In 2011 an estimated 81 per cent of households had a home computer. This was an increase of 16 percentage points since 2007. Internet and broadband connection has also increased substantially over this period, with an estimated 78 per cent now connected to the internet compared with 72 per cent in 2010 and 57 per cent in 2007. There has been strong growth each year in internet connections (CSO, 2011). In 2011 71 per cent of the population use the internet regularly (i.e. at least once a week), up 8 percentage points since 2010 and 4 percentage points above the EU average of 68 per cent.

For disadvantaged people the rate was 57 per cent, 4 percentage points above the EU average (European Commission, 2012). CSO figures show that in 2010 27per cent of adults never used the internet, a figure which declined to 21per cent in 2011 (CSO, 2011:32). In 2011 the Netherlands, had the highest rate of household internet access in the EU at 94 per cent, while Ireland, at 78 per cent, was ranked eighth. The EU average was 73 per cent of households (CSO, 2012).

These figures underscore the progressively important role that ICT plays in modern society and the level of progress being made in regard to access to digital technology in Ireland. 'Digital literacy is increasingly becoming an essential life competence and the inability to access or use ICT has effectively become a barrier to social integration and personal development. Those without sufficient ICT skills are disadvantaged in the labour market and have less access to information to empower themselves as consumers, or as citizens saving time and money in offline activities and using online public services' (European Commission, 2008: 4).

Digital competence is also one of the competencies highlighted as part of the key competencies required for lifelong learning by the European Commission in 2006. Factors such as disability, age and social disadvantage all have significant roles to play in increasing digital exclusion. Apart from the impact on the individual, there are also losses to the business community and the economy at large (McDaid & Cullen, 2008).

In 2012 the Government published its digital strategy for delivering public services. Covering the period 2012 to 2015, this strategy encourages greater sharing of data between Government public bodies, wider adoption of online payments and the use of smartphone optimised sites and apps. It also identifies a number of services which may be particularly suitable for electronic delivery, such as the renewal of adult passports, planning applications and objections and welfare applications.

While progress is being made, Government needs to show sustained commitment to counteract the issue of digital exclusion in particular for the more vulnerable sectors of society. Resources will continue to be required in this area. At an economic level this is essential to promote competitiveness and effectiveness, while at a social services level it is essential to ensure digital exclusion does not become another form of exclusion being experienced by people who are already vulnerable.

Telecommunications

Two issues are of note in this area. Firstly, Com Reg has put in place a system to ensure that a basic set of telecommunications services is available to all consumers throughout the country. This is known as a Universal Service Obligation (USO). The services to be provided include: meeting reasonable requests for connections at a fixed location to the public communications network and access to publicly available telephone service; provision of directory services and maintenance of the national directory database; public telephone provision; specific services for disabled users; affordability of tariffs and options for consumers to control expenditure (Commission for Communications Regulation, 2011: 13). Eircom is the designated Universal Service Provider (USP) and has a number of obligations regarding the supply of these services.

Social Justice Ireland welcomes the vigilence of Com Reg in maintaining the quality of the service provided under this obligation, taking into account any potential negative effects on disadvantaged members of the community were these obligations not to be met. After broad consultation, Eircom was re-designated as the Universal Service Provider in June 2012 with the term set to last until 30 June 2014 (Commission for Communications Regulation, 2012).

Secondly, as part of the Digital Agenda for Europe, the European Commission has set targets of 30mbps broadband for all citizens and 50 per cent of citizens subscribing to 100mbps by 2020. While progress has been made in the provision of basic broadband services (see section on Information and Communications Technology), Ireland is performing badly in relation to the roll out and take up of advanced broadband services. In January 2012 the penetration rate of fixed broadband was 24.3 per cent of the population, 3.4 percentage points below the EU average of 27.7 per cent (EU Commission, 2012). 'Given the weak telecommunications investment climate in Ireland, our dispersed population patterns and the recession, there is a strong risk, if appropriate action is not taken, that Ireland is likely to fall even further behind as other countries are moving ahead to deploy advanced telecoms networks' (Forfas, 2011:27).

With this in mind, the Government has recognised the need to address Ireland's performance in regard to advanced broadband technology. The National Broadband Plan was published in August 2012 committing to the role out of:

- 70Mbps – 100Mbps to more than half of the population by 2015;

- at least 40Mbps, and in many cases much faster speeds, to at least a further 20 per cent of the population and potentially as much as 35 per cent around smaller towns and villages; and
- a minimum of 30Mbps for every remaining home and business in the country – no matter how rural or remote (Department of Communications, Energy and Natural Resources, 2012:1).

These targets are ambitious and will require substantial investment to be achieved. However, there will be many advantages to businesses and individuals. The plan recognises the need to bring faster broadband to rural areas and where the market fails to deliver this Government will intervene. This is important to ensure access for all (Department of Communications, Energy and Natural Resources, 2012:2). It is also essential that consideration be given to the cost of broadband provision in Ireland to ensure it is accessible and the price is not prohibitive.

Free legal aid
Citizens depend on the law and associated institutions to defend their rights and civic entitlements. The free legal aid system is a central element of this system, particularly for those with limited incomes. The Legal Aid Board provides civic legal aid to people with incomes of less than €18,000 per annum, with recipients contributing a nominal sum. *Social Justice Ireland* believes that free legal aid is an important public service. In the current economic climate, with rising unemployment and decreasing income, the demands on the Legal Aid Board are continuing to grow. Most notably there has been an increase in demand for services regarding debt issues.

'In the four years since 2006 the number of applications is up by more than 70 per cent and the upwards trajectory of demand has continued into 2011. In 2010 ... there was an increase in applications to law centres alone of almost 22per cent" (Legal Aid Board, 2010: 13). The waiting time for a full appointment with a solicitor is over four months in more than half the centres.

The Board has indicated that the sustained increase in demand is being primarily driven by two factors. The first, and most significant, is the economic downturn which has resulted in many more people eligible for the legal services provided by the Board. Secondly, there appears to be a greater need for legal services during times of economic crisis, particularly in areas such as family law, debt issues and employment.

There has been a massive increase in demand for this service at a time when resources are being reduced. In 2010 Exchequer funding for the civil legal aid service was cut by 8 per cent to €24.22 million (The Legal Aid Board, 2010:16).

The budget allocation for general legal services (excluding refugee/asylum related matters) was reduced from €26.99 million in 2008 to €26.31 million in 2009, €24.23 million in 2010, and €24.13 million in 2011. Therefore, despite an increased throughput by the Legal Aid Board's staff in law centres, those people entitled to access the civil legal aid scheme have to wait longer. According to the Legal Aid Board, of the 4,877 people waiting in June 2012, some clients waiting for a solicitor in two centres in Dublin – Clondalkin and Gardiner Street – could expect to wait for 13 months and 11 months respectively for a solicitor's appointment. It is important to remember that justice delayed is justice denied.

Social Justice Ireland believes that the provision of, and adequate support for, this service is a basic requirement of governance. In light of the increasing pressure on this service, it is vital that it is adequately resourced and supported by the Government.

Sports

A report carried out by Indecon International Economic Consultants (2010) highlighted the contribution provided by sport to the Irish economy. It also showed the important role played by sport in assisting the development of social capital and in contributing to the health and quality of life of the population. Therefore the considerable rise in participation in sports from 34 per cent in 2009 to 46 per cent in 2011 is a very welcome trend identified in the Irish Sports Monitor (2011).

The draft *National Sports Facilities Strategy 2012-2015* published in September 2012 acknowledges the important role that sport plays in terms of health, economic and social benefits. It outlines three overall objectives (Department of Transport Tourism and Sport, 2012:3):

- participation in sport and physical activity at all levels;
- opportunities for the achievement of excellence at the elite levels of sport, both nationally and internationally; and
- social inclusion.

One aspect of sports policy which is important, according to the strategy, is the 'need to improve the provision and accessibility of sports facilities in socially disadvantaged areas' (Department of Transport Tourism and Sport, 2012:12). This is very welcome because people who are socially disadvantaged are less likely to participate in sport and, therefore, less likely to obtain the health benefits of physical activity.

It has also been noted that income plays a large role when it comes to participation, with only 38 per cent of those in the lowest income bracket playing sport compared with 56 per cent of those in the highest income bracket (The Irish Sports Council, 2011).

The National Sports Council has developed a creative initiative of local sports partnerships. Some of these are working effectively to address this problem. Further funding for local sports partnerships would be most worthwhile.

Volunteering is an important aspect of the sporting landscape in Ireland. In 2011 the proportion of people volunteering for sport increased from 7 per cent to 15 per cent. The 2010 Indecon study conservatively estimated that over 270,000 people participate in some form of sport-related voluntary activity; the Irish Sports Council Strategic Plan (2009) estimated that the number was closer to 400,000. The estimated value of volunteering is between €321 million and €582 million per annum (Indecon, 2010). People engaging in volunteering also bring numerous social benefits, both for the volunteers and for the community. Government needs to continue to support policies aimed at encouraging volunteerism and enhancing the experience of volunteers.

As sports policy is developed against the background of increasingly scarce public expenditure resources, *Social Justice Ireland* believes that more in-depth consideration needs to be given as to how the returns on these investments can be maximised. Income and time are both major barriers to sports participation and policy makers need to be cognisant of this in developing sports policy (Lunn and Layte, 2009). In many cases simple schemes to encourage participation and use of existing sports facilities are all that is required.

Regulation

Regulatory policy in Ireland has failed in many areas and requires significant reform over the next few years. This has been clearly demonstrated in the problems that have emerged in the financial services sector. While some of the required reforms have been put in place, a serious re-think is required to ensure that regulation plays a stronger and far more effective role to ensure there is no repetition of the huge failures of the past decade.

Central to our opinion on how regulation should develop is the view that all current and future be required to consider the societal impact of any reforms they propose. They should also have the capacity to monitor what is happening and to act effectively and quickly when problems are identified. Regulation should be judged on how it affects social, cultural and sustainability issues in society as well as on the economy. Implementing regulation with this as its central aim would certainly achieve better regulation for all. It would also ensure consistently better outcomes for consumers. Such an approach, for example, would have prevented the failure of the regulatory process in the current banking crisis.

Social Justice Ireland also believes that there should be solid and justifiable reasons for introducing regulation. It should not be introduced just to create choice/competition within the market. For example, to achieve competition in the electricity market the electricity regulator increased the price of electricity. While this may achieve competition, we question the benefit to people. Furthermore, assessment mechanisms should be established to allow an analysis of regulation pre and post its implementation. Examination of societal impacts should be central to such an assessment procedure. We also believe that inputs should be sought from interested parties, including the community and voluntary sector, as part of the assessment procedure.

The impact of regulation within the context of regional policy is another important consideration. Cross-subsidisation issues, in postal or electrical services, are important to retain equity between rural and urban dwellers. A further challenge for regulatory authorities must be to retain this inter-regional equity.

Regulation and regulatory law has profoundly failed Ireland in recent years. It should be framed in ways that ensure it is effective, timely, accessible and interpretable. Currently regulatory law is complex and in many cases requires those being regulated to divert a considerable quantity of resources to keep up with it. Complex regulation also makes it difficult for interested parties to actively participate in the pre and post-regulation assessment mechanisms. *Social Justice Ireland* believes it is important that where regulation has been judged to be a failure, Government should reform it at the earliest opportunity.

Key Policy Priorities for Public Services

- Focus policy on ensuring that there is provision of, and access to, a level of public services regarded as acceptable by Irish society generally.
- Ensure equality of access across all public services.
- Target funding strategies to ensure that far greater priority is given to providing an easy-access, affordable, integrated and high-quality public transport system. This should include adequate support for the Rural Transport Initiative that increases significantly the quality of life of those living in remote rural areas, particularly older people and women.
- Support the further development of library services throughout the country, including provision of open-access information technology.
- Ensure that financial institutions provide people with easily accessed and affordable basic bank accounts and financial facilities, as per the Strategy for Financial Inclusion (2011).
- Give more in-depth consideration to how public funds are used to encourage sport and sporting activity. In many cases simple schemes to encourage participation and use of existing sports facilities are required.
- Adopt further information technology programmes to increase the skills of disadvantaged members of society.
- With continued investment in advanced broadband systems consideration needs to be given to the cost of its provision in Ireland to ensure it is accessible to all.
- Take action to address the huge failures identified in the regulatory process during the crisis in banking and financial services. This process should ensure that all types of regulation take into account their potential impact on social, cultural and sustainability issues within society as well as on the economy. Implementing regulation with this balance as its central aim would achieve better regulation for all.

7. Housing and Accommodation

CORE POLICY OBJECTIVE:
HOUSING & ACCOMMODATION
To ensure that adequate and appropriate accommodation is available for all people and to develop an equitable system for allocating resources within the housing sector

Issues relating to housing and accommodation have featured prominently in policy debates in Ireland over recent years. Most of this has been concerned with the provision and cost of privately owned accommodation. However, more recent developments in the area of housing relate to challenges involving the large surplus housing stock, high levels of mortgage arrears, unfinished developments and increasing social housing need, as well as changes in tenure patterns and the focus of housing policy. All these issues are discussed in this chapter.

During the boom years Ireland experienced an astonishing growth in property construction and house prices. Initially the increase in housing was a response to rising demand, as a result of a sustained growth in the population, low interest rates and increasing income per capita. As noted in chapter 2, this situation changed and construction was promoted and supported as an end in itself because it appeared to generate economic growth. Construction became a major element and driver of the Irish economy. However, housing construction increased at a rate which was not supported by demand. The result was a housing bubble which has contributed to the current economic crisis. According to Kitchin et.al (2010), poor financial and planning regulations, along with tax incentives, served to support this negative phenomenon.

Housing: a New Philosophy

Given the changes which have occurred in the housing landscape in Ireland it is imperative that a new paradigm from which to progress housing policy into the future is identified. Drudy (2006) outlines the basic aspects of two approaches to housing – housing as a commodity or housing as a home.

When housing is viewed as a commodity the market is seen to be the ideal provider and state intervention is limited to facilitating and encouraging private provision through, for example, tax incentives. While some state provision of housing would exist, it would be limited to very low income groups. The implications of this standpoint is to develop a housing system which provides speculative profit for those with the resources, excluding people based on their ability to pay and generating a housing system which perpetuates inequality and segregation (Drudy, 2006).

The alternative to this is to view "housing as a home", placing the emphasis on– 'shelter, a place to stay, to feel secure, to build a base, find an identity and participate in a community and society' (Drudy, 2006:244). This view regards housing as a fundamental social requirement, in much the same way as education or health.

Social Justice Ireland strongly endorses the need to view housing as a fundamental social right. Over recent times it is clear that housing in Ireland has been seen as a commodity rather than a home and this has had major implications for Irish society. Had society adopted the approach of viewing housing as a social right over the past decade the Irish economy, and many Irish families, would not be in the precarious financial position they are now. It is time that we formally incorporated this approach into our national housing policy.

Government Housing Policy Statement 2011

The framework for the current national housing policy is found in the Government's Housing Policy Statement which was released in June 2011. It states 'Our vision for the future of the housing sector in Ireland is based on choice, fairness, equity across tenures and on delivering quality outcomes for the resources invested. The overall strategic objective will be to enable all households access good quality housing appropriate to household circumstances and in their particular community of choice' (Department of Environment, Community and Local Government, 2011b). The statement further specifies that it will not entice people to treat housing as a commodity.

The statement focuses on:

- the removal of incentives to purchase;
- the creation of a viable and well regulated private rental sector containing quality housing provision;
- the standing down of affordable housing programmes;
- the move to greater provision through options such as the Rental Accommodation Scheme and the long term leasing initiative;

- the remaining capital build programmes to focus, in particular, on regeneration and projects that cater for special needs; and
- bolstering the role of the voluntary and co-operative sector.

This has been accompanied by a massive reduction in capital spending on housing over the past number of years. The allocation for social housing in budget 2013 (Department of Finance, Budget 2013) was €585 million (i.e. €310 million in current spending and €275 million in capital expenditure). The Government claims this will result in an increase of 5,000 units of social housing in 2013. But there are close to 100,000 households on waiting lists for social housing and it is clear that Government has no credible plan to address this issue in the foreseeable future. The dramatic decline in the allocation for social housing illustrates the Government's approach to housing policy, with a reorientation of funding from construction towards leasing initiatives but no coherent approach to reducing the number of households on waiting lists.

Housing tenure in Ireland

Ireland's housing policy has resulted in very high levels of owner occupation to the detriment of other tenure types. Housing policy has favoured investment in residential development which, combined with policies of mortgage-interest tax relief and very favourable tenant purchase schemes, has resulted in a high level of home ownership. The abolition of local rates on residential property and the subsequent failure to implement a system of residential property tax ensured that owner occupation was additionally subsidised. Further to this, in the social housing sector people had the option of purchasing their own house and many did. In practice this transferred wealth to the purchaser as these houses were available for far less than their real market value. These policies over years produced a housing system that was not tenure neutral and led to the revisualisation of the rental sector, both public and private.

Using data from various Censuses of Population, table 7.1 shows how Irish tenure patterns have changed. In 2006 77.2 per cent of households were owner-occupiers, a figure which gave Ireland one of the highest rates of owner occupancy in the EU. Irelands traditionally high-level of home ownership is indicative of two factors: it shows the value which Irish people placed on owning their own home and it underscores the level to which Irish housing policy has supported owner occupation, placing little value on other tenure types.

This trend has begun to reverse with a substantial reduction in the level of owner-occupied dwellings in 2011 and a return to levels in renting which have not been seen since 1971 (see table 7.1). In 2011 owner occupied dwellings accounted for 70.8 per cent, down from 77.2 per cent in 2006, a reduction of almost 7 percentage points in this period and just less than 10 percentage points since 1991. There has also been a dramatic 47 per cent increase in the number of households in rented accommodation between 2006 and 2011, up from 323,007 to 474,788. The overall percentage of households renting their accommodation rose to 29.2[56] per cent, causing home ownership rates to fall sharply (see table 7.1) (CSO, 2012a). People's reluctance to buy property and to continue to rent instead may be due to such factors as the unavailability of mortgage finance and instability in the housing and employment markets.

Table 7.1: Nature of Occupancy of Private Households, Ireland 1961–2011

Year	Owner-occupied	Rented	Other
1961	59.8%	35.6%	4.6%
1971	68.8%	28.9%	2.3%
1981	74.7%	22.6%	2.6%
1991	80.0%	17.9%	2.1%
2002	79.8%	18.5%	1.7%
2006	77.2%	21.3%	1.5%
2011[57]	70.8%	27.6%	1.6%

Source: CSO, 2011:63 and CSO, 2012a:12

Total Housing Stock

Census 2011 revealed interesting insights into the total housing stock in Ireland. In April 2011 there were 1,994,845 permanent dwellings or housing units in the State. This is an increase of 225,232 units, or 12.7 per cent, on the level in 2006, representing an annual average growth rate of 2.4 per cent. This is a notable reduction on the increase in stock which occurred between 2002 and 2006, when

---

[56] "Other" refers to the category of people who indicated that they were living in their dwellings rent free. In the CSO publication *The roof over our heads* this category of people are included in the number of households renting, giving a total of 474,788 or 29.2%.

[57] The 2011 data cited in this table differs slightly from the publication released by the CSO *The roof over our heads*. This is because in order for the data to be comparable with other years it required that the category of people who "did not state" the nature of their occupancy be removed from the total number of dwellings prior to calculating the percentage of owner-occupied, rented and other. This is in keeping with other CSO publications, such as *Measuring Irelands Progress 2011*.

the housing stock increased by 309,560 (21%), representing an average annual growth rate of 4.9 per cent, which is the highest on record (CSO, 2012a:7). Comparing figures from census 2002, 2006 and 2011, it is clear that a significant slowdown in the housing stock growth has occurred − a slowdown which was inevitable due to the oversupply of housing which took place over the last 20 years.

Housing Stock and Population Growth

Table 7.2 shows the growth in housing stock compared to the growth in population over a 20 year period. The rise in housing stock was significantly greater than the growth in population (71.9% compared with 30.1%). There were 785 new housing units for every 1,000 persons added to the population between 1991 and 2011 (CSO, 2012a:7). This illustrates that the increase in housing which occurred over the 10 year period leading up to census 2011 was unsustainable, with more than one in four of all occupied dwellings in Ireland being built during this decade.

Table 7.2 Population and housing stock 1991-2011

Census Year	Population	% Change in Population	Housing Stock	% Change in Housing Stock
1991	3,525,719	–	1,160,249	–
1996	3,626,087	2.8	1,258,948	8.5
2002	3,917,203	8.0	1,460,053	16.0
2006	4,239,848	8.2	1,769,613	21.2
2011	4,588,252	8.2	1,994,845	12.7

Source: CSO 2012a:7

House completions

Table 7.3 outlines the rate of house completions in the various sectors between 1993 and 2011. The peak was in 2006 when over 93,000 units were completed. Since then the rate of dwelling completion has declined rapidly. The total number of house completions in 2010 was 14,602 and in 2011 it fell to 10, 480.

In 2009 the vast majority of new houses (80 per cent) were built by the private sector (down from 91 per cent in 2007). Local authorities built 3,362 new homes in 2009. The figures for 2009 also reveal a welcome growth in the levels of voluntary/non-profit and co-op housing.

These organisations built 2,011 dwellings during that year and they now account for over a third of all publicly assisted housing completions. This welcome trend underscores the growing role this sector is playing in Irish society. Currently the housing association sector manages over 27,000 homes (Irish Council for Social Housing, 2011). The government's housing policy statement indicates that the role of the voluntary and cooperative sector will be central in providing social housing into the future. With the elimination of the Capital Loans and Subsidy Scheme, it is essential that this sector is supported. *Social Justice Ireland* believes that the voluntary and co-operative sector has the capacity to make a significant contribution in addressing housing need in Ireland and that Government must provide the assistance needed to ensure its continued growth. With the government's housing policy statement focusing on the bolstering of this sector, it will be necessary to ensure its appropriate regulation, while also ensuring that sufficient funding and pathways to funding are available so that housing can be delivered on the scale needed to address the level of housing need in Ireland.

The Government has indicated that a return to large scale building of local authority housing is unlikely and has instead decided to focus resources in the area of social leasing initiatives and the rental accommodation scheme (RAS) in order to ensure social housing provision. 'While the current move to secure additional housing units through leasing rather than new build or acquisition is supported, the new policy approach should not rely solely on leasing. The depletion in the public housing stock that this would entail, coupled with demographic pressures which will become manifest in the medium-long term, would lead to a heavy burden on current expenditure. The policy approach pursued by D/EH&LG will therefore be to adjust the balance between leased and acquired and built units. This approach can be reviewed as broader developments occur' (Department of Finance, 2010:37). It is the contention of *Social Justice Ireland* that the Government should ensure continued investment in developing social housing in order to maintain a stock of local authority houses. Major scaling back in local authority stock will have long term consequences for people in housing need.

Table 7.3: House Completions, 1993–2011

Year	Local Authority Housing	Voluntary/Non Profit Housing	Private Housing	Total
1993	1,200	890	19,301	21,391
1994	2,374	901	23,588	26,863
1995	2,960	1,011	26,604	30,575
1996	2,676	917	30,132	33,725
1997	2,632	756	35,454	38,842
1998	2,771	485	39,093	42,349
1999	2,909	579	43,024	46,512
2000	2,204	951	46,657	49,812
2001	3,622	1,253	47,727	52,602
2002	4,403	1,360	51,932	57,695
2003	4,516	1,617	62,686	68,819
2004	3,539	1,607	71,808	76,954
2005	4,209	1,350	75,398	80,957
2006	3,968	1,240	88,211	93,419
2007	4,986	1,685	71,356	78,027
2008	4,905	1,896	44,923	51,724
2009[58]	3,362	2,011	21,076	26,420
2010	-	-	-	14,602
2011	-	-	-	10,480

Source: Department of Environment, Heritage and Local Government, Housing Statistics Bulletins (various editions).

Vacant housing stock

As the increase in housing stock significantly outstripped the growth in population it became increasingly clear that there would be insufficient demand to sustain this growth. Coupled with this, according to Kitchen (2010), the lack of a residential property tax ensured that local authorities adopted a model of funding which pursued income from development levies. This was further supported by central Government through tax incentive schemes and poor regulation of local planning. These factors have resulted in vacant housing stock in areas where there is the least demand as well as unfinished estates and developments across the country.

---

[58] There is a discrepancy of 29 in total house completions. This is as a result 39 voluntary and co-operative units completed in this year being represented by just 10 ESB connections due to the nature of the units.

In 2011 the overall vacancy rate was 14.5 per cent (if holiday homes are excluded the vacancy rate drops to 11.5 per cent). In 2011 the vacant units consisted of 59,395 holiday homes, 168,427 houses and 61,629 apartments. The total vacancy rate in 2011 fell by 0.5 per cent since 2006. However, the increase in total housing stock over this period means that the number of vacant units increased by 23,129 (see table 7.4).

The vacancy rate for 2011 varies considerably across the country. It is highest in Leitrim, at 30.5 per cent, followed by Donegal (28.6 per cent), Kerry (26.4 per cent) and Mayo (24.7 per cent). The lowest vacancy rate was recorded in South Dublin (5.4 per cent), followed by Fingal (7.0 per cent), Dun Laoghaire Rathdown (7.7 per cent) and Kildare (8.0 per cent). A vacancy rate of 10.2 per cent, or 24,638 units, was recorded for Dublin City (CSO, 2012b). Given the vacancy rate, the trend in house building in Ireland has been counter to what might be expected. Counties with the highest rates of vacant stock in 2006 subsequently enlarged their housing stock by the highest percentage in the ensuing years, and those counties with low vacancy increased their stock the least (Kitchin, et.al. 2010), with Cavan, Donegal, Leitrim and Longford recording a more than 18% increase in their housing stock over that period (CSO, 2012b).

Table 7.4 Vacancy rate and number of vacant units for years 1991, 1996, 2002, 2006 & 2011

Year	Vacancy Rate %	% Change on vacancy rate	Number of units vacant	Change number of units vacant
1991	9.1	————	105,142	———
1996	8.4	- 0.7%	105,250	+ 108
2002	9.8	+1.4%	143,418	+ 38,168
2006	15	+5.2%	266,322	+122,904
2011	14.5	-.5%	289,451	+ 23,129

Source: CSO 2012b

Unfinished housing estates
The plethora of unfinished housing estates throughout Ireland is largely a result of many local authorities disregarding good planning guidelines. Consideration was not given to "regional and national objectives, sensible demographic profiling of potential demand and the fact that much of the land zoned lacks essential services such as water and sewerage treatment plants, energy supply, public transport or roads' (Kitchin, et.al. 2010: 28).

The first report assessing the numbers of unfinished housing developments released in 2011 indicated that from a total of 2,876 housing development sites of two or more dwellings, there are 2,066 unfinished housing developments in the country. Of these, 1,822 were predominantly inactive at the time of inspection and only 245 active (Department of Environment, Community and Local Government, 2011a).

The Progress Report on Actions to Resolve Unfinished Housing Developments (Department of Environment, Community and Local Government, 2012a) indicates that as a result of recommendations from the Advisory Group on Unfinished Housing Developments (2011) the government's initial priority was to address public safety issues. But it also aimed to bring together the main stakeholders at national, regional and local level to ensure that there was a coordinated response; put in place stronger legislation with a view to ensuring the engagement of developers in resolving any unfinished estates and to build confidence in the housing sector by engaging in best practice in regard to utilising vacant housing for beneficial use.

This report revealed that one year later issues in respect of 211 unfinished estates had been resolved. Moreover, the rate of resolution of estates has varied hugely across the country[59] with limited progress in addressing issues relating to unfinished housing developments. This has obvious social and economic implications for people owning houses, often in negative equity and living in poorly finished estates. In some instances these home owners have few neighbours, no street lighting, paths or green areas and are located a good distance away from amenities or services (Kitchin et.al. 2010).

The current housing landscape in Ireland provides opportunities for the Government to address the on-going housing need which is apparent in our society. The Irish Council for Social Housing and the National Association of Building Cooperatives have indicated that 'opportunities exist for the voluntary and cooperative sector to have an impact on the issue of unfinished housing developments by working in partnership with Local Authorities to serve local social housing need" (Advisory Group on Unfinished Housing Developments, 2011:12). According to the Department of Environment, Community and Local Government (2012a) '3,200 homes have been indicated by NAMA as being available for potential use for social housing purposes and are being progressively assessed by housing authorities and approved housing bodies' (2012a:3). However, advancement has been slow.

---

[59] http://www.irishtimes.com/newspaper/ireland/2012/0706/1224319507369.html

Social Justice Ireland believes it is imperative that the government follow through on the commitment made to ensure that vacant homes which are in suitable locations are brought up to an appropriate standard in order for them to be utilised for social housing purposes. To this end it is vital that adequate funding should be made available to effectively resolve this on-going issue in order to ensure that houses can be brought into beneficial use to address the considerable housing need in Ireland.

Mortgage arrears

A further problem relating to housing in Ireland is the on-going issue of mortgage arrears. Central Bank figures (table 7.5) reveal the scale of this difficulty and also the level to which it has grown over the period from September 2011 to June 2012. The level of mortgage arrears has been increasing steadily.

At end-June 2012, there were 761,533 private residential mortgage accounts for principal dwellings held in the Republic of Ireland. Of these 83,251, or 10.9 per cent, were in arrears of more than 90 days. This compares to 62,970 accounts (8.1 per cent of total) that were in arrears of more than 90 days at end-Sept 2011.[60] At end of June 2012 there were a further 45,165 mortgages in arrears of less than 90 days, a slight fall off from 46,284 on March 2012. In total there were 128,416, mortgages in arrears of some form. This amounts to almost 17 per cent of the total residential mortgage loans at end of June 2012. A further 40,221 mortgages were classified as restructured but not in arrears at the end of June 2012. These figures are continuing to rise and highlight the scale of this issue.

With regard to this, the report of the Inter-Departmental Mortgage Arrears Working Group (2011) (The Keane Report) made a range of recommendations, including, the need for new bankruptcy legislation, non-judicial debt settlement options and further mortgage restructuring solutions. The report also recommended the establishment of mortgage-to-rent schemes. Such schemes would allow certain struggling mortgage holders to remain in the family home as social housing tenants.

A mortgage to rent scheme was rolled out by the Department of Environment, Community and Local Government in 2012. Under this approach the property is bought by an approved housing body (housing association or co-operative) at current market value and the household becomes a social housing tenant of the

---

[60] "The figures published represent the total stock of mortgage accounts in arrears of more than 90 days, as reported to the Central Bank of Ireland by mortgage lenders. They include mortgages that have been restructured and are still in arrears of more than 90 days as well as mortgages in arrears of more than 90 days that have not been restructured" (Central Bank, 2012) .

housing body. The purchase of the house is partly financed by a loan from the original mortgage lender and partly from the Exchequer. The government is budgeting for take up of the scheme from approximately 100 families in 2012. Eligibility criteria are as follows: the mortgage position should be deemed unsustainable under a Mortgage Arrears Resolution Process; the customer must agree to voluntary repossession and must qualify for social housing; the maximum value of the house must be €220,000 in Dublin and €180,000 in other parts of the country and the house must be suitable for the household's needs. Further to this the customer must not own any other property or have assets worth more than €20,000 and the maximum household net income must not exceed €25,000 to €35,000, depending on the regional area (Department of Environment, Community and Local Government, 2012b). This scheme is designed to assist the most distressed mortgage holders and should only be viewed as a small component in addressing the overall issue.

Table 7.5 Mortgage arrears

	Sept 2011	Dec 2011	Mar 2012	June 2012
Number of total residential mortgage loan accounts outstanding - at end of quarter	773,420	768,955	764,138	761,533
Total mortgage arrears cases outstanding at end of quarter which are:				
In arrears up to 90 days	47,627	48,238	46,284	45,165
In arrears 91 to 100 days	16,599	17,825	18,193	17,553
In arrears over 180 days	46,371	53,120	59,437	65,698
Total Arrears cases over 90 days outstanding (Number and Percentage)	62,970 8.1%	70,945 9.2%	77,630 10.2%	83,251 10.9%

Source: Central Bank, 2012

The Keane Report further recommended the need for the establishment of a mortgage support and advice service, recommending that this should be linked to MABS and that the expense of providing this service should be borne by the mortgage lenders. 'Given the complexity of the issue the Group is recommending the establishment of an independent mortgage advice service to guide mortgage holders through what can be a difficult and stressful process' (Inter-Departmental Mortgage Arrears Working Group, 2011:2). While nowhere near the scale of that recommended in the Keane Report, the Government established a financial advice service in 2012 which allows distressed mortgage holders to discuss with an accountant propositions made by the bank to deal with their mortgage difficulties, with the bank paying up to €250 for the consultation. Concerns with this scheme have been highlighted by FLAC (2012), which has said that distressed borrowers need sustained support and that this scheme does not address the difficulties faced by these individuals in the holistic manner required.

Housing needs assessment: Waiting lists – how many and how long?

Social housing support 'is broadly defined as accommodation provided, or arranged, by housing authorities or approved housing bodies for households who are unable to provide for their accommodation needs from their own resources' (Department of Environment, Community and Local Government, 2011c, pg.48). The most recent assessment of housing needs took place in March 2011. This provides a national picture of the level of housing need across the country. It must be noted that the approach used in the collection of the data in 2011 differs from that employed in previous years and therefore the figures are not strictly comparable (Housing Agency, 2011).

'Net need' refers to 'the number of households in need of housing support who are not currently receiving social housing support (those already in Local Authority, voluntary cooperative or RAS accommodation are excluded)' (Housing Agency, 2011:1). Table 7.6 presents a measure of the numbers of households who cannot be accommodated through the current stock available to housing authorities. The net need figure for 2008 shows that 56,249 households were in need of social housing support at 31 March 2008. This is an increase of 31 per cent on the level of need in 2005. While already acknowledged that the data from 2008 and 2011 are not strictly comparable, it is still alarming to see that the increase reported in net need from 2008 to 2011 amounts to 42,069 households. This is a 74.8 per cent increase over this period (see table 7.6). In 2008 the largest category of households on the lists was those labelled as being not able to meet costs of existing accommodation. In 2008 this group accounted for 53 per cent of the waiting list, or 29,583 households. The largest category of need in 2011 was again those people unable to meet the cost of accommodation. This category accounted for almost two thirds of all households, or 65,643 households. The next largest category in 2011 related to medical or compassionate reasons (9.7%), followed by involuntarily sharing (8.7 per cent). Overcrowding and unfit accommodation accounted for 4.7 per cent and 1.7 per cent respectively.

Table 7.6 Breakdown of the Local Authority Waiting List by Major Categories of Need 2005, 2008 and 2011

Category of need	2005[61]	as % of need 2005	2008	as % of net need 2008	2011	as % of net need 2011
Homeless	1,987	4.5	1,394	3	2,348	2.4
Traveller	1,004	2	1,317	2	1,824	1.9
Accommodation unfit	1,719	4	1,757	3	1,708	1.7
Accommodation overcrowded	4,073	10	4,805	9	4,594	4.7
Involuntary sharing	3,371	8	4,965	9	8,534	8.7
Young person's leaving care	256	.5	715	1	538	.5.0
Medical or compassion	3,504	8	8,059	14	9,548	9.7
Older Persons	1,658	4	2,499	4	2,266	2.3
People with a disability	455	1	1,155	2	1,315	1.3
Unable to meet Accommodation Cost	24,919	58	29,583	53	65,643	66.8
Total	42,946	100	56,249	100	98,318	100

Source: Department of the Environment, Heritage and Local Government, Annual Housing Statistics Bulletin 2008 & Housing Agency, 2011.

The household structure of those on the waiting list in 2011 shows that 48,748 households, or 49.6 per cent, were single adult households. Family households with one child accounted for 25.2 per cent, households with 2 children accounted for 12 per cent, households with 3 children accounted for 4.5 per cent and households with 4 or more children accounted for 2.6 per cent. Therefore, over 44 per cent of households in need of housing support consisted of households with children.

The majority of people in need of housing support are under 40 years of age (69 per cent), with the largest category (30.5 per cent) in the range of 31 – 40years.

[61] These figures are different from the figures reported in the 2005 Housing Needs Assessment as an adjustment was made to the 2005 figures in the 2008 Housing Statistics Bulletin for comparison purposes with the 2008 results.

The majority of households in need of housing support (70.5%) had Irish citizenship, while 20.2 per cent were EU citizens and the balance of 9.3 per cent were categorised as having refugee status, permission to remain in the state or subsidiary protection status.

There is a clear association between being in housing need and low income. According to the OECD (2011) people with low incomes are more likely to face poorer basic housing conditions and are also less likely to be satisfied with their housing arrangements. Table 7.7 shows that over three quarters (78.5 per cent) of households in need of social housing had incomes below €15,000. The majority of these had gross incomes between €10,000 and €15,000. Overall 89.6 per cent, or 88,064 households, had incomes below €20,000. Larger households are likely to have larger incomes coupled with larger living expenses. However, only 3.6 per cent of households had income levels above €25,000.

Table 7.7 Breakdown of Local Authority Housing Waiting List by Gross Household Income 2011

Income Band	No. of Households	%
Below € 10,000	27,065	27.5
€ 10,001 – € 15,000	50,118	51.0
€ 15,001 – € 20,000	10,881	11.1
€ 20,001 – €25,000	6,736	6.8
€25,001 – € 30,000	2,159	2.2
Over €30,000	1,359	1.4
Total	98,318	100

Source: Housing Agency, 2011.

The length of time spent by households on waiting lists once they have applied for social housing support is another area which deserves attention. In 2011, 22.5 per cent of households had applied to a local authority for housing less than one year previously. A total of 31,286 (31.8 per cent) households had been waiting for between two and four years and 24,138 households (24.6 per cent) had been waiting more than four years.

The level of housing need in Ireland appears to be increasing at a substantial rate. These numbers represent the most vulnerable people in Irish society. *Social Justice Ireland* calls for swift and significant action to address this situation.

The private rented sector

Traditionally the private rented sector has been the residual sector of the Irish housing system, characterised by poor-quality accommodation and non-secure tenure at the lower end of the housing market. Today, this sector is highly differentiated, with high-quality housing and relatively secure tenure at the upper end of the market and low-quality housing and insecurity of tenure at the lower end. Reliance on this sector as a housing option fell to its lowest point of 7 per cent in 1991. Since then, however, it has risen substantially. The census of 2011 showed that almost 19 per cent of all households are now renting from a private landlord (table 7.8). The private rental sector is increasingly becoming the tenure of choice for a substantial number of households (see table 7.8) as well as being viewed as means by which to address social housing provision.

Table 7.8 Percentage distribution of housing units by occupancy status, 1961-2011

Occupancy Status	1961	1971	1981	1991	2002	2006	2011
LA Rented	18.4	15.9	12.7	9.7	6.9	7.5	7.9
Private Rented	17.2	10.9	8.1	7.0	11.1	10.3	18.8
Owner Occupied	53.6	60.7	67.9	80.2	77.4	77.2	70.8
Other	10.8	12.5	11.2	3.0	4.6	5.0	2.5[62]
Total	100	100	100	100	100	100	100

Source: CSO, 2003, 2007 & 2012 Various Census Publications

As noted above, Irish Government policy did not prioritise the private rental sector; which was viewed as secondary to owner-occupation. Reflecting this approach, legislation and regulation of this sector was often lacking. In an attempt to address this, the Private Residential Tenancy Board was established in 2004. The role of the PRTB includes the establishment and maintenance of a register of all private rental residential accommodation, the provision of a cheap and efficient resolution service to handle tenant and landlord disputes and the undertaking of research into the private rental market (PRTB, 2010).

However, despite legal requirements and the linking of tax deductions to registration, a number of privately rented residences in the country are not registered with the PRTB. The total number of tenancies registered with the Board

---

[62] Other refers to households who indicated that they were living rent free or renting from a voluntary body.

at the end of 2010 was 231,818 (PRTB, 2010). This compares with findings in census 2011, in which 305,377 households indicated that they were renting from a private landlord.

The task of ensuring that the standard of accommodation offered by this sector is at an appropriate level falls to the Private Residential Tenancy Board (PRTB) and local authorities. The level and geographical distribution of inspections carried out by the local authorities of the registered properties indicates that in some areas inspections are common while in others they are far lower. The numbers of inspections carried out have been increasing year on year. In 2007, 14,008 inspections were carried out. This rose to 17,186 in 2008 and 19,801 in 2009. A fifth of the properties inspected in 2009 (4,306, or 21 per cent) did not meet regulatory requirements.

The governments housing policy statement recognises the need to deliver a well regulated rental sector, ensuring that rental is a real housing option for everyone. Further development of the work of the Private Residential Tenancy Board (PRTB) to ensure that higher minimum standards of accommodation are enforced will play an important role in this.

Considering the growth in the private rented market in Ireland and bearing in mind the figures relating to the registration and inspection of these tenancies, *Social Justice Ireland* believes that the Government must take the necessary steps to ensure that all local authorities carry out a reasonable number of inspections to guarantee the quality of the accommodation offered by this sector and that necessary steps are taken to ensure official registration of all private rented properties.

Rent supplement
When rent supplement was introduced it was only intended as a short-term housing support for those who suffered a sudden drop in income. However, this programme has seen a massive increase in participants and costs over the period from 2002 to 2011 (see table 7.9).

In December 2010 there were 48,073 households in receipt of rent supplement for a period of 18 months or longer. At the end of 2011 this cohort accounted for approximately 53,000 households. These are the target group for the Rental Accommodation Scheme (RAS) (Department of Social Protection 2011a:23). Increasingly people are in receipt of rent supplement for long periods of time as progression to social housing provision such as RAS has not occurred in line with demand.

Table 7.9: Rent Supplement Cost and number of Recipients for 2002, 2007, 2009, 2010, 2011

Year	Expenditure €000	Recipients
2002	252,203	54,213
2007	391,466	59,726
2009	510,751	93,030
2010	516,538	97,260
2011	502,748	96,803

Source: Department of Social Protection, 2011bSupplement

A further issue in regard to rent supplement relates to the maximum rent limits in operation. These should reflect local conditions and family composition. These were reviewed and reduced in 2012 while the minimum contributions from recipients were increased. The purpose of this review was to establish new maximum rent limits regionally which were in line with the most up-to-date market data available. However, some voluntary agencies are concerned that the new limits are making it difficult for some recipients to source good quality accommodation appropriate to their needs, forcing them into homelessness or substandard accommodation.[63] This is an issue of great concern which needs to be monitored closely.

Plans are in place to move the operation of rent supplement from the Department of Social Protection to the Department of Environment, Community and Local Government. Details on this are sketchy. The Department states: 'The housing policy framework contains the announcement of the transfer of responsibility in providing housing needs for long-term rent supplement recipients to housing authorities on a phased basis. A multi-agency steering group has been established by the Department of Environment, Community and Local Government to give effect to the Housing Policy Initiative and this group is currently developing proposals and operational protocols for the transfer of tenants' (Department of Social Protection, 2011a:23). This is a welcome move and will hopefully result in increased efficiency as well as ensuring better quality and more secure accommodation for tenants. It is also considered likely that this move will eliminate

---

[63] http://www.irishtimes.com/newspaper/ireland/2012/0807/1224321631185.html

the poverty trap associated with rent supplement as people will pay differential rents to allow them to proceed to work while retaining some of their housing support benefit.

Rental Accommodation Scheme (RAS) and Social Housing Leasing

The government has ruled out a return to large capital funded construction programmes by local authorities, instead focusing on the enhanced role that the Rental Accommodation Scheme (RAS) and the Social Housing Leasing Initiative will play in the delivery of social housing.

RAS was designed to address the needs of people on rent supplement for periods of over 18 months. It provides a longer term contract and more security of tenure than is associated with people who have their accommodation needs met under rent supplement. The local authority rents the unit from the landlord at reduced market rent for periods of between one and four years. Unlike rent supplement, which involves the tenant dealing with the landlord, under the RAS the local authority deals directly with the landlord.

With the longer term leasing option, suitable properties can be leased to either local authorities or approved housing bodies (AHB) for a period of 10 – 20 years. Unlike RAS, where the landlord retains responsibility for the upkeep and maintenance of the property, under this initiative the local Authority or the AHB take on this responsibility. In both instances people have increased security of tenure and improved quality of accommodation as the property must comply with standards for rented houses.

'Figures for the end of December 2011 from the Department of the Environment, Heritage and Local Government indicate that local authorities have transferred 21,900 rent supplement cases to RAS units. Housing authorities have also transferred a further 15,800 recipients to other social housing options, a total of over 37,700 transfers since 2005 of which 6,337 occurred in 2011' (Department of Social Protection, 2011a:23). With 98,318 households on local authority waiting lists in 2011, it is imperative that the Government take action and address this issue swiftly, making more accommodation available through RAS and other leasing options.

Homelessness

People experiencing homelessness are not a homogenous group and there are many reasons why people become homeless. 'Structural explanations locate the reasons for homelessness in social and economic structures and cite poverty, negative labour market forces, cuts and restrictions in social welfare payments and reductions or shortfalls in the supply of affordable housing as the leading causes. Individualistic accounts, on the other hand, focus on the personal characteristics and behaviours of homeless people and suggest that homelessness is the consequence of personal problems, such as mental illness and addiction' (O'Sullivan, 2008:21).

Census 2011 revealed that 3,808 persons were either sleeping rough or in accommodation designated for the homeless on the night of the count. Of these, 2,539 were male and 1,269 were female. Of the 64 persons found sleeping rough, all but six were males. Dublin accounted for 59 of the 64 rough sleepers. The proportion of persons with disabilities among the homeless population was significantly higher, at 42 per cent, than for the general population (13 per cent). Forty nine per cent reported that they did not have an educational qualification beyond lower secondary level compared to 25 per cent of the general population. Almost one third reported that their health was 'fair,'bad' or 'very bad' compared to 10 per cent of the general population (CSO, 2011c). These statistics show the myriad of difficulties surrounding the phenomenon of homelessness.

In addressing homelessness, policy needs to focus on both the structural and individualistic causes. Decreases in funding for homeless services place severe pressure on services dealing with the many complexities of this issue at a time when service providers are reporting a significant increase in demand for their services.

Another issue associated with homelessness relates to gaining an accurate measure of the numbers of people experiencing this difficulty. Clearly complications arise due to the complexity of matters surrounding homelessness and the level to which, by its very nature, it is a hidden problem. There is a gap between the administrative data (Local Authority Needs Assessment) held and the numbers of people accessing homeless services. While the census 2011 report provides figures for the level of homelessness and insights into the nature of homelessness issues still arise. It is not possible to carry out a comparison between 2008 figures and 2011 figures because the methodologies used in both counts are so different. Furthermore, the methodology employed does not make it possible to account for all people who are experiencing homelessness. For instance, people who are staying with friends and relatives with no other accommodation option, so called "sofa surfers", were not accounted for in the 2011 census count. In order to assess the impact which policies are having on homelessness *Social Justice Ireland* believes that it is important that resources are put in place to ensure that a comparable accurate regular count of homeless persons takes place.

In February 2013 Government published a Homelessness Policy Statement which commits it to prioritising the provision of long-term housing as early as possible, rather than putting homeless people through a process of short and medium-term housing 'steps'.

Social Justice Ireland believes it should be possible to end homelessness by 2016 if sufficient resources are targeted at the goal without delay.

To demonstrate that its commitment to addressing the issue of homelessness in Ireland is real and not just rhetorical *Social Justice Ireland* believes that Government should immediately allocate the resources required to end homelessness in Ireland by 2016.

Traveller accommodation
The number of people enumerated as Irish Travellers in Census 2011 increased by 32 per cent from 22,435 to 29,573, with all counties apart from Limerick and Waterford showing increases larger than the increase in the general population. Further findings in Census 2011 indicate that only 12 per cent of Irish Travellers lived in caravans and mobile homes, with almost 84 per cent of the Traveller population living in permanent housing. This is a significant fall from 2006, when one in four Irish Travellers lived in temporary accommodation (CSO, 2012d).

The All-Ireland Traveller Health Study (2010) showed that while the majority of Traveller families have basic household amenities (flush toilet, running water, waste disposal), there are still a disproportionately greater amount of Traveller families without these amenities than in the general population. Significant numbers of families in group housing or sites reported lack of footpaths, public lighting, fire hydrants and safe play areas. A quarter (24.4 per cent) of Traveller families in the Republic considered where they lived to be 'unhealthy' or 'very unhealthy' and significant numbers (26.4 per cent) considered their place of residence unsafe.

'Traveller accommodation is inextricably linked to almost all other aspects of Travellers' lives – their traditions, health, education, employment prospects and any number of other issues' (Coates et.al. 2008, pg.81). Despite many legislative and policy changes and increased support for Traveller specific accommodation, there is widespread consensus that in practice Traveller accommodation is a challenging area to address. According to Coates et al (2008), politicians, policy makers and local authorities as well as Traveller organisations and members of both the Traveller and settled community, are dissatisfied with the existing situation in regard to Traveller accommodation in Ireland.

Capital funding for Traveller accommodation has been significantly reduced, down from over €45 million in 2006 to €15 million in 2011 (Department of Environment, Community and Local Government, 2011d). According to Pavee Point (2011) there is a need for the Government to ensure that local authorities fulfil their obligations in relation to Traveller accommodation.

Housing and people with disabilities

'The housing options available to people with disabilities generally fall far short of those available to the general population. Limited understanding of disability and the needs and aspirations of people with disabilities on the part of society generally may result in inadequate policy responses to the housing needs of people with disabilities" (Browne, 2007: iv).

Additional housing costs are a feature of having a disability. Primarily these costs are for adjustments to residences to ensure access and continued use and there are several housing adaptation grants available for this purpose. The Government indicates in the *National Housing Strategy for People with a Disability 2011-2016*, that promotion of independent living for people with disabilities and the elderly is supported by the availability of such grants. However, the funding for these grants has been substantially reduced over recent years. According to the Department of the Environment, Community and Local Government, the overall budget for housing adaptation grants was down by €15 million in 2011 and was due to be reduced by a further €4.5 million in 2012 (2011d:11). *Social Justice Ireland* believes that given social and economic benefits of people remaining in their own homes, adequate funding should be made available to ensure that they can do so. This would also be in keeping with the recent *National Housing Strategy for People with a Disability 2011-2016*. Funding, however, is being reduced and therefore schemes are in danger of not assisting the number of people they should.

The national strategy represents a very welcome policy outline aimed at ensuring that the rights of people with disability are upheld. It sets out a framework for delivering housing to people with disabilities through mainstream housing policy. The vision underpinning this strategy is 'To facilitate access for people with disabilities to the appropriate range of housing and related support services, delivered in an integrated and sustainable manner, which promotes equality of opportunity, individual choice and independent living' (Department of the Environment, Community and Local Government, 2011c: 34). The National Implementation Framework to support this strategy was released in 2012. This framework identifies the manner in which the Government and other stakeholders will ensure the continued implementation of the objectives established in the strategy. It focuses on several aspects of housing in regard to people with disabilities. Among them are ensuring people with disabilities within the community are provided with the requisite supports to access and maintain housing which meets their needs and addressing the manner in which the transitioning of people from institutional care to more independent living is to be achieved. The Government should make available the appropriate level of funding to ensure the on-going implementation of this framework.

Housing and children
Factors which impact on child wellbeing and development are varied and interconnected. The OECD (2011) highlighted that housing conditions and child development outcomes are strongly linked because children spend the largest proportion of their time indoors. Poor housing affects children at different stages of their life. For example, lack of affordable housing may have an impact during early childhood as it weakens the family's ability to meet basic needs while neighbourhood effects are more likely to have negative impacts on adolescents. Furthermore, associations between poor housing conditions and child development are more often than not irreversible and transfer to adulthood. One of the objectives of the National Children's Strategy is to ensure that 'Children will have access to accommodation appropriate to their needs' (Department of Health and Children, 2000, pg. 65). One of the ways in which this was to be achieved was through the prioritisation of families with children for accommodation under the new streams of housing to become available under the Local Authority and Voluntary Housing Programmes.

However, the number of households with children in need of social housing increased from 2005 to 2008. In 2008, 27,704 households with children were identified as being in need of social housing. In 2005 this figure had been 22,335 (Office of Minister for Children and Youth Affairs, 2010). As indicated above, figures from 2008 and 2011 are not strictly comparable and it is difficult, therefore to assess the extent to which this trend has continued. Nonetheless, in 2011 a total of 43,578 households which were in need of social housing support included children. The special report relating to homeless people in census 2011 revealed a further disturbing finding that there were 457 children aged 14 and under in the homeless count, representing 12 per cent of the total number of homeless people in Ireland (CSO, 2012c).

As already highlighted, low income and low accommodation standards are associated with poor health levels and poor future educational and life opportunities. Given Ireland's already deplorable record in regard to child poverty, *Social Justice Ireland* believes that the area of children and housing requires urgent action.

Policy Priorities on Housing and Accommodation in Ireland

*   Take the required action to ensure the supply of social housing, including co-op and voluntary/non-profit housing, is on the scale required to eliminate local authority housing waiting lists.
*   Ensure continued investment in developing social housing in order to maintain a stock of local authority houses.
*   Ensure prompt delivery and adequate resources to support long term leasing initiatives such as the Rental Accommodation Scheme (RAS)
*   Make adequate funding available to resolve effectively on-going issues regarding unfinished housing estates so that suitable units can be brought into beneficial use.
*   Take the necessary steps to ensure that all local authorities carry out a reasonable number of inspections annually of private rented accommodation and that further efforts are made to ensure official registration of all such properties.
*   Allocate the resources required to end homelessness in Ireland by 2016.
*   Ensure that those facing major adjustments as a result of mortgage arrears are dealt with fairly by banks. This requires that under any repayment schedule they have sufficient income to provide a minimum adequate standard of living.[64]
*   Ensure that an accurate regular count of homeless persons takes place.
*   Provide sufficient funding for the on-going implementation and monitoring of the *National Housing Strategy for People with Disability 2011-2016*.
*   Provide continued investment in the Traveller accommodation programme to ensure local authorities are fulfilling their obligations in this area.

---

[64] Details of what these income levels should be are provided by the *Vincentian Partnership for Social Justice* in its studies – 2006 and 2010 – on this issue.

8. Healthcare

> ## CORE POLICY OBJECTIVE: HEALTHCARE
>
> To provide an adequate healthcare service focused on enabling people to attain the World Health Organisation's definition of health as a state of complete physical, mental and social wellbeing and not merely the absence of disease or infirmity.

Healthcare is a social right that every person should enjoy. People should be assured that care is guaranteed in their times of illness or vulnerability. Being so fundamental to wellbeing, healthcare services are important in themselves and they are also important as a factor in economic success in a range of ways, including improving work participation and productivity. The standard of care is dependent to a great degree on the resources made available, which in turn are dependent on the expectations of society. The obligation to provide healthcare as a social right rests on all people. In a democratic society this obligation is transferred through the taxation and insurance systems to government and other bodies that assume or contract this responsibility. These are very important considerations at this particular moment because Government is proposing to make fundamental changes in Ireland's healthcare system. This chapter outlines some of the major considerations *Social Justice Ireland* believes Government should bring to bear on such decision-making.

Poverty and Health

Health is not just about healthcare. The link between poverty and ill-health has been well established by international and national research. A World Health Organization Commission that reported in 2008 on the social determinants of health found that health is influenced by factors such as poverty, food security, social exclusion and discrimination, poor housing, unhealthy early childhood conditions, poor educational status and low occupational status. In Ireland, studies conducted by the Irish Public Health Alliance (IPHA) detail striking differences in life expectancy and premature death between people in different socio-economic groups. The Pfizer Health Index published in 2012 showed that those from a lower socio-economic background are more likely to be affected by a wide range of medical conditions (including heart disease, cancer, depression and arthritis) than middle class people (ABC1) (Pfizer, 2012).

Analysis of Census 2011 data by the CSO confirms the relationship between social class and health. While 95 per cent of people in the top social class enjoyed good or very good health, this proportion fell across the social groups to below 75 per cent in social class 7 (CSO, 2012a). In summary, poor people get sick more often and die younger than those in the higher socio-economic groups. Poverty directly affects the incidence of ill health; it limits access to affordable healthcare and reduces the opportunity for those living in poverty to adopt healthy lifestyles. A recent study by Eurofound reveals that the health status of Europeans has deteriorated during the economic crisis in respect of the prevalence of chronic diseases and that the gap between the self-reported health of low-income earners and that of the highest income earners is increasing (Eurofound, 2012). In Ireland a recent survey by the CSO measuring the economic downturn (CSO 2012), shows that more than half of all households have cut back their spending on groceries and this is of particular concern. Annex 8 discusses the social determinants of health and health inequality in Ireland in more detail.

Life expectancy

According to Eurostat's figures for 2010, Irish males had life expectancies of 78.7 years while Irish females were expected to live 4.5 years longer, reaching 83.2 years (Eurostat, 2013), figures which have gradually improved over the past decade. Based on these figures, Ireland's life expectancy performance is slightly above the European average. The EU average, however, is pulled down by low life expectancies, especially among men, in such countries as Estonia, Latvia and Lithuania (see table 8.1). Relative to the older member states of the EU the Irish figures are somewhat less impressive. Furthermore, life expectancy at birth for both men and women in Ireland is lower in the most deprived geographical areas than in the most affluent (CSO, 2010). For example, life expectancy at birth of men living in the most deprived areas was 73.7 years (in 2006/07) compared with 78 years for those living in the most affluent areas. For women the corresponding figures were 80 and 82.7 years (CSO, 2010).

Ireland's life expectancy figures should be considered in the context of many of the findings of the PHAI reports referred to above and in Annex 8 and the poverty figures discussed earlier (see chapter 3). Ireland's poverty problem has serious implications for health because of the link between poverty and ill health. Thus, those in lower socio-economic groups have a higher percentage of both acute and chronic illnesses.

Table 8.1: Life Expectancy at Birth by sex, 2010			
	Male **2010**	**Female** **2010**	**Difference**
France	78.2	85.3	7.1
Spain	79.1	85.3	6.2
Italy	79.8	85	5.2
Cyprus	79.2	83.9	4.7
Malta	79.2	83.6	4.4
Sweden	79.6	83.6	4.0
Finland	76.9	83.5	6.6
Luxembourg	77.9	83.5	5.6
Austria	77.9	83.5	5.6
Ireland	**78.7**	**83.2**	**4.5**
Slovenia	76.4	83.1	6.7
Belgium	77.6	83.0	5.4
Germany	78.0	83.0	5.0
Netherlands	78.9	83.0	4.1
EU(27 countries)	**77.0**	**82.9**	**5.9**
Portugal	76.7	82.8	6.1
Greece	78.4	82.8	4.4
United Kingdom	78.7	82.6	3.9
Denmark	77.2	81.4	4.2
Czech Republic	74.5	80.9	6.4
Estonia	70.6	80.8	10.2
Poland	72.1	80.7	8.6
Slovakia	71.7	79.3	7.6
Lithuania	68	78.9	10.9
Hungary	70.7	78.6	7.9
Latvia	68.6	78.4	9.8
Romania	70.1	77.6	7.5
Bulgaria	70.3	77.4	7.1

Source: Eurostat, 2013, tps00025

Access to Healthcare: Medical Cards and Health Insurance

International experts recently noted that Ireland is the only EU health system that does not offer universal coverage of primary care. People without medical or GP visit cards (approximately 60 per cent of the population) must pay the full cost of almost all primary care services and outpatient prescriptions. These experts also noted that gaps in population and cost coverage distinguish Ireland from other EU countries, as does an element of discretion and lack of clarity about the scope of some services, especially community care services, in which there are service and regional differences (World Health Organisation & European Observatory on Health Systems and Policies, 2012: 60).

CSO statistics (August 2011) showed that in 2010, 47 per cent of adults over 18 years had private health insurance, a percentage that had decreased since 2007. Thirty per cent reported they had a medical card only, while 23 per cent indicated they had neither a medical card nor private health insurance (CSO, 2011a). Department of Health figures suggest that in 2011, 1,694,063 persons had a medical card and 125,657 persons had a GP visit card (Department of Health, 2012).

According to the Department of Health, the centralisation of the process for obtaining a medical card was completed in 2011. While this development is seen as progressive, transparent and efficient for some, it has given rise to serious concerns for others. Among these concerns are that the system does not allow for discretionary measures regarding eligibility, that there are many people who do not have easy access to the technology or the capacity to use it and that the 14 days allowed for response relative to renewals is not user-friendly. In the past GPs often took care of their clients who were waiting for medical cards to be restored. Because of long delays, difficulties in getting the medical card restored and general cutbacks, GPs are now less likely to risk incurring expense that may not be recouped.

Provisions made as part of Budget 2013 will have a negative effect on access to healthcare. The overall decrease in health spending (€781 million) represents a cut of more than 5 per cent. This is despite international evidence that significant year-on-year variations in the level of statutory funding available for health services can be highly disruptive to the sustained delivery of services of a given quality and desired level of access (World Health Organisation & European Observatory on Health Systems and Policies, 2012). These international experts who reviewed the Irish healthcare system in 2012 concluded that continuing budgetary cuts and consequent adjustments raises 'serious concerns whether this can be achieved without damaging access to necessary services for certain groups' (World Health Organisation & European Observatory on Health Systems and Policies, 2012: 47).

As a result of Budget 2013, the equivalent of a further 3,500 full-time jobs in healthcare are to be cut and this will inevitably affect frontline services. According to the Department of Health there has already been a 9 per cent decline in jobs (whole time equivalents) between 2007 and 2012 in the public health services, Between 2011 and 2012 alone, there was a reduction of 3.7 per cent in nursing staff and of 3 per cent in health and social care professionals (Department of Health, 2012a). In addition, the tripling of prescription charges introduced in Budget 2013 will present a significant additional cost to many people, especially those whose medical conditions require several different medicines.[65] This, along with the increased threshold in the Drug Repayment Scheme, will cause some people to avoid accessing the medicines they need.

Social Justice Ireland believes these measures will most adversely affect people on low-incomes. It is difficult to see how this is compatible with Ireland having a decent healthcare service characterised by safety and high-quality outcomes.

The length of waiting lists remains a cause of major concern in the Irish healthcare system. The CSO study showed that in the third quarter of 2010, 8 per cent of the adult population (aged 18 and over) was on a hospital waiting list, compared to 6 per cent in 2007 (CSO, 2011a). Waiting times for out-patient appointments had also increased.

Full medical card coverage is necessary for all people in Ireland who are vulnerable. An international study of the Irish system has noted the existence of financial barriers to access, especially among those just above the threshold for a medical or GP visit card (World Health Organisation & European Observatory on Health Systems and Policies, 2012: 62). Despite this, the HSE National Service Plan for 2013 envisages a cut of €323 million in demand-led primary care schemes. The Plan provides for the withdrawal of approximately 40,000 medical cards. Some of these are higher earners aged over 70, but changes to the income eligibility criteria for others are also envisaged. Thus €20 million in savings are to be made through changes in the income criteria for awarding medical cards[66] (HSE, 2013, p.4). At the time of writing

---

[65] For example, evidence from TILDA, the Irish Longitudinal Study on Ageing shows that 20per cent of people over 50 take five or more medications; nearly 50 per cent of those over 75 take five or more medications (WHO and the European Observatory on Health Systems and Policies, 2012).

[66] In addition to €12 million due to changes in medical card eligibility for higher-earners aged over 70 whose medical cards will be replaced with GP only cards.

details of how the income eligibility criteria will be applied are not available But given the very low income thresholds that currently apply (€184 weekly for a single person living alone) further restrictions in access to medical cards for poor people are extremely worrying, especially as the current income threshold for obtaining a medical card is already well below the poverty line.

This creates, in effect, an employment trap as parents are often afraid to take up a job and consequently lose their medical card even though their income remains low. The 'doctor visit only' cards are an improvement on the previous situation only if they are upgraded to full medical cards in due course. At present they create new problems because many people are in the unenviable situation of knowing what is wrong with them but not having the resources to purchase the medicines they need.

Health expenditure
Healthcare is a social right for everyone. For this right to be upheld governments must provide the funding needed to ensure that the relevant services and care are available when required. The OECD has noted that Ireland's total healthcare spending rose as a percentage of GDP due to the recession and the resulting fall from 2008 in the country's GDP levels (2012). Comparative statistics are available for total expenditure on health (i.e. public plus private). Table 8.2 shows that Ireland spends 9.7 per cent of GDP on healthcare, in line with the EU-27 average of 9.8 per cent. In Gross National Income (GNI) terms this expenditure translates into a figure of 11.7 per cent.[67] In comparison, Belgium spends 11.8 per cent of its GDP; Germany spends 11.3 per cent and Austria 11 per cent. Ireland is ranked tenth on this basis among EU countries. This data, for 2009, is the most recent comparative data available from the CSO and Ireland's ranking may have changed since then.

Healthcare costs tend to be higher in countries which have a higher old age dependency ratios. This is not yet a significant issue for Ireland as the old age dependency ratio is low compared to the much higher EU average (11.6 per cent of the population is aged 65 years and over according to the 2011 Census and the old-age dependency rate is 17.4 per cent (CSO, 2012c)).

However, Ireland's public spending on healthcare has reduced since 2004. The decline since 2008, 10.4 per cent, has been particularly rapid, according to a study by international experts. This has resulted public expenditure falling below the OECD average as a share of all health spending for the first time in over a decade (WHO & European Observatory on Health Systems and Policies, 2012: 27, 30, 47).

---

[67] GNI is similar to the concept of GNP and has a similar value.

Table 8.2: EU-27 health expenditure as a percentage of GDP, 2009

Country	%	Country	%
Belgium	11.8	United Kingdom	9.3
France	11.7	Slovenia	9.1
Ireland (% GNI)	**11.7**	Slovakia	8.5
Germany	11.3	Luxembourg	7.8
Portugal	11.3	Czech Republic	7.6
Denmark	11.2	Malta	7.5
Austria	11.0	Bulgaria	7.4
Netherlands	10.8	Hungary	7.3
Greece	10.6	Poland	7.1
Sweden	9.9	Estonia	7.0
EU	**9.8**	Lithuania	6.6
IRELAND (% GDP)	**9.7**	Latvia	6.5
Finland	9.7	Cyprus	6.0
Spain	9.7	Romania	5.4
Italy	9.5		

Source: CSO, 2012:53

An open and transparent debate on funding of healthcare services is needed. Ireland must decide what services are expected and how these should be funded. Despite expenditure of 9.7 per cent of GDP going to fund healthcare there are still recurring problems in such areas as waiting lists, bed closures, staff shortages, long-term care and community care. However, this debate must acknowledge the enormous financial expenditure on healthcare. Public healthcare expenditure grew rapidly over the decade 2000 to 2010, from €5.334bn to €14.165bn. This was an increase of 160 per cent over a period in which inflation increased by 33 per cent. The difference is attributed in part to improved and expanded services, as well as to organisational changes such as home-helps, for example, becoming salaried members of staff within the HSE. However, the issue of medical inflation also needs to be addressed. International experts have noted that, despite increased investment during the previous decade, when the financial crisis occurred in 2008 Ireland still had poorly developed primary and community care services (WHO & European Observatory on Health Systems and Policies, 2012).

The Minister for Health has announced that €14,023bn has been allocated for 2013 on current and capital spending. In 2012, the budget allocation for gross public expenditure on healthcare was €14.034bn, which was 25 per cent of all projected government expenditure. (Comprehensive Expenditure Review 2012-2014 p.130).

Clearly there are significant efficiencies to be gained in restructuring the healthcare system. Obtaining value for money is essential. However, these efforts should be targeted at areas in which efficiencies can be delivered without compromising the quality of the service. *Social Justice Ireland* continues to argue that there is a need to be specific about the efficiencies that are needed and how they are to be delivered.

As well as a debate on the overall budget for healthcare, there should be discussion and transparency on the allocation to each of the services. Currently about 61.3 per cent of the budget is allocated to Primary, Community and Continuing Care, which includes the medical card services schemes (Department of Health, Key Trends 2012, figure 6.2). *Social Justice Ireland* recommends an increase in this percentage and greater clarity about the budget lines.

The model of healthcare
- Community-based health and social services require a model of care that:
- is accessible and acceptable to the communities they serve;
- is responsive to the particular needs and requirements of local communities;
- is supportive of local communities in their efforts to build social cohesion; and
- accepts primary care as the key component of the model of care, affording it priority over acute services as the place where health and social care options are accessed by the community.

Instead, the majority of cuts envisaged in the Budget 2013 will fall on community schemes (like older people's, disability and family services) and almost half of the overall savings (€323 million) are to come from demand-led primary care schemes such as medical cards (HSE, 2013).

Action is required in four key areas if the basic model of care that is to underpin the health services is not to be undermined. There areas are:

Older people's services
Primary care, primary care teams and primary care networks
Children and family services
Disability and mental health

Older people's services

Although Ireland's population is young in comparison to those of other European countries, it is still ageing. Those over 65 years of age increased by 14.4 per cent between 2006 and 2011 and those aged over 85 years increased by 22 per cent (CSO, 2012d). By 2025 the number over 85 years will have doubled (Department of Health, 2012c: 2). Ireland does not yet have a national strategy on ageing and a National Positive Ageing Strategy proposed in 2007 has not yet been published.

If the health of older people is to be addressed appropriately it is essential that they are supported in ways which enable them to live at home for as long as possible. This requires the provision of community-based services to meet their needs. The 2.6 per cent cut in services for older people envisaged in the HSE national service plan for 2013, therefore, (HSE, 2013: 15) is worrying and counter-productive. This is particularly so when the number of people aged over 85 is increasing rapidly as many of them are dependent on public services to continue to live with dignity.

Other Budget 2013 measures, such as the cut to the carers respite grant, changes to the Household Benefits Package and increased prescription charges, will have negative effects on many older people and their families. Furthermore, the level of overall cut to the health budget makes it inevitable that all services will affected, including those for older people. International experts have identified that the fall in Ireland's public health spending on over 65s will have fallen by approximately 32 per cent per head between 2009 and 2016[68] (World Health Organisation & European Observatory on Health Systems and Policies, 2012: 11).

Supports that enable people to live at home need to be part of a broader integrated approach that ensures appropriate access to acute services when required. To achieve this the specific deficits in infrastructure that exist across the country need to be addressed urgently. There should be an emphasis on replacement and/or refurbishment of facilities. If this is not done the inappropriate admission of older people to acute care facilities will continue, along with the consequent negative effects on acute services and unnecessary stress on older people.

Social Justice Ireland acknowledges the work done to date to develop services for older people. The introduction of '*A Fair Deal – The Nursing Home Care Support Scheme 2008*' was a step in the right direction. We are, however, concerned about

---

[68] Based on government estimates to 2014 and assuming that funding levels remain static for 2015 and 2016

an increase proposed as part of Budget 2013 in the proportion of the person's assets that may be used (from 15% to 22%) in this scheme. However, recent cutbacks have resulted in long waiting lists for the scheme, even after people are assessed and deemed in need of care. The HSE Service Plan for 2013 envisages that this will continue, with new places only being offered as budget allows (HSE, 2013: 16;60). This will inevitably lead to older people remaining in inappropriate care facilities such as acute hospitals, an outcome in the best interests of neither the individual nor the hospital. At the same time nursing home beds may be available but funding is not committed.

It is crucial that funding be released in a timely manner when a person is deemed in need of a 'Fair Deal' bed and that sufficient capital investment is provided to ensure that enough residential care beds are available to meet the growing demand for them. The focus on the development of community based services to support older people in their own homes/communities for as long as possible is welcome. But a commitment to supporting people at home is only aspirational if funding is not provided for home help services, day care centres and home care packages – areas that have received serious and unwelcome cuts in recent Budgets. One possible outcome of these cuts is that the service would become nothing more than a 'Bed and Breakfast' facility. This would be a travesty of what was intended and, more importantly, of what is required.

Social Justice Ireland believes that a total investment of €500 million over five years, i.e. €100 million each year, is required to meet this growing need. This would enable some 12 to 15 community nursing facilities with about 50 beds each to be replaced or refurbished each year. In addition to supporting the needs of older people, this proposal would also stimulate economic activity and increase employment in many local communities during the construction periods.

Primary care

Primary care is one of the cornerstones of the health system and was acknowledged as such in the strategy document *Primary Care – A New Direction* (2001). It has also been identified as an essential pre-requisite in the new health services reform strategy, *Future Health* (2012). Between 90 and 95 per cent of the population is treated by the primary care system. The model of a primary care adopted must be flexible so that it can respond to the local needs assessment. Paying attention to local people's own perspective on their health and understanding the impact of the conditions of their lives on their health is essential to community development and to community orientated approaches to primary care. A community development approach is needed to ensure that the community can define its own health needs, work out collectively how these needs can best be met and decide on a course of action to achieve this in partnership with service providers. This will ensure greater control over the social, political, economic and environmental factors that determine the health status of any community.

The principle underlining this model should be a social model of health, in keeping with the World Health Organisation's definition of health as a 'state of complete physical, mental and social well-being and not merely the absence of disease or infirmity'. Universal access is needed to ensure that a social model of health can become a reality and Government commitment to achieving this, which is contained in the *Future Health* reform strategy, is to be welcomed in principle. However, the strategy lacks detail on how its aims will be achieved. There are also areas in which the approaches outlined may well face serious challenges... Amongst them is how to deliver a truly integrated system of care, especially for people with complex or chronic conditions, within a system in which primary and hospital care is to be funded through the proposed Universal Health Insurance system but social care services, including long-term care, are not. Will access to social care services, for example, be universal as well as access to GP services? For the strategies outlined to be implemented there is a clear need for an increase in the proportion of the total healthcare budget being allocated to primary care and a more comprehensive and integrated approach to social care services to support people living at home.

Primary care teams and primary care networks
Ireland's healthcare system has struggled to provide an effective and efficient response to the health needs of its population. Despite a huge increase in investment in recent years great problems persist. The development of primary care teams across the country could have a substantial positive impact on reducing these problems.

Primary care teams draw together health professionals in an area to provide a local 'one-stop' shop, avoiding unnecessary presentations at acute hospital emergency departments.

Developing primary care teams and primary care networks is the basic 'building block' of local public health care provision. The Primary Care Team (PCT) is intended to be a team of health professionals catering for a catchment of 7,000 to 10,000 people who work closely together and with the local community to meet the needs of people living in that community. These professionals include GPs and Practice Nurses, community nurses (i.e. public health nurses and community RGNs), physiotherapists, occupational therapists and home-care staff. They provide the first point of contact when individuals need to access the health system.

It is expected that when the system is fully developed 519 primary care teams would cover the whole country. These are to be supported by 134 Health and Social Care Networks. PCTs are expected to link in with other community-based disciplines to ensure that health and social needs are addressed. These include speech and language therapists, dieticians, area medical officers, community welfare officers, addiction counsellors, community mental health nurses, consultant psychiatrists, etc. PCTs provide a single point of contact between the person and the health system. They facilitate navigation 'in', 'around' and 'out' of the health system. According to the HSE, there were 425 PCTs in place by the end of 2011 (Department of Health, 2012) although the HSE acknowledges that failure to fill posts of key team members has hampered progress to date (HSE, 2013). The work done on existing teams is very welcome but much more is needed to ensure they command the confidence and trust of local communities.

The Government proposal to introduce a new system of seven directorates to run the health system is of concern because this approach is likely to obstruct the delivery of an integrated healthcare system for service users at local level. There are real concerns that the proposed new approach will increase rather than reduce costs and bureaucracy. Instead of an integrated system based on primary care teams at local level, seven 'silos' could emerge, competing for resources and producing a splintered system that is not effective, sustainable or viable in the long term.

Social Justice Ireland believes that reform of the healthcare system is necessary but is seriously concerned that the proposed new structure will see each directorate establish its own bureaucracy at national, regional and local levels.

Children and family services
There is a need to focus on health and social care provision to children and families in tandem with the development of primary care team services. The obligation on the State to develop and provide services and facilities to support vulnerable and at risk children has been highlighted recently. The standard of care, as monitored by the Health Information and Quality Authority (HIQA), and the challenges posed for care providers by young people with complex needs, have proven difficult for both public and private service providers.

Many community and voluntary services are being provided in facilities badly in need of refurbishment or rebuilding. Despite poor infrastructure, these services are the heart of local communities, providing vital services that are locally 'owned'. There is a great need to support this activity and, in particular, to meet its infrastructural requirements.

Social Justice Ireland believes that a total of €250 million is required over a five year period to address the infrastructural deficit in Children and Family Services. This amounts to €27 million per area for each of the nine Children Services Committee areas and a national investment of €7 million in Residential and Special Care.

Social Justice Ireland has welcomed the appointment of a Minister for Children and Youth Affairs. This is an area with a substantial agenda that could, however, be addressed effectively in a relatively short period of time if the political will to do so were present. As well as the issue of Child Safeguarding, we believe the current key issues are the second National Children's Strategy, policy on early childhood care and education, child poverty, youth homelessness, disability among young people and the issue of young carers.

Disability
In 2011 the *Programme for Government* gave a commitment to complete the consultation required to establish 'a realistic implementation plan for the National Disability Strategy'. This is still awaited. There are many areas within the disability sector in need of further development and core funding. These areas need to be supported.[69] The commitment in the HSE national service plan for 2013 (HSE, 2013:16) to maintain personal assistance hours at 2012 levels is welcome. However, *Social Justice Ireland* is particularly concerned about the further 1.2 per cent cut envisaged in respect of services for people with disabilities. Additionally, the overall cut in health spending as well as specific Budget 2013 measures (such as the cut to the carers respite grant, the increase in prescription charges and the increase in threshold for the Drug Repayment scheme) will affect many people with disabilities and families that include sick children or adults.

Mental health
The National Health Strategy entitled *Quality and Fairness* (2001) identified mental health as an area needing development. The Expert Group on Mental Health Policy

---

[69] Other disability related issues are addressed throughout this review.

published a report entitled *A Vision for Change – Report of the Expert Group on Mental Health Policy* (2006). This report offered many worthwhile pathways to adequately address mental health issues in Irish society. Unfortunately, to date little has been implemented to achieve this vision.

There is an urgent need to address this whole area in the light of the World Health Report (2001) *Mental Health: New Understanding, New Hope.* This estimated that in 1990 mental and neurological disorders accounted for 10 per cent of the total Disability-Adjusted Life Years (DALYs) lost due to all diseases and injuries. This estimate increased to 12 per cent in 2000. By 2020, it is projected that these disorders will have increased to 15 per cent. This has serious implications for services in all countries in coming years.

In June 2011 the Institute for Public Health published a study of the impact of the recession on men's health, especially mental health. Entitled *Facing the Challenge: The Impact of Recession and Unemployment on Men's Health in Ireland,* the study showed that employment status was the most important predicator of psychological distress, with 30.4 per cent of those unemployed reporting mental health problems.

Social Justice Ireland has welcomed the appointment of a Minister of State with responsibility in this area and the allocation of €35 million in Budget 2012 for the development of Community Mental Health Teams. It is hoped that these teams will reduce the stigma of mental health and improve access to facilities and services for assisting those with mental health problems. However, delays in implementation meant that this money was not spent on mental health services in 2012. The allocation of a further €35 million in Budget 2013 is likewise welcome, but this must be matched by a commitment to actually make the investment in 2013. Furthermore, the proposal to reduce inpatient beds by 102 by the end of 2013 (HSE, 2013) must not be implemented before an adequate and effective community provision is in place.

Areas of concern in mental health
There is a need for effective outreach and follow-up programmes for people who have been in-patients in institutions upon their discharge into the wider community. These should provide:

- sheltered housing (high, medium and low supported housing);
- monitoring of medication;
- retraining and rehabilitation; and
- assistance with integration into community.

In the development of mental health teams there should be a particular focus on people with an intellectual disability and other vulnerable groups, including children, the homeless, prisoners, Travellers, asylum seekers, refugees and other minority groups. People in these and related categories have a right to a specialist service to provide for their often complex needs. A great deal remains to be done before this right could be acknowledged as having been recognised and honoured in the healthcare system.

The connection between disadvantage and ill health when the social determinants of health (housing, income, childcare support, education etc.) are not met is well documented. This is also true in respect of mental health issues.

Suicide – a mental health issue

Suicide is a problem related to mental health. For many years the topic of suicide was rarely discussed in Irish society and, as a consequence, the healthcare and policy implications of its existence were limited. Over time Ireland's suicide rate has risen significantly, from 6.4 suicides per 100,000 people in 1980 to a peak of 13.9 in 1998, and to 11.7 suicides per 100,000 people in 2008 (OECD, 2005 and National Office of Suicide Prevention, 2010:23).

In 1993, 327 suicides were recorded. A decade later the figure was 497. Over the following five years the annual number declined consistently, dropping to 458 in 2007. This downward trend, however, did not persist. There were 552 recorded suicides in 2009 and 525 in 2011, according to provisional figures. Of the latter, 439 were males and 86 were females.

Table 8.3 provides shows that suicide is predominantly a male phenomenon, accounting for approximately 80 per cent of such deaths. Young males in particular, are the group most at risk, although the rate for men remains consistently high at all ages up to age 65. At every age the rate is higher for men than for women (National Office for Suicide Prevention, 2012: 49). In the period 2003-2007 young males aged between 20-24 years had a suicide rate of 30.7 per 100,000 in the population – almost three times the national average. Among this age-group, suicide is one of the largest causes of death (National Office for Suicide Prevention, 2010:24 -25).

Table 8.3: Suicides in Ireland 2003-2011						
	Overall		Males		Females	
Year**	No.	Rate	No.	Rate	No.	Rate
2003	497	12.5	386	19.5	111	5.5
2004	493	12.2	406	20.2	87	4.3
2005	481	11.6	382	18.5	99	4.8
2006	460	10.8	379	17.9	81	3.8
2007	458	10.6	362	16.7	96	4.4
2008	506	11.4	386	17.5	120	5.4
2009	552	12.4	443	20.0	109	4.9
2010*	486	10.9	386	17.4	100	4.4
2011*	525	11.4	439	19.3	86	3.7

Source: National Office of Suicide Prevention (2010:23-24; 2012: 47-48)
Notes: * Provisional figures
          **Annual data is by year of occurrence (2003 to 2009) and by year of registration
          (2010 and 2011).
          Rate is rate per 100,000 of the population.

The sustained high level of suicides in Ireland is a significant healthcare and societal problem. Of course, the statistics in table 8.3 only tell one part of the story. Behind each of these victims are families and communities devastated by these tragedies. Likewise, behind each of the figures is a personal story which leads to victims taking their own lives. *Social Justice Ireland* believes that further attention and resources need to be devoted to researching and addressing Ireland's suicide problem.

Older people and Mental Health

Mental health issues affect all groups in society. Some 41,700 people in Ireland are estimated to be affected by dementia or Alzheimer's disease (Cahill, O'Shea and Pierce, 2012) Most are over 65 but the above figure includes people of all ages and some 3,600 of them are likely to be under 65. Older people with dementia are a particularly vulnerable group because they often "fall between two stools" (i.e. between mental health services and general medical care). A co-ordinated service needs to be provided for this group. It is important that this be needs-based and service-user led and should be in keeping with the principles set out in the World Health Organisation's 2001 annual report. Department of Health plans to introduce a national strategy for dementia in 2013 are welcome.

Research and development in all areas of mental health are needed to ensure a quality service is delivered. Providing good mental health services should not be viewed as a cost but rather as an investment in the future. Public awareness needs to be raised to ensure a clearer understanding of mental illness so that the rights of those with mental illness are recognised.

Future healthcare needs
A number of the factors highlighted elsewhere in this review will have implications for the future of our healthcare system. The projected increases in population forecast by the CSO imply that there will be more people living in Ireland in 10 to 15 years time. One clear implication of this will be additional demand for healthcare services and facilities. In the context of our past mistakes it is important that Ireland begin to plan for this additional demand and begin to train staff and construct the needed facilities.

The new health reform strategy, 2012-2015, *Future Health,* envisages major changes in the way that health services are organised and delivered, including the introduction of a system of Universal Health Insurance intended to facilitate access to healthcare based on need not income. This aim is a desirable one, but, as previously mentioned, the details of the strategy have not been provided so far and no evidence has been presented to explain the basis for such fundamental decisions. The time frame for its introduction (2016) is also relatively short, given the very complex health system that currently operates and the degree of budgetary cuts and consequent disruption that has occurred in recent years and is set to continue. It has not been established that the proposed system of a number of competing insurers will succeed in achieving the necessary improvements in equity, quality and efficiency. We look forward to the publication of the proposed White Paper on Health Insurance in 2013, which is to provide the basis for many of the actions that are to be taken to introduce the new system (Department of Health, 2012c).

We share the concerns of the Council for Justice and Peace of the Irish Episcopal Conference (2012) about a lack of focus on outcomes. We agree with it that the: 'public health strategy should ... not only spell out goals for public health but also set out the role that each major field of intervention is expected to perform in achieving those goals, the implications for resource allocation that arise from such roles and the mechanisms that will be used to ensure that spending actually goes to the areas where it will achieve greatest benefit.'

Key policy priorities on healthcare

- Recognise the considerable health inequalities present within the Irish healthcare system, develop strategies and provide sufficient resources to tackle them.
- Give far greater priority to community care and restructure the healthcare budget accordingly. Care should be taken to ensure that the increased allocation does not go to the GMS or the drug subsidy scheme.
- Resource and continue the roll out of the 519 primary care teams.
- Increase the proportion of the health budget allocated to health promotion and education in partnership with all relevant stakeholders.
- Focus on obtaining better value for money in the health budget.
- Provide the childcare services with the additional resources necessary to effectively implement the Child Care Act.
- Provide additional respite care and long stay care for older people and people with disabilities and proceed to develop and implement a coherent dementia strategy.
- Promote equality of access and outcomes to services within the Irish healthcare system.
- Ensure that structural and systematic reform of the health system reflects the key principles of the Health Strategy aimed at achieving high performance, person-centred quality of care and value for money in the health service.
- Develop and resource mental health services, recognising that they will be a key factor in determining the health status of the population.
- Continue to facilitate and fund a campaign to give greater attention to the issue of suicide in Irish society. In particular, focus resources on educating young people about suicide.
- Enhance the process of planning and investment so that the healthcare system can cope with the increase and diversity in population and the ageing of the population projected for the next few decades.
- Ensure the new healthcare structure is fit for purpose and publish detailed evidence of how the decisions taken will meet healthcare goals.

9. Education and Educational Disadvantage

CORE POLICY OBJECTIVE: EDUCATION AND EDUCATIONAL DISADVANTAGE

To provide relevant education for all people throughout their lives, so that they can participate fully and meaningfully in developing themselves, their community and the wider society

Education can be an agent for social transformation. *Social Justice Ireland* believes that education can be a powerful force in counteracting inequality and poverty while recognising that, in many ways, the present education system has quite the opposite effect. Investment in education at all levels can deliver a more equal society and prepare citizens to participate in a democracy.

Education in Ireland – the numbers
There are just over one million full-time students in the formal Irish education system. Of these, 514,852 are at primary level, 359,653 at second level and 169,209 at third level. The sector accounts for over 22 per cent of the population and the numbers at primary level have been increasing since 2001 (CSO 2012:100). Demographic growth and the knock-on pressure on the education system and the need to develop long-term policies to cater for increased demand have been acknowledged by the Minister for Education and Skills.[70] By 2017 there will be an extra 105,000 extra students in education in Ireland; 64,000 at primary level, 25,000 at second level and 16,000 at third-level.[71]

Ireland's expenditure on education equalled 6.5 per cent of GDP in 2009 (CSO 2012: 48), the latest year for which comparable EU-wide data is available. This compares to an EU-27 average of 5.4 per cent of GDP in that year. Over much of the last decade, as national income has increased the share allocated to education has slowly increased; a development we strongly welcome. Table 9.1 (CSO 2012:

---

[70] See address by Minister Quinn at Nordic Education Seminar 12/09/2012
http://www.education.ie/en/Press-Events/Speeches/2012-Speeches/SP2012-09-17.html
[71] ibid

47) details how real current public expenditure on education per student rose steadily until 2009. Since then it has reduced across all categories due to budgetary constraints. The increases in expenditure until 2009 can be partly attributed to increased pay. However, it can also be partly explained by an increase in student numbers at all levels. Between 2002 and 2011 the numbers of students in Ireland grew by 15.9 per cent at first level and by 5.2 per cent at second level. Over the same period, the number of full-time third level students increased by 28.5 per cent (CSO 2012: 47). The number of part-time third-level students dropped by 2.2 per cent in the same period. It should also be noted, however, that Ireland's young population as a proportion of total population is large by EU standards and, consequently, a higher than average spend on education would be expected.

Table 9.1: Ireland: Real current public expenditure on education, 2002-2011

Year	First Level* €	Second Level* €	Third Level* €	Real Current Public Expenditure** €m
2002	4,860	7,176	10,552	6,181
2003	5,356	7,775	10,473	6,644
2004	5,756	7,863	10,264	6,848
2005	5,856	8,202	10,612	7,082
2006	6,055	8,558	11,128	7,439
2007	6,197	9,014	11,037	7,761
2008	6,315	9,140	10,909	8,003
2009	6,532	9,204	10,325	8,251
2010	6,434	8,928	9,926	8,217
2011	6,368	9,113	9,091	8,207

*€ per student at 2011 prices   **€m at 2011 prices
Source: Department of Education and Skills, CSO (CSO 2012:47)

Real expenditure per student in Ireland increased over the period 2002-2011 by 31 per cent at first level and by a 27 per cent at second level. At third level there was a decrease of 13.8 per cent over the same period.

Investment and planning for future education needs

There is a history of minimal long-term strategic planning by the Department of Education in respect of investment in facilities at primary and second level. *Social Justice Ireland* has been proposing for the past decade that the Department of Education use the population projections by the CSO based on the census results to plan for future education needs, timing and spatial distribution.[72] Using these figures, the Department of Education now projects the following possible increases in enrolment across the system:

- an additional 32,500 places will be needed at primary level between now and 2014 and an increase in enrolments to 601,820 by 2020;[73]
- an additional 17,000 places will be needed at second level between now and 2014 with significant increases projected in the years after 2014, to peak at an enrolment of 413,118 in 2026;[74]
- at third level the number of students is expected to rise by 15,000 by 2015; between 205,000 and 210,000 students are expected by 2026/27.[75]

The Department of Education has published a capital works programme amounting to €2.2 billion between now and 2016 to address this issue and increase the number of places available through a five year School Building Programme. *Social Justice Ireland* believes it is critically important that Government, and in particular the Department of Education and Skills, pays attention to the population projection by the CSO for the years to come in order to adequately plan and provide for the increased places needed within the education system in the coming decades.

Education is widely recognised as crucial to the achievement of our national objectives of economic competitiveness, social inclusion and active citizenship. However, the overall levels of public funding for education in Ireland are out of step with these aspirations. This under-funding is most severe in early childhood education and in the areas of lifelong learning and second chance education – the very areas that are most vital in terms of the promotion of greater equity and

---

[72] The preliminary results of Census 2011 are available, a more comprehensive analysis and projection will be available later in 2012.

[73] http://www.education.ie/en/Publications/Statistics/Projections-of-full-time-enrolment-Primary-and-Second-Level-2012-2030.pdf

[74] ibid

[75] http://www.education.ie/en/Publications/Statistics/Projections-of-demand-for-Full-Time-Third-Level-Education-2011-2026.pdf

fairness. The projected increased demand outlined above in all areas of our education system must be matched by investment at all levels. Failure to invest in education would be unwise given the projections outlined above. Government policy in terms of investment in education must be focussed on protecting and promoting quality services for those in the education system.

Early Childhood Education

It is widely acknowledged that early childhood (pre-primary) education helps to build a strong foundation for lifelong learning and ensure equity in education. It also improves children's cognitive abilities, reduces poverty and can mitigate social inequalities (OECD 2012: 338). The most striking feature of investment in education in Ireland relative to other OECD countries is our under-investment in early childhood education relative to international norms. Ireland spends 0.1 per cent of GDP on pre-primary education compared with the OECD average of 0.5 per cent (OECD 2012: 339). The introduction of the Early Childhood Care and Education Scheme (ECCE) has been a positive move in addressing this under investment. However, Ireland still has quite a way to go to catch up with the OECD average. Ireland provides one universal pre-school year to all children through the ECCE scheme by paying a capitation fee to participating services. The ECCE scheme is availed of by over 65,000 children and is administered by the Department of Children and Youth Affairs at a cost of €175 million. [76]

Early Childhood Education and Care is the essential foundation for successful lifelong learning, social integration, personal development and later employability (European Commission, 2011), yet Ireland continues to under-invest in this area. Ireland will invest €175 million in early childhood education in 2013 and over €3 billion at primary level and second level education. It is important that adequate resources are invested in this area because early childhood education plays a crucial role in providing young people with the opportunity to develop to their fullest potential. Early childhood is also the stage where education can most effectively influence the development of children and help reverse disadvantage (European Commission, 2011). It has the potential to both reduce the incidence of early school leaving and to increase the equity of educational outcomes. Early childhood education is also associated with better performance later on in school. A recent OECD study found that 15 year old pupils who attended pre-primary education perform better on PISA testing (Programme for International Student Assessment) than those who did not, even allowing for differences in their socio-economic

---

[76] Budget 2013 estimate

backgrounds (OECD, 2012:338). Chart 9.1 below illustrates that the highest return from investment in education is between the ages of 0 to 5. This is the point in the developmental curve where differences in early health, cognitive and non-cognitive skills, which are costly sources of inequality, can be addressed most effectively. The evidence shows that early childhood education has the greatest potential to provide more equal educational opportunity to those students from lower socio-economic backgrounds. It is critically important that Ireland invest in this area and provide universal early childhood education services for children. The present situation, in which those parents with resources can afford to enrol their children in early childhood education programmes, while children of poorer parents cannot, reinforces educational disadvantage at a very early age.

Chart 9.1: The Heckman Curve

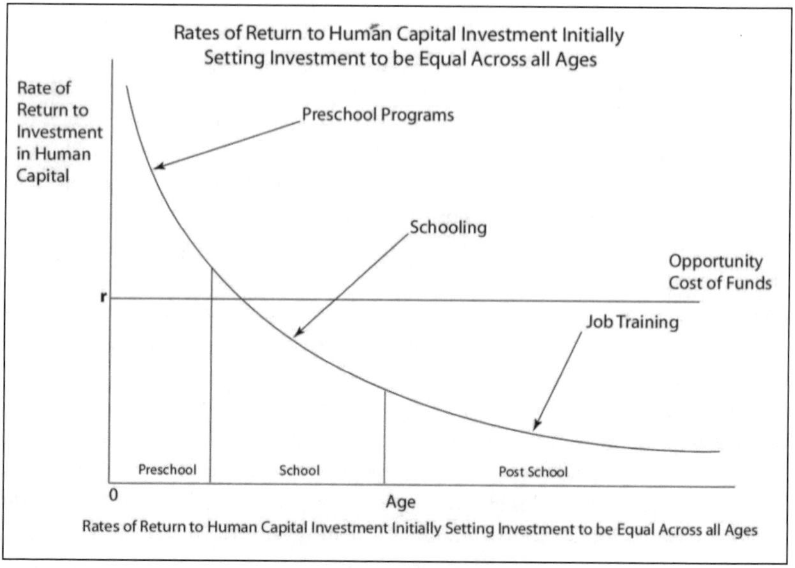

Rates of Return to Human Capital Investment Initially Setting Investment to be Equal Across all Ages

Rate of Return to Investment in Human Capital

Preschool Programs

Schooling

Opportunity Cost of Funds

Job Training

r

Preschool   School   Post School

0   Age

Rates of Return to Human Capital Investment Initially Setting Investment to be Equal Across all Ages

Source: Carneiro and Heckman, 2003

The importance of investment in education is widely acknowledged and the rewards for individuals are clear. The European Commission believes that Europe's future will be based on smart, sustainable and inclusive growth and that improving the quality and effectiveness of education systems is essential to this (European Commission, 2011). Achieving such growth, and honouring the educational commitments outlined in the Programme for Government and National Recovery in the process, will require significant strategic investment in early childhood education and lifelong learning through a policy making process that has long-term planning at its core. Our under-investment in early childhood education is a cause for concern. Our success in educating future generations of pre-school children will be a major determinant of our future sustainability.

Primary and Second Level Education

Ireland has a pupil teacher ratio (PTR) of 15.9 at primary level and 14.4 at second level (CSO, 2012:49), the tenth highest in the EU. The average class size in Ireland at primary level is 24.1, the second highest in the EU. In 2011 Ireland took part in the Progress in International Reading Literacy Study (PIRLS) and the Trends in International Mathematics and Science Study (TIMSS). These test primary school pupils in the equivalent of fourth class in reading, mathematics and science in over 60 countries. Ireland preformed relatively well, ranking 10th out of 45 participating countries in reading, 17th out of 50 participating countries in mathematics and 22nd out of 50 participating countries in science. A summary analysis has been published by the Educational Research Centre (Eivers and Clerkin 2012) with further detailed analysis to follow in 2013.

Some of the most interesting findings are in the differences in results for children in Northern Ireland and the Republic. Northern Irish primary school pupils performed better in reading and numeracy than any other English speaking country, coming 5th out of 45 participating countries in reading and 6th out of 50 participating countries in mathematics. A revised primary school curriculum and targeted literacy and numeracy programmes were introduced in Northern Ireland in 2007. The new curriculum is based on the skills that children should attain rather than on content to be covered, with a focus on preparation for learning and child-led learning. The revised curriculum has been a considerable success and provides an excellent example of how to redesign a school curriculum, putting quality programmes and services at the heart of the system. This is particularly relevant at a time when the Minister for Education and Skills claims to be implementing a reform agenda to radically improve teaching and learning in Ireland and the learning experience of students in the Irish education system.

The reform agenda referred to by the Minister for Education and Skills is being implemented at second level with the publication of the '*Framework for Junior Cycle*' and the phased replacement of the Junior Certificate examination with a new school-based approach to assessment. This framework was developed in response to weaknesses in the current model highlighted by the National Council for Curriculum and Assessment[77] and to address the issue of second level students not achieving their potential and the wake-up call in Irish education of students failing PISA tests[78]. *Social Justice Ireland* welcomes the new student centred approach to the Junior Cycle and the new emphasis on helping students who are not performing well in Irish schools. It is important that such reforms be followed through to the Leaving Certificate to ensure policy coherence and a truly student centred approach in the second level education system. It is equally important that policymakers, whilst implementing a reform agenda, remember that the primary focus of education is to prepare students for life, not just for work.

Literacy and Adult Literacy

The issue of literacy has been contentious in recent times. As long ago as 1997 an OECD survey found that a quarter of Ireland's adult population performed at the very lowest level of literacy.[79] Despite performing well in the PIRLS, results from the OECD's PISA study found that Ireland's fifteen-year olds rank 17th out of 34 for reading levels among OECD countries. They also highlighted that average reading levels have been decreasing across all ability levels over time in Ireland and that 17 per cent of students in Ireland are low-achieving in reading, meaning that they are 'below the basic level needed to participate effectively in society and in future learning' (OECD, 2010). It is of concern that the study also found that almost a quarter of male students achieved scores considered to be below the level of literacy needed to participate effectively in society, meaning they may lack the skills needed to function in today's labour market and can be at risk of leaving school early and struggling to find a job. Numeracy levels display a similar pattern, with Ireland ranking 26th in mathematics out of 34 countries.

The OECD's findings suggest that while reading levels among the school-going population are better than the population generally, this difference is much smaller than should be expected. However, there is something fundamentally wrong with an education system in which 1 in 6 students are unable to read at the most basic

---

[77] For more detail see Junior Cycle Briefing Note http://www.education.ie/en/Schools-Colleges/Information/Curriculum-and-Syllabus/A-Framework-for-Junior-Cycle-Briefing-Note.pdf

[78] See Speech by Minister Quinn http://www.education.ie/en/Press-Events/Speeches/2012-Speeches/04-October-2012-Speech-by-Ruair%C3%AD-Quinn-TD-Minister-for-Education-and-Skills-On-the-launch-of-his-Junior-Cycle-Framework.html

[79] Ireland is currently participating in the OECD PIAAC study of adult skills with results due to be published in 2013, a 16 year gap since the IALS survey in 1997.

level. It is clear that fundamental reforms are needed to Ireland's education system[80] to address this problem. Left unresolved, it will store up continuous socio-economic problems for decades to come.

Social Justice Ireland therefore welcomes the reforms to the Junior Cycle and the development and implementation of the national literacy and numeracy strategy to improve literacy and numeracy in schools. Entitled '*Literacy and Numeracy for Learning and Life*', the strategy sets out national targets and a range of significant measures to improve literacy and numeracy in early childhood education and in primary and post-primary schools. These measures include improving the performance of children and young people in PISA literacy and numeracy tests at all levels, fundamental changes to teacher education and the curriculum in schools and radical improvements in the assessment and reporting of student progress at student, school and national level. Progress on this issue is overdue and budgetary and economic constraints must not be allowed to impede the implementation of the strategy.

The Programme for Government and National Recovery states that the government will address the widespread and persistent problem of restricted adult literacy through the integration of literacy in vocational training and through community education. No updated targets are given and neither has a strategy been outlined or developed. Without renewed targets the Government is committing itself to the target that is already outlined in the 2007 NAPinclusion document. This target for adult literacy policy was set stating that 'the proportion of the population aged 16-64 with restricted literacy will be reduced to between 10 per cent to 15 per cent by 2016 from the level of 25 per cent found in 1997', with 'restricted literacy' defined as level 1 on the International Adult Literacy Scale. People at this level of literacy are considered to possess 'very poor skills, where the individual may, for example, be unable to determine the correct amount of medicine to give a child from information printed on the package' (OECD, 2000:xi). As table 9.2 shows, in numerical terms this implies that the aim of government policy is to have no more than 301,960 adults of labour force age with serious literacy difficulties in Ireland by 2016. In the opinion of *Social Justice Ireland* this target is simply unacceptable.

---

[80] A discussion paper by Áine Hyland for the HEA Summer School 2011 suggested that the emphasis on rote learning at second level might have affected our results as the PISA test is based on the application of prior knowledge.

Table 9.2: Irish Government Adult Literacy Target for 2016	
Adult population (under 65 yrs in 2016)	3,019,600
10% "restricted literacy" target	301,960
15% "restricted literacy" target	452,940

Source: Calculated from CSO (2008:27) using the lowest CSO population projection for 2016 – The MOF2 population projection assumption

How can policy be so unambitious? How will these people with serious literacy problems function effectively in the economy and society that is emerging in Ireland? How can they get meaningful jobs? In reality achieving this target could only be interpreted as representing substantial and sustained failure. With the latest PISA results showing that 23.2% of all male students aged 15 have a reading level below level 1a the need for a comprehensive strategy to tackle adult literacy has never been more pressing.

Overall, *Social Justice Ireland* believes that the Government's literacy target is illogical, unambitious and suggests a complete lack of interest in seriously addressing this problem. The lack of focus on this issue was further underscored by the decision in Budget 2013 to reduce funding for adult literacy programmes by 2 per cent. By 2015 funding for adult literacy will have been reduced by 11 per cent since 2010.[81] The current target for restricted literacy should be revised down dramatically and the necessary resources committed to ensuring that the revised target is met. *Social Justice Ireland* believes that the government should adopt a new and more ambitious target of reducing the proportion of the population aged 16-64 with restricted literacy to 5 per cent by 2016; and to 3 per cent by 2020. This would still leave approximately 150,000 adults without basic literacy skills in 2016. However, this target is more ambitious and realistic in the context of the future social and economic development of Ireland.

Key issues: Early school leaving and its consequences

One in ten 18 to 24 year olds are early school leavers (CSO 2011:7). Early school leaving not only presents problems for the young people involved but it also has economic and social consequences for society. Education is the most efficient means by which to safeguard against unemployment. The risk of unemployment increases considerably the lower the level of education. Early school leavers are:

---

[81] Department of Public Expenditure and Reform 2011 (Budget 2011reduced capitation grants for adult and further education courses by 5%, a 2% reduction in Budget 2012, 2% in 2013 and 1% in 2014 and 2015).

- at higher risk of poverty and social exclusion;
- confronted with limited opportunities to develop culturally, personally and socially;
- likely to have poor health status; and
- face a cyclical effect associated with early school leaving, resulting in the children of early school leavers experiencing reduced success in education (European Commission, 2011).

In Ireland in 2010 the rate of early school leavers from education and training stood at 10.5 per cent. This rate has been decreasing steadily from the period 2002-2010. While this is a very positive trend, in the Irish context early school leaving remains a serious issue and the Irish Government has committed to reducing this to 8 per cent (Department of An Taoiseach, 2012). The unemployment rate for early school leavers is 37 per cent, almost twice that for other persons in the same 18 to 24 age cohort. They also had an employment rate that was half that of their peers (21 per cent compared to 42 per cent) (CSO 2011:7). Government has invested heavily in trying to secure a school-based solution to this problem through, for example, the work of the National Educational Welfare Board (NEWB). In the current situation early school leaving presents is a major issue for government that requires a long-term policy response. Seventy nine per cent of early school leavers are either unemployed or classified as economically inactive, a situation that is simply unacceptable and cannot be allowed to continue. It may well be time to try alternative approaches aimed at ensuring that people in this cohort attain the skills required to progress in the future and participate in society.

Key issues: Lifelong learning
Equality of status is one of the basic democratic principles that should underpin lifelong learning. Access in adult life to desirable employment and choices is closely linked to level of educational attainment. Equal political rights cannot exist if some people are socially excluded and educationally disadvantaged. The lifelong opportunities of those who are educationally disadvantaged are in sharp contrast to the opportunities for meaningful participation of those who have completed a second or third level education. Unlike the rising earnings premium and earnings rewards enjoyed by those who have completed higher education, the earnings disadvantage for those who have not completed upper secondary education increases with age. Therefore, lifelong education should be seen as a basic need. In this context, second chance education and continuing education are vitally important and require on-going support.

Table 9.3: Summary of educational attainment and labour force participation 25-64 year olds, April 2011

Highest education level attained	%	Labour force participation rate	Employment rate	Unemployment rate
Primary or below	10	46	35	24
Lower secondary	15	67	54	21
Higher secondary	24	76	65	14
Post leaving cert	13	78	64	18
Third Level	38	87	81	7
Total persons aged 25 to 64	**100**	**76**	**66**	**13**

Source: CSO 2011:1

Table 9.3 clearly highlights the link between educational attainment and employment. Those aged 25 to 64 with only primary level qualification are three times more likely to be unemployed than those with a third level qualification (24 per cent versus 7 per cent). This gap has increased 10 percentage points since 2009, demonstrating the difficulties faced by Government in helping those with low levels of educational attainment up-skill and improve their prospects of getting a job. The Programme for Government makes reference to lifelong learning as a high priority for jobseekers. However, labour market activation cannot be the sole factor defining the lifelong learning agenda and education and training curricula. Various reports identify generic skills and competences as a core element of the lifelong learning framework. The Forfás Report 'Sharing our future: Ireland 2025' (Forfas 2009) highlights the increasing range of generic skills that individuals require to operate within society and the economy. These include basic skills such as literacy, numeracy, use of technology, language skills, people related and conceptual skills. The report of the Expert Group on Future Skills Needs 'Tomorrow's Skills – Towards a National Skills Strategy' (2007) indicates that there is substantial evidence to show that employers regard generic skills as equal to, if not more important than, technical or job specific skills.

The report by the Council of Europe and the European Parliament (2006) 'Key Competences for Lifelong Learning' identified eight key competences for lifelong learning:
- Communication in the mother tongue (reading, writing, etc.);
- Communication in foreign languages;
- Mathematical and basic competences in science and technology;
- Digital competence;

- Learning to learn;
- Social and civic competences;
- Sense of initiative and entrepreneurship;
- Cultural awareness and expression.
-

These key competences are all interdependent, with an emphasis in each on critical thinking, creativity, initiative, problem solving, risk assessment and decision taking. They also provide the framework for community education and training programmes within the European Education and Training 2010 work programme and the Strategic Framework for European Cooperation in Education and Training (ET 2020) (European Commission, 2011).

Access to educational opportunity and meaningful participation in the system and access to successful outcomes, are central to the democratic delivery of education. Resources should be made available to support people who wish to engage in lifelong learning, in particular those people who completed second level education but who chose not to progress to third level education at that point.

Key issues: contributing to higher education
There are strong arguments from an equity perspective that those who benefit from higher education and who can afford to contribute to the costs of their higher education should do so. This principle is well established internationally and is an important component of funding strategies for many of the better higher education systems across the world. People with higher education qualifications reap a substantial earnings premium in the labour market which increases with age (OECD, 2012:140). The earnings premium in Ireland for those with higher education has increased by 22 percentage points since 2000. Third-level graduates in employment in Ireland earn on average 64 per cent more that those with a leaving certificate only (OECD, 2011), and 81 per cent of people aged 25 to 64 with a third-level qualification are in employment compared with 35 per cent of those with a primary level qualification only. Ireland is the highest ranking country in the EU in terms of higher education attainment, with 48 per cent of all 25-34 year olds having a third-level qualification. At present third-level students do not pay fees but do incur a student contribution charge at the beginning of each academic year. This student charge has risen significantly from £150 (€191) in 1995/96 to €2,500 in 2013/14. There are a number of difficulties with this charge:

- There is no definition of what services the 'student charge' covers;
- It does not adequately cover the cost of providing 'student services' (HEA, 2010); and
- Upfront charges and payments such as the student charge act as a significant barrier to students from lower socio-economic backgrounds.

There has been much discussion regarding the future funding for Higher Education Institutions (HEIs) and how they might be configured in the future. In the '*National Strategy for Higher Education to 2030*' the Higher Education Authority (HEA) discusses broadening the base of funding for HEIs and sets out in detail how a student contribution framework might be developed and managed. Various policy options for student contributions are discussed in a report to the Minister (Department of Education, 2009) and the fiscal impact of these options are outlined in detail. Further research concludes that an income contingent student loan rather than a graduate tax system would be the most equitable funding option for Ireland (Flannery & O'Donoghue, 2011). *Social Justice Ireland* believes that Government should introduce a system in which fees are paid by all participants in third-level education with an income-contingent loan facility being put in place to ensure that all participants who need to do so can borrow to pay their fees and cover their living costs, repaying such borrowing when their income rises above a prescribed level. In this system:

- All students would be treated on the same basis insofar as both tuition and living cost loans would be available on a deferred repayment basis;
- All students would be treated on the same basis as repayment is based on their own future income rather than on current parental income; and
- Inclusion of all part-time students would reduce the present disparity between full-time and part-time students.

Were such a scheme introduced, *Social Justice Ireland* calculates that the gain to the Exchequer would be €445 million in a full year (2011 estimates) and proposes that €120 million of this should go towards early childhood education and adult literacy programmes.

Key Priorities on Education and Educational Disadvantage
- Invest in universal, quality early childhood education.
- Increase resources available to lifelong learning and alternative pathways to education.

- Adopt a new and more ambitious adult literacy target and significantly increase the funding provided to address adult literacy problems, including the funding provided to the National Adult Literacy Agency.
- Introduce an income-contingent loan facility for all third-level students and develop a system in which fees are paid by all participants in third-level education.

10. Migration and Intercultural Issues

CORE POLICY OBJECTIVE:
MIGRATION & INTERCULTURAL ISSUES
To ensure that all citizens have the opportunity to stay in Ireland and contribute to Ireland's future, and to ensure that Ireland is open to welcoming people from different cultures and traditions in a way that is consistent with our history, our obligations as world citizens and with our economic status.

Migration issues of various kinds, both inwards and outwards, present important challenges for Government. The circumstances that generate involuntary emigration must be addressed in an open, honest and transparent manner. For many migrants immigration is not temporary. They will remain in Ireland and make it their home. Irish society needs to adapt to this reality. Ireland is now a multi-racial and multi-cultural country and Government policies should promote and encourage the creation of an inclusive and integrated society in which respect for and recognition of their culture is an important right for all people.

The key challenge of integration
The rapid internationalisation of the Irish population in recent years presents Ireland with the key challenge of avoiding mistakes made by many other countries. The focus should be on integration rather than on isolating new migrant communities. Census 2011 showed that there were a total of 544,357 non-Irish nationals – representing 199 different nations – living in Ireland in 2011 (CSO, 2012: 8). It also showed that 268,180, or 15.1 per cent of the labour force, are non-Irish nationals (CSO, 2012: 19). These figures are unlikely to change significantly over the next few years, even when allowance is made for emigration.

Although this chapter focuses principally on the problems facing refugees, asylum-seekers and migrants, it is important to recognise that other groups, such as Travellers, also require their culture to be respected as a right. In the *Programme for Government and National Recovery 2011-2016* the Government commits to promoting 'greater coordination and integration of delivery services to the Traveller communities across Government, using available resources more effectively to deliver on principles of social inclusion particularly in the area of Traveller education' (Government of Ireland 2011: 53). While the structures recommended by the Task Force on Travelling People have been established, it is very important to ensure that the recommendations of the report are fully implemented.

Migrant Workers

Ireland has had one of the largest declines in foreign-born working population in the EU 27 states – a fall of 105,000 between 2008 and 2010 (Eurofound, 2011). The latest figures are presented in table 10.1. They show that there was an overall decline of 2.9 per cent in the number of non-Irish nationals in employment between the third quarter of 2011 and the third quarter of 2012, the latest figures available at the time of writing.

Table 10.1: Estimated number of persons aged 15 years and over in employment and classified by nationality Q3 2006-2012, by '000

	2006	2007	2008	2009	2010	2011	2012
Irish	1,792.80	1,831.60	1,799.40	1,656.70	1,614.20	1,568.20	1,571.60
Non-Irish	285.6	338	337	296.8	271.8	277.5	269.6
Including							
UK	56.7	54.8	54.5	49.9	49.5	44.9	47.4
EU15★	32.6	33.5	33	33.9	29.2	31	29.6
EU15/27★★	122.6	169	169.5	138.2	123.5	126.7	126.2
Other	73.8	80.7	80	74.8	69.6	74.8	66.4
Total	2,078.40	2,169.60	2,136.40	1,953.50	1,886.00	1,845.70	1,841.20

Source: CSO QNHS Series (2012). All figures from Q3. ★excluding Ireland and UK ★★EU15 to EU27 states.

There has been criticism of Irish immigration policy and legislation due to the lack of support for the integration of immigrants and a lack of adequate recognition of the permanency of immigration. Three significant areas of concern are:

- work permits are issued to employers, not to employees, which ties the employee to a specific employer, increasing their vulnerability to exploitation and reducing their labour market mobility;
- the Irish asylum process can take many years and most refugees coming onto the Irish labour market are *de facto* long-term unemployed. A process for training and education asylum seekers is needed so that they can retain and gain skills (ECRI, 2006 & Employers Diversity Network, 2009); and

- The presence of up to 30,000 undocumented migrants in Ireland. Without credentials they are denied access to basic services and vulnerable to exploitation by employers. The Irish Migrant Rights Centre has proposed an Earned Regularisation Scheme to provide a pathway to permanent residency.

Refugees and asylum seekers

Until recently the number of refugees forced to flee their own countries to escape war, persecution and abuses of human rights had been declining worldwide for many years. In its most recent report, however, the United Nations High Commission for Refugees (UNHCR) signalled a sizeable reversal of this positive trend. At the end of 2011 the total population of concern to UNHCR was estimated at 35.4 million people, including: 10.4 million refugees; 895,284 asylum seekers; 531,907 refugees who had repatriated in 2011 (almost double the 2010 figure); 26.4 million internally displaced persons; and an estimated number of 3.5 million stateless people worldwide (UNHCR, 2012: 41).

Irish people have a long tradition of solidarity with people facing oppression within their own countries but that tradition is not reflected in our policies towards refugees and asylum-seekers. *Social Justice Ireland* believes that Ireland should use its position in international forums to highlight the causes of displacement of peoples. In particular, Ireland should use these forums to challenge the production, sale and free access to arms and the implements of torture.

Despite this tradition of solidarity with peoples facing oppression, racism is an everyday reality for many migrants in Ireland. A recent report published by the Immigrant Council of Ireland (Immigrant Council of Ireland, 2011) highlights this and the lack of leadership in dealing with the issue. An integrated policy response is needed to address the root causes of racism within communities while political and institutional responses are required to prevent the problem escalating.

The establishment of Citizenship Ceremonies by the Minister for Justice, Equality and Defence and reforms to the procedure of assessing and processing citizenship applications are welcome and have the potential to promote inclusiveness and integration.

Table 10.2 shows the consistent decline in the number of applications for asylum in Ireland2000 and 2012, from over 10,000 to fewer than 1,000. Early indications are that the numbers seeking asylum in the European Union – particularly from

Syria – have increased in 2012 (Eurostat, 2012). Almost 2,700 people were deported from Ireland in 2012, of whom 2,260 were refused entry into the country at ports of entry (Department of Justice and Equality, 2013).

Table 10.2 Applications for Asylum in Ireland, 2000-2012					
Year	**Number**	**Year**	**Number**	**Year**	**Number**
2000	10,938	2005	4,323	2010	1,939
2001	10,325	2006	4,314	2011	1,290
2002	11,634	2007	3,985	2012	956
2003	7,900	2008	3,866		
2004	4,766	2009	2,689		

Source: Office of the Refugee Applications Commissioner (2012), Statistical Report December 2012.

The European Commission against Racism and Intolerance (ECRI) has identified difficulties in gaining recognition for professional qualifications as a major challenge facing refugees and asylum-seekers when they have been granted leave to stay in Ireland. It means refugees are often unable to find employment commensurate with their qualifications and experience, impeding their full integration into society. It also means their valuable skills, which could contribute to the Irish economy, are unused or underused (ECRI, 2006). *Social Justice Ireland* proposes that asylum-seekers who currently are not entitled to take up employment should be allowed to do so with immediate effect and that structures are established to recognise professional qualifications. Any recommendations to this effect contained in the forthcoming ECRI fourth report on Ireland, due in late 2012, should be implemented.

While asylum-seekers are assigned initial accommodation in Dublin, most are subsequently allocated accommodation at locations outside Dublin, pending the completion of the asylum-seeking process. The Reception and Integration Agency (RIA) was established to perform this task. The latest statistics from the RIA show that there are 35 accommodation centres throughout the country accommodating 4,822 people (RIA, 2012). The policy for 'direct provision' employed in almost all of these centres results in these asylum-seekers receiving accommodation and board, together with €19.10 direct provision per week per adult and €9.60 per child. Over time this sum has remained unchanged and its value has therefore been eroded by inflation. Between 2001 and 2012 the purchasing power of these payments has been decreased by almost 20 per cent. This situation, combined with the fact that asylum-seekers are denied access to employment, means that asylum-seekers are among the most excluded and marginalised groups in Ireland.

Social Justice Ireland proposes that asylum-seekers who currently are not entitled to take up employment should be allowed to do so with immediate effect and that the direct provision payments should be increased immediately to at least €65 per week for an adult and €38 per week for a child. Removing employment restrictions and increasing the direct provision allocation would cost €12.5 million per annum[82] and provide noticeable improvements in the subsistence life being led by these asylum-seekers.

Emigration

Emigration has increased dramatically since 2009. Welcome changes in the CSO's methodology entailed a revision of inter-censual migration figures so that migration statistics are more accurate. Net migration was negative in 2010, the first time since 1995 that more people left Ireland than returned or arrived from elsewhere. Net outmigration was 27,400 in 2011 and rose to 34,400 in 2012. During 2008 and 2009 the majority of those emigrating were from the new EU accession countries. However, from 2010 the largest group emigrating has been Irish nationals, of whom 42,000 left in 2011 and 46,500 left in 2012. Overall, emigration of all nationalities is estimated to have reached 87,100 in 2012. Table 10.3 below outlines the numbers of people leaving the country between 2006 and 2012, both Irish and non-Irish nationals.

Table 10.3: Estimated Emigration by Nationality, 2006 – 2012, by'000

Year	Irish	UK	EU 13*	EU 10/12**	Rest of World	Total
2012[83]	46.5	3.5	11.2	14.8	11.1	87.1
2011	42	4.6	10.2	13.9	9.9	80.6
2010	28.9	3	9	19	9.3	69.2
2009	19.2	3.9	7.4	30.5	11	72
2008	13.1	3.7	6	17.2	9	49.2
2007	12.9	3.7	8.9	12.6	8.2	46.3
2006	15.3	2.2	5.1	7.2	6.2	36

Source: CSO 2012, Population and Migration Estimates.
* EU 15 excluding UK and Ireland ** EU MS that joined in 2004 and 2007

---

[82] *Social Justice Ireland* calculation based on 2010 data.
[83] Preliminary.

The rate of emigration of Irish nationals has more than tripled since 2008. This demonstrates the lack of opportunities available for people in Ireland, especially for those seeking employment in the 15 to 44 age group. Of those who emigrated in 2012, more than 75,300 were in this age group, while 35,800 were in the 15 to 24 age cohort. The austerity programme is contributing to Ireland's loss of young people and this loss will pose significant problems for economic recovery.

This emigration 'brain drain', which in some quarters is perversely being heralded as a 'safety valve', is in fact a serious problem for Ireland. It may well result in a significant skills deficit in the long-term and hamper Ireland's recovery. Sadly, outmigration has been one of the factors keeping the unemployment rate down. The IMF estimates that had all the employees who lost their job at the outset of the crisis remained in the labour force, then unemployment would now be 20 per cent (IMF, 2012: 5).

Given the continuing weakness of domestic demand and investment in the economy induced by austerity budgets, it is likely that emigration will continue at a very high rate. Expecting the labour force to continue to fall due to declining participation and outmigration, the Government admits that with employment growth flat these two factors will reduce the unemployment rate in 2013 (Department of Finance, 2012: 22). Unless there are measures in place to increase employment by boosting domestic demand and investment, outmigration will continue.

Youth unemployment
Youth unemployment in the European Union – particularly in the peripheral countries most deeply affected by austerity and the Euro crisis – has become a European crisis. The latest Eurostat figures show that youth unemployment in Ireland – unemployment amongst those under 25 seeking work – now stands at 30.6 per cent, 7.7 percentage points above the EU 27 average (Eurostat, 2013). Youth unemployment has risen from 9.1 per cent in 2007 to 30.6 per cent in 2012. In Spain Eurostat estimated 2012 youth unemployment of 53.2 per cent, while in Greece the statistics agency has estimated youth unemployment in 2012 at just under 60 per cent (Eurostat, 2013; ELSTAT, 2013). Across the EU-27 youth unemployment is estimated to be 22.9 per cent. Addressing the issue of youth unemployment and its link to high emigration rates among young people must be a core policy priority for Government and the European Union. Radical initiatives to create jobs are urgently required.

The most recent figures released by the Higher Education Authority (HEA) show that graduates in 2008 with an honours degree had a 10 per cent unemployment rate, those with a postgraduate degree had a 12 per cent unemployment rate and those with a Masters or PhD had a 16 per cent unemployment rate, well above the corresponding rates in the preceding year. In 2008 almost 15 per cent of honours degree graduates and 17 per cent of PhD graduates were in employment overseas while 34 per cent were engaged in further studies. Ireland is relying on the "smart economy" as the foundation of economic recovery. The latest emigration and graduate employment statistics raise serious questions about the sustainability of such reliance.

Key policy priorities on migration and intercultural issues
- Address involuntary emigration and the long-term policy problems it presents for the State.
- Promote integration and an inclusive society, giving priority to recognising the right of all refugees and asylum-seekers to work.
- Introduce an Earned Regularisation Scheme similar to that proposed by the Migrant Rights Centre Ireland to provide a pathway to permanent residency for the 30,000 undocumented migrants in Ireland.
- Immediately increase the weekly allowance allocated to asylum-seekers on 'direct provision' to at least €65 per week for an adult and €38 for a child.

11. Participation

> ## CORE POLICY OBJECTIVE: PARTICIPATION
> To ensure that all people have a genuine voice in shaping the decisions that affect them and to ensure that all people can contribute to the development of society.

The changing nature of democracy has raised many questions for policy-makers and others concerned about the issue of participation. Decisions often appear to be made without any real involvement of the many affected by the decisions' outcomes. The context of the 2011 general election dissipated some of the voter apathy that had been widespread over previous years. Indeed, the election also reminded voters of the importance of governance and decision making in democratic societies. As chart 11.1 shows, voter turnout has been falling over time and reached a low point of 62.6 per cent in 2002.

Chart 11.1: Percentage turnout in Irish General Elections, 1973-2011.

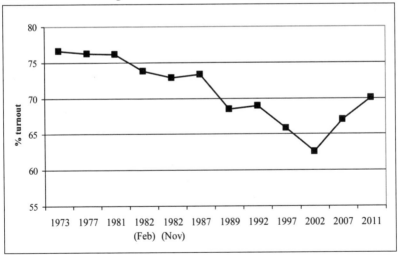

Source: CSO (2011:87) and Department of Environment, Heritage and Local Government (2011).

The 2011 turnout, at 70.9 per cent, was an improvement on previous elections and brought Ireland's turnout above the European average for the first time since the 1980s. The EU-27 average turnout is 69.7 per cent (CSO, 2010:44).[84] Progress made in terms of voter turnout has dissipated since the general election in 2011. It is clear that a significant number of voters have lost faith in their ability to influence the governance and decision making processes in Ireland and feel powerless to make any changes. The results of the Referendum on the Fiscal Stability Treaty held on 31st May 2012 and The Children Referendum held on 10th November 2012 both show a significant drop in voter turnout from the general election. In the referendum on the Fiscal Treaty only 50.6 per cent[85] of those eligible to vote did so and in The Children Referendum only 33.5 per cent[86] of those eligible voted. Such a significant drop in voter turnout in 12 months is a cause for alarm. It also highlights the need for a discussion on how to engage voters meaningfully in the decision-making process. A further problem alongside falling voter participation is the lack of female representatives in politics. Women are markedly underrepresented in Irish politics, accounting for just 15 per cent of TDs and 30 per cent of senators. (McGing, 2011). Government has moved to address this through The Electoral (Amendment) (Political Funding) Bill 2011 which introduced gender quota legislation. Under this legislation political parties will lose half of their central exchequer funding if the minority gender of their candidates accounts for less than 30 per cent of those seeking election in the next national election. Seven years after this the minimum threshold will rise to 40 per cent.

The most recent in-depth analysis of voter participation was undertaken in 2011 by the CSO. In a quarterly national household survey module on voter participation and abstention, issued in November 2011, the CSO provided an insight into how people regarded the electoral process. It found that the turnout of young people in the February 2011 general election had increased considerably since the previous survey in 2003. Just over 62 per cent of those aged 18 to 24 voted in the 2011 general election. This contrasts with participation figures of 92 per cent for older voters aged 55 to 64 years, highlighting that young people are still considerably less likely to vote than their older compatriots (CSO 2011: 3).

---

[84] The 2006 review of the accuracy of the electoral register may suggest that the official figures for 2002 and 2007 are somewhat understated.
[85] http://www.thejournal.ie/referendum-results-the-county-by-county-stats-471311-Jun2012/?r_dir_d=1
[86] http://www.referendum.ie/results-summary.php?ref=6

The survey also found that over one-third of those who did not vote were not registered to vote, 11 per cent of non-voters said they had 'no interest', 10 per cent were 'disillusioned' with politics and 11 per cent had difficulty getting to the polling station (this was particularly common among non-voters aged 55 and over). (CSO, 2011:4) The survey also found that those educated to primary level or below were most likely to say they did not vote because they were disillusioned with politics. These findings suggest that many people, especially young people and those who have lower educational attainment levels, have little confidence in the political process. They have become disillusioned because the political process fails to involve them in any real way, while also failing to address many of their core concerns. Transparency and accountability are demanded but rarely delivered. Many of the developments of recent years will simply have added to the disillusionment of many people. A new approach is clearly needed to address this issue. The low turnout over two referenda highlights apathy among the public towards the political system and the need for Government to engage with civil society in a deliberative democracy process. Although Government is engaging with members of civil society on eight specific issues as part of the Constitutional Convention,[87] it can ill afford to ignore the lack of trust and engagement of civil society in the democratic processes of the state. To date the remit of the Constitutional Convention has been extremely limited and it does not satisfy people's desire for engagement in the way that a genuinely deliberative process would.

The need for an agreed forum and structure for discussion of issues on which people disagree is becoming more obvious as political and mass communication systems develop. Most people are not involved in the processes that produce plans and decisions which affect their lives. They know that they are being presented with a *fait accompli*. More critically, they realise that they and their families will be forced to live with the consequences of the decisions taken. This is particularly relevant in Ireland in 2013, where people are living with the consequences of the bailout programme and repaying the debts of European banks through a programme of austerity and upward redistribution of resources. Many feel disenfranchised by a process that produced this outcome without any meaningful consultation with citizens. A lack of structures and systems to involve people in the decision-making process results in the exclusion and alienation of large sections of society. It causes and maintains inequality.

---

[87] For more information see https://www.constitution.ie/Convention.aspx

Any exclusion of people from debate on the issues that affect them is suspect, leaving those responsible open to the charge of arbitrary use of power. Some of the decision-making structures of our society and of our world allow people to be represented in the process. However, almost all of these structures fail to provide genuine participation for most people affected by their decisions. To facilitate real participation a process of 'deliberative democracy' is required. Deliberative democratic structures enable discussion and debate to take place without any imposition of power differentials. Issues and positions are argued and discussed on the basis of the available evidence rather than on the basis of assertions by those who are powerful and unwilling to consider the evidence. Deliberative democracy produces evidence-based policy.

Deliberative participation by all is essential if society is to develop and, in practice, to maintain principles guaranteeing satisfaction of basic needs, respect for others as equals, economic equality, and religious, social, sexual and ethnic equality. Modern means of communication and information make it relatively easy to involve people in dialogue and decision-making. The big question is whether the groups with power will share it with others?

Some progress has been made towards this objective in Ireland over the past decade. At local government level the development of Community Forums, Strategic Policy Committees and County/City Development Boards were moves in the right direction. So also were some of the developments in social dialogue at national level, most importantly the creation of the Community and Voluntary Pillar and the Environmental Pillar. However, these initiatives fell short of real deliberative processes. In practice, power differentials were used to undermine the validity of evidence-based policy proposals. While evidence-based proposals can be undermined in this way, the issue of real participation has quite some distance to go before the rhetoric of participation is matched by reality.

In October 2012 the Department of Environment, Community and Local Government published '*Putting People First: Action Programme for Effective Local Government*'. The document outlines a vision for local government as 'leading economic, social and community development, delivering efficient and good value services, and representing citizens and local communities effectively and accountably' (Department of Environment, Community and Local Government, 2012: iii). One of the stated aims of this process of local government reform is to create more meaningful and responsive local democracy (DECLG 2012:148) with options for citizen engagement and participative democracy outlined in the report.

The report also deals with the issues of good governance, strong leadership and democratic accountability and outlines the reforms identified by Government as necessary to ensure that:

- local government is accountable and effective;
- local objectives, national interests and the common good are balanced; and
- community involvement in the policy and decision making process is promoted.

Social Justice Ireland welcomes the stated commitments to make local democracy more meaningful and responsive and to ensure broader citizen engagement in local government as part of the alignment process of local government reform. We believe that a deliberative democracy process would be the most appropriate way forward and that such a structure and framework would enhance community involvement in decision making and the policy making process at a local level.

Deliberative Democracy
Social Justice Ireland believes a deliberative democracy process, in which all stakeholders would address the evidence, would go some way towards ensuring that local issues are addressed and would also ensure a high level of accountability among stakeholders. This process could be implemented under the framework of the Council of Europe's *Charter on Shared Social Responsibilities*.[88] The Charter states that shared social responsibility in terms of local government requires that local government 'frame local policies which acknowledge and take into account the contribution made by everyone to strengthening social protection and social cohesion, the fair allocation of common goods, the formation of the principles of social, environmental and intergenerational justice and which also ensure that all stakeholders have a negotiation and decision-making power' (Council of Europe, 2011). We believe these guidelines can be adapted to the Irish context and would be useful tools for devising a policy to promote greater alignment between local government and the community & voluntary sector in promoting participation at local level. This would involve:

- Local government, the community & voluntary sector and the local community working together to ensure the design and efficient delivery of services for local communities to cater for the specific needs of that particular local community.

---

[88] The Charter of Shared Social Responsibilities is also discussed in chapter 2 of this publication.

- Highlighting the key role of social citizenship in creating vibrant, participative and inclusive communities.
- Direct involvement of local communities, local authorities, state bodies and local entrepreneurs in the policy making and decision making processes.
- Ensuring all voices are heard (especially those of people on the margins of society) in the decision making process.
- Reform of current local government structures to better involve local communities in the governance of and decision making in their local area.
- An increased sense of 'ownership' over local government by the local community, which will only come about with increased participation. The community & voluntary sector has a key role to play in this.

Social Justice Ireland believes that these guidelines would be very relevant Ireland's needs. Reform of local government is designed to promote local community, social and economic development (Department of Environment, Community and Local Government, 2012: ii). Deliberative democracy guidelines would ensure that these reforms are both socially inclusive and sustainable. They could provide a key part of the framework aimed at creating a truly participatory and inclusive system of local governance involving all of the stakeholders equally. These guidelines would also provide a framework for achieving the high level objectives of a strong, democratic, participative and responsive local government providing services to socially inclusive and sustainable communities (Department of Environment, Community and Local Government, 2008).

A forum for dialogue on civil society issues

The failure to discuss openly a range of civil society issues that are of major concern to large numbers of people is contributing to disillusionment with the political process. When discussion or debate does take place, furthermore, many people feel that they are not allowed to participate in any real way.

The development of a new forum within which a civil society debate could be conducted on an on-going basis would be a welcome addition to Ireland's political landscape. Such a forum could make a major contribution to improving participation by a wide range of groups in Irish society.

Social Justice Ireland proposes that Government authorises and resources an initiative to identify how a civil society debate could be developed and maintained and to examine how it might connect to the growing debate at European level around civil society issues.

There are many issues such a forum could address. Given recent developments in Ireland, the issue of citizenship, its rights, responsibilities, possibilities and limitations in the twenty-first century is one that springs to mind. Another topical issue is the shape of the social model Ireland wishes to develop in the decades ahead. Do we follow a European model or an American one? Or do we want to create an alternative – and, if we do, what shape would it have and how could it be delivered? The issues a civil society forum could address are many and varied and Ireland would benefit immensely from having one.[89]

Impact on the democratic process

Would a civil society forum and a new social contract against exclusion take from the democratic process? Democracy means 'rule by the people', which implies that people participate in shaping the decisions that affect them most closely. What we have, in practice, is a highly centralised government in which we are 'represented' by professional politicians. The more powerful a political party becomes, the more distant it seems to become from the electorate. Party policies on a range of major issues are often difficult to discern. Backbenchers have little control over, or influence on, Government ministers, opposition spokespersons or shadow cabinets. Even within the cabinet some ministers seem to be able to ignore their cabinet colleagues.

The democratic process has certainly benefited from the participation of various sectors in different arenas. It would also benefit from taking up the proposals to develop a new social contract against exclusion and a new forum for dialogue on civil society issues.

The decline in participation is exacerbated by the primacy given to the market by many analysts, commentators, policy-makers and politicians. Many people feel that their views or comments are ignored or patronised, while the views of those who see the market as solving most, if not all of society's problems are treated with the greatest respect. This situation seems to persist despite the total failure of market mechanisms in recent years and despite the role these very mechanisms played in producing Ireland's range of current crises and the associated EU-level crises that are not currently being recognised by most decision-makers.

Markets have a major role to play. But it needs to be honestly acknowledged that they produce very mixed results when left to their own devices. Recent experience

---

[89] For a further discussion of this issue see Healy and Reynolds (2003:191–197).

has shown clearly that markets are extremely limited in terms of many policy goals. Consequently other mechanisms are required to ensure that some re-balancing, at least, is achieved. The mechanisms proposed here simply aim to be positive in improving participation in a 21st century society.

Supporting the Community & Voluntary Sector

The issue of governance is of major importance for Government and for society at large. Within this wider reality it is an especially crucial issue for the community & voluntary sector. There is a substantial role for civil society in addressing both the causes and the consequences of the multi-faceted crises Ireland currently faces (economic, banking, fiscal, social and reputational, as outlined in chapter 2). All communities are different and not every community has the capacity or the infrastructure to engage meaningfully with and participate in local government. This is where the community and voluntary sector has a key role to play in informing, engaging with and providing the local communities with the skills to participate in and contribute to local government. In light of the recommendations contained in the Final Report of the Steering Group on Local Government and Local Development Alignment Process, it is important that the community & voluntary sector is supported in promoting deliberative democracy processes and participation at local level.

The community & voluntary sector is playing a major role in responding to both the causes and the consequences of these crises. Support for this work is crucial and it should not be left to the welcome but very limited charity of philanthropists. Funding required by the sector has been provided over many years by Government. In recent years, however, the level of state funding has been reduced, with obvious consequences for those depending on the community & voluntary sector. It is crucial that Government appropriately resource this sector into the future and that it remains committed to the principle of providing multi-annual statutory funding.

Social dialogue is a critically important component of effective decision making in a modern democracy. The Community & Voluntary Pillar provides a mechanism for social dialogue that should be engaged with by Government across the range of policy issues in which the Pillar's members are deeply engaged. All aspects of governance should be characterised by transparency and accountability. Social dialogue contributes to both transparency and accountability. We believe governance along these lines can and should be developed in Ireland.

Key Policy Priorities on Participation

- Incorporate the shared social responsibility and deliberative democracy frameworks into the reform programme for local government and the local development process.
- Strengthen the mechanisms of engagement between the state and the C&V sector.
- Establish and resource a forum for dialogue on civil society issues. This initiative should identify how a civil society debate could be developed and maintained in Ireland and should examine how it might connect to the growing debate at European level around civil society issues.
- Significantly increase the funding to community & voluntary sector organisations which provide services, facilitating participation at national and local level and addressing both the causes and the consequences of Ireland's current series of crises.
- Ensure that there is real and effective monitoring and impact assessment of policy implementation using an evidence-based approach. Involve a wide range of perspectives in this process, thus ensuring inclusion of the experience of those currently excluded.

12. Sustainability

CORE POLICY OBJECTIVE: SUSTAINABILITY

To ensure that all development is socially, economically and environmentally sustainable

The search for a humane, sustainable model of development has gained momentum in recent times. After years of people believing that markets and market forces would produce a better life for everyone, major problems such as resource depletion and pollution have raised questions and doubts. There is a growing awareness that sustainability must be a constant factor in all development. Sustainability is about ensuring that all development is socially, economically and environmentally sustainable. This understanding underpins all the other chapters in this review. This chapter focuses in more detail on promoting sustainable development and on reviewing environmental issues.

Promoting Sustainable Development

Sustainable development is defined as 'development which meets the needs of the present, without compromising the ability of future generations to meet their needs *(World Commission on Environment and Development, 1987)*. It encompasses the three pillars; environment, society and economy. All three pillars of sustainability must be addressed in a balanced manner if development is to indeed be sustainable. Maintaining this balance is crucial to the long-term development of a sustainable resource-efficient future for Ireland. While growth and economic competitiveness are important, they are not the only issues to be considered and cannot be given precedence over others. They must be dealt with using a framework for sustainable development which gives equal consideration to the environmental, social and economic pillars. It is also important to note that, although economic growth is seen as the key to resolving many aspects of the current crisis across the EU, it is this very growth that may be damaging the possibility of securing sustainable development in the Global South.

Sustainable development is our only means of creating a long term future for Ireland, with the environment, growth and social needs met in a balanced manner with consideration for the needs of future generations. Sustainability and the adoption of a sustainable development model presents a significant policy challenge: how environmental policy decisions with varying distributional consequences are to be made in a timely manner while ensuring that a disproportionate burden is not imposed on certain groups e.g. low income families or rural dwellers. This policy challenge highlights the need for an evidence-based policy process involving all stakeholders. The costs and benefits of all policies must be assessed and considered on the basis of evidence only. This is essential in order to avoid the policy debate being influenced by hearsay or vested interests or the thoughtless exercise of power. Before the current recession began the global economy was five times the size it had been 50 years before and, had it continued on that growth path, it would be 80 times that size by 2100 (SDC, 2009). This raises the fundamental question of how such growth rates can be sustained in a world of finite resources and fragile ecosystems. Continuing along the same path is clearly not sustainable. Promoting a sustainable economy requires that we place a value on our finite natural resources and that the interdependence of the economy, wellbeing and natural capital are recognised (EC 2011).

Beyond 2015 – Towards Sustainable Development Goals
Discussions and negotiations at the RIO+20 summit in June 2012 culminated in the '*Future We Want*' outcome document which outlines UN commitments for a sustainable future and the development of Sustainable Development Goals (SDGs) to replace the Millennium Development Goals[90] (MDGs) after 2015. Work on developing SDGs began in earnest in January 2013 with the establishment of the Open Working Group on Sustainable Development Goals.[91] The '*Future We Want*' indicates that the SDGs should address and incorporate in a balanced way all three dimensions of sustainable development and their inter-linkages and should be universally applicable to all countries. All stakeholders should be included in the process of creating the SDGs and the measurable targets and indicators. While the development of SDGs is welcome, it is of concern that there is no mention of the common good in the '*Future We Want*', even though it does give significant consideration to sustained economic growth. This commitment to sustained economic growth indicates a failure to learn from past mistakes and the current crises by the international community – an issue that is of concern to *Social Justice Ireland*. The common good must be at the core of sustainable development to ensure that natural resources are protected for future generations.

---

[90] For a more detailed discussion on MDGs see Annex 14 of this socio-economic review
[91] For further information see http://sustainabledevelopment.un.org/index.php?menu=1549

Civil society organisations engaged with the post-2015 development agenda have given a cautious welcome to the development of the SDGs. They emphasise the need for a meaningful and inclusive framework to engage people who are affected by poverty and experience marginalisation in order to promote ownership of the SDGs. This was one of the failures of the MDG process because those who were to benefit from the MDGs being achieved were not involved in the development of these goals. It is also crucial that the SDG targets are equitable, that priority is given to meeting the challenge faced by the most disadvantaged and that fair allocation of resources is secured for both poor people and poor countries.

When formulating SDGs, the Open Working Group on Sustainable Development Goals must take into account the shortcomings of the MDGs, specifically their failure to address the structural causes of poverty, inequality and exclusion. The set of SDGs which are eventually agreed should be truly universal, integrate sustainable development and the environment and should confront the root causes of our current crises and the reality that the world needs to move towards a sustainable path in order to guarantee a future for generations to come.

The need for shadow national accounts
According to Repetto, Magrath, Wells, Beer and Rossini (1989:3) the 'difference in the treatment of natural resources and other tangible assets [in the existing national accounts] reinforces the false dichotomy between the economy and "the environment" that leads policy makers to ignore or destroy the latter in the name of economic development.'

Acceptance of the need to move away from money-measured growth as the principal economic target and measure of success towards sustainability in terms of real-life, social, environmental and economic variables must be central to any model of development with sustainability at its core. Our present national accounts are based on GNP/GDP as scorecards of wealth and progress and miss fundamentals such as environmental sustainability. These measures completely ignore unpaid work because only money transactions are tracked. Ironically, while environmental depletion is ignored, the environmental costs of dealing with the effects of economic growth, such as cleaning up pollution or coping with the felling of rainforests, are added to, rather than subtracted from, GNP/GDP.

It is widely acknowledged that GDP is 'an inadequate metric to gauge wellbeing over time, particularly in its economic, environmental, and social dimensions, some aspects of which are often referred to as sustainability' (Stiglitz Commission 2009:

8). A new scorecard or metric model is needed which measures the effects of policy decisions on people's lives as well as the environmental, social and economic costs and benefits of those policies. The United Nations High Level Panel on Global Sustainability recommends that the international community measure development beyond GDP and that national accounts should measure and cost social exclusion, unemployment and social inequality and the environmental costs of growth and market failures.

Development of 'satellite' or 'shadow' national accounts should be a central initiative in this. Already a number of alternative scorecards exist, such as the United Nations' Human Development Index (HDI), former World Bank economist Herman Daly's Index of Sustainable Economic Welfare (ISEW) and Hazel Henderson's Country Futures Index (CFI). A 2002 study by Wackernagel et al presented the first systematic attempt to calculate how human demands on the environment are matched by its capacity to cope. It found that the world currently uses 120 per cent of what the earth can provide sustainably each year.

In the environmental context it is crucial that dominant economic models are challenged on, among other things, their assumptions that nature's capital (clean air, water and environment) are essentially free and inexhaustible, that scarce resources can always be substituted and that the planet can continue absorbing human and industrial wastes. These are issues that most economists tend to downplay as externalities. Shadow national accounts would help to make sustainability and 'green' procurement mandatory considerations in the decision and policy making process. They would also go some way towards driving a civil society awareness campaign to help decouple economic growth from consumption.

Social Justice Ireland welcomes the publication by the Departments of Environment, Community and Local Government and Public Expenditure and Reform of the Action Plan for Green Public Procurement as a step on the road towards making green procurement mandatory in public sector procurement decisions.

Some governments and international agencies have picked up on these issues, especially in the environmental area and have begun to develop 'satellite' or 'shadow' national accounts that include items not traditionally measured. *Social Justice Ireland's* 2009 publication *Beyond GDP: What is prosperity and how should it be measured?* explored many of these new developments. It included contributions from the OECD, the New Economics Foundation, and other informed bodies and proposed a series of policy developments which would assist in achieving similar progress in Ireland.

There has, in fact, been some progress in this area, including commitments to better data collection and broader assessment of well-being and progress by the CSO, ESRI and EPA. However, much remains to be achieved and *Social Justice Ireland* strongly urges Government to adopt this broader perspective and commit to producing these accounts alongside more comprehensive indicators of progress. Measures of economic performance must reflect their environmental cost and a price must be put on the use of our natural capital.

The OECD Global Project on measuring the progress of society recommends that sets of key environmental, social and economic indicators be developed and that these should be used to inform evidence-based decision making across all sectors (Morrone, 2009: 23).

Social Justice Ireland recommends that government commit to producing shadow national accounts and that these accounts include indicators that measure the following:

- the use of energy and materials to produce goods;
- the generation of pollution and waste;
- the amount of money spent by industry, government and households to protect the environment or manage natural resources;
- natural resource asset accounts measuring the quantity and quality of a country's natural resources;
- sustainability of the growth being generated *vis-a-vis* our social and natural capital;
- natural resource depletion and degradation as a cost to society;
- the output of waste and pollution as a result of commercial activity as a cost within the satellite national accounts; and
- the measures of the GPI (Genuine Progress Indicator) which measure and deduct for income inequality, environmental degradation and cost of crime, amongst other items. By measuring and differentiating between economic activities that diminish natural and social capital and those activities that enhance them we can ensure that our economic welfare is sustainable (Daly & Cobb, 1987).

Stakeholder involvement

One of the key indicators of sustainability is how a country runs stakeholder involvement. Sustainable Development Councils (SDCs) are a model for multi-stakeholder bodies comprising members of all major groups – public, private, community, civil society and academic – engaged in evidence-based discussion.[92] The EU-wide experience has been that SDC's are crucial to maintaining a medium and long-term vision for a sustainable future whilst concurrently working to ensure that sustainable development policies are embedded into socio-economic strategies and budgetary processes.

Ireland established its sustainable development council (Comhar) in 1999 and disbanded it in 2011, transferring its functions to NESC (National Economic and Social Council). This is unfortunate in the light of the United Nations recommendation that the link between informed scientific evidence and policy making on sustainable development issues be strengthened (United Nations, 2012). While it is admirable that Government wishes to place sustainable development at the core of policy making and has asked NESC to ensure it gives sustainable development major consideration in all it does, it is also important to note that NESC is not in a position to do the detailed work done previously by Comhar.

All areas of governance, from international to national to local, along with civil society and the private sector, must fully embrace the requirements of a sustainable development future (United Nations, 2012). In order to facilitate a move towards a sustainable future for all, stakeholders from all arenas must be involved in the process. There is need for a deliberative democracy arena within which all stakeholders can discuss evidence without power differentials impeding outcomes.

Principles to underpin sustainable development

Principles to underpin sustainable development were proposed in a report for the European Commission prepared by James Robertson in May 1997. The report, *The New Economics of Sustainable Development*, argued that these principles should include the following:

- systematic empowerment of people (as opposed to making and keeping them dependent) as the basis for people-centred development;
- systematic conservation of resources and environment as the basis for environmentally sustainable development;

---

[92] For more information see http://www.eeac.eu/images/doucments/eeac-statement-backgr2011_rio_final_144dpi.pdf

- evolution from a 'wealth of nations' model of economic life to a 'one-world' economic system;
- evolution from today's international economy to an ecologically sustainable, decentralising, multi-level one-world economic system;
- restoration of political and ethical factors to a central place in economic life and thought;
- respect for qualitative values, not just quantitative values; and
- respect for feminine values, not just masculine ones.

At first glance these might not appear to be the type of concrete guidelines that policymakers so often seek. Yet they are principles that are relevant to every area of economic life. They also apply to every level of life, ranging from personal and household to global issues. They influence lifestyle choices and organisational goals. If these principles were applied to every area, level and feature of economic life they would provide a comprehensive checklist for a systematic policy review.

It is also important that any programme for sustainable development should take a realistic view of human nature, recognising that people can be both altruistic and selfish, both co-operative and competitive. It is important, therefore, to develop the economic system to reward activities that are socially and environmentally benign (and not the reverse, as at present). This, in turn, would make it easier for people and organisations to make choices that are socially and environmentally responsible. Incorporating social and environmental costs in regulating and pricing both goods and services, combined with promoting those goods and services which are sustainable, should also become part of sustainable development policy.

Any programme for sustainable development has implications for public spending. In addressing this issue it needs to be understood that public expenditure programmes and taxes provide a framework which helps to shape market prices, rewards some kinds of activities and penalises others. Within this framework there are other areas which are not supported by public expenditure or are not taxed. This framework should be developed to encourage economic efficiency and enterprise, social equity and environmental sustainability. Systematic reviews should be carried out and published on the sustainability effects of all public subsidies and other relevant public expenditure and tax differentials. Governments should identify and remove those subsidies which cause the greatest detriment to natural, environmental and social resources (United Nations, 2012:14). Systematic reviews should also be carried out and published on the possibilities for re-orientating public spending programmes, with the aim of preventing and reducing social and environmental problems.

Social Justice Ireland welcomed the publication entitled *'Our Sustainable Future – A Framework for a Sustainable Development for Ireland'* (Department of the Environment, Community and Local Government, 2012) which is a late but positive step on the road towards a sustainable development model. One area of concern, however, is the failure by governments to implement earlier sustainability strategies (2000 & 2007) and another is the lack of quantitative and qualitative targets and indicators to accompany the Framework itself. *Social Justice Ireland* welcomes the Framework's emphasis on the need for a whole of government approach to sustainability and the need for all areas of government policy to have regard for sustainable development. It will be important that the Cabinet Committee on Climate Change and the Green Economy and the High-Level Inter-Departmental Group on Sustainable Development are given the necessary resources to ensure that the framework is at the heart of policy making in all Government departments and that the recommendations of the report are incorporated right across Government.

Monitoring sustainable development
Many studies have highlighted the lack of socio-economic and environmental data in Ireland required to assess trends in sustainable development. A chapter by Carrie in the Feasta Review (2005) focused on the lack of long-run socio-economic data in respect of such issues as education participation, crime and healthcare. Another paper by Scott (ESRI, 2005) outlined the empirical and methodological gaps which continue to impede the incorporation of sustainable development issues into public policy making and assessment. It is only through a sustained commitment to data collection in all of these areas that these deficiencies will be addressed. We welcome recent developments in this area, particularly at the CSO, and look forward to all of these data impediments being removed in the years to come.

Comhar undertook a lot of work developing indicators in order to set targets and quantitative means of measuring the progress of sustainable development. *Social Justice Ireland* does not believe that the work of Comhar[93] has been satisfactorily adopted by NESC to date and a great deal of work needs to be done in the area of indicators. There should be real consultation between NESC, the CSO, and the Community & Voluntary Pillar (which has done extensive work in this area[94]) to

---

[93] http://www.comharsustainableindicators.ie/explore-the-indicators/comhar-indicators.aspx
[94] This work involved extensive engagement with a range of government departments on agreeing appropriate indicators to measure progress on the high-level goals contained in the national agreement *'Towards 2016'*. Much of this work remains valid despite the changing context.

---

ensure that these issues are addressed, appropriate indicators are immediately put in place and the necessary data collected. In a study of national strategies towards sustainable development in 2005 (Niestroy, 2005: 185) Ireland's sustainability strategy was criticised for:

- having no systematic monitoring system;
- having no general timetable; and
- lacking quantitative national targets.

Implementation, targets and monitoring will be crucial to the success of any policy approach that genuinely promotes sustainable development. It is important that these targets and indicators and the mechanisms for monitoring, tracking and reviewing them are developed and clearly explained to ensure that responsibility is taken across all departments and all stakeholders for its implementation.

The recent publication by the Central Statistics Office of *Sustainable Development Indicators Ireland 2013*, aims to achieve continuous improvement in the quality of life and well-being for present and future generations through linking economic development with protection of the environment and social justice (CSO, 2013). This is a positive step towards integrating sustainable development across the entire policy agenda in Ireland.

Environmental Issues

Maintaining a healthy environment remains one of the greatest global challenges. Without concerted and rapid collective action to curb and decouple resource depletion and the generation of pollution from economic growth, human activities may destroy the very environment that supports economies and sustains life (UNEP 2011: II).

Our environment is a priceless asset. It is also finite – a fact that is often ignored in current debates. Protection and conservation of our environment is of major importance as it is not just for our use alone; it is also the natural capital of future generations.

For environmental facts and details for Ireland see Annex 12.

The economic growth of recent decades has been accomplished mainly by drawing down natural resources without allowing stocks to regenerate and causing widespread degradation and loss to our eco-system. Careful stewardship of Ireland's natural resources is required to ensure the long term health and sustainability of our environment. Unsustainable use of natural resources is one of the greatest long-term threats to humankind (European Commission, 2012:3). It is crucial, therefore, that Ireland meets the challenges of responding to climate change and protecting our natural resources and biodiversity with policies that are based on scientific evidence and protecting the common good.

Climate change

Climate change is one of the most significant and challenging issues currently facing humanity. Increased levels of greenhouse gases, such as CO_2, increase the amount of energy trapped in the atmosphere which leads to global effects such as increased temperatures, melting of snow and ice and raised global average sea-level. If these issues are not addressed with urgency the projected effects of climate change present a serious risk of dangerous and irreversible climate impacts at national and global levels. Food production and ecosystems are particularly vulnerable.

Climate change and implementation of climate policy have been challenges for Ireland. Despite two National Climate Change Strategies (one in 2000 and one in 2007), there have been significant delays in implementing these policies. In some cases policies have still not been implemented. The mobilisation of vested interested has been a decisive factors in many of these delays and cases of non-implementation (Coughlin (2007). This is very disappointing because if these policies had been implemented on time and as specified Ireland's climate policy commitments could have been met from domestic measures. Now Ireland is faced with the prospect of not meeting its emissions targets, even if all measures are implemented immediately. It is, in fact, on course to overshoot its EU 2020 emissions targets as early as 2015 (EPA 2011).

Social Justice Ireland welcomes the publication of the *General Scheme of a Climate Action and Low Carbon Development Bill 2013* by the Department of Environment, Community and Local Government for consideration of the Oireachtas Joint committee on the Environment, Culture and the Gaeltacht and stakeholders. It is crucial that all expert and evidence-based advice should be made available in an accessible manner to increase Irish people's understanding, engagement and participation on climate change policy and also to enhance political accountability and transparency on climate policy. However there are a number of areas of concern:

1. *Social Justice Ireland* is concerned that the only mention of targets in the Bill are those that Ireland is committed to under European Union law to reach by 2020

and those under the Kyoto Protocol. The only target mentioned beyond 2020 is to reach a low carbon, climate resilient and environmentally sustainable economy by 2050. The absence of sectoral targets and quantitative measures and outputs has already impeded climate change policy progress internationally (UNEP 2011: vii). Without sectoral targets and a system whereby they are regularly reviewed, the monitoring of progress on climate change policy will be very difficult. The absence of these targets will also make enforcing responsibility and accountability for implementation of climate policy across all Government departments and stakeholders in all sectors extremely challenging.

2. As outlined in the Bill, the Minister for Environment, Community and Local Government will submit a national low carbon roadmap within 12 months of the passing of the Bill. This means that Government will not adopt a national policy position on climate legislation and the transition to a low carbon future until the end of 2013 at the earliest, while implementation of these policies will move out to at least 2014. This will give the Government just six years to reach the targets set in the EU 2020 strategy (European Commission, 2010). Given that we are on course to overshoot emissions targets by 2015, there is a real danger that short-term planning to limit our liabilities in respect of missed targets will overshadow the requirement for long-term planning and policy goals for a sustainable and low carbon future. The long-term goal of a low carbon economy beyond 2020 must be at the core of climate policy.

3. *Social Justice Ireland* is concerned that the Bill refers to the objective of achieving the national low carbon roadmap at the least cost to the national economy. By failing to take appropriate actions and measures on climate change and carbon emissions now Ireland's economy and society will bear a far greater cost in the future. It is important that the National Expert Advisory Body on Climate Change is not constrained by economic and cost issues and that its recommendations should be based solely on scientific evidence and best practice.

Emissions challenge

Ireland has two sets of emissions targets to meet: the Kyoto Protocol and the EU 2020 Targets. Ireland is on track to meet its Kyoto commitments when the effects of the EU Emissions Trading Scheme and forest sinks are taken into account. However, it is already facing significant challenges in meeting its future EU emissions targets for greenhouse gases under the EU Climate and Energy package for 2020 and further anticipated longer term targets up to 2050. This is despite substantial declines in greenhouse gas emissions in 2009 and 2010 and a projected fall of 6.7 per cent in 2011 which the EPA attributes primarily to the economic recession.

Under the *Climate and Energy Package*, as part of the EU 2020 targets Ireland is required to deliver a 20 per cent reduction in non-Emissions Trading Scheme (ETS) greenhouse gas emissions by 2020 (relative to 2005 levels). Ireland also has binding annual emissions limits over the period 2013 to 2020 to ensure movement towards the EU 2020 target. The latest EPA projections indicate that Ireland will exceed its annual binding limit in 2015 – 2017 and that it will exceed its obligations over the 2013 to 2020 period by 1.9-20.6 Mtonnes of CO_2eq.

Ireland's emissions profile is dominated by emissions from the energy supply, transport and agriculture sectors (EPA, 2012). The domestic sector comprises transport, agriculture and residential waste activities and is also responsible for 72 per cent of Ireland's total emissions. The immediate challenge for Irish climate policy is to meet the EU 2020 targets for the domestic sector, which is a reduction of at least 20 per cent on the 2005 emission levels by 2020. If achieved, the projected strong growth in the agriculture sector set out in the Department of Agriculture, Fisheries and Food vision *Food Harvest 2020* will likely result in agricultural emissions increasing by 7 per cent by 2020. There is a significant challenge for Government in achieving the binding EU 2020 targets whilst also pursuing its *Food Harvest* agenda.

Support for sustainable agricultural practice is important to ensure the long-term viability of the sector and consideration must also be given to how the projected increase in agriculture emissions can be offset. It is important that the agriculture sector be at the fore of developing and implementing sustainable farming practices and be innovative in terms of reducing emissions. Consideration should also be given to the European Commission proposals to establish a framework for land use, land use change and forestry (LULUCF) to be included in the emission reduction targets. This is important for Ireland because it is estimated that forest sinks could provide significant relief in reaching emissions targets (see Annex 12).

Transport and agriculture represent the most intractable sectors in terms of carbon offsets and emissions mitigations, with the transport sector recording a 121 per cent increase in emissions between 1990 and 2011.[95] A national sustainable transport

---

[95] Transport emissions have decreased for four consecutive years and are now 22% below peak levels in 2007.

network would represent a major step towards a low carbon, resource efficient economy. Capital investment will be required in sustainable transport infrastructure projects to ensure the reduction of transport emissions. Agriculture, which accounted for 32 per cent of total emissions in 2011, faces major difficulties in limiting emissions and meeting future targets. In the agriculture sector progress towards changing farm practices has been limited and incentives to reduce on-farm greenhouse emissions have not been delivered on a wide scale (Curtin & Hanrahan 2012: 9). The agriculture and food sector must build on its scientific and technical knowledge base to meet the emissions challenge.

The European Network for Rural Development has highlighted a number of opportunities for Ireland to use the development of renewable energy to mitigate the effects of climate change by delivering additional reductions to Ireland's CHG emissions. The opportunity and capability exist to significantly mitigate climate change through growth in afforestation and renewable energy sources. Forestry can play a significant role in combating climate change but the development of the forestry sector and renewable energy lack support in the Irish CAP Rural Development Programme (discussed further in chapter 13). It is important, therefore, that Government departments work together to tackle climate change and recognise that action on climate change is not just a challenge but a great opportunity to create jobs and develop a genuine, indigenous, low carbon economy.

Biodiversity
Nature and biodiversity are the basis for almost all ecosystem services and biodiversity loss is the greatest challenge facing humanity (EPA 2011: vii). Biodiversity loss and ecosystem degradation directly affect climate change and undermine the way we use natural resources (EEAC 2011: 114). Pollution, over-exploitation of natural resources and the spread of non-native species are causing a decline in biodiversity in Ireland. The Environmental Protection Agency (EPA) has identified the four main drivers (EPA 2011: 11) of biodiversity loss in Ireland all caused by human activity:

- habitat destruction and fragmentation;
- pollution;
- over-exploitation of natural resources; and
- the spread of non-native species.

Our eco-system is worth €2.6 billion to Ireland annually (EPA 2011) yet our biodiversity capital is decreasing rapidly. Ireland missed the 2010 target to halt biodiversity loss and lacks fundamental information on such issues as the distribution of species and habitats that inform planning and policy in other countries. *Social Justice Ireland* is concerned that responsibility for biodiversity now lies with the Department of Arts, Heritage and the Gaeltacht, whereas responsibility for all environmental issues lies with the Department of Environment, Community and Local Government. Both departments must work together to ensure that the policies they implement are designed to complement each other and will not have any negative consequences on other areas of environmental concern.

Biodiversity underpins our eco-system, which supports our natural capital and in particular the agriculture industry. It is critically important that our biodiversity is preserved and maintained and that the effects of policies and developments on biodiversity are monitored in order to inform environmental policy in the short and long-term. Ireland has less land designated as a Special Protected Area under the EU Habitats Directive than the EU average. The majority of Ireland's habitats listed under the Habitats Directive are reported to be in poor or bad conservation status (EPA 2012:76).

The economic value of biodiversity and how it contributes to our well-being needs to be better promoted and understood. Without biodiversity and our eco-system the development of a sustainable, low-carbon future for Ireland will not be possible and the value of our natural capital will be lost. Climate change will not go away and initial costs will have to be incurred in order to preserve and conserve our natural resources.

The long-term benefits of these investments, both for the present and future generations, will far outweigh the initial cost. It is important that the economic value of biodiversity be factored into decision making and reflected in national accounting and reporting systems. The EPA notes that the continuing loss of biodiversity is one of the greatest challenges facing us (EPA 2012:82). *Social Justice Ireland* believes that Government should implement the EPA's recommendations regarding evidence-based decision making on biodiversity issues and the integration of the economic value of ecosystems into the national accounting and reporting systems.

Environmental taxation
The extent of Ireland's challenge in terms of climate change and maintaining and preserving our national resources is clear from the information outlined above. One way of tackling this challenge whilst also broadening the tax base is through

environmental taxation. Eco-taxes, which put a price on the full costs of resource extraction and pollution, will help move towards a resource efficient, low carbon green economy. Carbon taxation was introduced in Ireland in Budget 2010 and was increased from €15 to €20 per tonne in Budget 2012. *Social Justice Ireland* welcomed the introduction of a carbon tax but is disappointed that Government has not used some of the money raised by this tax to target low income families and rural dwellers who were most affected by it. When considering environmental taxation measures to support sustainable development and the environment and to broaden the tax base, the Government should ensure that such taxes are structured in ways that are equitable and effective and do not place a disproportionate burden on rural communities or lower socio-economic groups.

Key Policy Priorities on Sustainability

- A common understanding of sustainable development must be communicated across all Government departments, policy makers, stakeholders and civil society.
- All public policy decisions across Government departments must be underpinned by the principles of sustainability.
- The economic value of biodiversity must be accounted for in all environmental policy decisions.
- Shadow national accounts should be developed to move towards a more sustainable, resource efficient model of growth.
- A progressive and equitable environmental taxation system should be developed in a structured way that does not impose a disproportionate burden on certain groups.
- A detailed roadmap towards the development of a low carbon sustainable economy, with targets to be met towards 2020 and beyond, should be published.
- Investment should be made in sustainable infrastructure projects which will have substantial long-term dividends.

13. Rural Development

CORE POLICY OBJECTIVE: RURAL DEVELOPMENT

To secure the existence of substantial numbers of viable communities in all parts of rural Ireland where every person would have access to meaningful work, adequate income and to social services, and where infrastructures needed for sustainable development would be in place.

Rural Ireland continues to change dramatically. Approximately 40 per cent of Ireland's population live in rural areas. The need for an integrated transition from an agricultural to a rural development agenda to improve the quality of life for all rural dwellers has never been more pressing. Agriculture, forestry and fishing now account for only 85,600 people classified as employed in Ireland (CSO, 2012). At present those in farming comprise just one-quarter of the rural labour force and are a minority of the rural population.

Farm incomes

Rural income data from the SILC reports was reviewed in chapter 3. This shows that rural Ireland has high dependency levels, increasing outmigration and many small farmers living on very low incomes. The data from the most recent SILC study (CSO 2011: 10) shows there is a very uneven national distribution of poverty. The risk of poverty in rural Ireland is 4.6 percentage points higher than in urban Ireland – 18.8 per cent and 14.2 per cent respectively.

Key farm statistics:

- Average family farm income was €24,461 in 2011, a 30 per cent increase on 2010. This can be attributed entirely to output gains (Teagasc, 2012). The preliminary Teagasc estimates for 2012 indicate that average family farm income fell by 12 per cent in 2012 to €21,500. This average reduction masks significant variations on individual farms.
- The number of farm households in which the farmer and/or spouse were engaged in off-farm employment was 49.5 per cent in 2011 (Teagasc, 2012).
- Teagasc classified 34 per cent of Irish farm households (35,640 farms) as being 'economically vulnerable', meaning the farm business is not

economically viable and neither the farmer nor the spouse worked outside the farm in 2011.

- The largest number of economically viable farms is in the Southeast region while the largest number of economically vulnerable farms is in the Border region.
- The results of the CSO Agricultural Census 2010 show that the number of farms in Ireland fell from 141,527 in 2000 to 139,860 in 2010 and that the average farm size had increased slightly over the same period.
- Direct payments comprised 73 per cent of farm income in 2011 and averaged €17,929 per farm.
- According to Eurostat, real agricultural income per worker in Ireland in 2012 decreased by 10.1 per cent.[96]

These statistics mask the huge variation in farm income in Ireland as a whole. Only a minority of farmers are at present generating an adequate income from farm activity and even on these farms income lags considerably behind the national average. An important insight into the income of Irish farmers is provided by Teagasc in its National Farm Survey 2011 and the IFA's Farm Income Review 2012. Table 13.1 below outlines the huge variations in farm income in Ireland in 2011, with 65 per cent of farms in Ireland having an income of less than €20,000.

Table 13.1: Distribution of Family Farm Income in Ireland 2011

€	< 5,000	5,000 – 10,000	10,000 – 20,000	20,000 – 30,000	30,000 – 50,000	> 50,000
%	23	21	21	9	11	15
Number	24,273	22,162	22,162	9,498	11,609	15,830

Source: IFA Farm Income Review 2012

The majority of farm families rely on income support and payments from the state to supplement their income. The latest CSO figures show that the value of subsidies less taxes on production to Irish farms was €1,661 million in 2012 (CSO, 2012). Table 13.2 shows that by the end of 2012 there were 11,200 families receiving the Farm Assist payment, an increase of 3,550 since 2006. This increase can be attributed to a combination of falling product prices and the loss of off-farm employment. Off farm employment and income is extremely important to farming households and

---

[96] http://ec.europa.eu/ireland/press_office/news_of_the_day/eurostat-estimates-agricultural-income_en.htm

the fall in availability of off farm employment due to the recession will increase the dependence of farms on direct subsidies to avoid rural poverty and social exclusion.

Table 13.2: Farm Assist Expenditure (€m) 2006-2012

Year	Expenditure (€m)	Number Benefiting	Average Payment (€/week)
2006	71	7,650	179
2007	79	7,400	205
2008	85	7,710	213
2009	96	8,845	209
2010	111	10,700	199
2011	112	11,300	190
2012(est)	106	11,200	182

Source: IFA Farm Income Review 2012

Agriculture and direct employment from agricultural activities have been declining in Ireland. The Department of Agriculture, Food and the Marine has outlined its vision of the future of Irish Agriculture in *Food Harvest 2020* (Department of Agriculture, Food and the Marine, 2011). It envisages that by 2020 the Irish agri-food industry will have developed and grown in a sustainable manner by delivering high quality, natural-based produce. This requires the industry to adopt a 'smart economy' approach by investing in skills, innovation and research. This signals a move away from traditional farming methods and to a method of collaboration across the agricultural, food and fisheries industries. In implementing this policy there needs to be significant investment in sustainable agriculture, rural anti-poverty and social inclusion programmes in order to protect vulnerable farm households in the transition to a rural development agenda.

Rural development
Rural development is often confused with agricultural development. This approach fails to grasp the fact that many people living in rural Ireland are not engaged in agriculture. This, in turn, leads to misunderstanding when the income from agriculture increases because many people fail to realise that not everyone in rural Ireland benefits from such an increase. As the number employed in agriculture declines a more comprehensive set of rural development policies is needed. Long-term strategies to address the failures of current and previous policies on critical issues, such as infrastructure development, the national spatial imbalance, local access to public services, public transport and local involvement in core decision-making,

are urgently required. The 1999 White Paper on rural development provided a vision to guide rural development policy (something Social Justice Ireland had advocated for over a decade previously). The current rural development policy has been developed within an EU framework and is dominated by the agri-model of rural development. It lacks an inclusive, overarching vision. Ireland's rural development policy is outlined in the CAP Rural Development Programme 2007-2013 under three main priorities (Department of Agriculture, Food and the Marine, 2011):

- improving the competitiveness of the agriculture sector;
- improving the environment and the countryside by support for land management; and
- improving the quality of life in rural areas and encouraging diversification of economic activity.

The rural development programme is funded through the European Agricultural Fund for Rural Development and member state contributions. The European Development Programme on which Irish rural development policy is based is divided into four axes:[97]

- Axis 1: to improve the competitiveness of the agricultural and forestry sector, including a range of measures that target human and physical capital in the agriculture, food and forestry sectors and quality production.
- Axis 2: to improve the environment and the countryside, providing measures to protect and enhance natural resources as well as preserving biodiversity, high nature value farming, forestry systems and cultural landscapes.
- Axis 3: to enhance the quality of life in rural areas and diversification of the rural economy, offering support to help develop local infrastructure and human capital in rural areas, to improve the conditions for growth and job creation in all sectors and the diversification of economic activities.
- Axis 4: based on the Leader experience, introduces possibilities for innovative governance through locally based, bottom-up approaches to rural development.

---

[97] For a more detailed breakdown see European Agricultural Fund for Rural Development: http://europa.eu/legislation_summaries/agriculture/general_framework/l60032_en.htm

In the Irish programme items under axes 3 and 4 are implemented together under LEADER. Table 13.3 outlines the expenditure on all four axes of the CAP Rural Development Programme in Ireland from 2007 to 2010, the last year for which detailed data is available.

Table 13.3: Financial Implementation of the Rural Development Programme and National Strategy Plan - Overall Summary of Progress on Implementation

Axis and Total	Funding Allocation in € million (2007 – 2013) (EAFRD + Matching National +Health Check + EERP funds) Cumulative	Actual Expenditure in € million				Cumulative Expenditure - 2007-2010 - € million	Expenditure to date as % of RDP Allocation
		2007	2008	2009	January to June 2010		
Axis 1	483.5	63.2	65.7	74.2	27.6	230.6	47.7%
Axis 2	4,147.1	699.6	568.9	564.3	136.6	1,969.4	47.5%
Axis 3	370.9	0.0	0.0	10.0	6.4	16.4	4.4%
Axis 4	95.5	0.0	0.0	8.8	4.6	13.5	14.1%
Total Axes 1 to 4	**5,097**	**763**	**635**	**657**	**175**	**2,230**	**43.7%**
Technical Assistance	6.0	0.00	0.28	0.24	0.12	0.64	10.7%
Overall RDP	**5,103.1**	**762.8**	**634.8**	**657.5**	**175.3**	**2,230.5**	**43.7%**
% of Total Expenditure - 2007-2010		34%	28%	29%	8%	100%	

Source: Indecon, Mid Term Evaluation of CAP Rural Development Plan

Less detailed data is available for the period to the end of 2011. Within the first five years of implementation the Irish programme used about 66 per cent of the total public expenditure planned and emphasis has been given to agri-environmental payments, which represent almost 52 per cent of total public expenditure of the programme up to December 2011.[98] In an Irish context, activities and programmes aimed at developing a more sustainable rural economy, diversification of economic activity and an improved quality of life in rural areas are lagging being the policies being implemented in axis 1 and axis 2. Measures under axes 3 and 4 only commenced in mid-2009, with €109 million of the allocated €428 million spent by 2011. This poses a challenge for government in trying to ensure that the Leader Local Action Groups have the infrastructure and capacity required to accelerate the allocation of funding to projects and actions so as to meet the programme targets.

The primary goals of axes 3 and 4 are to increase the diversification of economic activity in rural areas, enhance the opportunities for alternative business creation in rural areas and to improve the quality of life for rural dwellers. Actions contained in axes 3 and 4 are designed to:

- Increase economic activity and employment rates in the wider rural economy through encouraging diversification into non-agricultural activities;
- Support the creation and development of micro-enterprises in the broader rural economy;
- Encourage rural tourism built on the sustainable development of Ireland's natural resources, cultural and natural heritage;
- Improve access to basic services by rural dwellers e.g. inadequate recreational facilities;
- Regenerate villages and their surrounding areas by improving their economic prospects and the quality of life; and
- Maintain, restore and upgrade the natural and built heritage.

(Department of Agriculture, Food and the Marine, 2011)

These actions are in line with the *AGRI Vision 2015* report (Department of Agriculture, Food and the Marine, 2004), which stated that the primary purpose of rural policy development is to underpin the economic and social wellbeing of rural communities. This report highlighted the fact that many rural dwellers are not linked to agriculture and that in order to improve the standard of living and

---

[98] The figures for 2012 are not yet available. For 2011 data see
http://enrd.ec.europa.eu/app_templates/enrd_assets/pdf/RDP-information-sheets/D_Infosheet_IE.pdf

quality of life in rural communities opportunities must be created so that the rural economy can develop agriculture in conjunction with much needed alternative enterprises.

It is of concern that the mid-term evaluation of the Rural Development Plan (Indecon, 2010) highlights the need for careful monitoring of expenditure in axes 3 and 4 and the possibility that the expenditure targets will not be met because of the delay in implementing actions under these axes. It is also of concern that the Department of Agriculture, Food and the Marine notes that the on-going reduction in services and enterprise opportunities due to the disproportionate effect of transport and fuel costs represents a threat to the quality of life in rural areas. The National Rural Network should be given adequate funding to ensure that it can continue to be a valuable source of information and in particular can highlight the resources and opportunities available to local rural communities under axes 3 and 4, as well as play a role in ensuring this funding is allocated effectively. The latest funding update and output indicators show that Ireland is still a considerable distance from meeting output targets in axis 3 but has closed the gap slightly in axis 4. [99]

With the on-going challenges facing traditional rural sectors, including agriculture, the future success of the rural economy is inextricably linked with the capacity of rural entrepreneurs to innovate and to develop new business opportunities that create jobs and income in rural areas. Some of the key needs of rural entrepreneurs have been highlighted as:

- Better, more locally-led access to finance;
- Harnessing local knowledge at all stages of policy formulation, delivery and evaluation;
- Developing better communication between national, regional and local actors to ensure the needs of entrepreneurs can be met;
- Acknowledgement that rising costs and Government revenue raising measures can hit rural businesses disproportionately compared to their urban counterparts e.g. fuel is often a bigger cost for rural businesses and entrepreneurs who need to transport produce or goods greater distances. (EU Rural Winter Review 2011)

---

[99] http://enrd.ec.europa.eu/policy-in-action/rural-development-policy-in-figures/rdp-monitoring-indicator-tables/financial-and-physical-indicators/en/financial-and-physical-indicators_en.cfm

Lack of quality broadband in rural areas is a considerable barrier to the diversification and growth of the rural economy in Ireland. Case studies show that several large firms have moved out of the South West of Ireland as a result of poor broadband speed and quality (ECORYS, 2010:237:241). The provision of quality broadband to rural areas must be a priority in the future if rural development is to be facilitated in a meaningful manner. The commitment to between 40Mbps and 30Mbps broadband speed in rural areas contained in the National Broadband Plan for Ireland is insufficient to encourage diversification and economic growth in rural areas. A rural broadband strategy should be developed and implemented by Government as a matter of priority to support the development and growth of rural enterprise and the creation of employment in rural areas. Priority must also be given to developing an integrated public transport system.

The negotiations for reform of the Common Agricultural Policy (CAP) from 2014 are on-going at the time of writing and will have a significant impact on the future of rural development. The reform of CAP will be situated within the broader objectives of the Europe 2020 strategy of inclusive growth, smart growth and sustainable growth. Supporting the shift towards a low carbon economy and promoting social inclusion, poverty reduction and economic development in rural areas are among the six priorities outlined by the European Commission. It is important that the reform of CAP moves towards a broader rural development, rural diversification and biodiversity focus rather than maintaining the narrow focus on agriculture, farms support payments and food organisation of the current CAP system. Across Europe the secondary and tertiary sectors[100] are now the main drivers of economic growth and job creation in rural regions. These sectors support activities such as tourism, niche manufacturing and business services (ECORYS: 2010). For rural areas to become sustainable in the long-term these sectors must form an integral part of any future rural development strategy both in Ireland and in Europe.

The establishment of the Commission for the Economic Development in Rural Areas[101] is a welcome step towards the development of a long-term strategy for rural development in Ireland. The Commission is tasked with developing a draft strategy guiding medium-term economic development of rural areas for the period

---

[100] The EU traditionally splits economic activities into three sectors. Primary sector includes agriculture, forestry and fisheries; secondary sector includes industry and construction, tertiary sector includes all services.
[101] For more information see www.ruralireland.ie

to 2025. It is crucial that rural communities be fully involved in the development of this strategy and that job creation and sustainable development in rural areas be promoted and supported.

Rural transport

'The rural transport network is vital for rural communities as a reliable and sustainable transport service. We will maintain and extend the Rural Transport Programme with other local transport services as much as possible' (Government of Ireland 2011: 63).

The lack of an accessible, reliable and integrated rural transport system is one of the key challenges facing people living in rural areas. Rural dwellers at present shoulder a disproportionate share of the burden of insufficient public transport, according to a recent report (EPA 2011: 10), 45 per cent of the rural district electoral divisions in Ireland have a minimal level of scheduled public transport services with varying frequency and timing. Among the main identified issues contributing to rural deprivation and depopulation are:

- access to secure and meaningful employment;
- availability of public transport in order to access employment and public services;
- access to childcare; and
- access to transport.

(McDonagh, Varley & Shortall 2009: 16)

Small rural firms and rural entrepreneurs need to be supported in developing their businesses and in overcoming the spatial disadvantage to benefit from the growth in the 'knowledge economy'. Sustainable, integrated public transport serving rural Ireland and reliable high speed broadband must be given priority in order to support rural businesses and the development of the rural economy through diversification and innovation. The current strategy of relying on 'global demand' and foreign direct investment (FDI) has led to a widening of the development gap between urban and rural areas. One of the major problems faced by the government in trying to develop and promote sustainable rural communities is the restricted opportunities in secondary labour markets in rural areas.

Car dependency and the reliance of rural dwellers on private car access in order to avail of public services, employment opportunities, healthcare and recreational activities is a key challenge for policy makers. Transport policy must be included in planning for services, equity and social inclusion. The social inclusion element of an integrated rural public transport system can no longer be ignored. The links between better participation, better health, access to public services, access to employment opportunities and a public integrated rural transport service have been documented (Fitzpatrick, 2006). Thus far there has been a failure to incorporate this knowledge fully into rural development policy. The Rural Transport Programme (RTP) (formerly the Rural Transport Initiative) has certainly improved access in some areas. However, the lack of a mainstream public transport system means that many rural areas are still not served. People with disabilities, women, older people, low income households and young people are target groups still at a significant disadvantage in rural areas in terms of access to public transport. Policy makers must ensure that local government and the local community are actively involved in developing, implementing and evaluating rural transport policies as national planning has not worked to date. In 2000 there was a call for a national rural transport policy and the prioritisation of government funding in this area (Farrell, Grant Sparks, 2000). Thirteen years later this policy has yet to be delivered. By 2021 it is estimated that the number of people with unmet transport needs could number 450,000 and of this group an estimated 240,000 will be from the target groups of vulnerable rural dwellers outlined above.

As a result of the publication of the Value for Money Review of the Rural Transport Programme in 2012 the National Transport Authority (NTA) is now responsible for integrated local and rural transport and for implementing the recommendations of the review. The National Integrated Rural Transport Committee was established to oversee six pilot programmes to integrate all state transport services in rural areas and provide access for the whole community to health services, education, employment and retail, recreational and community facilities and services. While the integration of rural transport with national transport policy is welcome, it is important that the models of best practice that emerge from the pilot programmes are put into a national rural transport strategy without delay. A mainstreamed rural public transport service is required to service those in need of rural public transport and those who are potential users. Investment in a national sustainable rural transport network is required to support rural development. It is required to ensure access to employment, access to services and to ensure rural economies are supported in terms of economic diversification.

Improved rural public transport and improved accessibility to services also provide Ireland with an opportunity to deliver a key change which would in turn help deliver a significant reduction of climate harming gas (CHG) emissions (Browne 2011: 12). This is all the more pressing in terms of Ireland's EU 2020 emissions target and CHG emissions from private vehicles. By investing in a sustainable national public transport system covering all rural areas government could significantly reduce CHG emissions in the long run.

Future of rural Ireland

Rural Ireland and rural communities are coming under unprecedented pressures and many are fighting for survival. The cumulative impact of measures introduced in the 2012 and 2013 Budgets are likely to have a negative effect on rural families[102] and on the weakest people in rural Ireland as inflation rises, unemployment persists, the carbon levy is increased and services are either reduced or have their charges increased. The allocation to the Rural Economy was reduced by 78 per cent in Budget 2013. Such removal of resources from rural areas will make it difficult to maintain viable communities. Small rural schools are under threat, losing up to 100 posts due to the increase in the pupil threshold for teacher allocations in these schools introduced in budget 2012. A value for money review of smaller schools is currently being undertaken by the Department of Education and concern has already been raised about the significant socio-economic impact of the possible closure of these schools on rural communities. Combined with the closure of 139 rural Garda stations in 2012 and 2013[103], the quality of life for rural dwellers and the sustainability of our rural communities is facing a significant threat.

The impact of sustained high levels of unemployment and subsequent high levels of emigration among young people in rural communities cannot be overestimated. It has led to a loss of young people in rural communities. This in turn means that the development of the rural economy has been hindered and it will continue to struggle in any future upturn due to the lack of skilled workers and the corresponding emergence of an ageing population. By failing to support young people to stay in their communities Government is potentially failing to address a key aspect of sustainability while supporting an emergence of an ageing demographic profile for rural areas which undermines both employment and growth targets (ECORYS, 2010:249).

Government is also failing to deal with the new challenges an ageing population brings to rural areas in relation to health services, social services and accessibility

---

[102] For further detail c.f. Social Justice Ireland (2012) *Budget 2013 Analysis and Critique* p.11
[103] 39 Garda Stations were closed in 2012 and a further 100 closures are planned for 2013.

for older and less mobile people. Employment, diversification of rural economies, adapting to demographic changes and supporting young people to stay in their communities are areas that need immediate attention from Government. *Social Justice Ireland* believes that we are now reaching a crucial juncture that requires key decisions in ensuring the necessary structures are put in place so that rural communities can survive.

Key Policy Priorities on Rural Development

- Recognise that rural Ireland involves far more than agriculture, develop policies to promote the diversification of the rural economy and support local enterprise and local employment.
- Adopt integrated rural development policies which prioritise access to public services and rural transport.
- Support young people to remain in their communities and implement policies to ensure rural areas can adapt to a changing demographic profile in the longer-term.
- Prioritise rolling out high speed broadband to rural areas.
- Invest in the development of renewable energies in order to ensure the sustainability of the rural environment.
- Ensure that policies do not impact disproportionately on rural dwellers e.g. carbon levy.
- Ensure all policies are based on equity and social justice and take account of rural disadvantage.

14. The Developing World

CORE POLICY OBJECTIVE: THE DEVELOPING WORLD

To ensure that Ireland plays an active and effective part in promoting genuine development in the developing world and to ensure that all Ireland's policies are consistent with such development

---

There are 920 million people in the Global South living on $1.25 a day. In a world with resources many times what is required to eliminate global poverty this situation is intolerable. There has been some progress in Asia but the situation has changed little since the 1980s in Sub-Saharan Africa and in Latin America.

An indication of the size of underdevelopment and inequality is outlined in the United Nations Human Development Report. Table 14.1 presents an insight into the scale and extent of these problems using UN data from the *2011 Human Development Report*.

Tables 14.1 and 14.2 show the sustained differences in the experiences of various regions in the world. There are sizeable differences in income levels (GNI per person) between the most developed countries of the world, those in the OECD, and the rest (i.e. the vast majority) of the world. These differences go beyond just income and are reflected in each of the indicators reported in both tables. Today, life expectancies are 25 years higher in the richest countries than in Sub-Saharan Africa. Similarly, the UN reports that more than one in three Southern Asians and Sub-Saharan Africans are unable to read.

These phenomena are equally reflected in high levels of absolute poverty and in the various mortality figures in table 14.2. The 2011 *Human Development Report* shows that almost 13 per cent of all children born in Sub-Saharan Africa died before their fifth birthday. The comparable figure for countries with a very high development index was 6. There has been some progress on this front as the deaths of children under five declined from 12.4 million in 1990 to 8.1 million in 2009. Despite many successful health aid programmes, however, maternal mortality rates are still very high in developing countries. Table 14.2 shows that there are 537

---

deaths per 100,000 live births in Least Developed Countries as against 16 in OECD countries

Table14.1:United Nations development indicators by region and worldwide			
Region	GNI per capita (US$ PPP)*	Life Expectancy at Birth (yrs)	Adult Literacy %**
Least Developed Countries	1,327	59.1	59.2
Arab States	8,554	70.5	72.9
East Asia + Pacific	6,466	72.4	93.5
Europe + Central Asia	12,004	71.3	98.0
L. America + Caribbean	10,119	74.4	91.0
South Asia	3,435	65.9	62.8
Sub-Saharan Africa	1,966	54.4	61.6
Very High HDI^	33,352	80.0	n/a
Worldwide total	**10,082**	**69.8**	**80.9**

Source: UNDP (2011: 130, 161)

Notes: * Gross National Income (GNI) Data adjusted for differences in purchasing power.

** Adult defined as those aged 15yrs and above.

^47 Countries including the OECD with very high human development indicators.

The comparable rates for Ireland are: GNI per capita: $29,322; Life expectancy: 80.6; adult literacy: not available

Table 14.2: Maternal and Infant Mortality Rates

Region	Maternal Mortality Ratio#	Under-5yrs mortality rate★
Least Developed Countries	537	120
Arab States	192	49
East Asia + Pacific	79	26
Europe + Central Asia	29	19
L. America + Caribbean	80	22
South Asia	252	69
Sub-Saharan Africa	619	129
Very High HDI^	16	6
Worldwide total	**176**	**58**

Source: UNDP 2011:139, 158

Notes: # ratio of the number of maternal deaths to the number of live births expressed per 100,000 live births

★ Number of deaths per thousand live births

^47 Countries including the OECD with very high human development indicators.

The comparable rates for Ireland are: Maternal mortality: 2 (per 100,000); Under 5 mortality: 4 (per 100,000).

UN millennium development goals

In response to these problems the UN Millennium Declaration was adopted in 2000 at the largest-ever gathering of heads of state. It committed countries – both rich and poor – to doing all they can to eradicate poverty, promote human dignity and equality and achieve peace, democracy and environmental sustainability. World leaders promised to work together to meet concrete targets for advancing development and reducing poverty by 2015 or earlier. Emanating from the Millennium Declaration, a set of Millennium Development Goals (MDGs) was agreed. These bind countries to do more in the attack on inadequate incomes, widespread hunger, gender inequality, environmental deterioration and lack of education, healthcare and clean water. They also include actions to reduce debt and increase aid, trade and technology transfers to poor countries. These goals and their related targets are listed in Annex 14.

Progress on the MDGs has been mixed. The UN suggests that East Asia and the Pacific are progressing satisfactorily but that overall human development is proceeding too slowly. For example, Target One committed to halving the number of people living on less than a dollar a day between 1990 and 2015. A recent report shows that in Sub-Saharan Africa this figure reduced only from 57 per cent to 48 per cent between 1990 and 2008. (CSO 2013:1:3).

While the achievement of the MDGs would represent real progress, it is widely acknowledged now that these goals were dictated by donors, written by donors, and made sense in the Aid Effectiveness agenda and process (Paris 2005 – Accra 2008 – Busan 2011), rather than in the development agenda. As a consequence, there was very little ownership of the MDGs by development actors, very few countries attempted to localise them and most of the MDGs national reports were actually drafted by officers at UNDP country offices. Even the innovative UN Financing for Development process never really owned the MDGs agenda. The UN had to create in 2003/4 the Millennium Campaign to help build ownership among governments and stakeholders. In the years ahead a different approach is needed, one that engages the people who are meant to benefit from this process. It is also essential that the focus be on development that is sustainable (environmentally, economically and socially) and on all countries and not just the poorest.

Social Justice Ireland believes that the international community needs to play a more active role in assisting less developed countries achieve their potential. The provision of additional financial support is central to this, as is engagement by all with the search for a sustainable development model for all.

Poverty and its associated implications remain the root causes of regional conflicts and civil wars in many of these poor countries. States and societies that are poor are prone to conflict. It is very difficult for governments to govern adequately when their people cannot afford to pay taxes and industry and trade are almost non-existent. Poverty is also a major cause of environmental degradation. Large-scale food shortages, migration and conflicts lead to environmental pressures.

Clearly, poverty in the southern world threatens the very survival of all peoples. It is the major injustice in a world that is not, as a unit, poor. Now more than ever the Irish government must exercise its voice within the European Union and in world institutions to ensure that the elimination of poverty becomes the focus of all policy development.

Trade and debt
A further implication of the earlier tables is to underscore the totally unacceptable division that currently exists between rich and poor regions of the world. The

persistence of this phenomenon is largely attributable to unfair trade practices and to the backlog of unpayable debt owed by the countries of the South to other governments, to the World Bank, the International Monetary Fund (IMF) and to commercial banks.

The effect of trade barriers cannot be overstated. By limiting or eliminating access to potential markets the Western world is denying poor countries substantial income. In 2002 at the UN Conference on Financing and Development Michael Moore, the President of the World Trade Organisation (WTO), stated that the complete abolition of trade barriers could 'boost global income by $2.8 trillion and lift 320 million people out of poverty by 2015'. Research by Oxfam (2002) further shows that goods from poor countries are taxed at four times the rate of goods from rich countries and that 120 million people could be lifted out of poverty if Africa, Latin America and Asia increased their share of world markets by just 1 per cent. It is clear that all countries would gain from trade reform. Such reform is now long overdue.

The high levels of debt experienced by Third World countries have disastrous consequences for the populations of indebted countries. Governments that are obliged to dedicate large proportions of their country's GDP to debt repayments cannot afford to pay for health and educational programmes for their people. The Global Development Finance Report 2012 (p40) shows that in 2010 the external debt owed by developing countries had increased by $437 million to just over $4 trillion. The cost of servicing this debt was almost $600 billion. It is not possible for these countries to develop the kind of healthy economies that would facilitate debt repayment when millions of their people are being denied basic healthcare and education and are either unemployed or earn wages so low that they can barely survive.

The debt relief initiatives of the past 10 years have been very welcome. These initiatives need to be further developed as there is growing concern that the debts of the poorest countries are beginning to rise again. It is now important that Ireland campaigns on the international stage to reduce the debt burden on poor countries. Given Ireland's current economic circumstances, the Irish population now has a greater appreciation of the implications of these debts and the merit in having them reduced.

Social Justice Ireland believes that Ireland's representatives at the World Bank and the IMF should be more critical of the policies adopted by these bodies. The

Department of Finance's annual reports on Ireland's involvement in these organisations reveal an alarming degree of unconditional support. According to these reports Ireland has unconditionally supported the World Bank's positions in all of the following areas: poverty reduction, gender issues, private-sector development, governance issues and corruption, military spending, post-conflict initiatives and environmentally sustainable projects. This level of support does not match Irish public opinion. NGOs, such as the Debt and Development Coalition, which have done much work on these issues, are very critical of the World Bank in its policies on issues such as poverty reduction, gender and the environment. We believe that this criticism of Government is well founded.

Ireland's commitment to ODA
The international challenge to significantly increase levels of Overseas Development Assistance (ODA) was set out by the former UN Secretary General Kofi Annan shortly after the adoption of the MDGs. He stated that: 'We will have time to reach the Millennium Development Goals – worldwide and in most, or even all, individual countries – but only if we break with business as usual. We cannot win overnight. Success will require sustained action across the entire decade between now and the deadline. It takes time to train the teachers, nurses and engineers; to build the roads, schools and hospitals; to grow the small and large businesses able to create the jobs and income needed. So we must start now. And we must more than double global development assistance over the next few years. Nothing less will help to achieve the goals.'

These comments lay down a clear challenge to the international community and *Social Justice Ireland* believes that Ireland can lead the way in responding to that challenge; even in the context of our current economic circumstances.

As table 14.3 shows, over time Ireland has achieved sizeable increases in our ODA allocation. In 2006 a total of €814 million (0.53 per cent of GNP) was allocated to ODA – reaching the interim target set by the Government. Budget 2008 further increased the ODA budget to reach €920.7 million (0.6 per cent of GNP). However, since then the ODA budget has been a focus of government cuts and has fallen by €298.7 million – more than 32.4 per cent.

Table 14.3: Ireland's net overseas development assistance, 2005-2013		
Year	**€m**	**% of GNP**
2005	578.5	0.42
2006	814.0	0.53
2007	870.9	0.53
2008	920.7	0.60
2009	722.2	0.55
2010	675.8	0.53
2011	657.0	0.50
2012	639.0	0.50
2013	662.0	0.48

Source: Irish Aid (2011:73) and various Budget Documents.

Administered by Irish Aid, the current aid programme can be summarised as having six key principles:

- **A poverty focus.** Ireland's ODA programme has as its absolute priority the reduction of poverty, inequality and exclusion in developing countries.
- **A geographic focus.** Since 1974 Ireland's ODA has had a strong geographic focus on Sub-Saharan Africa. Approximately 80 per cent of our ODA goes to Africa.
- **Untied aid.** Ireland's aid, unlike that of other countries, is 100 per cent untied. This implies that aid is not conditional in any way to the use of Irish goods, services or labour. This approach is very welcome and reflects much of the research on aid which highlights that tied aid is less effective in its impact on development than untied aid.
- **Partnership.** An implicit part of the delivery of Ireland's aid programme is the close relationship and partnership with recipient countries, other donors and international organisations, NGOs and missionaries. Partnership with the recipient countries is important in fostering a country's ownership of its own development and in encouraging the development of sustainable structures for indigenous public administration.
- **Effectiveness and accountability.** Using Programme Country Strategies and performance indicators, the effectiveness of Ireland's ODA Programme is monitored to determine the impact it is having on various development targets.

- **Policy coherence.** ODA policies interact with and complement other areas of Government policy, for example policy on agriculture, trade, environment, fiscal issues and the basic development model. Looking to the future, maintaining policy coherence between the Global South and the Global North will be a challenge. Sustainability requires recognition of our interdependence in all spheres.

Rebuilding our commitment to ODA and honouring the UN target should be important policy paths for Ireland to pursue in the years to come. Not only would its achievement be a major success for government – and an important element in the delivery of promises made – but it would also be of significance internationally. Ireland's success would not only provide additional assistance to needy countries but would also provide leadership to those other European countries which do not meet the target. In 2011 Ireland was ranked ninth in the list of Development Assistance Committee donors in terms of their contribution as a percentage of GNI (CSO 2013, 1:5). Despite the challenges, we believe that we should care for those less well-off, particularly the world's poorest people. We welcome the commitment of the Government to the 0.7 per cent of GNP target for Overseas Development Aid to be achieved by 2015.

HIV/AIDS

Target seven of the UN Millennium Development Goals committed the international community to have halted by 2015 and begun to reverse the spread of HIV/AIDS".

Published in November 2012, the UN World AIDS Report evaluated the progress being made. It shows that in 2011:

- 34 million people globally are living with HIV;
- 2.5 million people became infected with HIV;
- 1.7 million people died from AIDS related illness; and
- 65 per cent of all people living with HIV are in Sub-Saharan Africa, representing five per cent of all adults in the region.

However the Report shows very welcome progress in the fight against AIDS. There was a 50 per cent reduction in the rate of new HIV infections across 25 low and middle income countries. Half of all reductions in new HIV infections in the past two years have been among new born children. Sub-Saharan Africa has reduced

AIDS related deaths by one third in the last six years and increased the number of people on antiretroviral treatment by 59 per cent in the previous two years.

However, two regions experienced significant increases in AIDS-related deaths; Eastern Europe and Central Asia (21 per cent) and the Middle East and North Africa (17 per cent). The Report also notes that seven million people eligible for HIV treatment still do not have access to it and 72 per cent of children living with HIV who are eligible for treatment do not have access.

The Report notes that there is a 30 per cent gap in the resources needed to fully fund the AIDS response by 2015. The international community must take its commitment seriously and act with urgency.

Social Justice Ireland urges Government to meet its commitments in this area, despite Ireland's current economic difficulties, and to play a key role internationally in responding to this human crisis.

Key Policy Priorities
- Ensure that Ireland delivers on its promise to meet the United Nations target of contributing 0.7 per cent of GNP to Overseas Development Assistance by the EU deadline of 2015.
- Take a far more proactive stance at government level to ensuring that Irish and EU policies towards countries in the South are just.
- Continue to support the international campaign for the liberation of the poorest nations from the burden of the backlog of unpayable debt and take steps to ensure that further progress is made on this issue.
- Continue to support the implementation of the Millennium Development Goals. However, it is crucial that Ireland plays a prominent role in the development of Sustainable Development Goals for the planet and, within these, maintains the focus on the key issues originally addressed in the Millennium Development Goals.
- Engage pro-actively and positively in the Post-Rio+20 process referred to in chapter 12 on sustainability.
- Work for changes in the existing international trading regimes to encourage fairer and sustainable forms of trade. In particular, resource the development of Ireland's policies in the WTO to ensure that this goal is pursued.
- Ensure that the government takes up a leadership position within the European and international arenas to encourage other states to fund programmes and research aimed at resolving the AIDS/HIV crisis.

15. VALUES

'Few can doubt that we have been in a period of economic transition. The financial collapse has shown that many aspects of the "new economy", so widely praised just a few years ago, are unstable and unsustainable. For years we were told that we had entered a brand new world of unlimited financial possibilities, brought about by sophisticated techniques and technologies, starting with the internet and the information technology revolution, spread through the world by "globalisation" and managed by "financial engineers" who, armed with the tools of financial derivatives, could eliminate risk and uncertainty. Now we can see that the new financial structure was a house of cards built on sand, where speculation replaced enterprise, and the self-interest of many financial speculators came at the expense of the common good.

'While there were many factors that contributed to the financial meltdown of 2008, they start with the exclusion of ethics from economic and business decision making. The designers of the new financial order had complete faith that the "invisible hand" of market competition would ensure that the self-interested decisions of market participants would promote the common good.'

(Clark and Alford, 2010).

When the initial shock of the meltdown was absorbed many questions remained. Why did we fail to see the crash coming? Where did the wealth go? People want to know who benefitted from the meltdown. The people who are bearing the cost of the economic crash are obvious: the unemployed, emigrants who were forced to leave Ireland, poor, sick and vulnerable people who have had their income and social services cut. We are conscious of much fear, anxiety and anger in our communities. Today, more and more people are questioning how the policies and decisions of the past decade could have failed Irish society so badly. One critical question now is how do we prevent a recurrence of this type of economic crash? While some people advocate good regulation as the solution, others are sceptical and search for more radical approaches.

These reflections and questions bring to the fore the issue of values. Our fears are easier to admit than our values. Do we, as a people, in reality accept a two-tier society at the same time as we deride it in principle? The earlier chapters of this review document many aspects of this divided society. It is obvious that we are becoming an ever more unequal world. Scare resources are being taken from poorer people to offset the debts of bankers and speculators. This shift of resources is made possible by the support of our national value system. This dualism in our values allows us to accept the status quo. In reality, that means we find it acceptable that almost one sixth of the population is excluded from the mainstream of life within our society, while substantial resources and opportunities are channelled towards other groups in society. This dualism operates at the levels of individuals, communities and sectors.

To change this reality requires a fundamental change of values. We need a rational debate on the kind of society in which we want to live. To be realistic, this debate should challenge our values, and support us in articulating our goals and formulating the way forward. *Social Justice Ireland* wishes to contribute to this debate. We approach the task from the concerns and values of Christian thinking.

Christian Values
Christianity subscribes to the values of both human dignity and the centrality of the community. The person is seen as growing and developing in a context that includes other people and the environment. Justice is understood in terms of relationships. The Christian scriptures understand justice as a harmony that comes from fidelity to right relationships with God, people and the environment. A just society is one that is structured to promote these right relationships so that human rights are respected, human dignity is protected, human development is facilitated and the environment is respected and protected (Healy and Reynolds, 2003:188).

As our societies have grown in sophistication, the need for appropriate structures has become more urgent. The aspiration that everyone should 'enjoy the good life', and the goodwill to make it available to all, are essential ingredients in a just society. But this good life will not happen without the deliberate establishment of structures to facilitate its development. In the past charity, in the sense of alms-giving by some individuals, organisations and Churches on an arbitrary and *ad hoc* basis, was seen as sufficient to ensure that everyone could cross the threshold of human dignity. Calling on the work of social historians, it could be argued that charity in this sense was never an appropriate method for dealing with poverty. Certainly it is not a suitable methodology for dealing with the problems of today. As recent world disasters have graphically shown, charity and the heroic efforts of voluntary agencies cannot solve these problems on a long-term basis. Appropriate structures should be established to ensure that every person has access to the resources needed to live life with dignity.

Few people would disagree that the resources of the planet are for the use of the people – not just the present generation but also the generations still to come. In Old Testament times these resources were closely tied to land and water. A complex system of laws about the Sabbatical and Jubilee years (Lev 25: 1-22, Deut 15: 1-18) was devised to ensure, on the one hand, that no person could be disinherited and, on the other, that land and debts could not be accumulated. This system also ensured that the land was protected and allowed to renew itself.

These reflections raise questions about ownership. Obviously there was an acceptance of private property, but it was not an exclusive ownership. It carried social responsibilities. We find similar thinking among the leaders of the early Christian community. St John Chrysostom, (4ᵗʰ century), speaking to those who could manipulate the law so as to accumulate wealth to the detriment of others, taught that 'the rich are in the possession of the goods of the poor even if they have acquired them honestly or inherited them legally' (Homily on Lazarus). These early leaders also established that a person in extreme necessity has the right to take from the riches of others what he or she needs, since private property has a social quality deriving from the law of the communal purpose of earthly goods (*Gaudium et Spes* 69-71).

In more recent times, Pope Paul VI (1967) said 'private property does not constitute for anyone an absolute and unconditional right. No one is justified in keeping for his or her exclusive use what is not needed when others lack necessities … The right to property must never be exercised to the detriment of the common good' (*Populorum Progressio* No. 23). Pope John Paul II has further developed the understanding of ownership, especially in regard to the ownership of the means of production.

One of the major contributors to the generation of wealth is technology. The technology we have today is the product of the work of many people through many generations. Through the laws of patenting and exploration a very small group of people has claimed legal rights to a large portion of the world's wealth. Pope John Paul II questioned the morality of these structures. He said 'if it is true that capital as the whole of the means of production is at the same time the product of the work of generations, it is equally true that capital is being unceasingly created through the work done with the help of all these means of production'. Therefore, no one can claim exclusive rights over the means of production. Rather that right 'is subordinated to the right to common use, to the fact that goods are meant for everyone'. (*Laborem Exercens* No.14). As everyone has a right to a proportion of the goods of the country, society is faced with two responsibilities regarding economic resources. Firstly, each person should have sufficient to access the good life. Secondly, because the earth's resources are finite and because 'more' is not necessarily 'better', it is time that society considered the question of putting a limit on the wealth that any person or corporation can accumulate. Espousing the value of environmental sustainability requires a commitment to establish systems that ensure the protection of our planet.

Interdependence, mutuality, solidarity and connectedness are words that are used loosely today to express a consciousness which resonates with Christian values. All of creation is seen as a unit that is dynamic – each part is related to every other part, depends on it in some way and can also affect it. When we focus on the human family, this means that each person depends on others initially for life itself and subsequently for the resources and relationships needed to grow and develop. To ensure that the connectedness of the web of life is maintained, each person, depending on their age and ability, is expected to reach out to support others in ways that are appropriate for their growth and in harmony with the rest of creation. This thinking respects the integrity of the person while recognising that the person can achieve his or her potential only in right relationships with others and with the environment.

As a democratic society we elect our leaders regularly. This gives an opportunity to scrutinise the vision politicians have for our society. Because this vision is based on values it is worth evaluating the values being articulated and checking whether plans proposed are compatible with the values articulated and likely to deliver the society we desire.

Most people in Irish society would subscribe to the values articulated here. However these values will only become operative in our society when appropriate structures and infrastructures are put in place. These are the values that *Social Justice Ireland* wishes to promote. We wish to work with others to develop and support appropriate systems, structures and infrastructures which will give practical expression to these values in Irish society.

Annexes

Please note each annex has the corresponding number of the chapter
to which it relates.

Annex 3: Income distribution

To accompany chapter 3, this annex outlines details of the composition of poverty in Ireland over recent years and also affords an overview of Ireland's income distribution over the past two decades. The material underpins the development of many of the policy positions we have outlined in chapter 3.

Poverty – Who are the poor?

Two interchangeable phrases have been used to describe those living on incomes below the poverty line: *'living in poverty'* and *'at risk of poverty'*. The latter term is the most recent, introduced following a European Council meeting in Laeken in 2001 at which it was agreed that those with incomes below the poverty line should be termed as being 'at risk of poverty'.

The results of the *SILC* survey provided a breakdown of those below the poverty line. This section reviews those findings and provides a detailed assessment of the different groups in poverty.

Table A3.1 presents figures for the risk of poverty facing people when they are classified by their principal economic status (the main thing that they do). These risk figures represent the proportion of each group that are found to be in receipt of a disposable income below the 60 per cent median income poverty line. In 2011 the groups within the Irish population that were at highest risk of poverty included the unemployed and those not at work due to illness or a disability. Almost one in five classified as being 'on home duties', mainly women, have an income below the poverty line. The 'student and school attendees' category represents a combination of individuals living in poor families while completing their secondary education and those attending post-secondary education but with low incomes. The latter element of this group is not a major policy concern, given that such people are likely to only experience poverty while they gain education and skills which should ensure they live with sufficient income subsequently. Those still in school and experiencing poverty are more aligned to the issue of child poverty, which is examined later in this chapter.

Despite the increase in poverty between 2009 and 2011 (see chapter 3), the table also reveals the groups which have driven the overall reduction in poverty over the period (falling from 19.7 per cent to 16 per cent). Comparing 2003 and 2011, the poverty rate has fallen for all groups other than students while there have been pronounced falls among the welfare-dependent groups, i.e. the unemployed, retired and those not at work due to illness or a disability.

Table A3.1: Risk of poverty among all persons aged 16yrs + by principal economic status, 2003-2011

	2003	2006	2011
At work	7.6	6.5	6.5
Unemployed	41.5	44.0	30.6
Students and school attendees	23.1	29.5	31.4
On home duties	31.8	23.8	21.6
Retired	27.7	14.8	8.9
Unable to work as ill/disabled	51.7	40.8	22.8
Total	**19.7**	**17.0**	**16.0**

Source: CSO SILC reports (2005:11, 2007:15, 2013:9), using national equivalence scale

One obvious conclusion from table A3.1 is that any further progress in reducing poverty should be driven by continuing to enhance the adequacy of welfare payments. However, recent budgetary decisions seem likely to undermine progress in this area and have begun to drive poverty up once again (see analysis in chapter 3).

The working poor

Having a job is not, of itself, a guarantee that one lives in a poverty-free household. As table A3.1 indicates, 6.5 per cent of those who are employed are living at risk of poverty. Despite decreases in poverty among most other groups, poverty figures for the working poor have remained static, reflecting a persistent problem with low earnings. In 2011, almost 105,000 people in employment were still at risk of poverty.[104]

This is a remarkable statistic and it is important that policy makers begin to recognise and address this problem. Many working families on low earnings struggle to achieve a basic standard of living. Policies which protect the value of the minimum wage and attempt to keep those on that wage out of the tax net are relevant policy initiatives in this area. Similarly, attempts to increase awareness among low income working families of their entitlement to the Family Income Supplement (FIS) are also welcome, although evidence suggests that FIS is

---

[104] See table 3.7.

experiencing dramatically low take-up and as such has questionable long-term potential. However, one of the most effective mechanisms available within the present system to address the problem of the working poor would be to make tax credits refundable. We have addressed this proposal in chapter 3 of this review

Child poverty

Children are one of the most vulnerable groups in any society. Consequently the issue of child poverty deserves particular attention. Child poverty is measured as the proportion of all children aged 17 years or younger that live in households with an income below the 60 per cent of median income poverty line. The 2011 *SILC* survey indicates that 18.8 per cent were at risk of poverty and, as table A3.2 shows, in recent years the rate of child poverty has begun to increase (2013:9).

Table A3.2: Child Poverty – % Risk of Poverty Among Children in Ireland.				
	2006*	**2007***	**2009**	**2011**
Children, 0-17 yrs	19.0	17.4	18.6	18.8

Source: CSO (various editions of SILC)
Note: * 2006 and 2007 data exclude SSIA effect.

Translating the data in table A3.2 into numbers of children implies that in 2011 almost 190,000 children lived in households that were experiencing poverty.[105] The scale of this statistic is alarming. Given that our children are our future, this situation is not acceptable. Furthermore, the fact that such a large proportion of our children are living below the poverty line has obvious implications for the education system, for the success of these children within it, for their job prospects in the future and for Ireland's economic potential in the long-term.

Child benefit remains a key route to tackling child poverty and is of particular value to those families on the lowest incomes. Similarly, it is a very effective component in any strategy to improve equality and childcare. It is of concern, therefore, that child payments were cut in recent Budgets and has been highlighted as a potential target for future cuts in Budgets 2014 and 2015. On foot of these policies, it is likely that child poverty will increase further over the next few years. This will represent a major setback in an area in which the state already has a dismal record.

---

[105] See table 3.7.

Older people

According to the CSO's 2011 *Census Results* there were 535,393 people aged over 65 years in Ireland in 2011. Of these, more than a quarter live alone, comprising over 87,000 women and 49,000 men (CSO, 2012:26, 27). The 2011 figures also show that 9.7 per cent of those aged above 65 years live in relative income poverty (CSO, 2013:97).

Among all those in poverty, the retired have experienced the greatest volatility in their poverty risk rates. As table A3.3 shows, in 1994 some 5.9 per cent of this group were classified as poor. By 1998 the figure had risen to 32.9 per cent and in 2001 it peaked at 44.1 per cent. The most recent data record a decrease in poverty rates, mainly driven by increases in old age pension payments. While recent decreases are welcome, it remains a concern that so many of this county's senior citizens are living on so little.

Table A3.3: Percentage of older people (65yrs+) below the 60 per cent median income poverty line.

	1994	1998	2001	2003	2004	2005	2009	2011
Aged 65 +	5.9	32.9	44.1	29.8	27.1	20.1	9.6	9.7

Source: Whelan et al (2003: 28) and CSO (various editions of SILC)

The Ill / Disabled

As table A3.1 showed, those not employed due to illness or a disability are one of the groups at highest risk of poverty, with 22.8 per cent of this group classified in this category. Much like the experience of Ireland's older people, the situation of this group has varied significantly over the last decade and a half. The group's risk of poverty climbed from approximately three out of every ten persons in 1994 (29.5 per cent) to over six out of every ten in 2001 (66.5 per cent) before decreasing to approximately two out of every ten in the period 2008-2011. As with other welfare dependent groups, these fluctuations parallel a period where policy first let the value of payments fall behind wage growth before ultimately increasing them to catch-up.

Overall, although those not at work due to illness or a disability only account for a small proportion of those in poverty, their experience of poverty is high. Furthermore, given the nature of this group *Social Justice Ireland* believes there is an on-going need for targeted policies to assist them. These include job creation, retraining (see chapter 5 on work) and further increases in social welfare supports. There is also a very strong case to be made for introducing a non-means tested cost of disability allowance. This proposal, which has been researched and costed in detail by the National Disability Authority (NDA, 2006) and advocated by Disability Federation of Ireland (DFI), would provide an extra weekly payment of between €10 and €40 to somebody living with a disability (calculated on the basis of the severity of their disability). It seems only logical that if people with a disability are to be equal participants in society, the extra costs generated by their disability should not be borne by them alone. Society at large should act to level the playing field by covering those extra but ordinary costs. The *NESC Strategy 2006* also supported this policy development, urging that 'the Government strongly consider the case for a separate "cost of disability payment" that, in line with its analysis in the Developmental Welfare State, would be personally tailored and portable across the employment/non-employment divide' (NESC, 2005:168). In its *2008 Pre-Budget Submission* DFI anticipated such a scheme would cost €183 million per annum (DFI, 2007).

Poverty and education

The 2011 *SILC* results provide an interesting insight into the relationship between poverty and completed education levels. Table A3.4 reports the risk of poverty by completed education level and shows, as might be expected, that the risk of living on a low income is strongly related to low education levels. These figures underscore the relevance of continuing to address the issues of education disadvantage and early-school leaving (see chapter 9). Government education policy should ensure that these high risk groups are reduced. The table also suggests that when targeting anti-poverty initiatives, a large proportion should be aimed at those with low education levels, including those with low levels of literacy.[106]

Poverty by region and area

Recent SILC reports have provided a regional breakdown of poverty levels. The data presented in table A3.5 suggests an uneven national distribution of poverty. Using 2011 data, poverty levels are recorded as higher for the BMW region compared to the South and East. Previous SILC data (not updated in 2013) demonstrated that within these regions Dublin had less than one in ten people living in poverty while figures were twice this in the Mid-West, South-East and the Midlands. The table also reports that poverty is more likely to occur in rural areas than urban areas. In 2011 the risk of poverty in rural Ireland was 4.6 per cent higher than in urban Ireland with 'at risk' rates of 18.8 per cent and 14.2 per cent respectively.

---

[106] We address the issues of unemployment and completed education levels in chapter 5 and adult literacy in chapter 9.

Table A3.4:Risk of poverty among all persons aged 16yrs + by completed education level, 2007-2011

	2007	2009	2011
Primary or below	24.0	18.6	18.6
Lower secondary	20.7	19.7	21.9
Higher secondary	13.8	12.8	18.9
Post leaving certificate	10.9	9.1	14.5
Third level non-degree	8.4	4.9	10.8
Third level degree or above	4.2	4.8	5.4
Total	**15.8**	**14.1**	**16.0**

Source: CSO (2008:15; 2013:9), using national equivalence scale and excluding SSIA effect for 2007.

Table A3.5: Risk of poverty by region and area, 2005-2011

	2005	2009	2010	2011
Border, Midland and West	–	16.2	13.8	20.4
South and East	–	13.3	15.0	14.3
Urban Areas	16.0	11.8	12.5	14.2
Rural Areas	22.5	17.8	18.1	18.8
Overall Population	**18.5**	**14.1**	**14.7**	**16.0**

Source: CSO (2008:15; 2013:9) using national equivalence scale.

Deprivation: food and fuel poverty

Chapter 3 outlines recent data from the SILC survey on deprivation. To accompany this, we examine here two further areas of deprivation associated with food poverty and fuel poverty.

Food poverty

A report on the nature and extent of income-related constraints on food consumption in Ireland entitled *Food Poverty and Policy* defined food poverty as "the inability to access a nutritionally adequate diet and the related impacts on health, culture and social participation" (Society of St.Vincent de Paul et al, 2004). It found that poverty imposed three main constraints on their food consumption. It:

- affected food affordability, both in terms of the choice and quantity of food that can be bought and the share of the household budget that could be allocated to food;
- restricted access to food retail options in terms of transport and physical ability; and
- interacted with issues such as personal skills and knowledge, social pressure and cultural norms as well as with structural and economic constraints to produce a complex set of factors contributing to food poverty.

Consequently, the experience of food poverty among poor people was that they eat less well compared to better off groups, have difficulties accessing a variety of nutritionally balanced good quality and affordable foodstuffs, spend a greater proportion of their weekly income on food and may know what is healthy but are restricted by a lack of financial resources to purchase and consume it.

A subsequent study entitled *Food on a Low Income* (Safefood 2011) confirms these findings and notes that the priority of most poor people was to put food on the table rather than ensuring nutritional value.

Fuel poverty

Deprivation of heat in the home, often also referred to as fuel poverty, is another area of deprivation that has received attention in recent times. A 2007 policy paper from the Institute for Public Health (IPH) entitled *"Fuel Poverty and Health"* highlighted the sizeable direct and indirect effects on health of fuel poverty. Overall the IPH found that the levels of fuel poverty in Ireland remain 'unacceptably high' and that they are responsible for 'among the highest levels of excess winter mortality in Europe, with an estimated 2,800 excess deaths on the island over the winter months' (2007:7). They also highlighted the strong links between low income, unemployment and fuel poverty, with single person households and households headed by lone parents and pensioners found to be at highest risk. Similarly, the policy paper shows that older people are more likely to experience fuel poverty due to lower standards of housing coupled with lower incomes.

More recently, The Society of St Vincent de Paul's (SVP) has defined energy poverty as the inability to attain an acceptable level of heating and other energy services in the home due to a combination of three factors: income, energy price and energy efficiency of the dwelling. The 2011 SILC study found that 12.2 per cent of individuals were without heating at some stage in that year; a figure which is 21.7 per cent for those in poverty (see table 3.11). The SVP points out that households in receipt of energy-related welfare supports account for less than half of the estimated energy poor households and over time these payments have been cut while fuel prices and carbon taxes have increased. Clearly, welfare payments need to address energy poverty. Other proposals made by the SVP include detailed initiatives on issues such as: the prevention of disconnections; investing in efficiency measures in housing; education and public awareness to promote energy saving; and the compensation of Ireland's poorest households for the existing carbon tax.[107]

Social Justice Ireland supports the IPH's call for the creation of a full national fuel poverty strategy similar to the model currently in place in Northern Ireland. While Government has made some inroad into addressing low-income household energy issues through funding a local authority retrofitting campaign, progress to date has been limited given the scale of the problem and its implication for the health and wellbeing of many low-income families. Clearly, addressing this issue, like all issues associated with poverty and deprivation, requires a multi-faceted approach. The proposals presented by the SVP should form the core of such a fuel poverty strategy.

The experience of poverty: Minimum Income Standards

A 2012 research report from the Vincentian Partnership for Social Justice (VPSJ) and Trinity College Dublin casts new light on the challenges faced by people living on low incomes in Ireland (Collins et al, 2012). Entitled '*A Minimum Income Standard for Ireland*', the research establishes the cost of a minimum essential standard of living for individuals and households across the entire lifecycle, from children to pensioners. Subsequently the study calculates the minimum income households require to be able to afford this standard of living.

A minimum essential standard of living is defined as one which meets a person's physical, psychological, spiritual and social needs. To establish this figure, the research adopted a consensual budget standards approach whereby representative focus groups established budgets on the basis of a households minimum needs, rather than wants. These budgets, spanning over 2,000 goods, were developed for 16 areas of expenditure, including food, clothing, personal care, health related costs, household goods, household services, communication, social inclusion and participation, education, transport, household fuel, personal costs, childcare, insurance, housing, savings and contingencies. These budgets were then benchmarked, for their nutritional and energy content, to ensure they were sufficient to provide appropriate nutrition and heat for families, and priced. The

---

[107] We address these issues further in the context of a carbon tax in chapter 4.

study establishes the weekly cost of a minimum essential standard of living for five household types. These included: a single person of working age living alone; a two parent household with two children; a single parent household with two children; a pensioner couple; and a female pensioner living alone. Within these household categories, the analysis distinguishes between the expenditure for urban and rural households and between those whose members are unemployed or working, either part-time or full-time. The study also established the expenditure needs of a child and how these change across childhood.

Table A3.6 summarises the findings of this research for two adult plus two children urban households dependent on unemployment benefit. When the weekly income of these households is compared to the weekly expenditure they require to experience a basic standard of living, the report found that almost all these households received an inadequate income. These households have to cut back on the basics to make ends meet (Collins et al, 2012:105-107). The report found similar results for rural welfare dependent households. It also found that many low income working households, in particular those working at the minimum wage, were unable to earn sufficient income to afford a basic standard of living – a phenomenon which underscores the focus on the scale of the working poor problem earlier in this review.

Table A3.6: Comparisons of minimum expenditure levels with certain income levels for a 2 adult 2 child urban household (€ per week)

Ages of Children	9 Months & Pre-School	Both Pre-School	Pre & Primary School	Both Primary School	Primary & Second Level	Both Second Level
Household Expenditure	464.03	421.14	451.5	481.87	547.77	613.67
Household Income	437.02	437.02	440.87	444.71	446.73	448.75
Income – Expenditure	**-27.02**	**+15.88**	**-10.64**	**-37.17**	**-101.04**	**-164.92**
Income Adequacy	Inadequate	Adequate	Inadequate	Inadequate	Inadequate	Inadequate

Source: Collins et al, 2012: 105-107.

Overall this study, which complements earlier research by the VPSJ (2006, 2010), contains major implications for Government policy if poverty is to be eliminated. These include the need to address child poverty, the income levels of adults on social welfare, the 'working poor' issue and access to services ranging from social housing to fuel for older people and the distribution of resources between urban and rural Ireland.[108]

Ireland's income distribution: trends from 1987-2010

The results of studies by Collins and Kavanagh (1998, 2006) combined with the recent CSO income figures provide a useful insight into the pattern of Ireland's income distribution over 23 years. Table A3.7 combines the results from these studies and reflects the distribution of income in Ireland as tracked by five surveys. Overall, across the period 1987 – 2009 income distribution was very static. However, within the period there were some notable changes, with shifts in distribution towards higher deciles in the period 1994/95 to 2004.

Table A3.7: The distribution of household disposable income, 1987-2009 (%)

Decile	1987	1994/95	1999/00	2004	2009
Bottom	2.28	2.23	1.93	2.10	2.39
2nd	3.74	3.49	3.16	3.04	3.64
3rd	5.11	4.75	4.52	4.27	5.03
4th	6.41	6.16	6.02	5.69	6.31
5th	7.71	7.63	7.67	7.43	7.66
6th	9.24	9.37	9.35	9.18	9.11
7th	11.16	11.41	11.20	11.11	10.96
8th	13.39	13.64	13.48	13.56	12.94
9th	16.48	16.67	16.78	16.47	16.15
Top	24.48	24.67	25.90	27.15	25.83
Total	100.00	100.00	100.00	100.00	100.00

Source: Collins and Kavanagh (2006:156) and CSO (2006:18-19, 2010: 24-58).
Note: Data for 1987, 1994/95 and 1999/00 are from various Household Budget Surveys. 2004 and 2009 data from SILC.

Using data from the two ends of this period, 1987 and 2009, chart A3.1 examines the change in the income distribution over the intervening years. While much

---

[108] Data from these studies are available at www.budgeting.ie

changed in Ireland over that period, income distribution did not change significantly. Compared with 1987, only two deciles saw their share of the total income distribution increase – the bottom decile and the top decile. However, the change for the former is small (+0.11 per cent) while the change for the latter is more notable (+1.34 per cent). All other deciles witnessed a small decrease in their share of the national income distribution.

Chart A3.1: Change in Ireland's Income Distribution, 1987-2009

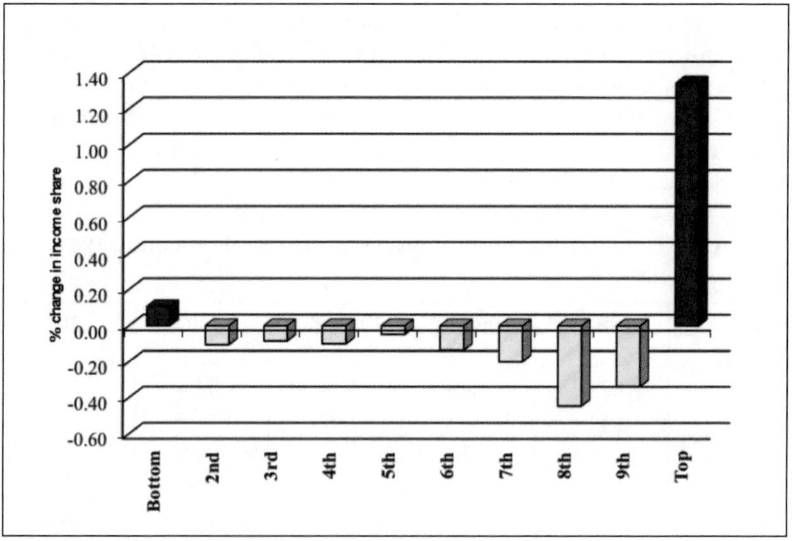

Source: Calculated from CSO, 2010:24-25

Looking at only the last six available SILC surveys (2004 – 2009), the CSO found that the share of income of the bottom two deciles increased. Similar to the earlier changes in the poverty figures, it is likely that these improvements were related to budgetary policy over that period which increased social welfare payments. The CSO data show that households in these deciles receive a large proportion of their income from social welfare payments (CSO, 2010: 24-25). As shown earlier, during this period they experienced increases in welfare payments representing a partial catch-up in their relative income position given the declines experienced in the late 1990s.

Preliminary data for 2011 suggests that changes in this reasonably static income distribution picture may have occurred. Although precise information on each decile share is not available yet, the CSO has reported that the overall level of income inequality has grown. Using the Gini coefficient measure of inequality, which ranges from 0 to 100, with higher scores indicating greater inequality, Ireland's inequality levels grew from 29.3 in 2009 to 31.1 in 2011. Furthermore, the initial 2011 data indicates that the share of the top 20 per cent of households has climbed further to reach 4.9 times the share of the bottom 20 per cent. The comparable ratio in 2009 was 4.3 times.

Annex 4: Taxation

This annex outlines the background data on taxation in Ireland. It compares the overall level of taxation in Ireland to that of other European countries and trace how this has changed over time. It then examines trends in income tax levels, outlines and compares income tax levels across the income distribution and examines the distribution of indirect taxes on household.

Ireland's total tax-take up to 2010

The most recent comparative data on the size of Ireland's total tax-take has been produced by Eurostat (2012) and is detailed alongside that of 26 other EU states in table A4.1. The definition of taxation employed by Eurostat comprises all compulsory payments to central government (direct and indirect) together with social security contributions (employee and employer) and the tax receipts of local authorities. [109] The tax-take of each country is established by calculating the ratio of total taxation revenue to national income as measured by gross domestic product (GDP). Table A4.1 also compares the tax-take of all EU member states against the average tax take of 35.6 per cent.

Of the EU-27 states, the highest tax ratios can be found in Denmark, Sweden, Belgium, France, Italy and Finland while the lowest are in Lithuania, Romania, Latvia, Bulgaria, Slovakia and Ireland. Overall, Ireland has the sixth lowest tax take, at 28.2 per cent, some 7.4 per cent below the EU average. Furthermore, Ireland's overall tax take has continued to fall over the past few years with the 2010 figure (which is the same as that recorded for 2009) representing the lowest tax take since Eurostat began compiling records in 1995 (see chart A4.1). The increase in the overall level of taxation between 2002 and 2006 can be explained by short-term increases in construction related taxation sources (in particular stamp duty and construction related VAT) rather than any underlying structural increase in taxation levels.

---

[109] See Eurostat (2012:268-269) for a more comprehensive explanation of this classification.

Table A4.1: Total tax revenue as a % of GDP, for EU-27 Countries in 2010

Country	% of GDP	+/- from average	Country	% of GDP	+/- from average
Denmark	47.6	12.0	Estonia	34.2	-1.4
Sweden	45.8	10.2	**Ireland GNP**	33.9	-1.7
Belgium	43.9	8.3	Czech Rep	33.8	-1.8
France	42.5	6.9	Malta	33.3	-2.3
Italy	42.3	6.7	Spain	31.9	-3.7
Finland	42.1	6.5	Poland	31.8	-3.8
Austria	42.0	6.4	Portugal	31.5	-4.1
Netherlands	38.8	3.2	Greece	31.0	-4.6
Germany	38.1	2.5	**Ireland GDP**	28.2	-7.4
Slovenia	38.0	2.4	Slovakia	28.1	-7.5
Hungary	37.7	2.1	Bulgaria	27.4	-8.2
Luxembourg	37.1	1.5	Latvia	27.3	-8.3
Cyprus	35.7	0.1	Romania	27.2	-8.4
United Kingdom	35.6	0.0	Lithuania	27.1	-8.5

Source: Eurostat (2012:180) and CSO National Income and Expenditure Accounts (2012:3)
Notes: All data is for 2010. EU-27 average is 35.6 per cent.

Chart A4.1: Trends in Ireland and EU-27 overall taxation levels, 2000-2010

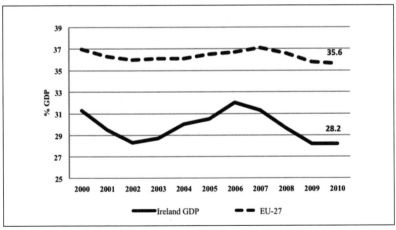

Source: Eurostat (2012:180) and CSO National Income and Expenditure Accounts (2012:3)

GDP is accepted as the benchmark against which tax levels are measured in international publications. However, it has been suggested that for Ireland gross national product (GNP) is a better measure. This is because Ireland's large multinational sector is responsible for significant profit outflows which, if included (as they are in GDP but not in GNP), exaggerate the scale of Irish economic activity.[110] Commenting on this, Collins stated that 'while it is clear that multinational profit flows create a considerable gap between GNP and GDP, it remains questionable as to why a large chunk of economic activity occurring within the state should be overlooked when assessing its tax burden' and that 'as GDP captures all of the economic activity happening domestically, it only seems logical, if not obvious, that a nations' taxation should be based on that activity' (2004:6).[111] He also noted that using GNP will understate the scale of the tax base and overstate the tax rate in Ireland because it excludes the value of multinational activities in the economy but does include the tax contribution of these companies. In this way, the size of the tax-take from Irish people and firms is exaggerated.

Social Justice Ireland believes that it would be more appropriate to calculate the tax-take by comparing either GNP or GNI (Gross National Income) and using an adjusted tax-take figure which excludes the tax paid by multi-national companies. As figures for their tax contribution are currently unavailable, we have simply used the unadjusted GNP figures and presented the results in table A4.1. In 2010 this stood at 33.9 per cent. This also suggests to international observers and internal policy makers that the Irish economy is not as tax-competitive as it truly is. This issue should be addressed by Government and appropriate adjustments made when calculating Ireland's tax-take as a percentage of GNP.

In the context of the figures in table A4.1 and the trends in chart A4.1, the question needs to be asked: if we expect our economic and social infrastructure to catch up to that in the rest of Europe, how can we do this while simultaneously gathering less taxation income than it takes to run the infrastructure already in place in most of those other European countries? In reality, we will never bridge the social and economic infrastructure gaps unless we gather a larger share of our national income and invest it in building a fairer and more successful Ireland.

---

[110] Collins (2004:6) notes that this is a uniquely Irish debate and not one that features in other OECD states such as New Zealand where noticeable differences between GDP and GNP also occur.
[111] See also Collins (2011:90) and Bristow (2004:2) who make a similar argument.

Effective tax rates
To complement the trends and data outlined in chapter 4, it is possible to focus on the changes to the levels of income taxation in Ireland over the past decade and a half.'Effective tax rates' are central to any understanding of these personal/income taxation trends. These rates are calculated by comparing the total amount of income tax a person pays with their pre-tax income. For example, a person earning €50,000 who pays a total of €10,000 in tax, PRSI and USC will have an effective tax rate of 20 per cent. Calculating the scale of income taxation in this way provides a more accurate reflection of the scale of income taxation faced by earners.

Following Budget 2013 we have calculated effective tax rates for a single person, a single income couple and a couple where both are earners. Table A4.2 presents the results of this analysis. For comparative purposes, it also presents the effective tax rates which existed for people with the same income levels in 2000 and 2008.

In 2013, for a single person with an income of €15,000 the effective tax rate will be 2.7 per cent, rising to 15.1 per cent on an income of €25,000 and 42.9 per cent on an income of €120,000. A single income couple will have an effective tax rate of 2.7 per cent at an income of €15,000, rising to 8.3 per cent at an income of €25,000, 26.6 per cent at an income of €60,000 and 39.3 per cent at an income of €120,000. In the case of a couple, both earning and a combined income of €40,000, their effective tax rate is 9.9 per cent, rising to 33.8 per cent for combined earnings of €120,000.

Table A4.2: Effective Tax Rates following Budgets 2000 / 2008 / 2013			
Income Levels	Single Person	Couple 1 earner	Couple 2 Earners
€15,000	13.9% / 0.0% / 2.7%	2.5% / 0.0% / 2.7%	0.8% / 0.0% / 2.0%
€20,000	13.9% / 0.0% / 11.1%	8.3% / 2.7% / 7.6%	6.1% / 0.0% / 2.3%
€25,000	24.0% / 8.3% / 15.1%	12.3% / 2.9% / 8.3%	11.0% / 0.0% / 2.5%
€30,000	28.4% / 12.9% / 17.7%	15.0% / 5.1% / 9.5%	14.6% / 1.7% / 5.6%
€40,000	33.3% / 18.6% / 24.8%	20.2% / 9.4% / 14.9%	17.5% / 3.6% / 9.9%
€60,000	37.7% / 27.5% / 33.9%	29.0% /19.8% / 26.6%	28.0% /12.2% / 17.7 %
€100,000	41.1% / 33.8% / 41.1%	35.9% /29.2% / 36.8%	35.9% /23.8% / 30.2 %
€120,000	41.9% / 35.4% / 42.9%	37.6% /31.6% / 39.3%	37.7% /27.2% / 33.8 %

Source: Social Justice Ireland (2012:8).
Notes: Tax = income tax + PRSI + levies/USC
           Couples assume 2 children and 65%/35% income division

While these rates have increased since 2008 for almost all earners they are still low compared to those which prevailed in 2000. Few people complained at that time about tax levels being excessive and the recent increases should be seen in this context. Taking a longer view, chart A4.2 illustrates the downward trend in effective tax rates for three selected household types since 1997. These are a single earner on €25,000; a couple with one earner on €40,000; and a couple with two earners on €60,000. Their experiences are similar to those on other income levels and are similar to the effective tax rates of the self-employed over that period (see Department of Finance, Budget 2013, taxation annex).

Chart A4.2: Effective tax rates in Ireland, 1997–2013

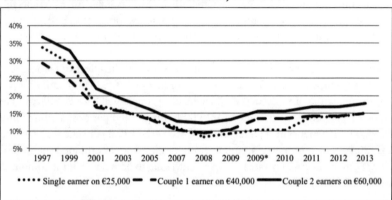

Source: Department of Finance, Budget 2013 and Social Justice Ireland (2012:8).
Notes: Tax = income tax + PRSI + levies/USC
Couples assume 2 children and 65%/35% income division
2009*= Supplementary Budget 2009 (April 2009)

The two 2009 Budgets produced notable increases in these effective taxation rates. Both Budgets required government to raise additional revenue and with some urgency – increases in income taxes providing the easiest option. Similarly, the introduction of the USC in Budget 2011 increased these rates, most notably for lower income earners. Budget 2012 provided a welcome reduction for the lowest earners through raising the income level at which the USC applies. Despite that change, the employee PRSI increase in Budget 2013 targeted lowest income earners hardest and increased effective taxation rate for almost all workers.

However, income taxation is not the only form of taxation and, as we highlight in chapter 4, there are many in Ireland with potential to contribute further taxation revenues to support the on-going budgetary adjustments.

Income taxation and the income distribution

An insight into the distribution of income taxpayers across the income distribution is provided each year by the Revenue Commissioners in its Statistical Report. The Revenue's ability to profile taxpayers is limited by the fact that it only examines 'tax cases' which may represent either individual taxpayers or couples who are jointly assessed for tax. A further disadvantage of these figures is that there is a considerable delay between the tax year being reported on and the publication of the data for that year. The latest data, published in 2012, is for 2010.

The progressivity of the Irish income taxation system is well demonstrated in table A4.3 – as incomes increase the average income tax paid also increases. The table also underscores the issues highlighted earlier in chapter 3, that a large proportion of the Irish population survive on low incomes. Summarising the data in the table, almost 20 per cent of cases have an income below €10,000, 55 per cent have an income below €30,000 and 90 per cent of cases are below €75,000. At the top of the income distribution, 5 per cent of households (almost 100,000) receive an income in excess of €100,000. The table also highlights the dependence of the income taxation system on higher income earners, with 27 per cent of income tax coming from cases with incomes of between €60,000 and €100,000 and 46 per cent of income tax coming from cases with incomes above €100,000. While such a structure is not unexpected, a symptom of progressivity rather than a structural problem, it does underscore the need to broaden the tax base beyond income taxes – a point we have made for some time and develop further in chapter 4.

Indirect taxation and the income distribution

As chapter 4 shows, the second largest source of taxation revenue is VAT and the third largest is excise duties. These indirect taxes tend to be regressive – meaning they fall harder on lower income individuals and households (Barrett and Wall, 2006:17-23; Collins, 2011: 102-103).

Table A4.3: Income taxation and Ireland's income distribution, 2010					
From €	**To €**	**No. of cases**	**Av. income**	**Av. Tax**	**% Total Tax**
–	10,000	387,175	€4,399	€12	0.05
10,000	12,000	71,719	€11,026	€35	0.03
12,000	15,000	109,788	€13,523	€56	0.06
15,000	17,000	72,768	€16,009	€70	0.05
17,000	20,000	122,603	€18,517	€114	0.14
20,000	25,000	200,619	€22,495	€476	0.97
25,000	27,000	74,917	€25,988	€892	0.68
27,000	30,000	102,601	€28,492	€1,196	1.25
30,000	35,000	152,930	€32,454	€1,738	2.71
35,000	40,000	137,680	€37,439	€2,554	3.58
40,000	50,000	198,857	€44,648	€4,242	8.59
50,000	60,000	130,636	€54,645	€6,665	8.87
60,000	75,000	124,574	€66,898	€9,497	12.05
75,000	100,000	102,146	€85,621	€14,659	15.26
100,000	150,000	63,191	€118,783	€25,612	16.49
150,000	200,000	17,101	€170,895	€43,216	7.53
200,000	275,000	9,308	€231,717	€62,667	5.94
Over	275,000	9,830	€522,062	€157,165	15.74
Totals		**2,088,443**	**€37,218**	**€4,700**	**100.00**

Source: Calculated from Revenue Commissioners (2012).

An assessment of how these indirect taxes affect households across the income distribution is possible using data from the CSO's Household Budget Survey (HBS), which collects details on household expenditure and income every five years. Chart A4.3 and table A4.4 presents the results of Barrett and Wall's examination of the 2004/05 HBS data. [112] They show that indirect taxation consumes more than 20 per cent of the lowest decile's income and more than 18 per cent of the income of the bottom five deciles. These findings reflect the fact that lower income households tend to spend almost all of their income while higher income households both spend and save.

Dealing specifically with VAT, the study also found that lower income households paid more at the 21 per cent (now 23 per cent) rate than did higher income

---

[112] A subsequent study by Leahy et al (2010) found similar results but provides less data on the income distribution impacts of indirect taxes.

households. Consequently in our *Analysis and Critique of Budget 2012*, *Social Justice Ireland* highlighted the way that that Budget's increase in VAT was regressive and unnecessarily undermined the living standards of low income households. Other, fairer approaches to increasing taxation were available and should have been taken.

Chart A4.3: VAT and excise duties as a % of household income, by decile

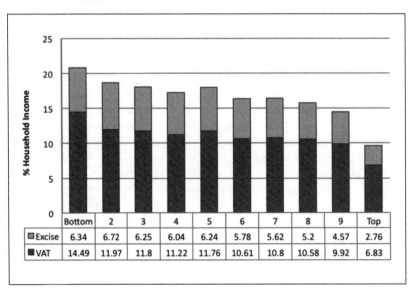

	Bottom	2	3	4	5	6	7	8	9	Top
▦Excise	6.34	6.72	6.25	6.04	6.24	5.78	5.62	5.2	4.57	2.76
■VAT	14.49	11.97	11.8	11.22	11.76	10.61	10.8	10.58	9.92	6.83

Source: Barrett and Wall (2006:19-20).

Table A4.4:VAT Payments at reduced and standard rates as a % of income, by selected deciles

% income paid in VAT	Bottom	2nd	3rd	8th	9th	Top
@ 13.5% rate (reduced)	3.6	3.0	2.7	2.0	1.8	1.3
@ 21% rate (standard)*	11.5	9.1	9.4	8.9	8.4	5.8

Source: Barrett and Wall (2006:19-20).
Note: * Rate subsequently decreased and increased – latest increase to 23% in Budget 2012.

Annex 5:
Work, Unemployment and Job Creation

Measuring the labour market

When considering terms such as 'employment' and 'unemployment' it is important to be precise about what these terms mean. Two measurement sources are often quoted as the basis for labour market data, the *Quarterly National Household Survey* (QNHS) and the *Live Register*. The former is considered the official and most accurate measure of employment and unemployment, although, unlike the monthly live register unemployment data, it appears only four times a year.

The CSO's QNHS unemployment data use the definition of 'unemployment' supplied by the International Labour Office (ILO). It lists as unemployed only those people who, in the week before the survey, were unemployed *and* available to take up a job *and* had taken specific steps in the preceding four weeks to find employment. Any person who was employed for at least *one hour* is classed as employed. By contrast, the live register counts everybody 'signing-on' and includes part-time employees (those who are employed up to three days a week), those employed on short weeks, seasonal and casual employees entitled to Jobseekers Assistance or Benefit.[113]

Labour force trends

The dramatic turnaround in the labour market after 2007 (see chapter 5) contrasts with one of the major achievements of the preceding 20 years, the increase in employment and the reduction in unemployment, especially long-term unemployment. In 1992 there were 1,165,200 people employed in Ireland. That figure increased by almost one million to peak at 2,169,600 in mid-2007. During early 2006 the employment figure exceeded two million for the first time in the history of the state. Overall, the size of the Irish labour force has expanded significantly and is today over 2.16 million people, almost 800,000 more than in 1992 (see chart A5.1).

However, in the period since 2007 emigration has returned, resulting in a decline in the labour force. Initially this involved recently arrived migrants returning home but was then followed by the departure of native Irish. CSO figures indicate that

---

[113] See Healy and Collins (2006) for a further explanation of measurement in the labour market.

during the first quarter of 2009 the numbers employed fell below two million and that since then they have continued to fall, reaching just over 1.8m in 2012 (see chart A5.1).

Chart A5.1:The Numbers of People in the Labour Force and Employed in Ireland, 1991-2012

Source: CSO, QNHS various editions

As chart A5.2 shows, the period from 1993 was one of decline in unemployment. By mid-2001 Irish unemployment reached its lowest level in living memory at 3.6 per cent of the labour force. Since then the international recession and domestic economic crisis have brought about increases in the rate. During 2006 unemployment exceeded 100,000 for the first time since 1999, with a total of 105,100 people recorded as unemployed in mid-2006. As chart A5.2 shows, it exceeded 200,000 in early-2009, 300,000 in 2010 and peaked at 328,000 in 2011. The chart also highlights the rapid growth in the number of long-term unemployed (those unemployed for more than 12 months).The CSO reports that there are now over 193,000 people in long-term unemployment and that this figure has increased six-fold since 2007. Quite simply, given the on-going economic crisis, many of those who entered unemployment between 2007 and 2010 have remained unemployed for more than 12 months and have therefore become long-term unemployed.

Chart A5.2: The Numbers of Unemployed and Long-Term Unemployed in Ireland, 1991-2012

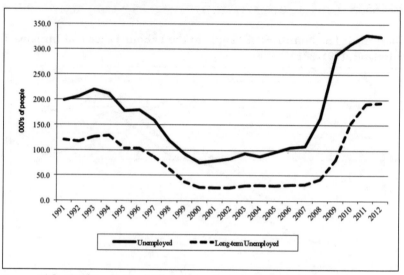

Source: CSO, QNHS various editions

Annex 8:
Social Determinants of Health and Health Inequalities

Social determinants of health

Health is not just about healthcare. For a number of years the World Health Organisation (WHO) has been concerned with what it terms the 'social determinants of health'. The WHO Commission established to study this topic produced its final report in 2008. This Commission found that health is influenced by factors such as poverty, food security, social exclusion and discrimination, poor housing, unhealthy early childhood conditions, poor educational status and low occupational status. These are important determinants of most diseases, deaths and health inequalities between and within countries. A follow up conference was held in Brazil in October 2011. At the end of the conference the Heads of Government 'expressed their determination to achieve social and health equity through action on the social determinants of health and well-being by a comprehensive inter-sectoral approach.' (WHO 2011: no. 1)

They noted that: 'Health inequities arise from the societal conditions in which people are born, grow, live, work and age, referred to as social determinants of health. These include early years' experiences, education, economic status, employment and decent work, housing and environment, and effective systems of preventing and treating ill health.' They continued: "We are convinced that action on these determinants, both for vulnerable groups and the entire population, is essential to create inclusive, equitable, economically productive and healthy societies. Positioning human health and well-being as one of the key features of what constitutes a successful, inclusive and fair society in the 21st century is consistent with our commitment to human rights at national and international levels.' (WHO 2011: no.6)

The reflections and outcomes of the conference are very relevant to the situation in Ireland at this time.

Health inequalities in Ireland

The Public Health Alliance of the Island of Ireland (PHAI) has provided a welcome insight into the extent of health inequalities in Ireland. This group is a north-south alliance of non-governmental organisations, statutory bodies, community and voluntary groups, advocacy bodies and individuals committed to work together for a healthier society by improving health and tackling health inequalities. It has published two detailed reports in the past decade: *Health in Ireland – An Unequal State* (2004) and *Health Inequalities on the island of Ireland: the facts, the causes, the remedies* (2007). These reports gather together the baseline information on health inequalities in Ireland and their findings merit serious attention. They detail striking differences in life expectancy and premature death between people in different socio-economic groups. For example:

- Between 1989 and 1998 the death rates for all causes of death were over three times higher in the lowest occupational class than in the highest.

- The death rates for all cancers among the lowest occupational class is over twice as high for the highest class; it is nearly three times higher for strokes, four times higher for lung cancer, six times for accidents.

- Perinatal mortality is three times higher in poorer families than in richer families.

- Women in the unemployed socio-economic group are more than twice as likely to give birth to low birth weight children as women in the higher professional group.

- The incidence of chronic physical illness has been found to be two and a half times higher for poor people than for the wealthy.

- Men in unskilled jobs were four times more likely to be admitted to hospital for schizophrenia than higher professional workers.

- The rate of hospitalisation for mental illness is more than six times higher for people in the lower socio-economic groups than for those in the higher groups.

- The incidence of male suicide is far higher in the lower socio-economic groups than for those in the higher groups.

- The most recent Survey of Lifestyle, Attitudes and Nutrition (SLAN) found that poorer people are more likely to smoke cigarettes, drink alcohol excessively, take less exercise and eat less fruit and vegetables than richer people. Poorer people's lifestyle and behavioural choices are directly limited by their economic and social circumstances.

The reports also found that some groups experience particularly extreme health inequalities. These include:

- Members of the Traveller community live between 10 and 12 years less than the population as a whole.[114]
- The rate of sudden infant deaths among Travellers is 12 times higher than for the general population.
- Many expectant mothers among asylum seekers in direct provision suffer malnutrition, babies in these communities suffer ill-health because of diet, many adults experience hunger.
- Homeless people experience high incidence of ill-health – a 1997 report found that 40 per cent of hostel dwellers had a serious psychiatric illness, 42 per cent had problems of alcohol dependency, and 18 per cent had other physical problems.
- The incidence of injecting drug use is almost entirely confined to people from the lower socio-economic groups.

The PHAI also compared the health of people in Ireland to that of the 14 other EU states (pre-EU enlargement). It found that Irish people compare badly with the experience of citizens in other EU counties. These findings included:

- Mortality rates in Ireland are worse than the EU average for a range of illnesses, particularly diseases of the circulatory system, breast cancer and death from smoking related illnesses
- Irish women have almost twice the rate of death from heart disease as the average European woman.
- The incidences of mortality for Irish women for cancers of the breast, colon, larynx and oesophagus and for ischaemic heart disease are among the highest in the EU.
- At the age of 65 Irish men have the lowest life expectancy in the EU. (PHAI, 2004:3-4).

In its 2007 study the PHAI summarised what the international research literature highlights as the most important influences on health and the causes of health inequalities. These are the economic, social and political environments in which people live including:

---

[114] For much greater detail on age-specific mortality rates among Travellers and a range of other Traveller health statistics cf. *All Ireland Traveller Health Study: Our Geels*, September 2010, published by the All Ireland Traveller Health Study Team, School of Public Health, Physiotherapy and Population Science, University College Dublin.

- level of income;
- early life experience;
- access to education and employment;
- food and nutrition;
- work opportunities;
- housing and environmental conditions; and levels of stress and social support.

Furthermore, it noted that "research has also established that the greatest determinant of health is the level of income equality in society. Societies with more equal distribution of income across the population have higher average life expectancies and better health outcomes than less equal societies" (PHAI, 2007:8).

The Pfizer Health Index 2012 looked at health information for over 6,000 Irish people collected over six years. It found that those suffering from any of a wide range of conditions (which included heart disease, cancer, depression and arthritis) are more likely to from a more socially disadvantaged background:

'Those from a lower socio-economic background are over-represented while many middle class people (ABC1) are under-represented' ((Pfizer, 2012: 20).

Analysis of Census 2011 data by the CSO confirms the relationship between social class and health: while 95% of people in the top social class enjoyed good or very good health, this proportion fell across the social groups to below 75% in social class 7 (CSO, 2012a).

Life expectancy at birth for both men and women in Ireland is lower in the most deprived geographical areas than in the most affluent (CSO, 2010). For example, life expectancy at birth of men living in the most deprived areas was 73.7 years (in 2006/07) compared with 78 years for those living in the most affluent areas. For women the corresponding figures were 80 and 82.7 years (CSO, 2010).

It is the nature of these inequalities and the fact that they are so interconnected with the social, economic and political environment of Ireland that places this issue as central to the agenda of *Social Justice Ireland*.

Annex 12: Ireland – some key environmental facts

(Information sourced from: CSO 2013, CSO 2012, EPA 2012, EPA 2013)

Greenhouse gases and climate change

- Greenhouse gas emissions fell substantially in 2009 and by 2010 Ireland was only slightly above the five years average limit set by the Kyoto Protocol.
- Ireland's greenhouse gas emissions on a *per capita* basis were the second highest in the EU in 2009, in large part due to the contribution of the agriculture sector to Ireland's greenhouse gas emissions, where methane and nitrous oxides accounted for 19 per cent and 13 per cent respectively of Ireland's total greenhouse gas emissions in 2010.
- Emissions of Nitrogen Oxide (NOx) in 2011 were above the specified EU emission ceiling. The road transport sector accounted for 55 per cent of total NOx emissions in 2011. Advances in emission controls in NOx have been largely off-set by increase in vehicle numbers and fuel use. In order to reduce these emissions a range of measures including travelling less by care and using newer, smaller vehicles is required.
- Agriculture and transport are the largest contributors to Irelands' greenhouse gas emissions making up 32.1 per cent and 19.7 per cent of total emissions respectively.
- Energy (20.8 per cent), agriculture (32.1 per cent), and transport (19.7 per cent) accounted for just over 72% of Ireland's greenhouse gas emissions in 2011. The remainder is made comprised of industry and commercial (14 per cent), the residential sector (11.5 per cent) and waste (1.8 per cent).
- Ireland is likely to breach its EU 2020 target and obligations on emissions from 2016 onwards (EPA, 2012).
- Forest sinks in Ireland could provide a removal of 4.6Mtonnes of CO_2 in 2020 and 32 Mtonnes of CO_2 over the 2013-2020 period.

Transport

- The number of licensed vehicles has increased by 164 per cent between 1985 and 2010.
- There has been a substantial increase in the number of low emission vehicles licensed since the introduction in 2008 of motor taxation rates based upon emissions. In 2011, 90 per cent of new private vehicles licensed were in emission bands A and B.

- There was a substantial fall in the number of air passengers travelling through Irish airports from 29.2 million in 2008 to 21.7 million in 2010.
- The transport sector accounted for 39.9 per cent of Ireland's final energy consumption in 2011, the highest for any economic sector in that year.
- The number of commuters using public buses fell by 23,277 between 2006 and 2011, a fall of 20 per cent. The number of commuters using a train, DART or Luas rose significantly between 1981 and 2011.
- Almost 40,000 more people took a train to work in 2011 than 30 years previously, doubling the share of commuters using the train from 1.7 per cent to 3.2 per cent.
- The number of female car drivers (551,638) surpassed male car drivers (515,813) among the working population for the first time with seven out of every ten women driving to work in 2011 compared with six out of 10 male commuters.
- More women walked to work (96,796) than men (73,714). Men accounted for the majority of those cycling with 29,075 (73 per cent), while the majority of public transport commuters were women (55.5 per cent).

Energy
- Ireland's primary energy requirement increased from 9.5 million tonnes of oil equivalent (t.o.e.) in 1990 to 16.5 million t.o.e. in 2008 but then decreased to 14.8 million in 2010.
- Transport accounted for 40 per cent of Ireland's final energy consumption in 2010.
- Oil accounted for 60 per cent of Ireland's total final energy consumption in 2010.
- Renewable energy accounted for 2 per cent of Ireland's total final energy consumption in 2010.
- The use of renewable energy sources as a proportion of total primary energy production fell from 41 per cent in 2009 to 31 per cent in 2010.
- Wind is the main sources of renewable energy used in the consumption of electricity, accounting for 11.1 per cent of electricity consumption in 2010.
- Natural gas, as a proportion of total primary energy production has fallen from54 per cent in 1990 to 17 per cent in 2010.
- Ireland had an imported energy dependency ratio of 88 per cent in 2011, the fourth highest in the EU.

Water

- Ireland ranked fourth among EU Member States in terms of compliance with bathing water quality guides in 2010.
- The proportion of Irish rivers classified as being unpolluted has declined from 77.3 per cent in 1987 –1990 to 68.9 per cent in 1997 –2009. The percentage of slightly polluted river water has increased steadily from 12 per cent in 1987 – 1990 to 20.7 per cent in the period 2007 –2009.
- The level of seriously polluted river water has remained at 1 per cent or less during the period 1987 – 2009.

Table 12.1: Irish River Water Quality 1987 - 2009

Quality polluted	Unpolluted polluted	Slightly polluted	Moderately	Seriously	Total
1987-1990	77.3	12.0	9.7	0.9	100
1991-1994	71.2	16.8	11.4	0.6	100
1995-1997	66.9	18.2	14.0	0.9	100
1998-2000	69.7	17.1	12.4	0.8	100
2001-2003	69.3	17.9	12.3	0.6	100
2004-2006	71.4	18.2	9.9	0.5	100
2007-2009	**68.9**	**20.7**	**10.0**	**0.4**	**100**

Source: Environmental Protection Agency 2010, Water Quality 2007 - 2009

Waste

- The amount of municipal waste generated fell from 800 kilograms per capita in 2006 to 620 kgs per capita in 2010. Ireland had the fourth highest level of municipal waste *per capita* in 2010.
- Municipal waste sent to landfill was just below 1.5 million tonnes in 2010, which was an improvement on the 2 million tonnes in 2007.
- In 2008 there were 9 kgs *per capita* of electrical waste collected from Irish households, which is more than twice the 4 kgs specified in the EU Waste Electrical and Electronic Equipment (WEEE) directive.
- By 2010, the recovery rate for packaging waste had reached 74 per cent.
- 46 per cent of that State's sewage treatment plants in urban areas fail to meet EU standards (EPA 2012).

Table 12.2 Ireland: Municipal waste, generated, recovered and landfilled			
Year	Waste generated (000 tonnes)	Waste recovered (% of waste generated)	Waste landfilled (% of waste generated)
2003	3,001.0	24.2	61.1
2004	3,034.6	30.3	59.9
2005	3,050.1	31.6	59.8
2006	3,384.6	33.1	58.5
2007	3,397.7	34.1	59.3
2008	3,224.3	36.1	60.1
2009	2,952.9	37.3	58.4
2010	**2,846.1**	**38.1**	**52.5**

Source: Environmental Protection Agency (2012), National Waste Report Series

Ireland has made significant improvements in increasing the amount of municipal waste recycled, which stood at 38 per cent in 2010. However, meeting the 2013 target for diversion of household waste from landfill to recycling of 50 per cent (EPA, 2012) remains a significant challenge.

Land Use
- In 2010, 10.7 per cent of Ireland's land was covered by forestry. This was the second lowest proportion of forest cover in the EU. The EU average forest cover in 2010 was 35.5 per cent of total land area.
- The area of forest owned privately in Ireland increased from 23 per cent in 1980 to 46 per cent in 2010.
- Although the area farmed organically increased by over 150 per cent between 1997 and 2009, Ireland had the third lowest percentage of agricultural land designated as organic in the EU in 2009.
- Ireland had the fifth largest cattle herd in the EU in 2010 with 6.8 per cent of total cattle numbers.
- House completions in Ireland peaked in 2006 with 93,400 completions and have since fallen to 10,500 in 2011. In 2011 there were 2.3 house completions per 1,000 population in Ireland.

Biodiversity and Heritage
- Ireland had the smallest percentage of land in the EU designated as a Special Protected Area, under the EU Birds Directive, at only 3 per cent of total land area in 2010.

- At 11 per cent, Ireland had less land designated as a Special Protected Area under the EU Habitats Directive than the EU average of 14 per cent in 2010.

Environmental Economy

- Revenue from environmental related taxes fell by €660 million between 2007 and 2010.
- Environmental taxes accounted for 8.5 per cent of Ireland's total tax revenues in 2009.
- Environmental subsidies in Ireland are entirely comprised of the Rural Environment Protection Scheme (REPS). REPS payments are made mainly to the agricultural sector and accounted for €153 million in 2010.
- The consumer price index for petrol and diesel increased by 13.5 per cent and 16.5 per cent respectively between December 2010 and December 2011.
- In 2011, Ireland imported €6.8 billion of fuel.

Annex 14:
UN Millennium Development Goals

The following are the UN Millennium Development Goals and the specific targets attached to each of these goals:

Goal 1: Eradicate extreme poverty and hunger
Target 1: Halve, between 1990 and 2015, the proportion of people whose income is less than $1 a day.
Target 2: Halve, between 1990 and 2015, the proportion of people who suffer from hunger.

Goal 2: Achieve universal primary education
Target 3: Ensure that, by 2015, children everywhere, boys and girls alike, will be able to complete a full course of primary schooling.

Goal 3: Promote gender equality and empower women
Target 4: Eliminate gender disparity in primary and secondary education, preferably by 2005 and in all levels of education no later than 2015.

Goal 4: Reduce child mortality
Target 5: Reduce by two-thirds, between 1990 and 2015, the under-five mortality rate.

Goal 5: Improve maternal health
Target 6: Reduce by three-quarters, between 1990 and 2015, the maternal mortality ratio.

Goal 6: Combat HIV/AIDS, malaria and other diseases
Target 7: Have halted by 2015 and begun to reverse the spread of HIV/AIDS.
Target 8: Have halted by 2015 and begun to reverse the incidence of malaria and other major diseases.

Goal 7: Ensure environmental sustainability
Target 9: Integrate the principles of sustainable development into country policies and programmes and reverse the loss of environmental resources.

Target 10: Halve by 2015 the proportion of people without sustainable access to safe drinking water.

Target 11: Have achieved by 2020 a significant improvement in the lives of at least 100 million slum dwellers.

Goal 8: Develop a global partnership for development

Target 12: Develop further an open, rule-based, predictable, nondiscriminatory trading and financial system (includes a commitment to good governance, development, and poverty reduction – both nationally and internationally).

Target 13: Address the special needs of the least developed countries (includes tariff and quota free access for exports, enhanced programme of debt relief for and cancellation of official bilateral debt, and more generous official development assistance for countries committed to poverty reduction).

Target 14: Address the special needs of landlocked countries and small island developing states (through the Programme of Action for the Sustainable Development of Small Island Developing States and 22nd General Assembly provisions).

Target 15: Deal comprehensively with the debt problems of developing countries through national and international measures in order to make debt sustainable in the long term

Target 16: In cooperation with developing countries, develop and implement strategies for decent and productive work for youth.

Target 17: In cooperation with pharmaceutical companies, provide access to affordable essential drugs in developing countries.

Target 18: In cooperation with the private sector, make available the benefits of new technologies, especially information and communications technologies.
(UNDP, 2003: 1-3)

REFERENCES

Abdelal, Rawi (2007) Capital Rules: the Construction of Global Finance. Harvard University Press: Cambridge MA.

Advisory Group on Unfinished Housing Developments (2011) *Resolving Irelands Unfinished Housing Developments Report of Advisory Group on Unfinished Housing Developments*. Department of Environment, Community and Local Government.

Alesina, Alberto and Francesco Giavazzi (2012) "The austerity question: 'How' is as important as 'how much'". *VoxEU.org*, April.

Alesina Alberto, and Silvia Ardagna (2010) 'Large Changes in Fiscal Policy: Taxes versus Spending'. *NBER Working Paper* 15438.

All Ireland Traveller Health Study Team (2010) *All Ireland Traveller Health Study: Our Geels Summary Of Findings.* Dublin: School of Public Health, Physiotherapy and Population Science. University College Dublin.

An Chomhairle Leabharlanna (2012) *Public Library Authorities Budgeted Expenditure.*

An Chomhairle Leabharlanna (2010) *Public Library Authority Statistics Actuals.*

Bank for International Settlements (2010) *Triennial Central Bank Survey of Foreign Exchange and Derivatives Market Activity.* Basel: BIS.

Barrett, A. and C. Wall (2005) *The Distributional Impact of Ireland's Indirect Tax System.* Dublin: Combat Poverty Agency.

Barry, Frank and Michael B. Devereux (2003) 'Expansionary fiscal contraction: A theoretical exploration'. *Journal of Macroeconomics*, 25, pp.1-23.

Batini, N., Callegari, G. and Melina, G. (2012) 'Successful Austerity in the United States, Europe and Japan'. *IMF Working Paper WP/12/190.*

Begg, D. (2003) "The Just Society – Can we afford it?" in Reynolds B. and S. Healy (eds.) *Ireland and the Future of Europe: leading the way towards inclusion?* Dublin: CORI.

Bennett M., D. Fadden,. D. Harney, P. O'Malley, C. Regan and. L. Sloyan (2003) *Population Ageing in Ireland and its Impact on Pension and Healthcare Costs.* Report of Society of Actuaries Working Party on Population Studies. Society of Actuaries in Ireland.

Bergin A., Fitz Gerald J. and Kearney I. (2002) *The Macro-economic Effects of Using Taxes or Emissions Trading Permits to Reduce Greenhouse Gas Emissions*, paper presented to ESRI conference entitled "The sky's the limit: efficient and fair policies on global warming". December, Dublin.

Blyth, Mark (2008) 'The Politics of Compounding Bubbles: The Global Housing Bubble in Comparative Perspective'. *Comparative European Politics*, 6, pp. 387–406.

Blyth, Mark (2002) *Great Transformations: Economic Ideas and Institutional Change in the Twentieth Century*. Cambridge: Cambridge University Press.

Bradley, John and Whelan, Karl (1997) 'The Irish expansionary fiscal contraction: A tale from one small European economy'. *Economic Modelling*, 14, pp. 175-201.

Bristow, J. (2004) *Taxation in Ireland: an economist's perspective*. Dublin: Institute of Public Administration.

Browne, D, Caulfield, B and O'Mahony, M (2011) Barriers to Sustainable Transport in Ireland. *Climate Change Research Programme (CCRP) 2007-2013 Report Series No. 7*. Dublin: EPA.

Browne, M. (2007) *The Right Living Space, Housing and Accommodation Needs of People with Disabilities*. A Citizens Information Board/Disability Federation of Ireland Social Policy Report.

Cafferkey, G and Caulfield, B (2011) *Examining the barriers to sustainable inter-city transport in Ireland*. Paper presented at ITRN, 31 August – 1 September 2011 University College Cork.

Cahill, S., O'Shea, E., & Pierce, M. (2012) *Creating Excellence in Dementia Care: A Research Review for Ireland's National Dementia Strategy*. Department of Health.

Carnegie Trust (2012) Refd. in chapter 6, Library services section

Carneiro, P and Heckman, J (2003) Human Capital Policy. *NBER Working Paper Series*. Cambridge MA: National Bureau of Economic Research.

Carrie, A (2005) "Lack of long-run data prevents us tracking Ireland's social health" in *Feasta Review No2 Growth: the Celtic Cancer* Dublin: Feasta.

Central Bank of Ireland (2012), *Residential Mortgage Arrears and Repossessions Statistics: Q3 2012*. Dublin: Central Bank.

Central Bank (2012) *Residential Mortgage Arrears and Repossessions Statistics: Q2 2012* Dublin: Central Bank.

Central Statistics Office (2013) *Earnings and Labour Costs – February.* Dublin: Stationery Office.

Central Statistics Office (2013) *Survey on Income and Living Conditions 2011 and revised 2010 results.* Dublin: Stationery Office.

Central Statistics Office (2013) *Sustainable Development Indicators Ireland 2013.* Dublin: Stationery Office.

Central Statistics Office (2013) *Goods Exports and Imports, December 2012.* Dublin: Stationery Office.

Central Statistics Office (2013) *Residential Property Price Index December 2012.* Dublin: Stationery Office.

Central Statistics Office (2012) *Measuring Ireland's Progress 2011.* Dublin: Stationery Office.

Central Statistics Office (2012) *Environmental Indicators Ireland 2012.* Dublin: Stationery Office.

Central Statistics Office (2012) *Statistical Yearbook of Ireland 2012.* Dublin:; Stationery Office.

Central Statistics Office (2012) *Quarterly National Household Survey Quarter 2 2011, Response of Households to the Economic Downturn – Pilot module.* Dublin: Stationery Office.

Central Statistics Office (2012) *Census 2011 Profile 4: A Roof Over Our Heads.* Dublin: Stationery Office.

Central Statistics Office (2012) *Census 2011: Profile 2 – Older and Younger.* Dublin: Stationery Office.

Central Statistics Office (2012) *Census 2011: Profile 8 Our Bill of Health – Health, Disability and Carers in Ireland.* Dublin: Stationery Office.

Central Statistics Office (2012) *Census 2011: Profile 6: Migration and Diversity.* Dublin: Stationery Office.

Central Statistics Office (2012) *National Income and Expenditure Accounts 2011*. Dublin: Stationery Office.

Central Statistics Office (2012) *This is Ireland: Highlights from Census 2011, Part 1*. Dublin: Stationery Office.

Central Statistics Office (2012) *Census 2011: Profile 10 Door to Door – Commuting in Ireland*. Dublin: Stationery Office.

Central Statistics Office (2012) *Census of Agriculture 2010 Final Results*. Dublin: Stationery Office.

Central Statistics Office (2012) *Environmental Indicators Ireland 2012*. Dublin: Stationery Office.

Central Statistics Office (2012) *Output, Input and Income in Agriculture 2012 – Advance Estimate*. Dublin: Stationery Office.

Central Statistics Office (2012) *Quarterly National Household Survey Q4 2011* Dublin: Stationery Office.

Central Statistics Office (2012) *Quarterly National Household Survey Quarter 3 2012*. Dublin: Stationery Office.

Central Statistics Office (2012) *Population and Migration Statistics*. Dublin: Stationery Office.

Central Statistics Office (2012) *Total Housing Stock by Province County or City, Census Year and Statistic*. Dublin: Stationery Office.

Central Statistics Office (2012) *Homeless persons in Ireland, a special Census 2011 report*. Dublin: Stationery Office.

Central Statistics Office (2012), *Population and Migration Estimates April 2012*. Dublin: Stationery Office.

Central Statistics Office (2011) *Information Society and Telecommunications in Households 2009-2011*. Dublin: Stationery Office.

Central Statistics Office (2011) *Measuring Irelands Progress 2010*. Dublin: Stationery Office.

Central Statistics Office (2011, *Statistical Yearbook of Ireland 2011*. Dublin: Stationery Office.

Central Statistics Office (2011) *Quarterly National Household Survey, Educational Attainment Thematic Report 2011*. Dublin: Stationery Office.

Central Statistics Office (2011) *Quarterly National Household Survey Voter Participation Quarter 2 2011*. Dublin: Stationery Office.

Central Statistics Office (2011) *Population and Migration Estimates April 2011*. Dublin: Stationery Office.

Central Statistics Office (2011) *Quarterly National Household Survey Quarter 3 2010, Health Status and Health Service Utilisation*. Updated, June 2012. Dublin: Stationery Office.

Central Statistics Office (2011) *Women and Men in Ireland*. February. Dublin: Stationery Office.

Central Statistics Office (2011) *Population and Migration Estimates,* Dublin: Stationery Office.

Central Statistics Office (2010) *Mortality Differentials in Ireland*. 22 December. Dublin: Stationery Office.

Central Statistics Office (2010) *Survey on Income and Living Conditions 2009 Results.* Dublin: Stationery Office.

Central Statistics Office (2010) *Quarterly National Household Survey: Special Module on Carers Quarter 3 2009*. Dublin: Stationery Office.

Central Statistics Office (2010) *National Disability Survey 2006 – Volume two*. Dublin: Stationery Office.

Central Statistics Office (2008) *National Disability Survey 2006 – First Results. Dublin*: Stationery Office.

Central Statistics Office (2006*) Industrial Earnings and Hours Worked*. Dublin: Stationery Office.

Central Statistics Office (2004) *Quarterly National Household Survey: Special Module on Disability Quarter 1 2004*. Dublin: Stationery Office.

Central Statistics Office (2004) *Industrial Earnings and Hours Worked*. Dublin: Stationery Office.

Central Statistics Office (various) *Quarterly National Household Survey*. Dublin: Stationery Office.

Central Statistics Office (various) *Survey on Income and Living Conditions Results*. Dublin: Stationery Office.

Chambers of Commerce of Ireland (2004) *Local Authority Funding – Government in Denial*. Dublin.

Clark C.M.A. (2002) *The Basic Income Guarantee: ensuring progress and prosperity in the 21st century*. Dublin: Liffey Press and CORI Justice Commission.

Clark C.M.A. and H. Alford (2010) *Rich and Poor: Rebalancing the economy*. London: CTS.

Coates, D. Kane, F. & Treadwell Shine, K. (2008) *Traveller Accommodation in Ireland Review of Policy and Practice (Housing Policy Discussion series 3*. Centre for Housing Research: Dublin.

Collins M.L. (2011) "Taxation". In O'Hagan, J. and C. Newman (eds.), *The Economy of Ireland* (11th edition). Dublin: Gill and Macmillan.

Collins, M.L. (2011) *Establishing a Benchmark for Ireland's Social Welfare Payments*. Paper for Social Justice Ireland. Dublin: Social Justice Ireland.

Collins, M.L. (2006) "Poverty: Measurement, Trends and Future Directions", in Healy, S., B. Reynolds and M.L. Collins, *Social Policy in Ireland: Principles, Practice and Problems*. Dublin: Liffey Press.

Collins, M.L. (2004) "Taxation in Ireland: an overview" in B. Reynolds, and S. Healy (eds.) *A Fairer Tax System for a Fairer Ireland*. Dublin: CORI Justice Commission.

Collins, M.L., B. Mac Mahon, G. Weld and R. Thornton (2012) *A Minimum Income Standard for Ireland – a consensual budget standards study examining household types across the lifecycle – Studies in Public Policy No. 27*. Dublin: Policy Institute, Trinity College Dublin.

Collins, M.L. and A. Larragy (2011) 'A Site Value Tax for Ireland: approach, design and implementation' *Trinity Economics Papers Working Paper 1911*. Dublin: Trinity College Dublin.

Collins, M.L. and M. Walsh (2010) *Ireland's Tax Expenditure System: International Comparisons and a Reform Agenda – Studies in Public Policy No. 24*. Dublin: Policy Institute, Trinity College Dublin.

Collins, M.L. and C. Kavanagh (2006) "The Changing Patterns of Income Distribution and Inequality in Ireland, 1973-2004", in Healy, S., B. Reynolds and M.L. Collins, *Social Policy in Ireland: Principles, Practice and Problems*. Dublin: Liffey Press.

Collins, M.L. and C. Kavanagh (1998) "For Richer, For Poorer: The Changing Distribution of Household Income in Ireland, 1973-94", in Healy, S. and B. Reynolds, *Social Policy in Ireland: Principles, Practice and Problems*. Dublin: Oak Tree Press.

Comhar (2002) *Principles for Sustainable Development*. Dublin: Stationery Office.

Comhar and Irish Rural Link (2009) *Towards a Sustainable Rural Transport Policy*. Irish Rural Link.

Commission for Communications Regulation (2012) *The provision of telephony services under Universal Service Obligation*.

Commission for Communications Regulation (2011) *Provision of Universal Service by Eircom, Performance Data – Q3 2011 (1 July 2011 to 30 September 2011)*.

Commission of Investigation into the Banking Sector in Ireland (2011) *Misjudging Risk: Causes of the Systemic Banking Crisis in Ireland*.

Commission on Taxation (2009) *Commission on Taxation Report 2009*. Dublin: Stationery Office.

Commission on Taxation (1982) *Commission on Taxation First Report*. Dublin: Stationery Office.

Considine, M & Dukelow, F (2009) *Irish Social Policy a Critical Introduction*. Gill and Macmillan: Dublin.

Cooper, Russell and Hempf, Hubert (2004) 'Overturning Mundell: Fiscal Policy in a Monetary Union', *Review of Economic Studies*, No. 71, pp. 371-396.

Costanza, R., Hart, M., Posner S. and Talberth, J. (2009) *Beyond GDP: The Need for New Measures of Progress*. Boston University: The Pardee Papers.

Coughlan, O (2007) Irish Climate Change Policy from Kyoto to the Carbon Tax: a Two-level Game Analysis of the Interplay of Knowledge and Power. *Irish Studies in International Affairs*, Vol. 18 (2007), 131–153.

Council of Europe (2011) *Draft text of the Council of Europe's charter of shared social responsibilities.* Brussels: Council of Europe.

Council of the European Union (2011) *Council Resolution on a renewed European Agenda for adult learning.* 20 December 2011. (2011/C 372/01).

Curtin, J and Hanrahan, G (2012) *Why Legislate? Designing a Climate Law for Ireland.* Dublin: The Institute of International and European Affairs.

Dalal-Clayton, B. & Bass, S. (2002) *Sustainable development strategies: a resource book.* OECD: Paris.

Daly, H.E and Cobb, J.B. (1987) *For the Common Good: Redirecting the Economy toward Community, the Environment and a Sustainable Future.* Boston: Beacon Press.

Department of Agriculture, Food and the Marine (2012) *Ireland CAP Rural Development Programme 2007-2013 (Revised).* Dublin: Stationery Office.

De Grauwe, Paul and Yuemei Ji (2013) 'Panic-driven austerity in the Eurozone and its implications', VoxEU.org, 21 February.

Department of Agriculture, Food and the Marine (2011) *Food Harvest 2020.* Dublin: Stationery Office.

Department of Agriculture, Food and the Marine (2004) *Agri-Vision 2015.* Dublin: Stationery Office.

Department of An Taoiseach (2012) *National Reform Programme for Ireland 2012 Update.* Dublin: Stationery Office.

Department of An Taoiseach (2006) *Towards 2016 - Ten-Year Framework Social Partnership Agreement 2006-2015.* Dublin: Stationery Office.

Department of An Taoiseach (2002) *Basic Income, A Green Paper.* Dublin: Stationery Office.

Department of An Taoiseach (2001) *Final Report of the Social Welfare Benchmarking and Indexation Group.* Dublin: Stationery Office.

Department of Communications, Energy and Natural Resources (2012) *Delivering a Connected Society – A National Broadband Plan for Ireland.* Dublin: Stationery Office.

Department of Education and Skills (2012) *A Framework for Junior Cycle.* Dublin: Stationery Office.

Department of Education and Skills (2012) Press Release *Minister Quinn protects frontline services in Budget 2013.* Dublin: Department of Education and Skills.

Department of Education and Skills (2012) *Report to the Minister for Education and Skills on the impact in terms of posts in Budget measures in relation to The Withdrawal form DEIS Band 1 and Band 2 Urban Primary Schools of Posts from Disadvantage Schemes pre-dating DEIS.* Dublin: Department of Education and Skills.

Department of Education and Sills (2012) Address by Minister for Education and Skills, Ruairí Quinn TD, at Nordic Education Seminar. Dublin: Department of Education and Skills.

Department of Education and Sills (2012) Speech by Minister for Education and Skills Ruairi Quinn, TD at the launch of his Junior Cycle Framework. Dublin: Department of Education and Skills.

Department of Education and Skills (2011) *An Evaluation of Planning Processes in DEIS Post-Primary Schools.* Dublin: Stationery Office.

Department of Education and Skills (2011) *An Evaluation of Planning Processes in DEIS Primary Schools.* Dublin: Stationery Office.

Department of Education and Sills (2011) *2011-2031, Twenty Years of Radical Reform* Speech by Minister for Education and Skills Ruairi Quinn, TD at the MacGill Summer School, Glenties, Co. Donegal.

Department of Education and Skills (2011) *Comprehensive Review of Current Expenditure.* Dublin: Department of Education and Skills.

Department of Education and Skills (2011) *Information Note regarding main features of 2012 Estimates for Education and Skills Vote.*

Department of Education and Skills (2011) *Literacy and Numeracy for Learning and Life, The National Strategy to Improve Literacy and Numeracy among Children and Young People 2011 – 2020.* Dublin: Stationery Office.

Department of Education and Skills (2011) *National Strategy for Higher Education to 2030.* Dublin: Stationery Office.

Department of Education and Skills (2009) *Policy Options for New Student Contributions in Higher Education: Report to Minister for Education and Science.* Dublin: Stationery Office

Department of Environment, Community and Local Government (2013) *General Scheme of a Climate Action and Low Carbon Development Bill 2013.* Dublin: Stationery Office.

Department of Environment, Community and Local Government & Department of Health (2012) *"National Housing Strategy for People with Disability 2011-2016, National Implementation Framework".* Dublin: Stationery Office.

Department of Environment, Community and Local Government (2012) *Putting People First:Action Programme for Effective Local Government.* Dublin: Stationery Office.

Department of Environment, Community and Local Government (2012) *Final Report of the Local Government/Local Development Alignment Steering Group.* Dublin: Stationery Office.

Department of Environment, Community and Local Government (2012) *Our Sustainable Future. A Framework for Sustainable Development for Ireland.* Dublin: Stationery Office.

Department of Environment, Community and Local Government (2012) *Green Tenders – An Action Plan for Green Public Procurement* Dublin: Stationery Office.

Department of Environment, Community and Local Government (2012) *Progress Report on Actions to Resolve Unfinished Housing Developments.* Dublin: Stationery Office.

Department of Environment, Community and Local Government (2012) *Mortgage to Rent Scheme Provides Certainty and Security for Low Income Families Most Affected by Economic Turmoil, 28/06/2012.* Dublin: Stationery Office.

Department of Environment, Community and Local Government (2011) *2011 National Housing Development Survey Summary Report.* Dublin: Stationery Office.

Department of Environment, Community and Local Government (2011) *Housing Policy Statement.* Dublin: Stationery Office.

Department of Environment, Community and Local Government (2011) *National Housing Strategy for People with a Disability 2011-2016.* Dublin: Stationery Office.

Department of Environment, Community and Local Government (2011), *Comprehensive Review of Expenditure Capital Review.* Dublin: Stationery Office.

Department of Environment, Community and Local Government (2011) *A Roadmap for Climate Policy and Legislation.* Dublin: Stationery Office.

Department of Environment, Community and Local Government (2011) *Review of National Climate Policy.* Dublin: Stationery Office.

Department of Environment Heritage and Local Government (2009) *Annual Housing Statistics Bulletin 2008.* Dublin: Stationery Office.

Department of Environment, Heritage and Local Government (2008) *Statement of Strategy.* Dublin: Stationery Office.

Department of Environment Heritage and Local Government, (2008) *The Way Home: A Strategy to Address Adult Homelessness in Ireland 2008 - 2013.* Dublin: Stationery Office.

Department of Environment, Heritage and Local Government (1998) *Branching Out - A New Public Library Service,* Dublin: Stationery Office.

Department of Finance (2013) *Finance Bill.* Dublin: Stationery Office.

Department of Finance (2012*) Budget 2013.* Dublin: Stationery Office.

Department of Finance (2012) *Medium-Term Fiscal Statement November 2012.* Stationary Office: Dublin.

Department of Finance (2012) *Finance Bill.* Dublin: Stationery Office.

Department of Finance (2011) *Budget 2012.* Dublin: Stationery Office.

Department of Finance (2011) *Medium Term Fiscal Statement.* Dublin: Stationery Office.

Department of Finance, (2010) *Infrastructure Investment Priorities 2010-2016 A Financial Framework.* Dublin: Stationery Office.

Department of Finance (various) *Budget Documentation* – *various years.* Dublin: Stationery Office.

Department of Health (2012) *Annual Output Statement for Health Group of Votes – 38 and 39.* Dublin: Department of Health.

Department of Health (2012) *Health in Ireland: Key Trends, 2012.* Dublin: Department of Health.

Department of Health (2012) Press Release: Minister Reilly pledges service protection a key priority as savings are made.

Department of Health (2012) *Future Health – A Strategic Framework for Reform of the Health Service, 2012-2015.* Dublin: Department of Health.

Department of Health and Children (2000) *National Children's Strategy, Our Children their Lives.* Dublin: Stationery Office.

Department of Justice and Equality (2013) *Immigration in Ireland – 2012 in Review.* Dublin: Stationery Office.

Department of Justice, Equality and Defence (2011) *Immigration in Ireland 2011 – a year end snapshot.* Dublin: Stationery Office.

Department of Public Expenditure and Reform (2011) *Social Housing Supports Comprehensive Review of Expenditure, Thematic Evaluation Series.* Dublin: Stationery Office.

Department of Social Protection (2011) *Comprehensive Review of Expenditure.* Dublin: Stationery Office.

Department of Social Protection (2011) *Annual Report 2011.* Dublin: Stationery Office.

Department of Social Protection (2011) *Statistical Information on Social Welfare Services 2011.* Dublin: Stationery Office.

Department of Social, Community and Family Affairs (2000) *Supporting Voluntary Activity.* Dublin: Stationery Office.

Department of Transport Tourism and Sport (2012) *National Sports Facilities Strategy DRAFT 2012-2015.* Dublin: Stationery Office.

Department of Transport, Tourism and Sport (2012) *Value for Money and Policy Review of the Rural Transport Programme.* Dublin: Stationery Office.

Department of Transport Tourism and Sport (2011) *Statement of Strategy 2011-2014.* Dublin: Stationery Office.

Department of Transport (2009) *A Sustainable Transport Future A New Transport Policy for Ireland 2009 – 2020.* Dublin: Stationery Office.

Disability Federation of Ireland (2007) *Pre-Budget Submission for Budget 2008.* Dublin: DFI

Dorgan, J., (2009) *Adult Literacy Policy: A Review for the National Adult Literacy Agency.* Dublin: National Adult Literacy Agency.

Dorgan, J., (2009) *A Cost Benefit Analysis of Adult Literacy Training: Research Report, March 2009.* Dublin: National Adult Literacy Agency.

Drudy, P.J., (2006) *Housing in Ireland, Philosophy Problems and Policies* in Healy, S. Reynolds, B. and Collins, M. (eds) *Social Policy in Ireland , Principles, Practice, and Problems.* Dublin: Liffey Press.

Duffy, D., J. Durkan, K. Timoney and E. Casey (2012) *Quarterly Economic Commentary Winter 2012.* Dublin: ESRI.

Dunne, T. (2004) "Land Values as a Source of Local Government Finance" in B. Reynolds, and S. Healy (eds.) *A Fairer Tax System for a Fairer Ireland.* Dublin: CORI Justice Commission.

Economic and Social Research Institute (2003) *National Development Plan Mid-Term Review.* Dublin: ESRI.

Economists Intelligence Unit (2009) *European Green City Index Assessing the Environmental Impact of Europe's major Cities.*

ECORYS Research and Consulting (2010) *Study on Employment, Growth and Innovation in Rural Areas.* Netherlands: ECORYS.

EEAC (2011) *The "Green Economy" Agenda in the context of SD Institutional framework for SD at National Level.* Brussels: EEAC.

Eichengreen, Barry and Kevin O'Rourke (2012) 'A tale of two depressions redux', *VoxEU.org*, 6 March.

Eivers, E. and Clerkin, A. (2012) *PIRLS and TIMSS 2011: Reading, Mathematics and Science Outcomes for Ireland.* Dublin: Educational Research Centre.

Employers' Diversity Network (2009) *Issues and Challenges in the Recruitment and Selection of Immigrant Workers in Ireland.* Dublin: Stationery Office.

Environmental Protection Agency (2013) *EPA Releases figures for key air pollutants. Press release.* Dublin: EPA.

Environmental Protection Agency (2012) *The EU Emissions Trading Scheme. A review of the first six years of operation.* Dublin: EPA.

Environmental Protection Agency (2012) *National Waste Report 2010.* Dublin: EPA.

Environmental Protection Agency (2012) *Ireland's Greenhouse Gas Emissions Projections 2011-2020.* Dublin: EPA.

Environmental Protection Agency (2012) *Ireland's Greenhouse Gas Emissions in 2011 – Key Highlights.* Dublin: EPA.

Environmental Protection Agency (2012) *Ireland's Environment 2012 – An Assessment.* Dublin: EPA.

Environmental Protection Agency (2012) *Ireland's Climate Strategy to 2020 and beyond - A contribution to the Programme for Development of National Climate Policy and Legislation 2012.* Dublin: EPA.

Environmental Protection Agency (2012) *A Focus on Urban Waste Water Discharges in Ireland.* Dublin: EPA.

Environmental Protection Agency (2012) *A Year in Review – Highlights from 2011.* Dublin: EPA.

Environmental Protection Agency (2011) *Biodiversity Action Plan 2011-2013.* Dublin: EPA.

Environmental Protection Agency (2011) *Biochange: Biodiversity and Environmental Change: An Integrated Study Encompassing a Range of Scales, Taxa and Habitats.* Wexford: EPA.

Environmental Protection Agency (2010), *Water Quality in Ireland 2007-2009.* Dublin, EPA.

Environmental Protection Agency (2010) *Environmental Protection Agency Biodiversity Action Plan.* Dublin: EPA.

Epstein, Gerald (2001) 'Financialization, Rentier Interests, and Central Bank Policy', Department of Economics and Political Economy Research Institute (PERI), University of Massachusetts.

Eurofound (2012) Third European Quality of Life Survey – Quality of Life in Europe: Impacts of the crisis. Luxembourg: Publications Office of the European Union.

Eurofound (2011) *Shifts in the job structure in Europe during the Great Recession.* Luxembourg: Publications Office of the European Union.

European Commission (2013) *A Decent Life for All: Ending Poverty and Giving the World a Sustainable Future.* Brussels: European Commission.

European Commission, (2012) *Digital Agenda for Europe, Digital Scorecard.* Brussels: European Commission.

European Commission (2012) *Rural Development in the EU Statistical and Economic Information Report 2012.* Brussels: European Commission.

European Commission (2011) A *resource-efficient Europe – Flagship initiative under the Europe 2020 Strategy.* Brussels: European Commission.

European Commission (2011) *Early Childhood Education and Care: Providing all our children with the best start for the world of tomorrow.* Brussels: European Commission.

European Commission (2011) *Our life insurance, our natural capital: an EU biodiversity strategy to 2020.* Brussels: European Commission.

European Commission (2011) *Proposal for a Regulation of the European Parliament and of the Council on support for rural development by the European Agricultural fund for Rural Development (EAFRD)*. Brussels: European Commission.

European Commission (2011) *Roadmap to a Resource Efficient Europe. COM(2011) 571*. Brussels: European Commission.

European Commission (2011) *Strategic framework for European cooperation in education and training (ET 2020)*. Brussels: European Commission.

European Commission (2011) *The Social Dimension of the Europe 2020 Strategy A report of the Social Protection Committee*. Luxembourg: Publications Office of the European Union.

European Commission (2011) *Commission Staff Working Paper Accompanying the White Paper - Roadmap to a Single European Transport Area – Towards a competitive and resource efficient transport system*. Brussels: European Commission.

European Commission (2010) *Eurobarometer 74 Autumn 2010 Report*. Brussels: European Commission.

European Commission (2010) *Europe 2020: A strategy for smart, sustainable and inclusive growth*. Brussels: European Commission.

European Commission (staff working document) (2008) *Digital Literacy Report: a review for the i2010 eInclusion Initiative Digital Literacy: High-Level Expert Group Recommendations*, Brussels: European Commission.

European Commission (2010) *Digital Agenda for Europe, Digital Scorecard*. Brussels: European Commission.

European Commission against Racism and Intolerance (2007) *Third Report on Ireland*. Strasbourg.

European Migration Network (2012) *Useful Statistics*. Brussels.

European Network for Rural Development (2012) *EU Rural Review No. 13 Autumn 2012*. Belgium.

European Network for Rural Development (2011) *Climate Change and Renewable Energy measures in EU RDPs 2007-2013 Member state profile – Ireland*. Belgium.

European Network for Rural Development (2010) *Climate Change and Renewable Energy measures in EU RDPs 2007-2013 Ireland*. Belgium.

Eurostat (2013) *Life Expectancy at birth, by Sex*. Luxembourg: Eurostat.

Eurostat (2012) *Taxation Trends in the European Union*. Luxembourg: Eurostat.

Eurostat (2012) *Population and Social Conditions, Asylum applicants and first instance decisions on asylum applications: third quarter 2012*. Luxembourg: Eurostat.

Eurostat (2012) *Agriculture, fishery and forestry statistics: Main results — 2010-11*. Luxembourg: Publications Office of the European Union.

Eurostat (2011) *Taxation Trends in the European Union*. Luxembourg: Eurostat.

Eurostat (2008) Satellite accounts sharpen the focus. *Sigma — The bulletin of European Statistics, 2008.03*. Luxembourg: Eurostat.

Eurydice Network (2012) *Key Data on Education in Europe 2012*. Brussels: European Commission.

Expert Group on Future Skills Needs (2012) *Addressing High Level ICT Skills Recruitment Needs Research Findings*. Dublin: Expert Group on Future Skills Need.s

Expert Group on Future Skills Needs (2007) *Tomorrow's Skills: Towards a National Skills Strategy. 5th Report*. Dublin: Expert Group on Future Skills Needs.

Farrell, C. McAvoy, H. Wilde, J. & Combat Poverty Agency (2008) *Tackling Health Inequalities an All-Ireland Approach to Social Determinants*. Dublin: Combat Poverty Agency/Institute of Public Health.

Farrell, Grant Sparks (2000) *Rural Transport — A National Study from a Community Perspective*. Dublin: ADM

Ferguson, Charles H. (2012). *Predator Nation: Corporate Criminals, Political Corruption, and the Hijacking of America*. Crown Business.

Fitzpatrick & Associates for Department of Transport (2006) *Progressing Rural Public Transport in Ireland*. Dublin: Stationery Office.

Flannery, D. and O'Donoghue, C. (2011) The Life Cycle Impact of Alternative Higher Education Finance Systems in Ireland. *The Economic and Social Review, Vol. 42, No.3, (Autumn, 2011):pp.237-270* Dublin: UCD.

Florio, Massimo (2002) "Economists, Privatization in Russia and the Waning of the 'Washington Consensus'", *Review of International Political Economy*, 9 (2), pp. 359-40.

Forfas and National Competitiveness Council (2012) *Ireland's Competitiveness Scorecard 2012*. Dublin: Stationery Office.

Forfás & National Competitiveness Council (2011) *Ireland's Competitiveness Challenge 2011*. Dublin: Stationery Office.

Forfas (2009) *Sharing our future: Ireland 2025*. Dublin: Stationery Office.

Forfas (2011) *Ireland's Advanced Broadband Performance and Policy Priorities*. Dublin: Stationery Office.

Free Legal Advice Centres (2012) Debtors need sustained support, not just once-off financial advice. Dublin: FLAC.

Gaudium et Spes, (1965) Vatican II Council, Maryknoll: Orbis Books.

Giavazzi F., and M. Pagano (1990) 'Can Severe Fiscal Contractions Be Expansionary? Tales of Two Small European Countries', *NBER Macroeconomics Annual*, Cambridge MA: MIT Press.

Global Development Finance Report (2012) *External Debt of Developing Countries*. Washington DC: The World Bank.

Glyn, Andrew (2006) *Capitalism Unleashed: Financial Globalisation and Welfare*, Oxford: Oxford University Press.

Goldberg, F.T., L.L. Batchelder and P.R. Orszag (2006) *Reforming Tax Incentives into Uniform Refundable Tax Credits*. Washington: Brookings.

Gordon, Robert J. (2011, 'The History of the Phillips Curve: Consensus and Bifurcation', *Economica*, Vol. 78, No. 309, pp. 10-50.

Gravelle, Jane G., 'Tax Havens: International Tax Avoidance and Evasion', *CRS Report for Congress*.

Government of Ireland (2013) *Action Plan for Jobs 2013*. Dublin: Stationery Office.

Government of Ireland (2012) *Pathways to Work*. Dublin: Stationery Office.

Government of Ireland (2012) *Ireland's National Reform Programme 2012 – Update*. Dublin: Stationery Office.

Government of Ireland (2012) *Action Plan for Jobs 2012*. Dublin: Stationery Office.

Government of Ireland (2011) *Jobs Initiative*. Dublin: Stationery Office.

Government of Ireland (2011) *Programme for Government and National Recovery 2011-2016*. Dublin: Stationery Office.

Government of Ireland (2010) *National Pensions Strategy*. Dublin: Stationery Office.

Government of Ireland (2007) *National Climate Change Strategy*. Dublin: Stationery Office.

H.M. Treasury (2004) *Financial Statement and Budget Report, 2004*. London: H.M. Treasury.

Haase, T. and Pratschke, J. (2012) *The 2011 Pobal HP Deprivation Index for Small Areas (SA)* Dublin: Pobal.

Health Service Executive (2013) *HSE National Service Plan 2013*. Dublin: HSE.

Healy, S and B. Reynolds (2011) "Sharing responsibility for Shaping the Future – Why and How?" in B. Reynolds and S. Healy (eds) *Sharing Responsibility in Shaping the Future*. Dublin: Social Justice Ireland.

Healy, S and B. Reynolds (2003) "Christian Critique of Economic Policy and Practice" in J.P. Mackey and E. McDonagh (eds) *Religion and Politics in Ireland at the turn of the millennium*. Dublin: Columba Press.

Healy, S. and M.L. Collins, M.L. (2006) "Work, Employment and Unemployment", in Healy, S., B. Reynolds and M.L. Collins, *Social Policy in Ireland: Principles, Practice and Problems*. Dublin: Liffey Press.

Healy, S., M. Murphy, S. Ward and B. Reynolds (2012) 'B*asic Income – Why and How in Difficult Economic Times: Financing a BI in Ireland*' Paper to the BIEN Congress 2012, Munich.

Heisenberg, Dorothy (1999) *The Mark of the Bundesbank: Germany's Role in European Monetary Co-operation*. London: Lynne Rienner.

Helleiner, Eric (1994) *States and the Re-emergence of Global Finance: from Bretton Woods to the 1990s*. Cornell University Press: Ithaca.

Higher Education Authority (2013) *Completing the Landscape Process for Irish Higher Education*. Dublin: HEA.

Higher Education Authority (2011) *National Strategy for Higher Education to 2030*. Dublin: HEA.

Higher Education Authority (2012) *Towards a Future Higher Education Landscape*. Dublin: HEA.

Higher Education Authority (2012) *Springboard 2011 First Stage Evaluation*. Dublin: HEA.

Higher Education Authority (2012) *10/11 Higher Education Key Facts and Figures*. Dublin: HEA.

Higher Education Authority (2011) *Report on the Social and Living Conditions of Higher Education Students in Ireland 2009/2010*. Dublin: HEA.

Higher Education Authority (2011) *10/11 Higher Education Key Facts and Figures*. Dublin: HEA.

Higher Education Authority (2010) *What do graduates do? The Class of 2008*. Dublin: HEA.

Higher Education Authority (2010) *Review of Student Charge*. Dublin: HEA.

Higher Education Authority (2010) *National Plan for Equity of Access to Higher Education 2008-2013 Mid-Term Review*. Dublin: HEA.

Higher Education Authority (2010) *A Study of Progression in Irish Higher Education*. Dublin: HEA.

Hoegen, M (2009) *Statistics and the quality of life. Measuring progress – a world beyond GDP.* Bonn: InWent.

Holland, Dawn and Portes, Jonathan (2012) 'Self-defeating austerity?', *VoxEU.org*, 1 November.

Holton, Sarah and Fergal McCann (2012) 'Irish SME credit supply and demand: comparisons across surveys and countries'. *Central Bank of Ireland Economic Letters Series.*

Honohan, P. et. al. (2010*) The Irish Banking Crisis: Regulatory and Banking Stability, 2003-2008.* Dublin: Stationery Office.

Honohan, Patrick and Brendan M. Walsh (2002) "Catching Up with the Leaders: 'The Irish Hare'", *Brookings Papers on Economic Activity,* 33, pp. 1-78.

Houses of the Oireachtas (2013) Report of the Joint Committee on Jobs, Enterprise And Innovation: *Creating Policies that Work - Actions to Address Youth and Long-Term Unemployment.* Dublin, Houses of the Oireachtas.

Housing Agency (2011) *Housing Needs Assessment 201.* Housing Agency.

Hutton, Will (2003) *The World We're In.* London: Abacus.

Hyland, A (2011) *Entry to Higher Education in Ireland in the 21st Century.* (Discussion Paper for the NCCA/HEA Seminar 2011) Dublin: HEA.

IMD (2007) *IMD World Competitiveness Yearbook.* Lausanne: Switzerland.

Immigrant Council of Ireland (2011) *Taking Racism Seriously: Migrants experiences of violence, harassment and anti-social behaviour in the Dublin Area.* Dublin: Immigrant Council of Ireland.

Indecon (2012) *Mid-Term Evaluation of the rural Development Programme Ireland (2007-2013).* Dublin: Stationery Office.

Indecon (2012) *Review of Certain Aspects of the Irish Horse Racing Industry final Report for Department of Agriculture, Food and the Marine.* Dublin: Indecon.

Indecon (2010) *Assessment of Economic Impact of Sports in Ireland.* Dublin: Indecon.

Indecon (2005) *Indecon Review of Local Government Funding – Report commissioned by the Minister for Environment, Heritage and Local Government.* Dublin: Stationery Office.

Institute for Public Health (2007) *Fuel Poverty and Health.* Dublin: IPH.

Institute for Public Health (2011) *Facing the Challenge: The Impact of Recession and Unemployment on Men's Health in Ireland.* Dublin: IPH.

Inter-Departmental Mortgage Arrears Working Group (2011) *Report of the Inter-Departmental Mortgage Arrears working Group.*

International Monetary Fund (2013, *World Economic Outlook Update.* Washington D.C.: International Monetary Fund.

International Monetary Fund (2012) *World Economic Outlook October 2012.* Washington D.C.: International Monetary Fund.

International Monetary Fund (2008) *World Economic Outlook.* Washington DC: IMF.

International Monetary Fund (2004) *World Economic Outlook.* Washington DC: IMF.

Irish Aid (2011) *Annual Report 2011.* Department of Foreign Affairs and Trade.

Irish Farmers Association (2013) *Farm Income Review 2012.* Irish Farmers Association.

Irish Fiscal Advisory Council (2012) *Fiscal Assessment Report: September 2012.*

Irish Sports Council (2009) *Building Sport for Life: The Next Phase. The Irish Sports Council's Strategy 2009-2011.* Irish Sports Council .

Irish Sports Council (2011) *Irish Sports Monitor 2011 Annual Report.* Irish Sports Council .

James, Harold (2013) 'Design Flaws of the Euro', 2013 Whitaker Lecture. Central Bank of Ireland.

Kelly, E., S. McGuinness and P. O'Connell (2012) *Literacy and Numeracy Difficulties in the Irish Workplace: Impact on Earnings and Training Expenditure.* Research Series Number 27 September 2012. Dublin: ESRI.

Kelly, E., S. McGuinness and P. O'Connell (2012) *Literacy, Numeracy and Activation among the Unemployed.* Research Series Number 25 June 2012. Dublin: ESRI.

Kinsella, Stephen (2012) 'Is Ireland really the role model for austerity?.' *Cambridge Journal of Economics*, 36(1), pp. 223-235.

Kirschner, Jonathon (2003) 'Money is Politics', Review of International Political Economy. 10: 645–60.

Kitchen, R. Gleeson, J. Keaveney, K. & O' Callaghan, C. (2010) *A Haunted Landscape: Housing and Ghost Estates in Post Celtic Tiger Ireland Working Paper Series no. 59.* National Institute for Regional and Spatial Analysis, NUI Maynooth.

Krugman, Paul (2012) *End this Depression Now!.* London: W. W. Norton & Company.

Krugman, Paul (1994) *Peddling Prosperity.* W.W Norton & Company: London.

Lavery, Brian and Timothy L. O'Brien (2005) 'For Insurance Regulators, Trail Leads to Dublin. The New York Times, April 1, 2005.

Leahy, A., M. Murphy, S. Mallon and S. Healy (2012) *Ireland and the Europe 2020 Strategy – Employment, Education and Poverty.* Dublin: Social Justice Ireland.

Leahy, E., S. Lyons and R.S.J. Tol (2010) 'The Distributional Effects of Value Added Tax in Ireland' *ESRI Working Paper 366.* Dublin: ESRI.

Legal Aid Board (2011) Annual Report 2011. Legal Aid Board.

Levy, Jonah D. (1999) *Tocqueville's Revenge: State, Society, and Economy in Contemporary France.* Cambridge MA: Harvard University Press.

Lucas, K. Grosvenor, T. & Simpson, R. (2001) *Transport, the Environment and Social exclusion.* York: Joseph Rowntree Foundation.

Lunn, P. and Layte, R. (2009) *The Irish Sports Monitor Third Annual Report.* Irish Sports Council.

Maddison, Angus (2005) *Growth and Interaction in the World Economy: the Roots of Modernity.* Washington, D.C.: American Enterprise Institute Press.

Mallon, S. and S. Healy (2012) *Ireland and the Europe 2020 Strategy – Unemployment, Education and Poverty.* Dublin: Social Justice Ireland.

Martin, M.O., Mullis, I.V.S., Foy, P., & Stanco, G.M. (2012) *TIMSS 2011 International Results in Science.* Chestnut Hill, MA: TIMSS & PIRLS International Study Center, Boston College.

Mc Daid, S. & Cullen, K. (2008) *ICT accessibility and social inclusion of people with disabilities and older people in Ireland: The economic and business dimension.* Dublin: NCBI.

McCoy, S, Byrne, D, O'Connell, P, Kelly, E & Doherty C (2010) *Hidden Disadvantage? A Study on the Low Participation in Higher Education by the Non-Manual Group.* Dublin: HEA.

McDonagh, J, Varley, T and Shortall, S *(eds)* (2009) *A living countryside?: the politics of sustainable development in rural Ireland.* Ashgate: England.

McGee, Harry (2012*) 'IFSC lobby group powerful in shaping policy'.* The Irish Times, October 8 2012.

McGing, C (2011) *'Geographical Perspective on Women in Local Government in Ireland'* paper presented at Feminist Open Forum Panel Discussion 20 October 2011.

McGinnity, F. and H. Russell (2008, *Gender Inequalities in Time.* Dublin: ESRI.

McGrath, B. Rogers M.& Gilligan, R. (2010), *Young People and Public libraries in Ireland: Issues and Opportunities.* Dublin: Department of Health and Children.

McGuinness, S., A. Bergin, E. Kelly, S. McCoy, E. Smyth and K. Timoney (2012) *A Study of Future Demand for Higher Education in Ireland.* Research Series Number 30 December 2012. Dublin: ESRI.

Moore, Malcolm (2012) 'Stiglitz says European austerity plans are a 'suicide pact'', *The Daily* Telegraph.

Morrone, Adolfo (2009) "The OECD Global Project on Measuring Progress and the challenge of assessing and measuring trust" in Reynolds, B. and Healy S. (eds.), *Beyond GDP: what is progress and how should it be measured.* Dublin.

Mullis, I.V.S., Martin, M.O., Foy, P., & Arora, A. (2012) *TIMSS 2011 International Results in Mathematics.* Chestnut Hill, MA: TIMSS & PIRLS International Study Center, Boston College.

Mullis, I.V.S., Martin, M.O., Foy, P., & Drucker, K.T. (2012) *PIRLS 2011 International Results in Reading.* Chestnut Hill, MA: TIMSS & PIRLS International Study Center, Boston College.

Mundell, Robert A. (1961) 'A Theory of Optimum Currency Areas', *The American Economic Review,* Vol. 51, No. 4, pp. 657-665.

National Action Plan for Social Inclusion 2007-2016 (2007). Dublin: Stationery Office.

National Anti-Poverty Strategy Review (2002) *Building an Inclusive Society*. Dublin: Stationery Office.

National Anti-Poverty Strategy (1997) *Sharing in Progress*. Dublin: Stationery Office.

National Disability Authority (2006) *Indecon Report on the Cost of a Disability*. Dublin: NDA.

National Economic and Social Council (2012) *Ireland and the Climate Change Challenge: Connecting 'How Much' with 'How To'. Final Report of the NESC Secretariat to the Department of Environment, Community and Local Government*. Dublin: NESC.

National Economic and Social Council (2009) *Ireland's Five-Part Crisis*. Dublin: NESC.

National Economic and Social Council (2006) *NESC Strategy 2006: People, Productivity and Purpose*. Dublin: NESC.

National Economic and Social Council (2005) *The Developmental Welfare State*. Dublin: NESC.

National Economic and Social Council (2003) *An Investment in Quality: Services, Inclusion and Enterprise*. Dublin: NESC.

National Economic and Social Forum (2006) *Improving the Delivery of Quality Public Services*. Dublin: NESF

National Office for Suicide Prevention (2012) *Annual Report 2011*. Dublin.

National Traveller Accommodation Consultative Committee(2010) *Annual Report 2010*.

Niestroy, I (2005) *Sustaining Sustainability*.Brussels: EEAC.

Nolan, Brian (2007), 'Long Term Trends in Top Income Shares in Ireland' in Atkinson, A. B. and Piketty, T. (editors) *Top Incomes over the Twentieth Century. A Contrast Between Continental European and English-Speaking Countries*, Oxford: Oxford University Press.

Nolan, B. (2006) "The EU's Social Inclusion Indicators and Their Implications for Ireland", in Healy, S., B. Reynolds and M.L. Collins, *Social Policy in Ireland: Principles, Practice and Problems*. Dublin: Liffey Press.

O'Gráda, Cormac (2011) 'Five Crises', 2011 Whitaker Lecture. Central Bank of Ireland.

O'Siochru, E. (2004) "Land Value Tax: unfinished business" in B. Reynolds, and S. Healy (eds.) *A Fairer Tax System for a Fairer Ireland*. Dublin: CORI Justice Commission.

O'Sullivan, E. (2008) *Researching Homelessness in Ireland Explanations, Themes and Approaches* in, Downey, D. (eds) *Perspectives on Irish Homelessness, Past Present and Future*. Dublin: The Homeless Agency.

O'Toole, F. and N. Cahill (2006) "Taxation Policy and Reform", in Healy, S., B. Reynolds and M.L. Collins, *Social Policy in Ireland: Principles, Practice and Problems.* Dublin: Liffey Press.

OECD (2012) *OECD Health Data, 2012: How does Ireland compare?* Paris: OECD.

OECD (2012) *Revenue Statistics.* Paris: OECD.

OECD (2012) *Equity and Quality in Education: Supporting Disadvantaged Students and Schools Spotlight on Ireland.* Paris: OECD.

OECD (2012) *Education at a Glance 2012: OECD Indicators.* OECD Publishing.

OECD (2011) *Employment Outlook 2011.* OECD Publishing.

OECD (2011) *How's Life? Measuring well –being.* Paris: OECD Publishing.

OECD (2011) *Busan Partnership for Effective Development Cooperation.* www.busanhlf4.org

OECD (2010) *PISA 2009 Results: Ireland.* OECD Publishing.

OECD (2008) *Economic Survey of Ireland.* Paris: OECD.

OECD (2004) *OECD Factbook.* Paris: OECD.

OECD (2000) *Literacy in the Information Age: Final Report of the International Adult Literacy Survey.* Paris: OECD.

Office of Minister for Children and Youth Affairs (2010) *State of the Nation's Children Ireland 2010.* Government Publications: Dublin.

Office of the Refugee Applications Commissioner (2012) *Monthly Statistical Report January 2012* .

Office of the Refugee Applications Commissioner (2012) *Statistical Report December 2012*.

Office of the United Nations High Commissioner for Refugees (2012) *Global Trends 2011*. United Nations.

Oxfam (2002) *Make Trade Fair Campaign*. www.maketradefair.com

Padoa-Schioppa, Tommaso (2000) *The Road to Monetary Union: the Emperor, the Kings and the Genies*. Oxford: Oxford University Press.

Pavee Point (2011) *Irish Travellers and Roma, Shadow Report, A response to Ireland's Third and Fourth Report on the International Convention on the Elimination of all Forms of Racial Discrimination (CERD.,* Pavee Point Travellers Centre: Dublin.

Perotti, Roberto (2011) 'The "Austerity Myth": Gain Without Pain?'. Bank for International Settlements.

Pfizer (2012) *The 2012 Pfizer Health Index*. Pfizer Healthcare Ireland.

Piketty, Thomas and Saez, Emmanuel (2007) 'Income and Wage Inequality in the United States 1913-2002' in Atkinson, A. B. and Piketty, T. (editors) *Top Incomes over the Twentieth Century. A Contrast Between Continental European and English-Speaking Countries*. Oxford: Oxford University Press.

Pope John Paul II (1981) *Laborum Exercens,* Encyclical Letter on Human Work. London: Catholic Truth Society.

Pope Paul VI (1967) *Populorum Progressio,* Vatican City: Rome.

Private Residential Tenancy Board (2010) *Annual Report and Accounts 2010*.

Public Health Alliance for the Island of Ireland (2007) *Health Inequalities on the Island of Ireland – the facts, the causes, the remedies*. Dublin: PHAI.

Public Health Alliance for the Island of Ireland (2004) *Health in Ireland – An Unequal State*. Dublin: PHAI.

Rajan, Raghurman G. (2010) *Fault lines: How Hidden Fractures still Threaten the World Economy*. Oxford: Princeton University Press.

Rapple, C. (2004) "Refundable Tax Credits" in B. Reynolds, and S. Healy (eds.) *A Fairer Tax System for a Fairer Ireland*. Dublin: CORI Justice Commission.

Reception and Integration Agency (2012) *Monthly Statistics Report November 2012*.

Reception and Integration Agency (2011) *Annual Report 2010*.

Regling, K. and M. Watson (2010) *A Preliminary Report into the Sources of Ireland's Banking Crisis*. Dublin: Stationery Office.

Rehn, Ollie (2013) '22 February 2013 letter to ECOFIN ministers'. Brussels: European Commission.

Repetto, R., W. Magrath, M. Wells, C. Beer and F. Rossini (1989) *Wasting Assets, Natural Resources in the National Income Accounts*. Washington: World Resources Institute.

Revenue Commissioners (2012) *Analysis of High Income Individual's Restriction 2010*. Dublin: Stationery Office.

Revenue Commissioners (2012) *Statistical Report 2011*. Dublin: Stationery Office.

Revenue Commissioners (various) *Effective Tax Rates for High Earning Individuals*. Dublin: Stationery Office.

Reynolds, B. and S. Healy (eds) (2012) *Does the European Social Model Have a Future?*. Dublin: Social Justice Ireland.

Reynolds, B. and S. Healy (eds) (2011) *Sharing Responsibility in Shaping the Future*. Dublin: Social Justice Ireland.

Reynolds, B. and S. Healy (eds) (2010) *The Future of the Welfare State*. Dublin: Social Justice Ireland.

Reynolds, B. and S. Healy (eds) (2009) *Beyond GDP: What is prosperity and how should it be measured?*. Dublin: Social Justice Ireland.

Robertson, J (2007) *The New Economics of Sustainable Development report to the European Commission*. Brussels: European Commission.

Ross, George (1995) *Jacque Delors and European Integration*. Polity: Cambridge.

Ruggie, John Gerard (1982) 'International Regimes, Transactions and Change: Embedded Liberalism in the Postwar Economic Order', *International Organisation*, Vol. 36 (2), pp. 379-415.

Russell, H., B. Maitre & N. Donnelly (2011) *Financial Exclusions and Over-indebtedness in Irish Housholds*. Dublin: Department of Environment, Community and Local Government

Safefood (2011) *Food on a Low Income*. Safefood.

Scarpetta, S, Sonnett, A & Manfredi, T (2010) *Rising Youth Unemployment during the Crisis: How to Prevent Negative Long Term Consequences on a Generation?* Paris: OECD Social, Employment and Migration Working Papers.

Schwartz, Herman M. (2009) *Subprime Nation: American Power, Global Capital and the Housing Bubble*. Ithaca: Cornell University Press.

Scott S. and Eakins, J. (2002) *Distributive effects of carbon taxes,* paper presented to ESRI conference entitled "The sky's the limit: efficient and fair policies on global warming" December: Dublin.

Scott S. (2005) *Environmental Economics: Fertiliser Taxes - Implementation Issues, Final Report*. Dublin: EPA/ESRI

Skidelsky, Robert (2000) *John Maynard Keynes: a biography, Vol. 3; Fighting for Britain, 1937-1946*. London: Macmillan.

Smith, David (1986) *The Rise and Fall of Monetarism*. London: Penguin.

Social Justice Ireland (2012) *Analysis and Critique of Budget 2013*. Dublin: Social Justice Ireland.

Social Justice Ireland (2012) *Policy Briefing: Budget Choices*. Dublin: Social Justice Ireland.

Social Justice Ireland (2011) *Analysis and Critique of Budget 2012*. Dublin: Social Justice Ireland.

Social Justice Ireland (2010) *Building a Fairer Taxation System: The Working Poor and the Cost of Refundable Tax Credits*. Dublin: Social Justice Ireland.

Society of St. Vincent de Paul, Combat Poverty Agency and Crosscare (2004) *Food Poverty and Policy*. Dublin: Combat Poverty Agency.

Steering Group on Financial Inclusion (2011) *Strategy for Financial Inclusion Final Report*. Department of Finance.

Stewart, J. (2011) 'Corporation Tax: How Important is the 12.5 % Corporate Tax Rate in Ireland?', *IIIS Discussion Paper 375*. Dublin: Trinity College.

Stiglitz, Joseph (2012) 'After Austerity', *Project Syndicate*, May 7.

Stiglitz, Joseph (2002) *Globalization and it's Discontents*. London: Penguin Books.

Stiglitz Commission (2008) *Report by the Commission on the Measurement of Economic Performance and Social Progress*. Paris .

Swann, Dennis (2000) *The Economics of Europe: From Common Market to European Union*. London: Penguin Books.

Sweeney, P. (2004) "Corporation Tax: leading the race to the bottom" in B. Reynolds, and S. Healy (eds.) *A Fairer Tax System for a Fairer Ireland*. Dublin: CORI Justice Commission.

Teagasc (2013) *Outlook 2013 Economic Prospects for Agriculture*. Teagasc.

Tegasc (2012) *National Farm Survey 2011*. Teagasc.

The Carnegie UK Trust (2012) *A New Chapter Public Library Services in the 21st Century*. Carnegie UK Trust.

Trichet, Jean-Claude (2004) *Structural reforms and growth, as highlighted by the Irish case*. European Central Bank.

Triffin, Robert (1960) *Gold and the Dollar Crisis: the Future of Convertibilit*. New Haven: Yale University Press.

UK Statistics Authority and Department of Work and Pensions (2011) *Statistics on National Insurance Number Allocations to Adult Overseas Nationals Entering the UK*. London: UK Statistics Authority.

UNAIDS Global Report (2012) Data Tables. United Nations Publications.

UNEP (2011) *Decoupling natural resource use and environmental impacts from economic growth, A Report of the Working Group on Decoupling to the International Resource Panel*. Paris: UNEP.

UNEP (2011) *Keeping track of our changing environment from RIO to RIO +20 1992-2012*. Nairobi: UNEP.

UNEP (2011) *Towards a Green Economy: Pathways to Sustainable Development and Poverty Eradication*. Norway: UNEP.

United Nations Development Programme (2011) Millennium Development Goals Report 2011. New York: United Nations Publications.

United Nations Development Programme (2011) Human Development Report 2011. New York: United Nations Publications.

United Nations Development Programme (2003) Human Development Report. New York: United Nations Publications.

United Nations General Assembly (2012) *Future We Want Resolution 66/288*. United Nations .

United Nations High Commission on Refugees (2011) *UNHCR Statistical Yearbook 2010* United Nations.

United Nations Secretary-General's High-Level Panel on Global Sustainability (2012) *Resilient people, Resilient planet: A Future Worth Choosing*. New York: United Nations.

Vatican Council II (1966) *Gaudium et Spes.* New York: Orbis.

Vincentian Partnership for Social Justice (2010) *Minimum Essential Budgets for Households in Rural Areas*. Dublin: VPSJ.

Vincentian Partnership for Social Justice (2006) *Minimum Essential Budgets for Six Households*. Dublin: VPSJ.

von Hagen, Jürgen and Barry Eichengreen (1996) 'Federalism, Fiscal Restraints, and European Monetary Union' *The American Economic Review*, 86 (2), pp. 134-138.

Wackernagel, Mathias et al (2002), *Tracking the ecological overshoot of the human economy*. National Academy of Sciences

Weir, S & Archer P (2011) *A Report on the First Phase of the Evaluation of DEIS*. Dublin: Educational Research Centre.

Weisbrot, Mark and Helene Jorgensen (2013) *Macroeconomic Policy Advice and the Article IV Consultations: A European Union Case Study*. Centre for Economic and Policy Research.

Whelan, C.T., R. Layte, B. Maitre, B. Gannon, B. Nolan, W. Watson, J. Williams (2003) *Monitoring Poverty Trends in Ireland: Results from the 2001 Living in Ireland Survey*. ESRI Dublin, Policy Research Series No. 51, December.

Wilkinson, R. & Mormot, M. (eds) (2003) *Social Determinants of Health, The Solid facts (2nd ed)*. Denmark : World Health Organisation .

Woods, C.B., Tannehill D. Quinlan, A., Moyna, N., and Walsh, J. (2010) *The Children's Sport Participation and Physical Activity Study (CSPPA)*. Research Report No 1. School of Health and Human Performance: Dublin City University and The Irish Sports Council, Dublin: Ireland.

World Commission on Environment and Development (1987) *Our Common Future (the Bruntland Report)*. Oxford University Press.

World Economic Forum (2012) *Global Competitiveness Report 2012-13*. www.weforum.org.

World Economic Forum (2011) *Global Competitiveness Report 2011-12*. www.weforum.org.

World Economic Forum (2008) *Global Competitiveness Report 2008-09*. www.weforum.org.

World Economic Forum (2003) *Global Competitiveness Report 2003-04*. www.weforum.org.

World Health Organisation and European Observatory on Health Systems and Policies (2012) *Health System responses to pressures in Ireland: Policy Options in an International Context*. Department of Health .

ONLINE DATABASES [all accessed February 2013]

CSO QNHS online database, web address: http://www.cso.ie/px

CSO Live Register online database, web address: http://www.cso.ie/px

Eurostat Income and Living Conditions online database, web address: http://epp.eurostat.ec.europa.eu